CLEAR WATERS
RISING

A Mountain Walk across Europe

Nicholas Crane

VIKING

for Annabel

VIKING

Published by the Penguin Group
Penguin Books Ltd, 27 Wrights Lane, London w8 5tz, England
Penguin Books USA Inc., 375 Hudson Street, New York, New York 10014, USA
Penguin Books Australia Ltd, Ringwood, Victoria, Australia
Penguin Books Canada Ltd, 10 Alcorn Avenue, Toronto, Ontario, Canada m4v 3b2
Penguin Books (NZ) Ltd, 182–190 Wairau Road, Auckland 10, New Zealand

Penguin Books Ltd, Registered Offices: Harmondsworth, Middlesex, England

10 9 8 7 6 5 4 3

Typeset in 10.5/14pt Adobe Palatino
Typeset by Datix International Limited, Bungay, Suffolk
Printed in England by Clays Ltd, St Ives plc

A CIP catalogue record for this book is available from the British Library

isbn 0-670-86839-6

Contents

Acknowledgements   vi
List of Illustrations   vi
List of Maps   vii

Beginnings   1
The Sierras   11
The Pyrenees   75
The Cévennes   119
The Alps   149
The Carpathians   199
The Balkan Ranges   331

Index   365

Acknowledgements

Many kind people helped with the preparation of this book. In particular I thank my grandmother Dr Ruth Dingley for letting me use her journals; Chris Brasher, Hol and Naomi Crane, Agustín Egurolla and David Hamilton for reading bits of the manuscript; Bela Cunha, Matt Dickinson, Andrew Franklin and Eleo Gordon for their editing skills; Colin and Alison Huxley for moral support and a desk; Derek Johns, my agent; and most of all Annabel, my wife, whose love and support made the project possible.

Illustrations

The start of the journey at Cape Finisterre (photograph © Annabel Huxley).
Santiago de Compostela: the market after rain.
Vilarello, below the Sierra de Ancares.
José and his *palloza* in Piornedo.
La Paredina and the Picos Blancos from the north-east.
Naranjo de Bulnes in the heart of the Picos de Europa, from Torre de los Horcados Rojos, 2,506 metres.
Ordesa canyon from the Faja de Pelay.
Morning on Pico de Aneto.
Château de Peyrepertuse, Corbières.
High wind on the San Jorio pass.
A typical day in the Bavarian Alps.
Hallstatt during a lull in the snowfalls.
Thaw in the Salza valley, mid-March.
Old Bratislava.
One of the lace-makers' cottages in the Carpathian village of Čičmany.

In the High Tatras, the Valley of the Five Polish Lakes, still frozen in late May.

The strip-fields below the High Tatras – Naomi and Hol provide parental guidance.

Jan Staszel-Furtek, a Górale shepherd in the High Tatras.

Cheese-making in the Hutzul country of Ukraine.

Hutzul shepherds of Ukraine.

A Górale shepherd making cheese.

Shepherds of the Transylvanian Alps.

A shepherd in the Pirin mountains.

A shepherd's hut lost on the lower slopes of Svidovets in Ukraine.

Sucevița monastery and its painted church.

In Bukovina, northern Romania, after one year's walking (photograph © Anthony Coleman).

Szeklers in a Transylvanian village.

The summit of Romania's highest mountain, Moldoveanu, with rain on the way.

Rila monastery.

The end of summer in the Pirin mountains.

Rozhen monastery.

Across the Golden Horn (photograph © Annabel Huxley).

Reunited with Annabel on Europe's eastern shore.

All the photographs were taken by the author except where indicated.

Maps

The Author's Route   viii-ix
The Cantabrian Mountains   12
The Pyrenees   76
The Cévennes   120
The Alps   150
The Carpathians   200
The Balkan Mountains   332

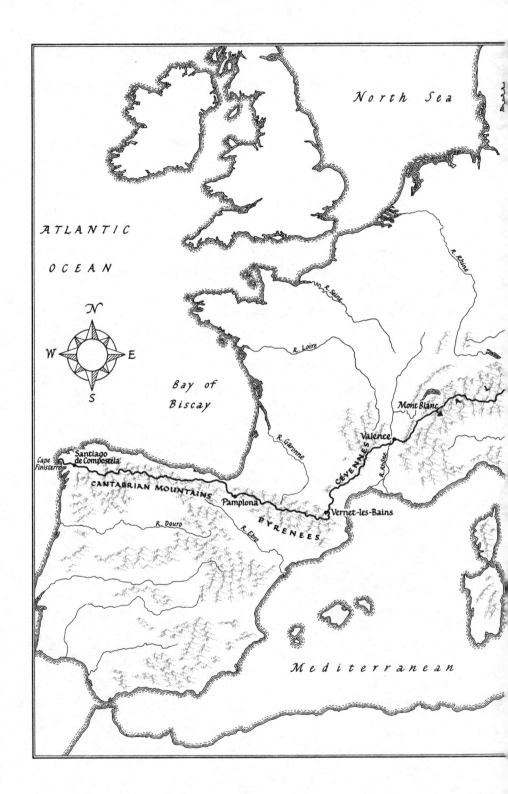

THE AUTHOR'S ROUTE

The route followed the continental divide across Europe from west to east and the total walking distance amounted to approx. 10,000 km.

0   100   200   300   400   500 km
0   100   200   300 miles

Baltic Sea

R. Oder

R. Vistula

R. Elbe

CARPATHIAN MOUNTAINS

R. Dniester

R. Prut

R. Danube

HALF-WAY POINT 'THE FULCRUM'

Vienna

Old 'Iron Curtain'

P S

R. Sava

Turnu Severin

R. Po

R. Danube

Black Sea

BALKAN MOUNTAINS

Istanbul

R. Tiber

Aegean Sea

Sea

Beginnings

I Will

'Nicholas Crane is away for one year. Please leave any messages for Nicholas, or for Annabel Huxley, after the beep.'

'Bother!'

Outside the telephone-booth darkness had fallen and so had the temperature. Slicks of ice glinted in the thin moonlight. I hefted the rucksack on to a low wall, wormed my arms through the shoulder straps, then pushed myself upright. Beyond the village I pulled myself up the gorge wall on tree branches and found a place to sleep. No water again; with the streams frozen or buried by snow I'd not been able to wash for a week. Inside the tent I lit the candle, opened my pen and began writing a letter to Annabel.

Annabel is six years younger than myself, tall, green-eyed, physically and emotionally strong. Before we met, she had spent two years wandering the Far East on her own, crossing Russia, trekking in Tibet and joining the Base Camp of a Himalayan mountaineering expedition, where she had been accidentally set on fire by Colonel John Blashford-Snell. To be torched by a famous explorer seemed to me an honourable initiation into the world of serious travel and I was slightly envious. Annabel had travelled alone and this had given her an unusual level of self-reliance and independence. We met in London, at that Pantheon to the Empire's great explorers, the Royal Geographical Society.

I lost count of the number of times I had failed to ask Annabel to marry me. One weekend I drove her down to Devon, where I knew of a headland whose north–south orientation guaranteed a romantic sunset. We had curled into a grassy nook, which I'd spotted on an earlier reconnaissance. I waited as a pool of sunlight raced across the sea towards our sheltered bower. Just as we were about to be bathed in celestial rays, Annabel stood up: 'Time to go; let's walk on.'

We went to Ecuador, whose varied topography would – I thought – provide several opportunities for proposal. The dug-out trip down the headwaters of the Amazon looked promising until Annabel sank into black slime and had to be dragged out, shoeless and covered in leeches.

In London I acquired an old sports car. Annabel was unimpressed but, undaunted, I suggested a weekend in Skye, intending to propose to her *en route*, on the summit of Bealach na Ba, the highest and most spectacular road-pass in the country. We left London after work on a Friday night, and, eleven hours later, incoherent with sleep deprivation, I nosed the MG up the hairpins of Bealach na Ba. At the top of the pass I pulled off the road. Where there should have been a spectacular view across a silvery sea to Skye, there was an impenetrable milky mist. Annabel was already asleep; I slumped exhausted on to the steering wheel, to wake hours later with an MG trade mark embossed on the skin of my forehead. The next day the engine disintegrated and we returned to London in a breakdown recovery vehicle.

My final set-piece was the result of extended research. Annabel had spent part of her childhood in Cyprus, where the weather is predictably good. We flew there in August, with a copy of Lawrence Durrell's *Bitter Lemons* in our luggage.

After a candlelit dinner on the terrace of Bellapaix Abbey I led her up a flight of ancient steps on to the abbey's ruined roof. We reached the top of a pinnacle of masonry which was just large enough to accommodate both of us. The vertical drops lent an edge to the precariousness of my own courage. Everything was perfect: the dizzy eyrie; the angle of the moon; the glow-worm lights of the fishing boats far below; the heady perfume of jasmine; the encouraging cicadas, whose scratchy calls seemed to be saying 'yeees . . . yeees . . . yeees . . .'

'Annabel . . .'

In the long pause while I drew breath I could hear my ventricle valves flapping like loose tappets.

'Mmmmm . . .'

'This is very beautiful . . .'

'Mmmmm . . .'

'A beautiful moment . . .'

'It is . . .'

'You're not about to go, are you?'

'No . . .'

'I'd like to ask you something . . . Will you marry me?'

A fleet of ships could have sailed upon that silence. The cicadas willed the response: 'yeees . . . yeees'. I wondered whether this tip of crumbling wall was safe; maybe I should have chosen something a little more ... secure. Wasn't that what wives wanted? Security? The wine, gravity and vertigo began to get the better of my balance. I could feel Annabel swaying, and for a moment thought that we might topple into the night, to fall locked and unresolved to the dry rocks of Bellapaix. Then she spoke: 'I feel sick.'

'Is that a "yes" or a "no"?'

'It's a "yes" ... I think.'

For our first Christmas together we took a series of trains to Istanbul. Snowstorms and Balkan timetables tied us up in Transylvania and we spent Christmas Day in a Bucharest flat eating hard-boiled eggs. Thereafter the journey became an extended exercise in endurance as snow banked up inside decrepit carriages. I sought escape in the map of Europe we'd brought with us.

There was, I noticed, a continuous line of mountains which stretched across the continent from the Atlantic to the Black Sea. From Cape Finisterre at the north-west tip of Spain, it followed the sierras east through the Basque Country, then the Pyrenees, Cévennes and Alps to Vienna, where it swung north to trace a sickle-curve through the Carpathians to the Iron Gates on the Danube, at which point it swerved south again through the Balkan mountains, then east to run into the sea at Istanbul. The line was what Americans call a continental divide; the crest dividing the two halves of the landmass. But Europe's continental divide was more than a geographical watershed separating northern cooler temperature Europe from southern warmer Mediterranean Europe. It had other, more extraordinary qualities. The precise mid-point on the line was marked by what used to be the Iron Curtain; on each side of this fulcrum were an identical number of countries: six in the west; six in the east. And the first town on the line was Santiago de Compostela, one of the greatest shrines in Christendom, while the last was Istanbul, the European gateway to Islam. The line was a mirror plane which reflected north and south, west and east, Christian and Muslim. This was the continent's magic axis, Europe's Golden Mean.

'It's a refuge too,' I'd said excitedly to Annabel. 'This line ties together Europe's mountain cultures. And its wildlife. Bears. Wolves. It defines Europe's last wilderness.'

Time added another dimension. For half a century the eastern portion of the line had been Communist territory and largely out of bounds.

That door had recently opened but, in a recurrence of Balkan tribalism, parts of the eastern ranges were already impenetrable fiefdoms. So the line existed like a wrinkle in the sand between the tide-marks, all the more beautiful for its transience.

By the time we were heading back from Istanbul through the blizzards to Belgrade, the journey was fully formed: 'I think I'd like to walk it,' I said to Annabel. 'But I'd like to do it alone.'

'Alone?'

'I've never travelled alone, at least not on a major journey.' We ran through all the advantages of solo travel: the test of one's self-dependence, the amplified effects of highs and lows, the freedom to live by whims, mobility.

'Well . . .' agreed Annabel. 'You'll get more out of it, travelling on your own. The tough part is keeping your spirit up. You'll have to be as interested in the bad times as in the good times.'

When we returned to London I wrote to Patrick Leigh Fermor. A letter quickly came back: 'I'm enormously impressed by – and rather envious of – the tremendous journey you're embarking on. It's a perfect itinerary,' he continued '. . . full of geographical logic and ethnographical possibilities, with plenty of elbow room for adventure.'

Encouraged, I began to make a few estimations. The distance was slightly alarming; Cape Finisterre to Istanbul was twelve thumb-lengths on my atlas, or about 10,000 kilometres of walking. I was unfamiliar with the practicalities of epic pedestrianism, but then lack of knowledge was one of my motives for going. Ignorance is an underrated virtue. To give the journey a temporal circularity I decided to shoehorn the walk into a cycle of four consecutive seasons, from spring to spring.

I would abide by two rules: first, I'd avoid mechanical contrivances: no cars, carts or cable-cars, no trains or tractors, bicycles, buses, escalators or elevators. I would walk every centimetre of the way across the continent. I would step back into a world which hosted the original human blueprint: a biped moving faster than a cow and slower than a horse. Second, I would make the journey without a break, so that I could live through each changing season.

We talked it over. 'Are you sure it'll take only a year?' asked Annabel. Her question raised a final, uncomfortable symmetry; we had been married for only a year.

Don't

The approach of a fortieth birthday adds momentum to any physical project. Suddenly life looks finite: you are half-way there; half-way to the end; your friends are balding and comparing notes on middle-schools; that fleshy flange that rides over the trouser belt has become a permanent fixture; it's too late to do the stack of things you'd been postponing since your twenties: run a sub-three-hour marathon, change career, build a house. Forty is as good a time as any to panic.

I began to worry about ageing early, around my third birthday, when I clearly remember not wanting to be old enough to go to school. As it became clear that there were certain aspects of growing up that were unavoidable, I relied increasingly on risk as a means of derailing the inevitable. Bad behaviour at school led to canings and detentions, which helped to disrupt the predictability of a week's timetable. And in the holidays my parents, Hol and Naomi, took my two sisters and me off on adventures in the back of a canvas-topped Land Rover, to France, or Cornwall, or Wales. We camped and dammed rivers and climbed mountains.

Hol knew things other dads didn't and his mystical way with Morse code, simultaneous equations, carburettor blockages, logic and egg-custard had always been a source of wonder. We had no television and were the only children in our road to have index-linked pocket-money. We could also earn paper credits called 'Cranar', which could be traded at a drawer in the living-room that contained toys and tools. Cranar, being a non-convertible currency, remained constant in value and never suffered from inflation. So a 1969 Cranar token for photographic goods bought the same quantity of photographic goods today, as it would have in 1969.

Hol had taught me about magnetic deviation and 'dead-reckoning navigation' – the estimation of walking times on set bearings which allows you to cross difficult terrain in nil visibility. As a test, he took my cousin and me to the centre of Dartmoor with a tent and food and told us that he would meet us at a grid reference on the southern edge of the moor in two days' time. Stephen and I were sixteen years old. For the next forty-eight hours the moor was obscured by mist and rain. We arrived at the rendezvous twenty minutes early, and I remember the shame and sadness of having lost my aluminium camping spoon.

I would have been around this age when Hol invited me on the first of his winter mountaineering trips. Since the 1940s he had headed north with friends to Scotland for two weeks' climbing over New Year. The ultimate destination would never be fixed until the border was crossed and snow conditions assessed. Some years we went right up to Cape Wrath, climbing those isolated giants Foinaven and Arkle. Other years we tackled the ridges above Torridon or Dundonnell, or remote peaks behind Glen Shiel, or the Cuillins, Red and Black. The weather was often Arctic and our kit was mostly second-hand or bought in War Department junk shops. My jacket was a gaberdine mac which my mother had cut off at the waist. When I eventually graduated from wearing Dad's cast-off camouflage trousers (which had so many patches and holes that bits flew off them in high winds), I bought myself a second-hand pair of Fleet Air Arm trousers which were so enormous that in updraughts the legs inflated like barrage balloons. On my feet I wore my army cadet boots from school, which soaked up water as if they were made from cardboard, which they probably were. My cousin Richard, who was my age, used to wear a pair of tweed trousers that he'd been given while acting as an extra in a mining drama in Durham. With ice-axes and hemp ropes that froze into unmanageable iron bars, we cut steps along Aonach Eagach and the Fasarinen Pinnacles, rising before dawn and returning to the valleys by torchlight. When one of the more affluent members of the group bought a waterproof cagoule, he was derided for breaking with tradition. Hol taught us to lead, to make route decisions, to estimate food requirements, to set the schedules for climbing a particular peak and to decide when to turn back.

Later, these were the skills that Richard and his younger brother Adrian used to make a foot traverse of the Himalayas, from end to end. And they were the skills that Richard and I used to cross Tibet and the Gobi desert on bicycles. There were more sombre excursions too: a visit to a refugee camp up near the Ethiopian border of Kenya; and a 1,000-kilometre journey on horseback with the charity Afghanaid, through the Hindu Kush mountains. With two Afghanis and one other Briton, I was asked to make a war-damage survey and to run checks on aid distribution. The Soviet Union was still an occupying force and we had to travel clandestinely, under the umbrella of the local *mujaheddin*. The valleys of bomb craters and tank-littered battlefields, the millions of anti-personnel mines and the obliterated villages changed my understanding of wilderness, and altered my image of mountains as a benign playground.

Preparations to walk across Europe had to be squeezed into the evenings and weekends, between Christmas and May. I accumulated stacks of notes, some clothing, a rucksack. Mistakenly I attempted some physical training. After work one evening, I tried to run a complete lap of Regent's Park, a distance of about three miles. But my legs were let down by my lungs, which felt as if they had turned inside-out. I walked most of the lap. After two weeks of daily outings I could run about three-quarters of the way around the park. Then, one night in the dark, the instep of my right foot landed on the edge of an unseen kerb. The pain was considerable. I had to hop home. Two days later, I still could not run. I went to the local doctor.

'You have periostitis on the calcaneum spur,' he said.

This sounded unhealthy.

'What would you say,' I asked, 'to a patient with periostitis on the calcaneum spur who told you that he is about to walk non-stop for 10,000 kilometres?'

The doctor pushed his glasses up his nose: 'Don't!'

The Sierras

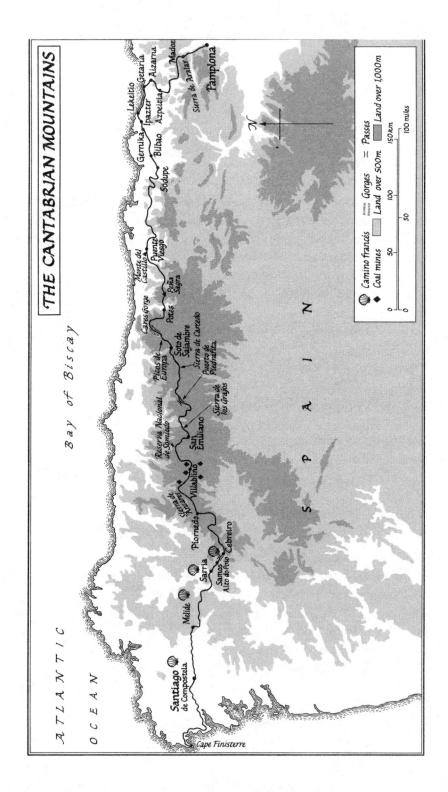

THE CANTABRIAN MOUNTAINS

ATLANTIC

OCEAN

Bay of Biscay

Cape Finisterre

Santiago
de Compostela

Melide

Sarria

Samos
Alto do Poio Cebreiro

Plornedo

Villablino

San
Emiliano

Reserva Nacional
de Somiedo

Sierra de
Riscaros

Picos de
Europa

Sierra de
los Grajos

Puerto de
Piedrafita

Sierra de Carcedo

Soto de
Sajambre

Potes

Peña
Sagra

Cares Gorge

Monte del
Castillo

Puente
Viesgo

Sodupe

Bilbao

Gernika

Lekeitio

Ipazter

Azpeitia

Getaria

Aizarna

Madoz

Sierra de Aralar

Pamplona

S   P   A   I   N

N

Legend

Camino francés

Gorges

Passes

Coal mines

Land over 500m

Land over 1,000m

0   50   100   150 km

0   50   100 miles

Finisterre

Off the cape, three fishing boats butted through the swell. We were on a fingertip of disintegrating granite that jabbed into the ocean from the coast of Galicia. Like the Celtic promontories of Brittany and Kerry, Finisterre and its coast – the Costa da Morte – had a reputation for wrecking ships. Long before the Romans reached *Finis Terrae* this was a magnet for lost souls. Pagan pilgrims used to come here to watch the sun fall through the surface of the ocean into the Underworld.

As we climbed up the rocks, I turned to Annabel: 'D'you think I've made a big mistake?'

'No . . . Not yet . . .'

Annabel had come to Spain to walk with me for the first five days to Santiago de Compostela. It was the last week in May and this hundred-kilometre amble was the prologue, a gentler way of saying goodbye. Above the rocks a path mounted the headland between brands of blazing gorse. The sound of the sea faded and cropped turf took the place of granite. Skylarks sang and a warm wind blew us towards a horizon of hills. We were soon caged between the valley and cloud. Rain squalls drove us into bars where we warmed ourselves over *cafés con leche* and tried to convince each other that we relished the challenge.

One morning we stood in a field of wet grass while I choked back the urge to confess a premonition of absolute catastrophe; the marriage would not survive; I would not survive. The brilliant vision had been overwhelmed by desolation and a sobbing sky. If Annabel had told me not to go, I wouldn't have been in this field, about to leave her. But she hadn't said no; she hadn't said I couldn't go. Neither, as far as I could remember, had she said that she *wanted* me to go . . .

Unwilling to share our last nights together in a sodden bivouac bag, we slept in village inns, ramshackle places with broken plumbing, serving dinners of freshly caught *merluza*. I remembered that I had not paid my subscription to the Royal Geographical Society; I signed my Last Will and Testament. At an inlet called Ria de Muros y Noya, we left the salt

Atlantic, an estuarine dribble folded by mud the colour of wet liver. I wondered when I'd next smell the sea.

Like the other lands of the Celtic water margin, these Galician hills looked ready to steal back hard-won fields the instant a farmer turned his back. Soil lay in pockets scooped from rock and heath. We walked along deserted country lanes, channelled by drystone walls. The gutters streamed with rainwater. When our road climbed above the muddy plots of spring crops we walked by moors and through forests of pine and eucalyptus. Up here, free breezes carried the scents of resin and pollen, a sweet contrast to the sour smell of freshly turned soil and sea.

Our toes looked like partly peeled onions. I was wearing nylon running shoes, which I had chosen for their lightness, but they soaked up Galician precipitation as surely as sponges. The exercise, or perhaps the distraction of the present, had however cured my injured heel. We lived in a waterworld. The water followed us indoors as wet skin and condensation. Long afternoons of slanting rain switched with sudden monsoons of silver pins. The locals, says Gabriel García Márquez in his essay *Watching the Rain in Galicia*, are all born under the sign of Pisces.

On the evening of the fifth day, we slithered down the streaming flank of Monte Pedroso into Santiago de Compostela, the city of pilgrims.

Annabel stayed on for a last candlelit dinner. I estimated that, if each of my strides covered an average of half a metre, I would be making twenty million steps between Santiago and Istanbul. I thought back to our wedding the previous year, and the eternity of time that had elapsed during the thirty steps we'd made together down the aisle. Twenty million steps was beyond comprehension, almost infinity; I might as well be hiking to Mars. My doubts bottomed at such a depth that it would have been easy to say over coffee that I had decided to fly back to London with Annabel.

'Nick, this will be the greatest adventure of your life. And it's a huge challenge for me too.'

I'd lost my tongue.

'Whatever happens,' she smiled, 'it will change us . . . and for the better.'

The next morning, on Plaza de Galicia, Annabel stepped into a taxi and was gone.

Que Chova?

I woke alone in a room overlooking a small, sunlit square filled with birdsong and skirling Galician bagpipes. Scents of coffee and pastries rose on thermals from the warm pavement below my balcony.

Annabel was gone; her sudden disappearance left me naked, unprotected from my doubts and guilts. We were both fairly self-contained individuals and were well equipped for our respective isolations, but there was no way of knowing how much this depended on being able to communicate with each other. Sending messages out to Annabel, by post or by public telephone, would be relatively easy, since I'd always know where to find her. But Annabel's chances to contact me would be rare. I remembered the moment when I had stood on the mountain pass marking the border between Pakistan and Afghanistan, looking ahead into the shark's teeth of the Hindu Kush and thinking that this was the point of no return. Contact with home was always the last and most exciting severance.

I needed an umbrella. A street vendor behind the cathedral gave me the address of his supplier.

At his *fabrica de paraguas* on Calle Curros Enriquez, I was greeted by Jorge Ferrer. He wore a blue lambswool pullover with an enamel brooch in the shape of a powerboat. Jorge had recently inherited the factory from his father. He looked troubled.

'Normally,' Jorge explained, as we stood in a catacomb beside metal racks stacked from floor to ceiling with umbrella skeletons, 'we could sell 300,000 umbrellas in one year, especially in October, November and December. Those are the best months. There is always much rain and our business depends on rain. But this is a very dry year in Spain. Once there were three umbrella factories in Santiago. Now there is just us.' He looked at the skeletons, the shafts and ribs, waiting for the fabric crowns to be stitched into place, 'We import these from an eastern country. But we make the umbrellas here. We sell many to Mr Fulton, in London. Many hundreds. Do you know Mr Fulton?'

'I don't think I do.'

Jorge introduced me to the company director. Antonio was the technical expert. He led me to the boardroom, where a rack of umbrellas stood against the far wall. With a deft flourish Antonio opened each umbrella and described its attributes. There were umbrellas with short or long shafts; with beech, plastic or malacca handles; models with eight and ten ribs and one the diameter of a military satellite dish, with sixteen ribs.

'Please,' said Jorge after Antonio had finished. 'We would like to give you an umbrella for your journey.' He thought for a moment, then chose a ten-ribbed, beech-handled model with a tubular steel shaft and black fabric. 'This is good for walking,' he said, handing it to me. 'It is strong.'

As I was leaving, Jorge handed me his business card. On it was a coloured illustration showing two Galicians in local dress sitting on a bench, the man in riding boots, the woman in wooden clogs. They were kissing beneath a large brown umbrella which was being pummelled by rain. Beneath the entwined couple was the slogan *Que chova?*

'In the *galego* language,' explained Jorge, 'it means "What rain?"'

It was the perfect apothegm for a journey which depended to some degree upon self-delusion.

St James

Framing the Pórtico de la Gloria against the inky Galician sky rose two encrusted stalagmites. Every centimetre had been chipped and bevelled into volutes, towers and niches, green with lichen. In the midst of the chaos stood the diminutive figure of St James, staff in hand, striking the bemused pose of a lost explorer in an exotic jungle. For arriving pilgrims, the Churrigueresque architecture of the Obradoiro façade is intended to be the divine climax to months of purgatorial travel. For me, it was the best place to gather information about the road ahead.

Pentecost has always been a good time for pilgrims to walk into Santiago. The thanksgiving was marked by the swinging of the fifty-four kilogram silver-plated *botafumeiro*, the biggest censer in the world. The spectacle overwhelmed the service. All eyes followed the *botafumeiro* as the supporting boss was tied to the end of a rope as thick as a ship's hawser, which hung from a pulley out of sight in the darkness of the cathedral roof. With a rattle, the *botafumeiro* was lifted, lit and given a shove. The seven *tiraboleiros* heaved on the knotted ropes attached to the other end of the hawser. The censer shot heavenwards. As it swung back towards the nave, they heaved again to accelerate the *botafumeiro* through the lowest part of its parabola up towards the transept roof. With each swing, the height of the pendulum increased till the burner was swooping through the transept and across the altar at seventy kilometres per hour, a plummeting meteorite, glowing red at its core and trailing a plume of white smoke. Ducking each time the *botafumeiro* scalded the air above my head, it was impossible not to dwell upon the day in 1499 when the chains gave with a sharp crack and the censer sailed out of the Platerías door to smash on the flags of the plaza.

To a medieval pilgrim with little experience of science or cities, the mechanics of the *botafumeiro* must have seemed miraculous. It is remarkable, even today, that six men and a rope can so swiftly unleash such force. The secret is in the different-sized drums, mounted co-axially on the *botafumeiro*'s pulley, which multiply the effect of each pull on the rope.

It was science's flip-side, faith or superstition, which brought pilgrims to Santiago. For one millennium they have been drawn to this remote corner of Europe by the remains of St James. The apostle's story (beheaded in the Holy Land in AD 44; brought in a stone coffin to Galicia where he lay undiscovered till 814, when Bishop Theodomir was guided to the spot by a star) created a shrine and then a city. The myth-breakers argue that St James was just a device to extend a lifeline to the Christian fringe of Islamic Spain. Santiago became a symbol of the 'Reconquest' which was eventually to drive the Moors back across the Straits of Gibraltar, and St James himself was adopted as the military icon, Santiago Matamoros, St James the Moor Slayer. The flood of international pilgrims brought prestige to Spain and prosperity to the villages, towns and monasteries along the *Camino francés*, the ancient route from France. Pagans on their way to Finisterre in pre-Christian times had already established a thoroughfare across northern Spain, so the Christians were able to adopt an existing route. The traditional assertion that 'Compostela' derives from *campus stellae* ('field of stars') has been replaced by a more prosaic explanation, following the discovery beneath the cathedral of a *camposanto*, or cemetery.

Only Rome and Jerusalem could match Santiago's pull for European Christians. In the Middle Ages the *Camino francés* was carrying half-a-million pilgrims a year; so constant was the stream of righteous itinerants across the *meseta* of northern Spain that the Milky Way came to be called

El Camino de Santiago. Today, people come to the crypt below the altar of Santiago's cathedral at a rate of one-and-a-quarter million a year. Of these about 7,000 arrive by bicycle, horse or foot and thus qualify for a 'Compostela', the document earned by those who can prove that they have walked or travelled by hoof or bicycle-wheel along at least one hundred kilometres of the *Camino francés.*

The pilgrims arrived daily in the Plaza de Obradoiro. They looked a strange breed, with sun-bleached hair and clothing weathered by wind and rain. Most carried the scallop shell, the symbol of the Santiago pilgrim, used in earlier times to scoop water from springs and broth from communal pots. Initially I was wary of these travel-stained professionals; the camaraderie they showed to each other, fostered during long, painful days crossing the high *meseta*, emphasized the singular and unorthodox nature of my own journey. Yet for the time being I was tied to them. For the first 150 kilometres of my route from Santiago, until I reached the high mountains, I would be following the *Camino francés*, albeit the 'wrong' way.

One evening, after nightfall, I stalked up to a man gazing at the Obradoiro façade. 'You have come far?' I asked.

'Yes, far,' replied the man in English. 'From Poland.'

'Is this a special event for you? To arrive here?'

'Yes, it is special.'

'My name is Nick, I am from London. I am making a kind of pilgrimage too.'

'My name is Professor Gruca,' replied the man. 'I am from Gdansk. I am attending a symposium on surgical infections.'

I had more success the following morning by ambushing a man who was wearing a dusty rucksack. We went to a bar off Calle de Franco, where he showed me the soles of his boots. The corners on the rubber treads were gone, rounded and scarred by sharp stones. Victor's olive-green army trousers were faded and his skin tanned to the colour of cork bark. He was sixty and had taken seventy-three days to walk the 2,100 kilometres from Antwerp.

'Do not ask me the reasons why I am doing it. It is an adventure. To feel the vibrations of the stones under my feet; to prove I can do it. A lot of the people do not start as a pilgrim, but become one on the road. On the road, you open your mind; you get rid of your mental ballast and open yourself to other things.' Victor paused, then looked metaphysical: 'In a full jar, you can put nothing.'

'But do you believe in the story of St James?'

'I was helped by St James. People along the way asked me to pray in Santiago for them. When they asked me, it felt uncomfortable, because to be asked makes you feel a little special. But if these people believe in St James, why not me?' Victor leaned forward, confidentially: 'You know,' he added. 'It's *easier* to have a belief.'

The following morning, I found my photograph on the back page of *La Voz de Galicia* newspaper at the head of the daily *Nombres Propios* column. 'Crane', the caption read, *'inició una peregrinación de Fisterra a Estambul.'* The article below announced that, on foot, I was about to cross *'las grandes cordilleras montañosas de Europa'*.

In print it looked so simple.

Sock Rotation

The aisles were deserted. Through the Pórtico de la Gloria I could just hear the asthmatic whine of a *gaitero* inflating his air-bag. I climbed the steps behind the High Altar, on tiptoes, as if he might hear me then swivel and shout *'Hola!'* My hands ran over the cold gold of his shoulders, polished by pilgrims' palms. Past his left ear, I could look the full length of the nave. A few women in charcoal cardigans sat bowed, at prayer. Leaning forward, I found myself whispering into St James's ear.

I left the cathedral through the old 'Door of France', the pilgrims' entrance, and walked through Plaza de Cervantes chewing an *empanada*, then up Casas Reales to the Puerto del Camino, where the morning traffic was beginning to lock horns. This was the start of the inner journey; the experiment in alone-ness. Some kind of cerebral engine jump-started and the creaky cams and pistons that had carried me from Finisterre now accelerated into a chuckling blur. Casas de los Concheiros swept up in a curve of cobbles to the hill of Monxoi – from *'Mons Jovis'* or Mounts of Jupiter, the player of thunder, storm and rain who gave his name to the hilltop cairns built by the ancients to help travellers find their way.

The morning was warm. The *Camino francés* was marked by dashes of yellow paint and followed back-roads through woods and fields and hollyhocks. The solitariness was so novel that I kept glancing over my shoulder to see if I was being followed. My companion was an elastic

Charlie Chaplin shadow, baggy-trousered and swinging an umbrella. The umbrella had already achieved talismanic status and when pointing out notable landmarks I addressed it as 'Que Chova'.

I passed the airport and collected a pair of boots which Annabel had put on a plane in London, to replace my continually damp shoes. I'd first used Brasher Boots eight years earlier, during a bicycle ascent of Mount Kilimanjaro, and had been favourably impressed by their light weight, durability and suppleness. And unlike traditional leather boots they did not need breaking in! Invincibly shod, I spent most of the afternoon lost in a forest. At dusk I came to the hamlet of Rua. Geraniums frothed over the gunwale of an old hay-cart. A drinking fountain tinkled. A sign pointed to a *hostal-residencia*. Elated by the day's progress I celebrated over a bottle of Ribeiro. I calculated that I had walked 120 kilometres since living Finisterre fourteen days earlier. On this basis, the 10,000 kilometres to Istanbul would take another four years. Annabel was unlikely to be amused.

About me in the room lay my possessions. I had one set of clothes. I lived in a pair of cotton trousers and a cotton shirt with two breast pockets in which I carried my passport, money and compass. For evenings I had a warm jacket and for bad weather a windproof cotton coat. For cold nights I carried a set of thermal underwear.

My one sartorial extravagance was a second pair of socks. In London, an expert traveller had pointed out that weight could be saved by carrying only *one* spare sock. Thus equipped with a total of three socks, the professional circulates them on the principle of crop rotation. Each morning, yesterday's right sock is moved to the left foot; yesterday's left sock is taken out of circulation for washing and mending; and yesterday's fallow sock, now clean and dry, is put on to the right foot. It is an ingenious system, but I anticipated two disadvantages: first, the diurnal rotation could become very muddling, and second, the system had the more serious drawback that the left foot would always be encased in a two-day-old sock. Reversing the direction of rotation would not be an option, since it would merely subject the right foot to the same low standard of comfort and hygiene. On balance, I decided that the extra calories I would burn by having to carry two spare ankle socks rather than one would be more than compensated for by the pleasure derived from starting each day with both feet cushioned in laundered cotton.

The item of clothing which had consumed the most research was my hat. I needed a head-covering with an all-round brim which would keep the sun from my eyes and neck and shelter my spectacles from rainwater and snow. The hat also needed to be lightweight and foldable, so that it could be stowed away in high winds. I eventually settled on a peat-brown Herbert Johnson 'Travelling' trilby, which weighed only a hundred grams and could be rolled into a cornet shape and carried in a pocket.

My old down sleeping-bag had been with me through the mountains of the Hindu Kush. It was worn and thin, but had been made to my own specifications, with no zips to reduce the weight. The bag had great sentimental value but not much warmth. To keep off the dew and rain, I had a waterproof bivouac bag which I had also used in Afghanistan. Unfortunately, I had not checked it for wear and tear before leaving England, and now found that it was perforated with no fewer than twenty-four holes. An oversight with potential for extreme discomfort was resolved when I remembered that I had brought with me a roll of self-adhesive tape for mending my clothes.

My kitchenware comprised a stainless-steel mug, a spoon, a penknife and a tin-opener. My plastic teaspoon had been with me since I had found it in a US Army ration pack in Pakistan. It was lighter weight than steel and extruded to military specifications and thus less liable to snap than the five-millilitre hospital spoon which I had carried across Tibet on a bicycle. The smallness of the American spoon gave it the double advantage of being less heavy than a dessert spoon and of making a small meal last longer.

My twin-bladed knife was a 'Pocket Pal', the smallest of the Swiss Army knives. I intended to use the longer blade for cutting food, and perhaps a bit of spreading, while the shorter blade I kept sharp and clean for emergency chiropody.

The can-opener had been with me for years and was a triumph of functional design. Only thirty-eight millimetres long, it consisted of a tiny crescentic blade hinged to a longer 'handle' which had been strengthened by having a rib pressed into it longitudinally. This gave it sufficient leverage to cut open the unusually thick metal which encased Latvian mackerel, while its ability to cut round a tight radius meant that it was one of the few opening devices which could manage the right-angled turns in the lids of the smallest sardine (or anchovy) cans. I had bought it for thirteen pence at Lawrence Corner, a military hardware store in London, which sells other useful urban accoutrements such as tin helmets and second-hand parachutes.

Sealed against the wet in a plastic bag, I had a wad of maps, bought at Stanford's of Covent Garden. For daily use I planned to use large-scale maps, normally 1:50,000 or 1:100,000, augmented by any extra sheets I could buy locally. For planning the entire journey I had a topographically shaded map covering the whole of Europe, from which I had cut the heavy card cover. To save weight I had arranged with Annabel that she would send the maps in batches to post offices along the route. In London I had found no maps for the second half of my journey, through eastern Europe, but that was a problem so distant that I would deal with it when – and if – I got to Vienna. In a plastic bag I called my 'office', I carried my notebook, cartridge pen and spare cartridges; airmail paper and envelopes; a list of addresses, cuttings from various books and a Spanish dictionary.

After some deliberation I had increased the size of my medical kit from three sticking plasters to four. My sister Liz, a dietician, warned me that a diet which excluded fruit and vegetables for twelve months or more would not be conducive to strenuous physical activity. She prescribed vitamins B and C and the mineral zinc. I bought 1,000 tablets, to be posted by Annabel in little pots with my maps.

There were two items which had no practical application. From one of our wedding photographs I had trimmed myself and a bush in the background, leaving Annabel standing radiant, clasping a spray of cream lilies. And the scallop shell which Annabel had picked off a beach at Finisterre was now wrapped in tissue inside my spectacle case.

On the Camino francés

Under the umbrella I followed the cart-tracks and footpaths of the *Camino francés* over an undulating green sponge threaded with streams that went slowly nowhere. Coming in the opposite direction were the pilgrims. Most had walked from St-Jean-Pied-de-Port in the French Pyrenees, but a few had set off from further afield. One or two, such as the bearded man who'd walked from Paris, were dressed in full medieval kit: wide-brimmed hat, calf-length cloak and a scallop shell and gourd swinging from a stout staff.

I interrogated each pilgrim, filling my notebook with a census of the passing traffic, as if the sheer weight of collected detail would teach me how to make a walking journey and help me to understand my own motives. But no rules emerged from the accumulating data. None of the pilgrims had left home with the belief that hundreds of kilometres of hot hiking would really win them the promised remission of purgatory. Some however had experienced spiritual awakenings. Most were on holiday. The maddest were the ones who had walked the furthest, which was a worrying omen.

I met the twins early one morning in a eucalyptus forest. They were suntanned, with grey trimmed beards and dressed in plus-fours and khaki blouses. Each had a gourd swinging from his matching knapsack. As we greeted each other their breath flooded the forest with the sugary scent of distilled alcohol. A silver flask appeared. 'You would like some? *Aguardiente*. It is like *grappa*.' We all swigged from the flask. They had been walking for fifty-one days, from Le Puy.

'And where is your home?' I asked.

'Germany!' they both hooted.

'What keeps you going?' I enquired. 'Is it the thought of reaching the shrine of St James?'

'No! It's the whisky!'

They sped on towards the finish line, mirror-images marching to an invisible metronome.

At noon I bought bread and cheese in the village of Boente and walked on to Regato Valverde, a valley spanned by water-meadows and seas of blowing grass with a small, granite cottage with apple-green window frames and a heap of scythed hay before the door. The day was possessed of so many pleasures that the kilometres passed easily. In the fields, reapers sliced the knee-high hay. I had to stand aside as a pair of oxen dragged a creaking, wooden-wheeled cart along a tunnel of trees. Laundry hung like bunting between two trees at a village wash-place. With East Anglian echoes of oak woods and lazy rivers and waving corn this could have been the countryside of Cotman or Constable.

My progress eastwards was slowed by having to make headway against the current of pilgrims, united in their goal and bonded by allegiances made during their shared weeks beneath the same sky. I met twenty or more a day. There were loners, lovers and losers. And there were families and friends, all moving west, one step at a time, dusty and sore. They looked like the earth's last evacuees, escaping along the only open road.

The blank expressions hid biographies whose latest chapter had sometimes been revelatory. 'Life's an open road!' exclaimed Werner, the Bavarian carpenter, seriously. Another man had taken the *Camino* to his heart and written a book about Galicia called *One Million Cows*. By a ford I met three German girls who insisted that I sit with them and watch the nymphs. And then there was Melchor, one of five Basque cyclists I shared dinner with in a *refugio para peregrinos* on a wind-blown moor, the pilgrim I'd meet again, in odd circumstances.

The liveliest of my contraplex encounters on the *Camino francés* occurred one afternoon when a perfectly formed, middle-aged pilgrim wearing tight blue shorts came to attention before my outstretched legs as I idled under an oak. He was Swiss and distressed: 'Have you seen the vicar?'

'No. I'm afraid I haven't.'

He pursed his lips. 'There is a vicar. He is making the pilgrimage to Santiago and he is *riding a bicycle!*'

'A vicar on a bicycle?'

'Yes, on a bicycle. And he is wearing his collar.'

'A dog collar?'

'Yes! And you know where he is from?'

'I don't.'

'England!' he spat.

'How interesting,' I smiled, 'I am from England too.'

'So . . . You have walked from St-Jean-Pied-de-Port?'

'No. From Santiago.'

'But you must walk *to* Santiago. That is the way.'

'I am walking *from* Santiago. To Istanbul.'

There was a long pause. Then he banged his ski-stick on the ground. '*Why* do you English have to be *different*?'

First Sierra

As the days passed, time and detail moved into new dimensions. Instead of looking at my watch, I came to glance at the sun. The concept of 'minutes' became irrelevant; the day now divided into two parts, before noon and after noon. I had the time to wait for a raindrop to slide from a dandelion petal. Unlike the monotonous tones of London's streets, the sounds changed every few steps, so that the rattle of pollarded oaks could be followed by the trumpeting of bullfrogs and then the sudden sigh of scrieving swifts. Wildlife grew less nervous; I saw my first pine marten, arched on the track like a watch-spring.

The rainless interlude in Galicia's otherwise watery calendar brought everyone to the fields. Rows of beer bottles lined drystone walls while barns were filled with swishing pitchforks. Countryside that had been abandoned to falling water since Finisterre now hummed to a harvest chorus. As I gained height towards the sierras, the two-storey villas and tidy cottages were replaced by dwellings with enormous, gently angled roofs of slate which overhung the low stone walls like over-sized berets.

Darkness was falling when I reached the walls of Samos monastery, where a monk scolded me so roundly for walking the 'wrong way' along Santiago's road ('Istanbul! Istanbul!' he had muttered as he pulled me into one of the cloister's seats. 'We must talk . . .') that I hadn't the nerve to ask for a bunk in the pilgrims' dormitory.

Through a gap between the houses I followed a flight of steps down to the vegetable plots on the river bank. Under a wild cherry at the water's edge I unrolled my sleeping-bag. As the light faded I dined from a tin of mussels, mopped up with stale bread, and familiarized myself again with the noisiness of night. The river roared, insects sounded like aeroplanes and the occasional 'plop' of a cherry falling on my sleeping-bag felt more like the impact of an apple dropped from a cliff-top. Then there was that primitive fear of being found, alone and defenceless in sleep. I drove Que Chova into the meadow grass by my head, within easy reach.

From Samos, the road began the long climb up to my first pass, the 1,337-metre Alto do Poio. Mountain passes have a way of accumulating mystique. They are places of battles with weather and between men. They mark borders. They are places of redemption (who has not crested a high pass and thanked God?); they are places to rest or to die.

Near the top of the climb I spent a second night under the stars, in the lee of a windbreak of flowering broom, then crested the summit early the following morning while the sun was low and the day cool. Behind me the blue hills of Galicia rolled away towards the Atlantic; ahead, the land fell towards the haze of the *meseta*. On a mountain spur beyond the pass was the hamlet whose name had been on the lips of virtually every pilgrim I'd met.

Cebreiro was the last hurdle for Santiago-bound pilgrims, the highest point on the *Camino francés* west of the Pyrenees. The church and clutch of buildings would almost reach the summit of Ben Nevis. Pilgrims dread Cebreiro's winds, fogs and freak blizzards. Among the millions who had rested here was Walter Starkie, the author and fiddle-wielding professor of Spanish at the University of Dublin, who passed by in 1954. Starkie – whose path I hoped to cross again, in the Carpathians – had fallen in with a fellow Celt, a young *gaitero* called Eladio, who'd played his pipes perched on a beech stool outside one of Cebreiro's ancient *pallozas*. The crude stone walls and immense thatched roofs of the *pallozas* are thought to have changed little since the Stone Age but most of them were now being used as barns. One was a museum. Inside its heavy walls the thick thatch shut out the light from the smoke-blackened interior. There were pieces of furniture about, but without their owners the place was dead. If I'd been told that afternoon that I would soon meet families for whom a *palloza* was still a home, I would not have believed it.

At Cebreiro I would be leaving the well-trodden rut of the *Camino francés* and striking out alone, on my own route, into the mountains. I was jumping the tracks, from the single line defined by St James to the vast web of footpaths and rough tracks, millions of kilometres of them, which fan out and interconnect across the continent's uplands. In theory I could reach Istanbul without my boots bending to bitumen. In practice I would resort to road-walking occasionally, for variety or to reach food and shelter.

My main arteries would be the drove roads which have been used for 2,000 years by shepherds to move their flocks and herds between pastures. This seasonal migration, transhumance, forms the basis of pastoral life from Cantabria to the Carpathians. In spring the animals are moved from the dry plains to the high grasslands, and in autumn the migration is reversed. It's a dying practice, but I hoped that I'd find some of the old drove roads intact. It was these tracks, and the thousands of minor capillaries that fed them, that I wanted to use as my highways as I made my way from the sierras of Spain, through the Pyrenees and uplands of France to the Alps, Carpathians and so to the Balkans.

Spain's drove roads – the *cañadas* – were the longest and most heavily used in Europe. Flocks of a thousand Merinos used to make the migrations, moving in walls of dust for up to thirty kilometres a day for four to six weeks, escorted by a pastor, his four assistants and five mastiffs, who were entitled to the same amount of food each day as the shepherds. Wolves shadowed the tail of the flock, and sometimes bears and thieves. Associations such as the Casa de Ganaderos in Aragón and the infamous Mesta in Castile, were established to protect the rights of its members. In the Middle Ages the Mesta wielded formidable powers; almost any land became subject to grazing rights and shepherds (the 'Brethren of the Mesta') were allowed to clear woodland, a concession that changed the landscape of Spain permanently. Farmers were prohibited from fencing their land and any infringements of shepherds' liberties were penalized by one of the Mesta's travelling magistrates. In addition to their generous pay, shepherds received one-seventh of the ewes' cheese from the flock under their care and one-fifth of the lambs. By the eighteenth century, four and a half million sheep were migrating to and fro across Spanish grasslands. Spain depended on the wool and the man with the crook was king.

Next morning, I climbed through the mist on to a verdant mountainside spread beneath a sky of purest blue. Streams tumbled down terraced slopes, a cuckoo called and my track unravelled through woods of oak, birch and sweet chestnut. In places the trees closed above my head so that I felt as if I was walking underwater, through a long, thin, sun-filled aquarium. That night I lay down under an oak and slept too deeply to dream.

Since Finisterre I'd watched the summer solstice creep closer. With no torch and most of my nights spent outdoors, I was dependent on daylight. I'd become used to being able to stay out on the hills until close to midnight, while first light would wake me two or three hours before the villages stirred.

Perhaps it was because I was beginning to adapt from my artificial, chaotic urban life to the well-ordered rhythms of the natural world, that I sensed this solstice giving birth to a melancholic little bug. I lived by the daylight. To move, I needed the sun. From now until the winter solstice, in six months, I would be living in declining time.

I marked the solstice by climbing up on to the main ridge of the Sierra de Ancares, the first range of mountains on my route. A track angled gently upwards into a clammy mist, then narrowed to a path, which rose to saw-tooth pinnacles. In the cloud, on the apex of that ridge, I could see only my own feet and the immediate rock they walked upon. There was no forwards or backwards. No future or past. Nobody could see me. Nobody knew I was there. I moved in a formless void. I might have been treading water in the midst of an ocean, or drifting through space.

In the afternoon the mist cleared and I came down through heather to an abandoned summer pasture, a *braña*, and an ancient shepherd's hut rotting beneath its heavy slate roof. Descending to warmer air, I passed snowy beds of speedwell, callianthemum and saxifrage and the inky bells of purple gentians. The surface underfoot changed from rock to mud and then to granite slabs, and at dusk I reached Vilarello. Light rain fell on the conical thatch roofs of the *pallozas*. A drunk wearing wooden clogs staggered across a yard matted with wet straw and manure. He told me that there was nowhere to stay in Vilarello, so I decided to walk to the next village, Piornedo. But it became dark while I was still on the track between the two villages and so I slept under a dripping chestnut with the umbrella over my head.

Old Ways

The last *palloza* dwellers in Piornedo were José, sixty-one, and his sister Luzdivina. In the centre of their uneven beaten-earth floor burned a pile of sticks. Luzdivina moved about the *palloza* with a stoop. She had a lined, oval face and fingers bent like birds' claws. José sat still, looking at the flames. Five chickens scuttled about Luzdivina's feet. Their beaks knocked on the hard floor like woodpeckers. Cats took turns to melt in and out of the gloom. Luzdivina laid another stick on the fire looking at the flames, sighing. She talked to herself, quietly. On the other side of a partition, the head of a cow itched up and down on the wood. It was very cold. There was a door at each end of the *palloza* and the wind, which was wet from the rain outside, came through in gusts.

Luzdivina brought breakfast to the table. There were three bowls of hot milk. Under the table, the cock crowed hideously. The brother and sister tore up some bread and dropped it into the milk. Then they added sugar and a sprinkle of coffee. A cow-bell clashed beyond the partition and there was an outbreak of scuffling. When he had finished eating, José took the cows out to his field. Luzdivina swept the chicken shit from the floor and began to cut potatoes.

The *palloza* had two beds, like ships' bunks, set into the wooden partition. Each was hidden from view by a cotton curtain. There was no chimney so the smoke filled the roof space then crept down and oozed out of the two doors. The roof beams were as shiny as coal. José returned. Luzdivina had filled with water the black cauldron which hung by a chain over the fire. Now José was back, she tipped in the potatoes, some cabbage, garlic, oil and salt.

A friend of José's came by. The two men sat with cigarettes beside each other on the bench, talking, watching the flames. The soup, traditional *caldo gallego*, slowly cooked. Outside, the rain streamed off the thatch on to the granite flags in an uninterrupted rattle.

José said that there were twenty-eight *pallozas* in Piornedo, but all were now empty, or used only for cows. Except for theirs. The Xunta had promised to re-house the two of them but their new flat showed no sign of completion. 'We'll be here for ever . . .' said Luzdivina. José had put up a sign outside the *palloza*, inviting passers-by to take a look for 1,000 pesetas.

The rain fell all afternoon as I walked over a low pass, the Puerto de Ancares. These wet forgotten hills hid the last remnants of a lost age. Beside the *pallozas* I saw a few pairs of wooden clogs – *madreñas* – still being worn, distinct from Dutch clogs by virtue of the three prongs projecting from the soles to keep them clear of farmyard mire. But the tally of traditional artefacts was tiny compared to the vast inventory compiled in the 1890s by Dr Hans Gadow, the Pomeranian-born reader in morphology of vertebrates at Cambridge University, who travelled through these northern sierras uncovering unlikely rustic pieces, among them a 'writing bone' – one of the cow's shoulder blades, which were popularly used as jotters in shops. In a village below the Sierra de Ancares, however, I did come across an abandoned farm cart that looked as if it had been left behind by the Romans. This was a rare *carro chirrión* ('screaming cart'), so called because of the shrieking of its wooden axle. A miniature bronze cart to the same design was unearthed at Città Castellana, Italy, and a century ago Gadow was writing of their 'queer, humming, drumming, singing sound'. In plan, the cart I saw at Degrada had a platform shaped like the outline of a boat, and from its 'prow' projected a long 'bowsprit' to which could be hitched oxen. The wheels were spokeless and had been cut from three immense slabs of oak and bound with bands of iron, then lightened by cut-outs in the shape of two half-moons – an echo it is said of prehistoric moon-worship. Instead of wheels revolving on a fixed axle, both wheels and axle were a fixed unit, which made the cart stronger but heavier. Farmers used to claim that the persistent shriek of wood grinding on wood placated their oxen and prevented collisions at blind crossroads. Townspeople were less amused by the din and insisted that carters smear their axles with soap or tallow before driving through the streets.

On the far side of the pass I splashed down towards a grey village. In the weeping dusk, Balouta presented a dismal, impoverished picture. The alleys between *pallozas* had turned to streams. Through the door of one *palloza*, I found myself staring at an entire family – father, mother, children, a grandparent – squatting around an open fire in the centre of an earth floor.

A farmer returning to the village with his cows said that he would find me a place to stay. He showed me to the house of Manuel Cadenas and his wife, Sara, who offered to let me sleep in their kitchen. It was a small room with a table, three benches, a coal-fired oven and a wooden cupboard. When I arrived, their son was there, a giant in his twenties with arms like oak branches and half of one little finger missing.

'It is dangerous to sleep in the mountains,' said Sara.

'There are wolves,' added the son. 'We hear of five or ten wolves a year.' He saw my interest and said: 'They do not attack people. Only cows and deer.'

Manuel had to go out to buy some cows. While he was away, Sara cooked me a plate of eggs and potato. We watched television. First there was a game-show with the first prize of an electric concrete-mixer. Then we watched a bullfight whose balletic young star was a matador called Enrique Ponce. About midnight Manuel returned with several men and they all drank red wine from a large plastic bottle to celebrate the purchase of the cows.

Lying on one of the benches in the kitchen, I was woken in the night by the door banging open. It was the son. His face was flushed and eyes puffed. He sat beside my head and ladled mouthfuls of bread and milk into his mouth, which sounded in the dead of the night like the slurps and splashes of a paddle-steamer.

The Dark Heartland

At the top of the pass above Balouta, a painted pole marked the border with Asturias and the wet air resonated with the rumble of falling rock. The track led down the northern side of the pass to a group of cottages on the edge of a cliff. The cottages, which were empty, had low roofs of split stone, leaning against the wind, rain and snow which sweep down from the Sierra de Campuliares. Some of the cottages had already fallen into the void, one was cut in half; the ground was webbed with cracks. In the gloom below the cliff, ponderous yellow insects crawled to and fro on the floor of the hole in the mountain. Periodically a wail rose from the hole, the insects froze in their tracks and a section of the cliff buckled and collapsed.

In the valley a figure, blackened from head to foot, pushed a chain of battered trucks along a miniature railway line whose rails ran into a mouth in the mountainside. The rain had mixed with the coal-dust to form a black treacle which slithered along the road. Dust coated every leaf and rock. The miners lived in terraced houses on the mountainside. Further up, miners on higher grades had clad their bungalows in painted ceramic tiles so that they looked like parts from a bathroom suite. Even the chimneys were glazed.

I walked through these dishevelled mountains for three days. In secluded corners there were still notional sanctuaries. Early one morning, while the dew lay on the leaves, I followed an ancient paved footpath down through the Bosque de Muniellos, one of Europe's largest forests of primeval oaks and the world's last refuge of the *urogallo*, a type of capercaillie. With me was an old man from the village of Sisterna, where I'd spent the night. The old man was pulled along by a dog on a length of string and around his neck he wore a pair of huge binoculars. We didn't see any *urogallos* and I pressed on alone into the Ibias gorge, the boundary of a sanctuary for the Asturian bear, protected and roaming among the peaks and forests of the Coto Nacional de Muniellos. But I saw only butterflies.

In these once inaccessible heights, Pelayo the Goth and his guerrillas had kept the Christian heart of Spain beating long after the rest of the Iberian peninsula had fallen to Moorish armies. Yet the heart of these mountains had now been torn out. My map was dotted with *Minas de carbón* symbols. Where I crossed the high passes on mule-tracks I found more mines, some abandoned, others still worked by isolated knots of men whose grandfathers had made history back in October 1934 when they rose with the rallying cry of *'Uníos, Hermanos Proletarios!'* against the conservative government of Gil Robles, forming revolutionary committees to run the province and a Red Army of 30,000. Directed from Madrid by General Francisco Franco, the Foreign Legion and Moroccan troops put down this working-class revolution with a loss of nearly 2,000 Asturian lives. The Civil War followed. Even after Franco's final success, these mountains continued as an enclave of resistance to his regime.

Under a grimy sky I walked up the valley of the Narcea. Spoil heaps poured down the mountainside; concrete and rusting metal poked from undergrowth. I rested at a mine, the Mina Juan, desolate and spilling its stains into the river. In the smashed shower-room sets of overalls lay sprawled amid the grit and broken glass. Lying about were boots, bits of rag and split rubber gloves. In a book on the floor were the daily tallies of coal excavated and dynamite used. The record came to a halt on 12 February 1987. On that snowbound day, fifty-two wagons of coal had been brought to the surface.

The road ended at a grey village, Monasterio de Hermo. Blue overalls and worn-out towels hung on washing lines and mist hung about the slate roofs. There was no monastery, nowhere to stay. It was already dusk. I asked two miners how I could find the way to the pass. They laughed. 'There are no paths. You must go back!' But there were paths; the map was covered with them. An Alsatian dog chased me out of the village.

A track led up into the mist. Darkness fell. From the main track, others branched off into the forest. As I climbed, an electrical whine carried through the still trees. There were other noises: dull thumps, a clatter like ships' chains running out, and the sporadic roar of large engines. It was as if a hideous beast inside the mountain was dying in agony. I wanted to run; to hide from the noise, the miners, the forest, the dark and the rain which would surely come in the night.

None of the tracks tallied with those marked on my map. At every junction, I took the track which climbed the steepest. The higher I could climb, the better the chance of understanding the lie of the land. Bit by bit I could see from the compass bearing that I was being led in a curve round to the south and then back to the west, till I'd turned full circle and was headed back to Finisterre.

High on the mountainside I came to a tunnel bored into the rock, lit by a line of electric light bulbs. A generator bellowed. I was passing the tunnel entrance when three figures stepped into the pool of light.

The men's faces were streaked black and their helmet-lamps shone with Cyclopean malice. The three stood, side by side, in front of me. They did not smile. One of the men said: 'Where are you going?'

'Cerredo.'

'It is impossible!'

My map marked a track over the mountain to Cerredo. 'Does this track go to Cerredo?'

'No. You must go back. To the valley.'

The man on the left said: 'We will take you. The truck comes for us in ten minutes.'

'Thank you, but I must walk. I am making a *peregrinación*. Everywhere I must walk. No cars, no buses. No trucks.'

The eyes and lamps stared back, unblinking.

'*Buenas noches, amigos . . .*'

I retraced my steps down the mountain, looking for a place to lie down. When I regained the valley floor, dogs came at me, howling and snarling. I unsheathed Que Chova and parried the attack. Through the darkness and mist I caught a glimpse of a figure. I yelled. He called the dogs off.

The farmer had driven up from Monasterio de Hermo to lock up his cattle for the night. He wore a beret and a watch-chain swung incongruously from his waistcoat pocket. He wanted to take me back down to the village in his jeep.

I asked if I could sleep with his cows. He was uncertain, but I pleaded. Between us we cleared a heap of farm junk off the back of a wooden cart, then wedged the cart's pole in the barn's planking so that the bed of the cart was level. I unrolled my sleeping-bag on the cart. '*Muchas gracias.*'

'*De nada,*' shrugged the farmer. 'Do not interfere with the cows.'

It had not crossed my mind.

'*Hasta luego.*'

'*Hasta luego.*'

In the morning I woke to the sighs and gasps from my bed mates, and plank-rattling belches broken by bellows of impatience. To these early-morning discomforts were added interminable nasal snuffles, sinister gaseous whistles and Niagaric expulsions of urine.

'You didn't touch the cows?' asked the farmer when he returned.

I rolled my sleeping-bag and he showed me the almost invisible track through the trees towards the Collado Alto. Bathed in dawn sunlight, the headwaters of the Narcea looked sublime. The track was intermittently paved and must once have been a drove road – perhaps an extension of the *cañadas reales* which reached into these sierras from the plains of Extremadura – into the old land of Laciana, whose southward flowing rivers, the Fletina, the Chanada, the Orallo, the San Miguel and Sosas fed meadows long favoured by cattle. My map now speckled Laciana's valleys with crossed pick-and-shovel symbols. The pass was carpeted with purple heather that opened into a narrow glen split by brooks and filled with the music of many bells. The dawn sun was lifting steam from the green bed of the valley.

Idling in this sauna was a herd of cattle. Unlike the slack-bellied beasts I'd just slept with, these were Asturian mountain cows, hardy and strong, prized for their limited yields of rich milk. Confronted by a wolf, it is said that they will form a corral and skewer the attacker on their dagger-like horns. I walked slowly among them. They looked part-bull with massive haunches rippled with muscle, and their thick necks bound by heavy leather collars hung with clanking bells. Their short-haired coats, in cream and chestnut, glistened in the sunlight. These were surely the cattle of Geryon, the three-bodied Spanish giant whose beasts Hercules had to steal and drive to Greece for his Tenth Labour.

The magicality evaporated from the valley as I lost height and the sun rose. There were more abandoned mines. Some looked as if they had been deserted the day before, others had been pillaged years ago. Rusting trucks lay in piles, with twisted strands of railway line, boilers, broken glass and miscellaneous oxidizing entrails.

Holding my cigarette lighter ahead of me, I walked into one of the tunnels. My boots splashed into water. Drips stung my head. The flame caught pieces of rail line emerging from the flooded floor ahead of me. The roof was too low to stand at full height. By my elbows, pine pit-props staggered under battens which in some places had burst apart from the pressure; silence itself seemed to support the unimaginable weight above my head. I stood in the dark, listening to the hollow plops of falling water echo off the inside of the mountain.

I thought of my own journey to work: a few steps from the coffee-pot in the kitchen to my desk with the view on to the whitebeam outside my window. And then I thought of the men who till recently had crept each day into this hole. The swallowing blackness, the din of generators, the chipping of picks, the clash and grate of the metal trucks, the continual catching of shins and elbows on raw rock, the sweaty helmet, the dust. And the fear. The fear of rockfalls, of gas, of flooding, of the unexploded detonator pulled mistakenly from the rock. I was beginning to understand fear. Or rather, I was beginning to understand that there could be no fear. Constant danger concentrated the mind on the practicalities of staying alive, of not making a mistake. It was a mechanical, absorbing business which demanded a combination of set rules and intuition.

Real fear showed up when control was snatched by the claws of fate. Played the right way, fate stood little chance.

Columella's Dogs

Villablino was waking to a clear dawn as I walked out of the town along the railway line beside the River Sil towards the old hunting grounds of the Leonese kings, wild mountains whose unintelligible language became known as *bable*. To this day, being 'away in Babia' is a lowlander's euphemism for having done a bunk. The peaks of Babia – higher and sharper than anything I'd yet met – all fell within the Reserva Nacional de Somiedo, the home of boar, deer and bears.

The inconveniently spaced railway sleepers gave me the gait of a man who couldn't remember which leg had been amputated, and I was relieved when the railway curved off to visit the mines of a side valley and I was able to continue up the Sil along an empty road lined with cow-parsley and buttercups. Drystone walls divided the lower slopes into a matrix of silver squares which rose to cliffs of shining limestone, a scene taken, blade and stone, from the Derbyshire Dales of England. Only the gliding eagles spoke of a stranger, wilder land.

Beyond meadows spotted with purple thistles and scarlet poppies, the road ended at La Cueta, where a woman wearing an apron and a wide smile broke off from chasing errant sheep along the lane so that she could show me the track up the valley towards the pass and the Picos Blancos. Ants ferried away my crumbs as I picnicked on bread and cheese and a tomato under the shade of a rustling poplar, with my feet trailing in the clear water.

I tiptoed across a romantic watercolour: a field of cobalt gentians spread before a cluster of thatched *cabañas*, half of them in ruins, and beyond the pass a lake lay ringed by peaks, the blues and whites and greens colour-washed by the pollinated haze of a late spring day. Above the lake the path angled up the mountain to a circular thatched hut, the miniaturized *palloza* of a shepherd who'd moved to lower quarters. Thin mists began to thread the spires of the Picos Blancos. I still had time before dusk to reach the Lagos de Saliencia, whose still pools were said to be guarded by *xanas*, fairy princesses, whose sunken treasures are used to please their lovers on the night of St John. I would sleep on the lake-shore.

I followed the hoof-prints of a recent horseman up on to an elongated tableland of grass as the hard red disc of the sun dipped below the Picos Blancos and a milky light spread across the silent plateau. I was watching my boots tread the spongy turf when the dogs erupted from the dusk. They closed in, snarling and barking, with quivering lips drawn back from curved teeth. There were eight of them. I singled out the youngest and began talking. It stopped barking, then trotted closer and nuzzled my hand. As I moved further from the flock of sheep, the other dogs peeled away, one by one, howling down the moon. Far off, a shepherd appeared and ran at them with a stick. Only the young dog remained, flopping its tail to and fro and nudging me with its nose.

My hand reeked from the dog's cream coat. 'Get out of it! Go on! Off home!'

He looked up, tongue to one side. I considered adoption. But how would the fanatically hygienic Swiss react to a tramp with a stinking shepherd dog? I would have to get papers and the dog would need injections. And I would have to add dog-food to my already irksome luggage. It was a very big dog. It probably ate more than I did. And how would it manage in the deep snow and sub-zero temperatures of a five-month winter?

The dog led me towards the edge of the plateau, where the ground became more broken. Having been chased by so many dogs since Finisterre, I was deeply touched by this uncharacteristic reversal of temperament. I bent to pick up a rock. The dog stopped in its tracks. Its tail slowed then hung still, its face communicating betrayal. The dog was still sitting there when I turned around for a last time as I dropped off the plateau. Darkness had fallen. I skipped the lakes and pressed on miserably to the Collado de Balbaran where I lay in a heathery cradle staring at the stars.

It was an anomalous hound. The sheepdogs I'd met during countless blood-curdling encounters were not the high-IQ collies that round up flocks on British fells, but gigantic proto-hounds left over from one of the Great Extinctions, fantastically ugly with oversized teeth and claws, programmed to attack anything that didn't bleat, particularly wolves, bears and lynx. They were not for driving sheep but guarding them.

Spanish shepherds (and, as I was to find to my cost, those of the Carpathians too) still followed the instructions laid down in dactylic hexameters in 60 BC by the agriculturalist Junius Moderatus Columella. Sheepdogs, wrote the Roman in his twelve-volume *De Re Rustica*, should be white in order for them to be distinguishable from wild beasts, and they should be powerful and aggressive in order to fulfil their primary role 'to pick quarrels and to fight'.

To sharpen their wits, Columella adds, neither 'dogs nor bitches must be allowed to have sexual intercourse until they are a year old; for if they are allowed to do so when they are quite young, it enfeebles their bodies and their strength, and causes them to degenerate mentally'. Later, it occurred to me that my young cream companion was less likely to have been befriending a stranger than trying to seduce one.

In the morning I climbed the ridge above my bivouac site and looked down on to the *Camino Real*, the Roman road which crosses the Cantabrian crest, linking the *meseta* to the sea. One of the maps I had bought in Villablino told part of the story: the ridge on which I stood was marked as the Heights of the Lookouts, and the pass below me as the Puerto de la Mesa. This would have been the gateway to the dangerous passage through the mountains. The road was now no more than a grassed shelf but it still ran in a clearly defined line along the empty valley, with embankments and well-engineered curves. Walking northwards along it for a while, I came to sections of the original limestone paving.

Under a blue sky at the end of the second millennium AD this was a benign amble. But it was easy to imagine how nerve-wracking this walk must have been to young soldiers sent out of Rome. Gaul had fallen to the Romans in only seven years; crushing the tribes of Iberia occupied the Imperialists for nearly 200 years. Notable setbacks for the invaders included the resistance of the shepherd-leader Viriatus, who recaptured parts of western and central Spain, and then the legendary defence of the city of Numancia, which took two decades to fall. The tribes of these northern mountains were the last in Hispania to hold out against the Romans. Even after the leaders had been nailed to crosses, the resistance continued. Hispania, like the province of Dacia (also on my route) far away on the north-eastern fringe of the Empire, was not a walkover.

By the side of the *Camino Real* a spout of water poured from the rock. As many before me must have done, I cupped my hands and drank long, cool, echoing draughts as splintering diamonds dashed against my feet. I'd never tasted water so sweet.

Just as Columella's dogs had shattered my paradise the day before, my Roman reveries were spoiled by another blindside attack; coming down the *Camino Real* my right leg began to ache. By the time I was passing beneath the shattered rocks of Peña Ubiña, a fine 2,417-metre pyramid I wanted to climb, I could barely walk. I took a few steps at a time, pausing in the strips of shade cast by the roadside trees. The muscles down the front of my leg seemed to have been pulled or torn.

At Torrebarrio I stopped at a bar and sat with my back to the sun to dry the sweat from my shirt and to rest my leg.

A monk pulled up a chair to my table. He was dressed in vestments and a pair of orange baseball boots. He said that he was eighty and had retired. He was on his annual one-month holiday, from his home in Gijón. 'You must climb Ubiña,' he insisted. 'The views are excellent!'

With every minute I sat in that chair, my body grew heavier. 'Is there anywhere to stay here?' I asked.

'Yes, yes, a *fonda* I think. In San Emiliano, the next village.' He clapped my back and added, 'Then you can climb Ubiña tomorrow.'

'Perhaps.'

'Come with me,' said the monk, standing. 'I will drive you to San Emiliano.'

'Thank you, no. I like to walk.'

He shrugged and smiled, then climbed into his battered car, reversed into the bar wall, then bounced off the grass bank and swayed away leaving behind a blue smokescreen.

My right leg was swollen from knee to ankle, the muscle inflamed and hot. I staggered on down the valley. Splinters of pain pierced my calf with every step. Just before dark, I limped into San Emiliano and checked into Hostal Asturias.

Hanging On

I woke with hay fever, an aching tooth, stomach cramps, a cold sore on my mouth and a throbbing calf. The soles of my feet were so bruised that I had to crawl to the sink. I did not feel well. Outside my window, a stork raised itself from its nest and called across the roofs of San Emiliano. 'Tacka-tacka-tacka-tacka-tacka!'

In the night I'd worked out what had gone wrong. Had I followed the rules of Roman marching, I would have travelled in bursts of three days, separated by one day's rest; I'd just walked eighteen days from Santiago without a rest. I spent the day on the edge of the bath running cold water over my leg.

The only other guest was Carlos, a radio journalist from Madrid. He was up in Babia for a weekend's fishing. He was thin and highly strung and, like me, was terrorized by the *hostal* proprietor who lurked behind a door marked PRIVADO glowering over the range, wearing a dressing-gown stained to tones of farmyard brown with highlights of grease on the cuffs and lapels. She was a superb cook.

'Let me tell you a traditional poem about Babia,' said Carlos over dinner:

> 'For trout, River Luna,
> For fat, Laciana.
> And for a marriage with pleasure
> take a maiden from Babiana.'

Then he grimaced and asked: 'Are you married?'

I held up my wedding-ring and replied: 'I'm very pleased to say that I am.'

I spent two nights in San Emiliano, then walked gingerly up the valley of the Alcantarilla, back into the mountains. Rain had returned to the Cordillera and I was beginning to doubt whether I'd find settled weather before the Pyrenees. Momentum was the answer; forward progress, whatever the difficulties, satisfied the twin needs of hope and interest. Change was always the cure-all. About one hundred kilometres to the east rose the limestone towers of the Picos de Europa, marking the mid-point of my traverse along the Spanish sierras. I set my sights on the distant massif, knowing that this milepost in the sky would point the way to lighter lands.

The track climbed to a plateau covered in cattle, with a building off to one side. The Casa de Mieres was busy with *vaqueros* playing cards, arguing, leaning on the bar, handing wads of money to each other beneath the table. The cattlemen said that I could cut across the Sierra de los Grajos to reach the Puerto de Pajares, but shortly after I left, the rain began to fall and the sierra was enveloped in grey mist and I was soon lost. I had no map for this sierra and so selected a cattle-track with the compass and was led to the edge of the plateau, below a cliff. This was the night before a new moon and the coming darkness would be as black as soot. The plateau was bleak and featureless and my leg had begun to ache again. At dusk I reached a huddle of round stone huts with clods of turf insulating their conical roofs. From one of the doorways seeped smoke.

As I approached the hut a man emerged wearing clogs and a frayed jacket. He was carrying a saucepan. He was about fifty and had dew-drops on the ends of his moustache. He looked up and saw a wild-eyed foreigner with a battered trilby and a bent umbrella. He waved me inside.

The hut had no windows and was lit by flames from a stack of kindling in the centre of the floor. There was a small table, two chairs and a bed. Without a chimney, the smoke swirled about our heads before creeping towards the cracks around the ill-fitting door. Manuel lived in this hut for four months every summer, tending seventy cattle. He came from a village to the north, towards the sea. When the pan of spaghetti had cooked Manuel divided it and gave me half. I declined, unwilling to take another man's dinner. Manuel rose from his chair and crashed the wine bottle to the table: 'Eat!' he shouted. 'Drink!'

I was so exhausted that for seconds I teetered between hugging this big-hearted cattleman and bursting into tears. As I lay next morning on a wooden shelf in one of the empty huts I wondered how I would react to a stranger banging on my door in London and asking for shelter. Would I leap up and divide my dinner in two? Would I even open the door?

By morning the weather had worsened. Manuel was disparaging about my chances of crossing the Sierra de los Grajos. I left him a bottle of olives I had carried up from San Emiliano and followed his directions to the Puerto de Cubilla, a pass nearby which he told me would lead off the plateau and around the edge of the sierra. A path angled down into a forest. I cut and trimmed a staff, to take the weight from my leg and to warn sheepdogs that I was armed.

For the next five days I was isolated in a world of rain and mist as I threaded my way through and over the Sierra de Casomera, the Sierra de Sentiles, Picos de Mampodre and Sierra de Carcedo. I walked on ill-trodden paths beneath the umbrella, crossing eight passes, half of them too obscure to carry a name. I existed in a self-contained capsule of day-dreams and practical calculations about food and sleep, interrupted at random by intrusions from the world beyond the umbrella crown: a fox, coming down the path towards me, head down in the rain till we almost collided: Luis, who sought me out as I sheltered from a freezing wind in a Romanesque monastery church on the Puerto de Pajares and who in-sisted I take as a gift a copy of the 300-page *Catálogo de su Archivo y Apuntes para su Historia*, which listed every document in the monastery archive from the date of 1071 onwards. 'Maybe you would like to read it, in the evenings . . .' he suggested, as I wedged its enormous bulk into my rucksack.

Churches and cowsheds were the only wayside buildings that reliably had open doors. I sheltered and prayed in churches and slept in the cowsheds, which I'd now categorized according to quality. To qualify for a *palacio* grading, a cowshed had to be dry, rat-free and stocked with hay from which I could make a mattress. A *casa grande* was liberally coated with fresh dung and needed sweeping before I could move in. A *desesperado* was tenanted and therefore acceptable only as a last resort. In the wet weather I had little alternative. So long as it had a roof, the dungiest byre was preferable to a night spent zipped into a clammy bivouac bag.

East of the Puerto de Pajares I tried to hurry my escape to more congenial climes by walking great distances, for fifteen hours one day, over three passes, the highest a bleak 1,900-metre notch whose only exit was a cloud-filled gully echoing with rockfall. Cresting the final sierra before the Picos de Europa, I was picking my way downward between misted cliffs when a footfall caused me to pause. Seven *rebecos* stood balanced on ledges, watching my clumsy progress. These nimble-footed athletes, part antelope part goat, then bounced across the face of the cliff tossing their horns with devil-may-care agility. I felt like an elephant at a ballet school. On the far side of the valley I climbed to the village of Soto de Sajambre at the foot of the Picos de Europa. An ominous wind blew down the gorge from the north.

Picos de Europa

I woke in a room like a battery-chicken shed, full of bunk-beds. Heaps of clothing, the sloughed skins of wet mountaineers, lay in dank mounds on the floor or hung stiffly from bed-ends. Through the murk of sock-gas and condensing perspiration came the surf-like sounds of breathing, punctuated by glottic gurgles and the clockwork ticks of partially blocked nostrils.

Outside, a champagne rain fizzed through silver mist. The grey street through Soto de Sajambre swam in soft focus, the morning-after effect of the bottle of Rioja I'd taken as an antidote to the microbiology of the mountain hut. Gutters trickled. The shop was closed. So was the bar.

The bad weather was unhelpful. Only twenty kilometres from the Atlantic Ocean, the Picos de Europa are one of Europe's angriest maritime ranges. Mists and storms are frequent and rainfall is high. They are also limestone, the pale rock loved by climbers and cavers for its abrasion and fissures and its spectacular sculptures. Carbonic acid in rain attacks the limestone and weathers it into canyons and spires. Rivers run underground, falling down through rock which is as hollow as old Gruyère. It's a lunar landscape, perforated by the crater-like *hoyos*, as if the rock has been pulverized by swarms of asteroids then parched and cracked apart. Maps of limestone mountains are notoriously useless. Even if it were possible for a cartographer to record the contortions of every mountain, he could not register the mayhem which exists between the contour lines. It is not a good idea to get lost in limestone country.

The Picos de Europa divide into three massifs: the Cornión, below which I now stood; the Urrieles in the centre, from which rose 2,648-metre Torre Cerrado, the highest peak in the range; and the smallest massif of the three, Andara, to the east. Between the Cornión and Urrieles massifs cut the Cares gorge, and in the bed of the gorge lay the hamlet of Caín. I would try to reach Caín before nightfall.

I left Soto de Sajambre beneath Que Chova's reassuring canopy on a track which climbed up through forest to the wet pasture of Vegebaño. A cowherd, standing beneath a tree wearing a dripping poncho, pointed me in the direction of the climbers' hut, at one side of the pasture. Inside, a huddle of young stubbled men clasped steaming mugs before a fire. They said that the traverse of the Cornión would take seven hours. I warmed up with a coffee then went back out to the wind and rain.

Beyond the hut, the track contoured around the flank of the mountain, skipping streams and threading through rocks and trees. In the thick mist I could see no further than ten metres. As I climbed, the wind became too strong to use the umbrella. I could feel the rainwater running inside my trousers.

I came to 'El Roblón', the massive oak which the climbers in the hut had mentioned. It is an old landmark on the route up the Cornión. Its top had been smashed off by lightning or wind, but the trunk lived. The path climbed steeply through the tree-line. With the compass out, I linked splashes of blue and yellow paint and occasional cairns. At the next pass, the Collado del Frade, the wind began to boom.

Now the route curved to the north, still climbing, but on scree and rock. My boots skidded and my hands became so cold that opening the compass lid became a clumsy struggle. I had always intended that my spare pair of socks would double as gloves, but now that I needed them, I was reluctant to get them wet. I could feel the water sluicing between my toes.

The path began to climb in zigzags up the Canal del Burro, the Gully of the Mule. The wet cotton of my trousers stuck to my thighs, stiffening my legs. At the Collado del Burro, I crouched from the wind and checked the map. I had reached 2,100 metres. I reset the compass to the new bearing and noted the time on my watch. When I stood, the wind cut through my sodden clothes. The route across the broken plateau was marked by small piles of stones.

After twenty-five minutes I reached the ruin of the old Vega Huerta hut. In the lee of one of its walls, I checked the map again. Water, wind and the cold seemed to be penetrating every part of my body. I had also crossed a fold on the map and now had to extract it from its plastic bag, re-fold it and then fit it back into the bag. In the high wind, this took five minutes, long enough for me to start shivering uncontrollably.

I was on the verge of becoming hypothermic. In less than one hour my brain would become confused, my body sluggish. Then I would become incapable of moving. I had only a few minutes to either make a move, or stop and make an emergency bivouac. In my rucksack I had dry thermal underwear and my sleeping-bag, and the bivouac bag with its repaired holes. But if the storm lasted another twenty-four hours I would become colder still. I might not have the strength to get off the Cornión. I had been fighting the wind and rain for seven hours, and was at the highest and most inaccessible point of the massif. There was no easy way off. My original plan, to descend into the Cares gorge, offered the least dangerous option.

Through the blurring rain, it was difficult to decipher the contours on the map. I could see the pecked lines indicating a path, from Vega Huerta to a col marked as Puertos de Cuba. But I knew from what I had seen already that this 'path' would be no more than a conceptual line over bare rock. Beyond the Puertos de Cuba I saw on the map a series of roundels, where the contours gathered in diminishing circles. It must be a tall, conical peak. If I could reach the Puertos de Cuba, all I had to do was reset the compass for the conical peak, which, having a defined summit, would fix my position accurately for the descent into the Cares gorge.

Leaving my rucksack at the ruin, I began to search for signs of the path to Puertos de Cuba. On a series of bearings fanning out from the ruin, I explored the ground to the east. The white rock blended into the thick mist. Snow filled the chasms in the limestone. I could not tell what was compact, firm snow strong enough to tread upon, and what was a fragile snow-bridge which would collapse.

After twenty minutes of searching I had still not found a sign of the path. Back at the ruin I ate some chocolate. I made a last attempt to find the path. This time I found a small tent, pitched on a patch of grass, islanded by rock. I shouted at its sodden, flapping fabric. A hand appeared, and a face. Inside, three men lay wedged against each other. They looked miserable. In an incoherent exchange, they confirmed that they were OK where they were and that the route down to the gorge did indeed begin by descending the snow-filled crevasses I'd already investigated.

I picked my way down the rock and ice. At each of the chasms, I either jumped, scrambled, or skirted the rim, picking up my compass bearing again on the far side. A cliff loomed out of the mist, bristling with towers, and a grass ramp, leading up to a notch in a ridge. The Puertos de Cuba. A dozen *rebecos* stood and stared, then sprang back into the mist.

I climbed the ramp at a rush. At the notch I peered into the cloud. Vague shapes took form. The rock appeared to fall away in front of me.

Then, for one or two seconds, a window was rent in the cloud. I was standing on the edge of a deep tapering hole. There was no sense in its shape, no conical mountain. Then the mist closed in again. The hole had been shaped like an inverted cone.

I stared at the concentric contours on the map, not wanting to believe that I had been so easily deceived. The concentric contours beyond the Puertos de Cuba did not describe a conical mountain, but an enormous, tapering *hoyo*. Looking closely at the map I could even see its name: Hoyo Verde, with a spot height at its bottom. This hole was 300 metres deep. Apart from volcanic craters I'd never seen anything like it.

I began to climb down slippery grass and rock into the hole. There was no wind. It was utterly silent. The mist prevented me seeing the bottom of the hole. I zigzagged down, past a skeleton. A sheep. Eventually the slope stopped. The hole had a flattish bottom strewn with bones. In several places were 'sink-holes', the drain holes which funnelled rainwater and snow melt into the underground caverns which riddled the massif.

I was standing in the centre of this still, quiet pit when a shriek volleyed to and fro between the flared walls. I swivelled around, surprised to see that the mist had lifted from the eastern rim of the hole, where there was a notch. I caught a glimpse of a tiny silhouette of a man holding an open umbrella.

I set the compass on the notch and began scrabbling upwards. On the far side of the notch, where the ground fell away, a faint path led down to a group of ruined *cabañas*. Two of the *cabañas* had good roofs, and in one, on the table, rested a handful of recently picked mushrooms. The man with the umbrella must have been a shepherd.

Beyond the *cabañas* was the brink of a cliff. Peering over the edge, I could see the path snaking down the precipice, into the mist. Ten hours had passed since I'd left Soto de Sajambre. As I stared down, silver and black streaks started to etch themselves into the enveloping screen of water droplets. A point of detail, a rock spire, took form. Then I realized that I was looking at sunlight striking the far wall of the Cares gorge. After an eternity of sightlessness, I could see again. I hurried down a few more switchbacks in the cliff path, through the underneath of the cloud till I could see rocks and cliffs, the khaki of the scrub, the uncoiling path. One thousand metres below, at the end of a green cleft patched with tiny pastures, I could see red roofs. Caín.

A dog appeared at my knee. I turned as the shepherd came

springing down the track. He was wearing low-sided rubber overshoes and walked quickly and noiselessly. His name was Umberto. It was he who had shouted at me in the Hoyo Verde. He said that he had wanted to show me the way out of the hole, towards the *cabañas*.

Umberto had one hundred sheep up on the mountain. Four times a week, he climbed the mountain from Caín to check the sheep and feed his three dogs, who stayed up with the flock. 'There are wolves,' he said. Three years ago he had lost thirty sheep in a single night. 'The wolf tore out their throats, like *this!*' he snarled, clawing at his own neck. 'It is not good to be alone in the mountains,' he added. 'Now we must go.'

Umberto led the way down the cliffs to Caín. As he walked, he used his stick to brush the water from overhanging foliage, so that his trousers kept dry. Everything about the way he moved was light and efficient. He reminded me of the *rebecos* I'd seen earlier in the day.

We came down to the pastures above the village. Umberto scooped a handful of recently cut hay. '*Malo!*' he said. 'No good!' He handed me the hay to smell. It was musty, damp. Umberto said that there had not been enough sun. We walked on down the track to his own fields. Here the hay stood piled in small domes. He said that he would leave it for another three or four days, then bring it into the barn. Umberto had spent five years working in a German factory. He still wore his blue German boiler suit.

At the bar, we drank a *vino tinto* each then parted, Umberto to his family, me to the village *fonda*. The river roared all night.

A characteristic of misadventures is that their sequels are often heaven-sent; the calm after the storm brings pleasures whose intensity is sharpened by the ghastliness of that which went before. I woke in Caín warm, dry and safe with the rest of my life stretched ahead like an eternal summer. The clouds were lifting; good weather was on the way.

Like the *levadas* of Maderia, the path down the Cares gorge teetered along cliff faces, burrowed through rock tunnels and leapt into space on slender iron bridges. Rock walls leaned overhead, topped by pinnacles wreathed in smoky clouds. I spent the night in Bulnes, a roadless hamlet of exquisite stillness, then climbed into the massif of Urrieles, where I found a rock overhang and built two low stone walls to keep the wind off my sleeping-bag.

I woke in the night. The sky had a deep blue glow and was thick with the phosphorescent sparkle of stars. Leaning over my head was the massive tombstone of Naranjo de Bulnes – 'El Picu' to locals – a sheer granite face 2,519 metres high, first climbed eighty-eight years earlier by the Marqués de Villaviciosa and Gregorio Pérez, the shepherd from Caín who became known as 'El Cainejo.' In the moon-glow I could see the top of the flake that they had reached before traversing across to the North Chimney, whose tricky moves climaxed in the awkward bulge of the Panza del Burro, the Donkey's Belly. Descending Naranjo de Bulnes led the pioneering duo into mild difficulties; when they reached the Donkey's Belly, El Cainejo lowered the Marqués on the hemp rope over the bulge until he rested on easier rock. Then the shepherd knotted his end of the rope, jammed it in a fissure and slid down to join the Marqués. El Cainejo then cut off the section of rope which he could not reach. The skills of abseiling had yet to reach the wilds of northern Spain.

At dawn I began across the massif. Snow and scree had painted in the walls of the twin basins of the Jou Sin Terre and Jou de los Boches and I crossed their uneven floors shadowed by skittish *rebecos* and dwarfed by encircling peaks. A burrow in blue ice led me up to the col below Horcados Rojos. Up in the clear air of the col, every peak looked within arm's reach. I left my rucksack behind a rock and floated unburdened upwards, as if the ring of gravity around the earth had wobbled off into space, the stone at my palms no longer an obstacle, but a celestial ladder.

The slabs on the summit of Torre de los Horcados Rojos were as warm as a stove-top. I was level with the top of Naranjo de Bulnes; level with its neighbours; balanced on a bed of nails, basking in the pleasure of being on the point of it all after the trials of mist and water since leaving Finisterre forty-one days earlier. An ocean of silver cloud frothed about the lower flanks of the Picos de Europa. As I stood alone on my peak, the soft wind felt like the breath of the mountain gods.

Recollections of the world below began to rise like whispers. Potes lay about thirty kilometres away. Potes had my mail. And food and baths. If I was quick I could reach the town before dark. Beyond the screes, pastures dotted with cows led to an old track which crept around the southern flank of Pico del Buey past stands of oak and a lone crag then dived towards the valley, into balmier airs that trembled with butterflies. The hay had been cut. While I had been in the mountains, the seasons had moved on. In the valleys, it was summer.

I felt conspicuously ragged. The seat had been ripped from my trousers, my jacket was torn, my socks full of holes and my boots down at the heels. I needed a bath and a shave. Fifteen hours after waking in my cave beneath El Picu I limped into Potes and took a room in an old town house with uneven floorboards and double doors opening on to an iron railing high above a cobbled lane.

Casa Cuba

Sitting above the bubbling Deva against a backdrop of peaks and forest, Potes had a dangerously beguiling charm. The problem with hot water, good food and utilities such as tables and chairs (which I missed most of all; I hate writing on my knee) was that their intoxicating sensuousness subverted the will to return to itinerancy.

At the *correos* I collected my mail and sat down to a Cantabrian breakfast of *churros* – hot fingers of deep-fried dough sprinkled with sugar – and a half-litre of hot chocolate the consistency of magma. The sugar-rush made me want to fight bears and do a thousand push-ups. There were three letters from Annabel. One of them began: 'What an odd thing for us to be apart.' I hardly dared read on. She suggested that we meet in Pamplona, before I turned up into the Pyrenees. Since parting in Santiago I had managed to write to Annabel every day, and so she had received a drip-feed of news which had kept her up to date with my progress. But – with the exception of a couple of telephone calls – I'd heard little of Annabel's life. 'I'm still riding high,' she wrote in one of her letters. 'The initial excitement, pride and novelty of the experience haven't worn off. And won't for some time.' She was concerned about my mental health; further down the letter she echoed an earlier warning: 'Don't expect to be thrilled by everything all the time.' I knew that Annabel was right. But the journey was already a runaway train and I was enjoying the ride too much to think of what might lie ahead. There is a point when expectations become kinetic; where the fulfilment of one hastens the need for the next. I'd never felt so alive.

One of Potes' many pleasures was the Casa Cuba, a bar hung with hams and run by three women who also served in the dining-room, which functioned as a club room for local male retirees. The servings were gargantuan. Soups were either noodle, or bean or *fabada*, a tureen of black pudding, broad beans, pork belly, *chorizo*, garlic and onions fabled for its ability to create a curmurring stomach and a nervousness of naked flame. A typical main dish would be a single discus-sized plate bearing chick peas, a couple of chicken necks, some egg pancakes, a slab of beef, a black pudding, a few slices of *chorizo*, boiled cabbage, a few potatoes, carrots and a slab of fat. After each meal I was brought a 'gift' from the house such as a bowl of cherries or a glass of *aguardiente*. On my third visit I was treated to a mountain of Cabrales, a crumbly grey cheese made from a mixture of milk from cow, goat and ewe and left to mature in caves. Like Roquefort, it is soft and veined and cured in a dark, constant temperature, but the French cheese is made from ewes' milk and is mellow, almost tasteless, compared to the olfactory assault course defending a pat of rotting Cabrales. After a few mouthfuls I had a numb nose and a locked epiglottis. Cabrales is the world's most extreme example of lactic putrefaction; I was woken next morning by a gangrenous pillow.

After two days in Potes I was on the brink of staying for ever. I bolted on a Saturday evening. One hour's hike returned me to the hills. The villagers of Aniezo were out in evening sun, the men stripped to the waist, shining with sweat, the women beside them, in shawls and skirts, raking the hay. They worked wordlessly, the air occupied by the rhythmic slice of the scythes and the rasp of the hay rakes. Down in Potes, the young men would be gathering in the bars to catch up with the Tour de France on TV (a Basque was winning) and to jab the games machines or riffle through *Alerta* for the football scores.

High on the open slopes of the Sierra de Peña Sagra I found a deserted *refugio* surrounded by cattle whose doleful bells serenaded the moon.

The Last Cantabrian

Julio Garcia Gomez appeared at the *refugio* shortly after sunrise. He had slept alone on the sierra and had come down to fetch water from the spring. He was startled to see me. 'It's unusual,' he said, 'for people to come to Peña Sagra.'

Far below us, the valley of the Deva was still filled with mist and the distant cliffs of the Picos de Europa appeared to be floating on a cushion of cloud.

'Do you know about Peña Sagra?' asked Julio.

'I don't, no . . .' It was just another sierra on my map, one of many I'd be crossing on my way to the Pyrenees.

'For us Cantabrians, this is a special place,' he said. Julio had read Florus (Lucius Annaeus), whose erratic history of Rome gave the Cantabrians a starring role in the Iberian campaigns, promoting them as rampaging freedom fighters determined to hold off the Romans to the last man.

'After all of Spain had been defeated by the Romans,' continued Julio, 'the last free Cantabrians retreated to Mons Vindium – the Picos de Europa. The Cantabrians were mountaineers, you see. Florus says the Cantabrians thought that the Roman Army was less likely to climb to those heights than were the waters of the ocean. But they were wrong, and the Romans did climb Mons Vindium. So the Cantabrians retreated to Mons Medullus, here, where we are now.' Julio pointed up to the summit of Peña Sagra, a bristling rampart of rocks against the blue sky. 'This was where the last Cantabrian battle took place.'

Julio went on to describe the eighteen-mile earthwork that circled the mountaintop, and the months of siege endured by the desperate Cantabrians. Like so many of the 'barbarian' tribes, they finally chose mass suicide rather than surrender. Some threw themselves on to fires, others stabbed themselves or took the poison of the yew tree. 'As Florus says,' concluded Julio, 'it is better to die standing than as servants of the enemy.'

After the battle the name of the mountain was changed from Mons Medullus to Peña Sagra, the Holy Mountain.

We spent the day together, walking over the sierra. On the flank of the mountain Julio showed me a 'beehive' hut about four metres high. 'It is a Celtic *castro*,' he announced, lifting his arms before the hut's tall dome. The doorway was so low that we had to crawl to reach the interior, and it was built from rock picked from the mountainside, without any use of mortar. 'It is not original,' apologized Julio. 'It has been repaired.'

Julio seemed a survivor himself, roaming the sierras with his tribal ancestors for company. In the weekdays he worked in an office in Santander. He was in his early twenties. There were, he said, only about fifty bears left in these sierras.

'Still they are getting shot,' he smiled sadly. He spoke in the Cantabrian dialect. The word for road, pronounced normally as *camino*, became in Cantabrian *camin-yo*; dog, *perro*, became *perru* and *pico* – as we know – became *picu*.

When I left him, he signed his name in my notebook: *El último guerrero Cántabro*, The last Cantabrian warrior.

The Knight of the Sad Countenance

In 1903, the thirty-seven-year-old director of the College of Arts and Crafts in Torrelavega, Don Hermilio Alcalde del Rio, discovered an enormous cave on Monte del Castillo. By 1914 archaeologists had excavated down through eighteen metres of detritus, uncovering harpoons, ceremonial staffs, pieces of stag and horse, scrapers and bone points, hand-axes and bits of rhinoceros. When they reached the fourteenth and final layer they discovered the remains of cave bears, reindeer and marmots. And signs of hearth fires, built by troglodytes who carried their birch-bark tinder and bracken into this cave, and spun their wood-drills to produce tiny coals that flowered into flame.

I joined the back of a tourist group and stooped through a dark opening into the guts of the mountain. Passages and cavities fed off each other, wet and shiny and various hues of bilious yellow. Bulging veins threaded through disquieting reddish stains and warty excrescences leered from unexpected corners. From the ceiling dangled tentacles of damp stone while others stretched from the floor, as high as a man. Black recesses oozed rivers of stilled globules and puddles of petrified slime. In places catastrophe had struck, renting the walls to jagged blocks frilled with tendrils of torn matter. In these intestinal voids, tattooists from the beginning of time had left their indelible marks: pictures of bison and elephant and stencilled hands which reached out from tunnel walls.

The caves made an eerie connection back to the beginnings of Iberia – and to the mountain culture that has drawn more attention than any other in Europe. Early anthropologists argued that the Basques were the last survivors of Europe's aborigines; the continent's oldest inhabitants. Serologists provided some of the most intriguing evidence, presenting figures that showed a disproportionate percentage of Basques to belong to the 'O' blood group and that the groups 'B' and 'A/B' were less frequently found among Basques than in other Europeans. Surveys also established that an abnormally high percentage of Basques were 'Rhesus negative'. Basques were also claimed to be two to three centimetres taller than French and Spanish races, and more muscular. Neither does Euskara, the Basque language, conform to European norms. Once believed to have been carried to Iberia by Noah's grandson, Tubal, after God's resolution of the Tower of Babel's linguistic chaos, Euskara has faint similarities to Georgian, Circassian and the Berber languages of the Atlas mountains. The frequency of Euskara words derived from *aitz* (stone) has encouraged some to claim that the Basques are the only survivors of Europe's late Stone Age, marooned in their forest fastness as the continent was swamped by the Indo-European migrations of the Bronze Age, from 2500–1000 BC. This was the last corner of southwestern Europe to convert to Christianity and the last part of the continent to build towns. It is the evidence of the archaeologists, the serologists, the philologists and the anthropologists that has been wielded to such effect by politicians that the Basque Country has become the most autonomous province in Europe, with its own tax system, police and education.

In Puente Viesgo I met a Basque friend. Twelve years earlier, on his forty-seventh birthday, I had come across Agustín at Cape Wrath, the wind-blasted corner of Northern Scotland. He was on a woman's bicycle which he had converted to a 'male' with a wooden crossbar, and had pedalled from the English Channel with a harmonica in his pocket and a huge Basque beret tilted on his head. We had corresponded since and I had come to look forward to reading the next sequel in Agustín's adventures as he criss-crossed the Spanish *meseta* on his bicycle.

For two days we walked together over the hills towards the border of the Basque Country. Agustín had grown up in Extebarria, a Basque hamlet thirteen kilometres up the Artibai river from the coast. His father had been a professional *pelota* player, away from home for a year at a time and Agustín had inherited a toughness which he inadvertently revealed when I mentioned my calf problem of the previous month. 'No *vayas al médico como no sea con la cabeza bajo el brazo,*' he scolded. 'It's a Spanish saying: Don't go to the doctor unless you're carrying your head under your arm.'

Agustín could see his old country changing every year. As we walked the overgrown byways he swiped at the undergrowth with the staff he had cut from a hedge. 'I feel myself [*swipe*] like Don Quixote [*swipe*] fighting windmills [*swipe*] and phantoms [*swipe*].' The target was modern youth. 'They are greedy, lazy and slovenly,' he continued. 'They want every consumer luxury and fancy. They're not prepared to work for it. The young people in Spain, they copy the Americans. [*swipe*] Youth is being depraved by lack of moral standards, and this [*swipe*] is typified by a lust for cars and pornography [*swipe! swipe!*].'

Nettles, clumps of cow-parsley and stray briars buckled before the Knight of the Sad Countenance. '*Erreztazunak dakar narraztazuna!*' exclaimed my companion. 'Easy living brings laziness!'

We stopped in a hayfield to picnic and Agustín unpacked his harmonica. Boisterous Basque dances bounced down the green slopes.

'*Fandango*, *Arin-Arin* and *Bideko*!' announced Agustín when he had finished. 'Three tunes I learned when I was young. And now I will play *Donostiako iru Damatxo*, "The Three Damsels of San Sebastian". It's about three young girls who always complain about their work, and then as soon as there is any fun going on around the corner, some young lads or whatever, they wake up and go down to the street with any excuse. It is . . . *piquant* and not too heavy!'

While Agustín played, I lay back, with my rucksack as a pillow.

The concert climaxed with a rendering of one of the greatest symbols of Basqueness: 'It is the popular Basque national anthem,' explained Agustín. 'It was written about one hundred years ago by José María de Iparraguirre, who was one of the most famous of Basque troubadours. It is called *Gernikako Arbola*, "The Tree of Gernika".' Agustín was apologetic: 'It is a difficult song for one person to sing. I shall sing it, although it will be a very poor and puny rendering. It should be sung by a big male voice choir. Then it sounds great: solemn, strong and powerful, although I have to say that it does have a softer, wistful middle part.'

Agustín raised himself to his feet and lifted both arms to the sky. He drew a deep breath, and, with his considerable chest swelled, embarked upon the Basque anthem, pumping his voice at the sky to imitate massed voices, directing an unseen orchestra with his arms and, when an instrumental interlude was called for, curving his mouth into a trumpet bell and mimicking an army of horns.

'What does being Basque mean to you, Agustín?'

'It is a big question . . . being Basque means to me many things of course, but first of all is having a distinct identity from Spanish, French or anything else. Of course I personally consider myself European, a citizen of the world. But at a more immediate level I am a Basque. I was born Basque, I can't help it. I'm not better or worse than anybody.' Agustín paused for a moment, then elaborated: 'Our problem is that we feel quite different from the rest of Spain, just as the French Basques feel different from the rest of France. But our boundaries are not definite and clear; we are Spanish but we are also Basques and there is a kind of dichotomy or a slight anxiety, a doubt if you like. We carry that with us more or less all the time. I like the Spanish people, I like the Spanish nation. But it's only when the two concepts – Spanish and Basque – conflict that there is an element of friction, an element of tension.' Agustín drew breath for his conclusion: 'So that is perhaps at the root of so many of the problems in the Basque Country: that lack of definite identity which can only be whole by having your own Basque passport, Basque currency, police, everything else. In other words being totally independent, which of course in practice is very, very difficult, though perhaps possible . . .'

Agustín's words were to follow me along the European watershed; they could have applied to any one of the compromised minorities I met along my mountain route.

We walked over the hill and down towards the valley of Pisueña, where we lost our path and were forced on to the road. The hurtling cars stoked another of Agustín's diatribes: 'These are a symbol of this country's mad excesses!' He lunged at a passing car and gathered breath: 'This obsession with cars is destroying Spain's ancient pathways. When I was a boy, I remember the market day in Markina. There were donkeys everywhere. To cycle from home in Etxebarria, to Markina, I had to thread my way past loaded donkeys and the women who led them. Then, within a few years, there were no donkeys. They had all gone! Now the paths around Markina have been turned into roads, or they have been abandoned and are now so overgrown they are impassable.'

After we parted, I had trouble crossing the cliffs to the valley of the Asón, and was then terrorized by increasingly heavy traffic as I was funnelled down towards Bilbao.

Beyond Sodupe the road became wedged in the bed of a gorge beside the river and the railway line. I was walking in the same direction as the Sunday evening rip-tide of traffic returning to Spain's sixth biggest city after a day in the country. Motorcyclists and cars swerved past my elbow at breakneck speeds. There was no pavement, so I walked in the gutter. Once an hour a white-painted *Cruz Roja* ambulance whisked past, taking the recently maimed to Bilbao. The next day, the papers would carry the gory photographs. Tufts of dog and cat stuck to the tarmac like scraps of old carpet. On my Michelin map, the road was edged in green to denote its scenic merit. My quixotic companion, Agustín, had once cycled this way. 'It is a hell . . .' he had warned me. 'Another kind of hell.'

La Cuadra sat in the gorge floor cut off by the road, rail and river. Without a car, train or boat, the village might as well be on the moon. I asked in a shop whether it was possible to cross the river and follow tracks down the far side of the gorge. A man with a goitre reaching from his ear to his shoulder shook his head. 'You must go by car or bus,' he said.

'It's not possible to walk?'

The goitre wobbled again.

Back in the gutter, I scrutinized the passing litter for an envelope of banknotes, jewels, dropped letters; anything interesting. But it was disappointing detritus: beer bottles; cans; car parts; cigarette packets; food wrappings; plastic bags, knotted and partially inflated by their own gases; corks and the ubiquitous polyethylene terephthalate bottle, the disposable cola container which clutters gutters the world over. I watched a man stand at the foot of his garden with his arms outstretched, releasing first one, then another black plastic dustbin sack, neatly tied at the neck, into the river. They fell with a slap into the current. Then he watched, hands on his hips, as his refuse began its voyage down to the Bay of Biscay. He wore an expression of sublime wonder.

Towards the bottom end of the gorge, the air began to smell; the river grew a chemical froth and the valley's ceiling became criss-crossed with the steel threads of cables and pylons, as if someone had made a botch job of darning a hole in the sky. The road climbed above grimy acres of industrial buildings tethered to a chimney sprouting a finger of flame that stuck up at the sun as it sank into a sickly yellow haze. To leave the gorge, the road climbed above the city to the Alto de Castrejana. From here I could look down upon a grey mass of factories, apartment blocks and streets, bagged and knotted by the enclosing hills and curled loops of the highways and the River Nervión, as brown as turkey gravy.

In the Casco Viejo, the old quarter, I found a room whose windows rattled like castanets to the percussion of hammer-drills and air-compressors boring holes in the ground to build a new underground railway. For two nights I walked the streets, mesmerized by the shop windows, lit like giant TV screens. I crossed the uliginous Nervión to amble along teeming Calle San Francisco, with its foot traders, prostitutes and bandaged rejects. I idled in tapas bars, whose chalked menu boards startled me at first with their exotic catalogue of seafood. I had forgotten that I was close to the ocean again. I snacked on *pinchos* of tuna and bread, laid with stripes of pimento and deep-fried in batter, and wrote my notes at night beside a plate of *merluza* baked in octopus ink. I hadn't eaten a cooked meal for a week. Bilbao's effete seafood was far removed from the simple flavours of the mountains.

In between the Basque Archaeological, Ethnographical and Historical Museum and the Museo de Bellas Artes I collided with Melchor, the bicycling pilgrim I'd shared a night with weeks earlier on the *Camino francés*. For an IBM employee suddenly confronted by a tramp, he performed a remarkably graceful welcome. 'You will like to join me and my colleagues for lunch?' he asked. Sitting in a city restaurant with six men dressed in dark suits was an experience so unreal that I felt as if I had hopped over the wall of a zoo. Melchor, slim from his cycling, with fine-boned, boyish looks, took vicarious pleasure in my adventure; he wanted to help. Annabel, he said, should fly to Bilbao, where he could collect her from the airport, give her a night with his family and then put her on a bus for Pamplona, where she could meet me in two weeks' time. Humbled by Melchor's kindness, I found it difficult to leave: 'Melchor, I'm going now.'

'Now?'

'Now. Tonight.'

'Then I will walk with you.'

'Really that's not necessary. It's going to rain.'

'I am coming with you. I will telephone my wife.' Melchor thought for a moment, and asked: 'Where are you going to walk to, from Bilbao?'

'Gernika.'

'Ah . . . Gernika!'

Dressed in his sharp grey suit, Melchor walked with me through the wet *ziri-miri* – the local mist – over the mountain and into the night.

Gernika

The spiritual home of the Basques nestled sleepily between forested bolsters. Children ran between the flower gardens and a shirt-sleeved policeman with a bunch of keys and a revolver guarded the Parliament house. The neo-classical Casa de Juntas stands on a rise above the town, beside the sacred oak – 'Gernikako Arbola' – under which the rights of Basques, the *fueros*, were reconfirmed by successive rulers until their repudiation in 1876. The withered trunk of the original oak, destroyed by the French in the Peninsular War, is enshrined in a pillared Pantheon close to the younger tree grown from its seed.

Gernika would have remained an idiosyncratic backwater had it not been the victim of the world's first large-scale aerial atrocity. During the Civil War forty-three aircraft of the German Condor Legion spent the afternoon and evening of 26 April 1937 dropping 29,000 kilograms of bombs on Gernika in an attempt by General Franco's nationalists to bring the Basques to their knees. When the planes left, over seventy per cent of Gernika's houses were totally destroyed. The town was in ruins. The number of Basques who died has never been accurately established because the town was choked at the time with refugees. There could have been as many as one thousand deaths.

Several days later, after seeing three black and white photographs of the aftermath on the front page of a French newspaper, Picasso began the sketches for the painting which became an icon for civilian martyrs. The soundless shout of terror on the faces of Gernika's dying citizens was so profoundly etched into my mind that I found it impossible to equate that smoking cemetery with a sunny market town whose loudest sounds were the children's laughter.

In a bar overlooking the flower gardens, I fell into conversation with a retired *pelota* player, Felipe Arrien. He had been in Gernika the afternoon the planes came. 'It was a Monday, market day, but not many people had come because the planes had been around. Young people were playing handball. I was at the *frontón*. At two p.m., the game was suspended because of the planes. At 4.30 one plane came over for a look. After that four or five groups of three planes in each came and started dropping bombs. There were many bombs, fire bombs too. It was frightening.'

Felipe described his dash for the shelter. When he reached it, there were so many people there already, that they told him to go away. 'A bomb hit the shelter and they all died . . . The bombing finished at 7.30 in the evening. Only two or three of the buildings in Gernika were left: the Casa de Juntas, the school and the buildings at the end of the garden. Afterwards, the papers were saying that the Basques had burnt the town but that wasn't true.'

'Are you angry about the bombing?'

'No. Not angry. You forget.'

Felipe talked about the days before the bombing. The *frontón* had been the hub of Gernika's existence; here, every Monday afternoon, the ball games took place, and here too were staged the silent movies and dances, boxing matches and stone-pulling contests. As one of Gernika's professional *pelota* players, Felipe was well established at the top of the town's social hierarchy. As I sat beside him in the sun, nearly sixty years on, he told me to hold his bicep. It was hard and knotted like old oak.

In Gernika's *frontón* that evening I went to a *festival* of *cesta punta* (literally 'basket point'), a variant of *pelota*. Felipe's photograph, taken back in the thirties when a Firestone advertisement covered the *frontón*'s façade, hung in the entrance hall. The game was as strange as any Basque sport. The matches began at ten p.m. and lasted through midnight to the early hours. The court was rectangular, with walls on three sides like a squash court, and the players walked on wearing white flannels, shoes and helmets, and white and blue shirts. Each wielded a *txistera*, a banana-shaped scoop which looked as if it had been parented by a baseball bat and an oversized soup ladle.

After a few drinks the match began to assume a blurred, balletic quality: the white players against the black court moved with the elastic thread of the streaking ball as it volleyed to and fro between wall and *txistera*, drawing each player in, then out, then in, then out. Each *txistera* worked like an extension of the player's arm, whirling in propeller blurs to catch the ball, then fire it from the tip of the *txistera*'s scoop back towards the wall.

Unrestrained by the conventions of more mannered ball-games such as cricket or tennis, the spectators milled about the seats and bar, drinking, smoking and chatting, or roaring approval if their attention should be caught by a fine rally. Cutting the smoke rising from the heads of the spectators was a continual crossfire of small balls containing scribbled bets, hurled to and fro between the punters and a line of bookies standing along the edge of the court with their backs to the players.

Buffeted by the hubbub, I sat over my beers wondering how a small town could recover so quickly from near annihilation. Felipe was an ordinary, relaxed pensioner. For him, the atrocity would not be healed by cogent emotions like 'forgiveness', or 'reconciliation' or even 'revenge', but by the erosion over time of the brain's ability to remember; the inevitability that human beings ultimately *forget*.

Fiesta

From Gernika I walked northwards till I crested a round, green hill and saw the horizon fill from side to side with blue ocean. A slim, dark-haired woman with a light-hearted smile overtook me, then waited at the next corner. 'Where are you going?' she asked.

'Ipazter. To the fiesta.'

'Do you mind if we walk together? Ipazter is only fifteen minutes from here.'

'You are walking very fast.' I winced.

'I am a mountaineer.' She climbed regularly in the Pyrenees and lived in Bilbao. She had family in Ipazter. Her name was Begoña. I had trouble matching her pace and as we raced towards the village I could feel my hips popping.

The siesta was coming to a close and knots of slow-moving people were beginning to congregate beneath the bunting about the church.

'We'll eat first,' said Begoña, 'then go to the fiesta.'

Begoña's sister lived in a modern apartment a few strides from the village centre. I'd walked for several hours in the sun since leaving Gernika after breakfast, and was sticky and sore. When I scratched my shoulder, a large flap of shirt ripped away in my hand. The family were gathered in the sitting-room for a rolling feast of local fare. Begoña's husband, Ibon, brought cider and home-made cakes. Sabin, Begoña's brother-in-law, rinsed a bag of mushrooms collected that afternoon on the Sierra de Urbasa, then sliced them into scrambled eggs and served them with a salad of fresh tuna which had been brought ashore at the neighbouring port of Lekeitio in the morning. Then we nibbled *mariscos* collected by Sabin during five hours of hunting on the seashore. Later we went down to join the fiesta and drank glass after glass of 'Tonica Sabin' – tonic water and Navarre *rosé*, poured over a mountain of ice. Sabin had spent his working life in a wine syndicate. 'I am *experto*,' he said, reminding me not to stir my drink.

Sabin's chilled tonics and the hot July night amplified the crowds and the clamouring rock music until, after several hours, they coalesced into pulsing thunder. When dawn broke I found myself part-way up the mountain above Ipazter, in my sleeping-bag, wedged between two eucalyptus trees, with a hangover.

I went to Mass with Sabin. Afterwards, he took me for fried egg and *chorizo* in the PNV building. As he tore the bread, Sabin explained that the Partido Nacionalista Vasco took up to eighty-five per cent of the local vote. I agreed with him that the PNV were impressive and explained that, where I come from, one of the political parties regards eggs as poisonous; another would be unable to agree what an egg is; and the third would insist that consumers pay an egg royalty, to be accrued in a Poultry Pensions Fund so that retired chickens could be eased towards old age on golf courses appropriated from the bourgeois. I was not surprised that a political party which could deliver on a plate, a fried egg, had attracted almost unanimous support.

After the eggs Sabin took me to the *frontón* to see the dancing. A stage for the musicians had been built at one end of the court, and a bar along one side. We drank shots of *tinto*, tossed down in one. The ritualized dances were performed by troupes of women, or of men, stamping and kicking and twirling in blurs of white and red and black. In the glaring sun, swords flashed and staves clashed; bells jingled at stuttering ankles and the Basque flag swirled to the drums and pipes of the band.

For the *Kaxarranka* the pace slowed as six barefoot fishermen walked with funereal solemnity on to the *frontón* bearing long oars in their right hands and the weight of a massive coffin-shaped chest – the *kaxa* – on their left shoulders. Teetering on top of the *kaxa* – traditionally used for storing the papers, money and valuables belonging to the fishermen's guild of Lekeitio – was 'St Peter', a young man dressed in a top hat and tails who performed three dances of increasing tempo and precariousness while his six bearers winced under the shock-loading of his bouncing feet.

'He fell off once . . .' whispered Sabin.

'When was that?'

'Oh . . . about 1690. Or 1700, I think.'

Sabin went home for his siesta and I found myself in the midday furnace of the village plaza. Dangling from the belfry by a rope was a human effigy. Two women were swabbing the loggia of the church with disinfectant. A carved stone plaque on the front wall of the building serving as the bar commemorated the building's service as a military hospital for Basque volunteers during the Peninsular War. The gloomy interior was occupied by the huddled forms of a few survivors clinging resolutely to their tumblers of blood-red *tinto*. I joined the walking wounded. Later, every able-bodied villager was conscripted to run a race through

Ipazter's lanes. The last home was a small, round girl of perhaps eight years, walking alone up the long hill to the plaza, convulsed with hiccuppy sobs. 'There, but for the grace of God . . .' I thought to myself.

I doubted my ability to survive another night of Sabin's tonics and so decided to leave Ipazter while I was still conscious. In one of those partings you make with new-found friends you know you'll never see again, we all said 'We must meet again!' little knowing that this would indeed happen.

Salt-water Trespass

Bamboo thickets of masts, aerials and fishing rods rose from the sterns of hundreds of tuna boats tied up along Lekeitio's quays. A brass band played before the church's flying buttresses and the waterfront was thick with couples and families *en paseo*, strolling arm in arm as the sun dissolved into the ocean. Relishing this trespass away from the mountains, I slept in a room above a bar and spent the next morning soaking up the salt air.

Behind the harbour and its grand glass-fronted houses, a thin, dark cobbled slot called Arranegui Ezpeleta ran the length of the old town. The houses overhung the alley, rising up four or five storeys and clung about with balconies, galleries and washing which sagged like limp topgallants. Caged canaries sang from spars projecting from open windows. A parrot eyed me and screeched, its green head tilted quizzically. Water dripped continually, as if I was creeping through the leaking hold of a ship. But the sources of the drips were the rows and rows of geranium pots underlining every window. The alley was busy with women bringing hot bread back from the baker and with the smells of cooking *alubias* and fish soup. Huge pulley wheels hung from second-floor warehouse doors. At an intersection of alleys, four women stood over painted trolleys selling wet fish.

In a curious mimicry of pastoral transhumance, the sons of communities like this used to sail each spring across the Atlantic to catch cod and whales, returning to the Basque coast in the autumn with their holds loaded with dried fish, blubber and oil. At Red Bay in Labrador, the remains of a Basque whaling station have revealed a *chalupa*, or whaleboat, and three small galleons; it is possible that Red Bay and others like it were founded before the coast of North America was sighted by John Cabot and Jacques Cartier.

For the next three days I walked along the coast, unable to tear myself from the uncomplicated space on my left and fuelled by *rapé* that was as sweet and firm as lobster, or fresh sardines served smoking from quayside grills and washed down with raw, fruity *txakoli*, the Basque white wine. I slept in bosomy clefts overlooking the ocean, with my back turned to the mountains. From my sleeping-bag I watched day melt into night and the waking eyes of ships' lights being brushed by the sweeping strobes of lighthouses. In the milky light of dawn, waiting for the dew to dry from my sleeping-bag, I saw fishing boats creep out from the ports below me, sliding across a sea of beaten pewter. I understood why people gravitate to the lands by the sea.

My coast-walking came to an end at the fishing village of Getaria, the birthplace of Placido Domingo's mother, and the home-port of the world's greatest explorer.

Juan Sebastián Elcano

On an August day thirteen years after Columbus died at Valladolid in 1506, thirty-two year-old Juan Sebastián Elcano sailed from Seville in one of the five vessels under the command of the Portuguese seafarer Ferdinand Magellan. Nearly forty years old, lame from battle wounds and a veteran of East Indies exploration, Magellan was intent upon finding a route to the Spice Islands from the west.

Magellan took with him 280 men, among them Antonio Pigafetta, in his late twenties, from Vicenza. Pigafetta was the only 'tourist' on board, an adventurer with a journalist's eye for a story. Among the crew was one Englishman, the chief gunner, Master Andrew from Bristol. Forty of the crew were Basques.

Magellan's ships crossed the Atlantic by way of Tenerife and sighted the South American coast off Pernambuco (now Recife, in Brazil). Sailing south down the coast of the New World, the fleet searched for a route through to the west. The ships explored the estuary of the River Plate and then continued south into colder latitudes. They met tribes who were immensely tall and called them 'Patagonians', after their large feet. Magellan wintered on this coast, quelled a mutiny among his men, then continued south to find the Cape of the Eleven Thousand Virgins, the entrance to the long sought passage through to the west. He emerged thirty-eight days later from what has come to be called the Straits of Magellan and then set a course across the 'Great South Sea'.

For ninety-eight days the fleet, now reduced to three ships, was pushed along by kind winds. Magellan called this sea 'Pacific'. Scurvy and malnourishment wore down the crews; they were reduced to eating ox-hides, sawdust and rats. Once they reached the Philippines, Magellan set about claiming the islands for Spain. The cross and the flag of Castile were raised on Humunu, then Mussava and Cebú. But on Mactan the chief refused to pay the full tribute and Magellan rashly attacked.

Pigafetta was with the admiral: '. . . twice they knocked his sallet from his head . . . (An) Indian threw a bamboo spear into his face . . . the captain tried to draw his sword and was able to draw it only half-way, because he had been wounded in the arm with a spear . . .' Pigafetta adds that he himself 'was wounded in the head by a poisoned arrow'.

With Magellan dead, the crews elected the admirals Serrão and Duarte Barbosa as joint commanders, but both were killed – along with twenty-five sailors – when the ruler of Cebú turned upon the foreigners during a banquet. The expedition looked ready to founder; Elcano's ship, the *Concepción*, became so unseaworthy that it had to be scuttled, leaving just the *Trinidad* and the *Victoria* to continue. Two years and two months after leaving Spain, the surviving two ships reached the Moluccas – the Spice Islands. Magellan's aim to find the western route to the islands was complete, but the remnants of the fleet now had to find a way back to Spain. The *Trinidad* was found to be unfit for the return to Europe and was to be reconditioned before attempting to recross the Pacific. That left the eighty-ton *Victoria*. She had on board forty-four Europeans and thirteen Indians, who now faced a voyage across the Indian Ocean, around the Cape of Good Hope and up the Atlantic, in a battered ship along a sea-lane patrolled by Portuguese ships whose orders were to seize or sink Spanish vessels. Fortunately for the crew of the *Victoria*, she was commanded by Juan Sebastián Elcano. Three years after leaving Spain, the *Victoria* crept up the Guadalquivir to Seville bearing eighteen emaciated survivors.

The first circumnavigation of the globe was the greatest single journey ever made. By comparison, all subsequent journeys have been increments on the known; after 1522 the world as a whole could be comprehended. On the day the leaking *Victoria* returned home, Elcano wrote in his letter to Emperor Charles V that 'we have given practical proof that the earth is a sphere', and as if he felt the need to qualify his amazing evidence of the world's roundness, he added: 'having sailed round it, coming from the west, we have come back through the east'. There has not been any event in the history of exploration which provoked among the general population such a sense of the miraculous.

Pigafetta's journal revealed fantastic lands: he was told by natives of an island where 'there are only women who conceive by the wind', and of a great tree on the Gulf of China with fruit called *buapangganghi* that were larger than water melons. And he heard of the *garuda* bird, so enormous that it could carry off buffalo and elephant. Yet Elcano is hardly known outside the Basque Country; he was not found a pedestal beside Marco Polo and Columbus or even Magellan. Many will argue that it is easier to complete a journey than to embark upon it, but every expedition needs its Elcano; the team-member who can assume leadership when all appears lost.

I found Elcano's statue as soon as I walked into Getaria. He blazed in the heatwave, dressed in white stone with one hand on his tiller and an Odyssean gaze on his face. On the pedestal below his thigh-boots were cut thirty-one names (a further thirteen survivors had returned later from the Cape Verde islands, after having been captured by the Portuguese).

The fifth name on the list was that of Antonio Pigafetta, whose journal of the voyage survives as the principal account. It's a record which would credit any modern front-line journalist, but it fails to mention Elcano, for the Italian disapproved of Elcano and was one of many who wanted Magellan – the Portuguese – to take the glory. When the eighteen reached Seville, Pigafetta visited the Emperor independently of Elcano, to present his own version of events. Since Pigafetta's account of the journey is the one that has endured (no log or journal attributed to Elcano seems to have survived), it is his version of the journey that has been handed down through history.

Staring at the sunlit names on the stone brought these heroes back to life. Among the survivors were seamen from places I'd passed through: Diego Carmona and Vasco Gomes Galego from Galicia, Juan de Arratia from Bilbao. One or two of the foreigners had come home: Hans, the gunner from Aachen, and Richard de Fodis, the carpenter from Evreux who could not write (did Richard ever return to the green fields of Normandy telling tales of the Big Feet?), and Nicolas the Greek from Naples. And little Juan, at fourteen the youngest to sail in the fleet, made it back to Seville. The Englishman's name is not there.

High Land Games

From Getaria footpaths led me back inland for half a day to Aizarna. Elcano came here to give thanks for his safe deliverance, climbing up the rock of Santa Engrazia to the lonely hermitage where hangs a great bronze bell said to have been dragged up the stone path by an enormous ram clashing like thunder. Later the bell was used to warn the locals of approaching storms. The village lay in the centre of a green bowl rimmed by hills. I was back in limestone country. Aizarna had no rivers or streams, or apparent water, yet its fields shone with verdant health. It has always been a mystical place. The caverns beneath the fields into which rainwater drains are said to be the homes of goblins and witches. Santa Engrazia is one of several hermitages that encircle the village.

At the end of the deserted plaza rested one of the great stones used in the test of oxen pulling-power in which a team of two animals attempts to drag weights of up to 1,500 kilograms the length of a measured course. Trials of strength are as necessary to a Basque as tests of patience are to an Englishman. In the country games – *Herri Kirolak* – men compete to carry fifty-kilogram weights – *txingas* – in each hand up and down a ten-metre cobbled court. Granite blocks weighing up to 300 kilograms are lifted; speed, strength, endurance and skill are tested in grass-cutting competitions, log-sawing and log-chopping; there are tugs-of-war – *sokatira* – and sheepdog trials. The *zakua* is a smugglers' race which involves a sprint with an eighty-kilogram sack across the shoulders.

These tests of rustic aptitudes have no urban equivalent. I once heard of a commuters' race in London, in which cyclists were pitted against pedestrians, motorists and public transport, but the cyclists won easily and it was hardly a fair competition. I thought of my own urban skills, accumulated through years of practice and experimentation, but could see little scope for converting them into competitive events. The city equivalent of *Herri Kirolak* would have to include events such as finding hidden phone-boxes; racing against accelerating buses; cutting through obstacle courses of dog excrement with a pram; traffic-jam endurance competitions; riding bicycles between converging taxis ... There are no Urban Games because there's no pride in city skills; they're not being handed down through the generations as wholesome celebrations of the human spirit.

From Aizarna I walked over the hills towards Azpeitia and the great fiesta which is staged every year on the last day of July to mark the death of St Ignatius of Loyola. Few places in the Basque Country are as spiritually loaded as this tight-packed town sitting under the 1,000-metre wall of Izarraitz. Cervantes made this the home of Don Sancho, the choleric Basque who cut off Don Quixote's ear then paid for his mistake by receiving such a blow from the enraged knight that blood spurted from nose, mouth and ears 'as if a mountain had fallen on him'. But Azpeitia's better-known son was Iñigo Lopez de Recalde, born in a tower house beside the River Urola on Christmas Eve in the year before Columbus set sail for the New World. He was the youngest of thirteen children. After learning to read and write the boy was sent as a page to the court of Ferdinand and Isabella and then took up arms under the Duke of Nájera. When Iñigo was twenty-nine a cannon-ball shattered one leg and wounded the other while he was helping to defend Pamplona against the French. Operations to set his leg led to complications and he received the last sacrament, whereupon he embarked upon a miraculous recovery. While he convalesced in the family tower house, Iñigo read *The Life of Christ* by Ludolphus of Saxony and the popular biographical collection called *Flowers of the Saints*. Thus began the conversion which led to his founding of the Society of Jesus – the Jesuits. In Azpeitia 600 stonemasons built a great basilica and Joaquín de Churriguera (whose style was adopted for Santiago de Compostela's cathedral) devised a method for supporting a sixty-five-metre-high dome. Marble was brought down from the heights of Izarraitz; jasper, lapis lazuli, alabaster and porphyry came from further mountains. Floor, walls and ceilings were worked with polychrome stone so that it looked like the inside of a jewel casket. The basilica and wings were built around the Loyola tower house, enveloping it within layers of Renaissance stone.

I arrived to find the narrow streets clogged and was carried by the crush to the Plaza de Toros where two men in green and yellow uniforms were selling tickets. 'How much?' I asked.

'Nothing!' laughed the first man.

'Yes,' said his companion. 'Give him the ticket. He's a tourist!'

They gave me a prized '*Sombra*' ticket. I squirmed up the steps with my rucksack, propelled by a steward to a place at the top with a good view. In front of me a bull bowed and bled. A matador tiptoed about his swirling cape. The bull pawed the dust then threw its horns.

Half of the bullring lay in the shade, half was filled with colour: the gold of the matador's waistcoat, the crimson blood, and white fans fluttering like hundreds of butterfly wings. This was a small bullring; every spectator looked within arm's reach of the bull. The matador slid his sword into the bull's neck. By the time I could bring my eyes back to the ring, the bull was a stilled black carcass on the sand.

I saw the next fight in its entirety. First into the ring were the *cuadrillas*, dancing with their pink capes to tease out the bull's humour; to gauge his mood for the ensuing duel. Then came the *picadores* on their armoured horses, wielding medieval lances. For a short while the fight seemed even as horse and bull wheeled and thrust. Then the bull hooked his horns under the horse's belly, driving the swaying *picador* back against the wooden planking at the side of the ring. The horse tossed and pawed frantically. The *picador* tumbled to the sand and rolled clear then scampered over the ringside. But this was a short reversal of fortune, for the bull was quickly drawn away from its prey by a squad of newcomers, nimble *banderilleros* armed with two-metre darts. Drawn by feints from the *cuadrillas*, the bull was lured into the range of each *banderillero*. The adversaries were face to face, for to place their darts on the bull's neck, each *banderillero* had to stand before the charging bull and thrust past the horns. The bull could smell his own blood. The crowd roared.

The *banderilleros* retired and the matador made his theatrical entry. Niño de la Capea succeeded in turning the bull six times without a break. Each time the horns swept past his abdomen the crowd bellowed a louder '*Olé!*' The dance of death swirled and turned, as the red of cape and blood and flashing gold shone in the evening sun while the matador quick-stepped about his lumpen black adversary. Suddenly both were still. The bull panted, head down, dripping. The matador thrust his groin at the pointing horns and, with hand on hip, strutted before the bull. The emotion was now contempt. The bull was lost. His chance to gore his tormentor had passed. The crowd hushed. The silence of the crypt fell on the ring.

The blade was drawn. The matador walked slowly forward. He halted and held his final stance, the sword at shoulder height, a horizontal extension of a straight arm, a long finger of steel running from the matador's eye to the bull's heart.

The bull started forward. The *coup de grâce* was delivered rapidly. The blade entered the bull cleanly and deeply, a single thrust over the lunging horns until the steel was buried to the hilt. For a few seconds the bull loped, charged and faltered with the sword handle a rosette on his neck. The *banderilleros* rejoined the matador, goading the dying bull until it coughed and buckled at the knees. Then it fell, dead.

The matador stood by the stilled bull. The crowd was on its feet. A team of two horses cantered into the ring. Nooses were looped over the bull's horns. The bull was dragged quickly around the ring and out through the arch, leaving a large, bloody question mark in the dust.

While men with rakes cleaned the ring, Niño de la Capea was showered with hats and roses. Handkerchieves waved. In one hand the matador held up a bouquet of flowers, in the other the two ears of his bull.

It was not until the third and final matador was introduced to the crowd that I realized that I had met him before. He stepped slightly smiling into the sunlight, slim-calved and glittering with gold brocade. The great Ponce! I'd spent a night with Enrique Ponce back in the highlands of Asturias, watching him on television in Sara's kitchen, in Balouta. He seemed an old friend, not as handsome as Pepe Luis, but familiar nevertheless. But poor Ponce won few friends in Azpeitia. Come the kill, his sword penetrated only half-way into the bull's neck. Ponce was forced to leap clear. While the animal raged and pawed the ring, one of the *banderilleros* had to recover the partly embedded sword using a long hook, so that the matador could try again.

Afterwards, my steward friend took me down to watch the dead bulls being loaded on to a truck with a road digger. It was this image, of beasts being shovelled ignominiously for later disposal, which I carried from this place. Perhaps this grotesque and anachronistic opera has endured because it has always been so defiantly contradictory; the bullfight appeals to two parts of the same character; grace and grossness, humiliation and honour, heart and head; and these opposing polarities repel a concerted verdict. We are addicted to the theatre of death, be it in the bullring or on the TV screen.

After the departing matadors, picadores and *banderilleros* had climbed (still resplendent in their dress) into their ordinary saloon cars I headed with thousands of others back into town for beer and a *bocadillo*. It was a long, hot night. Instead of dissipating with the setting sun, the heat increased until the air clung like a damp rag. Market stalls laid with leather-work and trinkets were set out in the streets, manned by Moroccans or Negroes from further south, or by Vietnamese. In the bars men stood shoulder to shoulder, wet with sweat and wine. I found it hard to imagine St Ignatius smiling benignly on a fiesta which celebrated his life-work with animal sacrifice and mass drunkenness.

The sky eventually cracked. Bolts of lightning burst above the plaza, followed by rumbling thunder and hot smacks of rain. For an hour the streets were pelted with rods of water. Gangs of hysterical teenagers huddled in doorways. Sparks and molten metal cascaded from fused wiring on the streaming walls. Later, as the rain moved on beyond the black mass of Izarraitz, the crowd reassembled on the river bank. Coloured rockets, Roman candles and showers of emeralds were interrupted by a firework which left earth with a boom and then, an eternity later, when it must have been twice as high as the sierras, blew up like an atom bomb, rattling every window and leaving ears ringing. The climax could have been caused by the *maestro bombardero* tossing a lighted rag into the remaining fireworks. The north bank of the river seemed to lift to the sky. A terrible roll of thunder and overlapping starbursts made Azpeitia's sky look as if it was giving birth to new galaxies. Lightning from the departing storm continued to flare. Orange sparks fell upon the town as thick as rain while fiery clouds of red and green smoke rolled across the dark water. Without taking his eyes from the sky, the teenage boy in front of me beat a burning ember from his smoking backside.

After midnight a twelve-piece band appeared on the stage in the packed central plaza, playing Glenn Miller's *In the Mood*, followed by *Tie a Yellow Ribbon* sung in Euskara by three girls in lamé dresses and bouffant hair-dos. I woke up to find that I had been sleeping on someone's front lawn.

Tricky Mathematics

Leaving Azpeitia I passed an old cast-iron signpost indicating the distance to three villages, accurate to three decimal places. Regil was 9.143 kilometres from where I stood, Vidania was 15.269 kilometres and

Urrestilla was 2.907 kilometres. Why should anyone need to know how far it was, to the nearest metre, to these villages? This seemed perverse in a country where I'd found that questions relating to distance produced neural blackouts.

It was late morning by the time I had walked the 2.907 kilometres to Urrestilla and evening by the time I had crossed the Mandubia pass to Beasain and the rare luxury of a hotel bed. The town was still sleeping when I stepped across the railway lines, past the apartment blocks towards the mouth of the Agaunza valley. I had to reach Pamplona by the following morning, if I was going to make my date with Annabel. Pamplona was still two days' or one day and one night's march away.

I followed the road up towards the western end of the Sierra de Aralar, the magic mountain of the ancient Basques. Its limestone heights are dotted with dolmen and menhirs; the stone chambers and standing stones left by the megalithic tribes. Near the far end of the sierra, alone on a mountaintop, is the Sanctuary of San Miguel. Aralar – 'the land of stones' – surrounded by cliffs and rising to 1,400 metres, sits astride the eastern border of the Basque Country and marks the end of the Cantabrian sierras; the next range east of here would be the Pyrenees.

The last village I passed was Ataun, hard under the western end of the Sierra de Aralar. It was a Sunday. Every shop was closed, except for the butcher's. I bought twenty slices of dried sausage and asked: 'Is there a path from Ataun to San Miguel?'

'Yes, there's a clear path.'

'How long will it take me to walk?'

The butcher pulled in his stomach. 'Not long! For me, I can run from Ataun to San Miguel in three hours.'

This seemed improbable. San Miguel was at least twenty kilometres away, and 700 metres higher than Ataun. 'Three hours? That's very fast.'

'When I was younger, I used to run it in less time. Often!'

'How old are you?'

'Fifty-five.'

The butcher gave me directions from the village. A narrow road led steeply up from the village, through a slot in the wall of the sierra. Crags hung over the road. I felt as if I was entering a hidden world, through a keyhole. Aralar's fiesta was being held that day and the steep road was busy with sweat-slicked old men stripped to singlets prodding their way uphill with sticks, and cars crammed with families clutching picnic baskets and wearing wide-brimmed hats. The road became a track then a footpath. A man ran past me. It was the butcher from Ataun. I called; 'Are you going to San Miguel?'

'Yes!'

'Then we can go together.'

'No, no, I must run. I have to get back to the fiesta in time to eat!' And with that, the bouncing butcher sped eastwards.

The track led to the high pasture where the fiesta was being held, beside a group of shepherds' cottages. Baskets were being unpacked on to cloths spread on the grass. Bottles stood in buckets of water. The accordionists' wild dances carried on the wind with me on the long climb eastwards, towards the heart of the sierra.

I had run out of water. Sweat glued my hatband to my forehead. Each time I looked up, the skyline seemed no closer. It always looked the same: a bald monochrome curve set against a blank backdrop. It was easier not to look; to stare at the short blades of grass and patches of dry granulated soil which passed each side of my scuffed boots. I felt sentimental about my boots; they had carried me across Spain and had I been able to re-sole them locally, they would have carried me another one or two thousand kilometres. But the heels were worn down and the treads smoothed away. In Pamplona Annabel would bring me a new pair.

I must have been looking down for some time, because when I lifted my head the bounding figure was almost upon me, black against the glare of the sky, arms outstretched. The turf juddered. A yell and he passed. The butcher! I tried to make a sound. But he was gone. I caught his brief backward glance; it was a look of pity.

At about 1,200 metres the ridge opened on to the table-top of the sierra. Ahead lay a confusing topography of hummocks and holes. An ancient track led to the dolmen, built at intervals along the south slope of the ridge, with vast views across the Araquil valley to the ramparts of the Sierra de Andia. Around each dolmen was a mound of stone about eighty paces in circumference. The chamber of one dolmen was large enough for me to slip inside. I lay in the dark with my cheek on the cool limestone. Among the theories surrounding these megalithic mounds is one proposing that they were summer shelters for shepherds who returned to them year after year.

A short walk further, at the Sanctuary of San Miguel, I met Xebe Peña, a wiry white-haired man in slacks and a sports shirt. Xebe (pronounced Chevy) managed the café; he was eighty-four and knew a short-cut off the sierra. 'There is a good *camino*,' he said as he took my arm. 'This way . . .'

Xebe led me down the narrow rocky ridge below the café. To the east, the Sierra de Aralar stretched in a series of sharp reefs. Bolts of lightning flashed against the cliffs of the Sierra de Andia. I followed Xebe's finger through the reefs. 'Go down this ridge, to the road. Then follow the path up to that rock, then down into the forest, where you will find another path all the way to Madoz. From Madoz there is a road to Pamplona. It is one day to walk.'

As we shook hands, a rattle of thunder echoed across the sierra. I fled down the ridge into the forest chased by flickers of lightning. An owl hooted; rain began to spatter my back. I unfurled Que Chova and felt protected from the lightning. The muddy valley path began to tilt and green dots of glow-worms winked in the black night. With no treads left on my boots and no torch, I fell frequently.

At ten p.m. I passed through Madoz. The insanity of the situation, tempered by the anticipation of seeing Annabel again after two months apart, raised my spirits. I marched out of the village into the black night with the rain pounding Que Chova's crown, down the cliffs of the sierra towards the headlights crawling along the Araquil valley.

I reached the main road at midnight and snacked off *tortilla* and bread in a bar full of drunks, then walked all night. There was little traffic. The rain had stayed behind on the sierra. Every hour I climbed over the fence beside the road and unrolled my sleeping-bag in the adjacent field, pulled off my boots and socks and lay back for ten minutes staring at the stars while I nibbled bread and sausage. Past the pyramidal hill of Santa Catalina the septic electric redness of the city spread across the plain ahead. Factories passed by; a dog lay on the bitumen, its entrails glistening under the glare of a street light. At 5.30 a.m. I crossed the river and climbed up through the great arch in the city walls.

I'd been walking for twenty-two hours. The city was still. Leaning my pack on a park bench I took off my shirt and, with the remaining water I carried, washed myself and combed my hair. I pulled on my spare pair of socks. Annabel would be arriving in about four hours. I wandered through narrowing streets towards the cathedral. Bars began to open for the office workers. I bought a newspaper and chose a café; selected a window table, put my pack in the corner, stretched out my legs, took the first sip of *café con leche*, a *grande*, and began reading the front page of the newspaper. I saw that 500 years ago on this day, Columbus had set sail for the New World in the *Santa María*.

I looked below the masthead of the newspaper and dribbled in disbelief: 3 *de agosto*. I'd arrived in Pamplona two days early.

Pamplona

When Annabel stepped down from the Bilbao bus, the sierras that had separated us for so long melted away and we clung as tightly as we had on that spring morning in the Plaza de Galicia. But something had changed: 'You look younger . . .' I laughed, realizing too late that it was I who felt older.

We walked out of the bus station and along Avenida San Ignacio, past the flaming geraniums and cooling fountains, to Calle San Nicolas, where we left Annabel's rucksack in the room with a balcony that I'd taken. And then we continued up the cobbled street for a late breakfast of chocolate and *churros* in the corner of Plaza del Castillo. The route was important; I'd planned it in advance, to provide a precise sequence of restorative stimuli. But the plan was only partially successful; at first we were both slightly nervous. Annabel was burdened with trying to make progress in her work and, in the bleaker moments felt unsupported, unhappy and alone.

Our five days in Pamplona were full of talk and laughter and tears as we both reckoned with the need to continue our lives without the physical comfort and support of the other. Neither of us regretted this challenge, yet we were about to part, each sick in the stomach, with a sense of the solitariness and enormity of what we still faced. Ironically, I would not have had the courage to embark upon the journey as a single man; it was the security of marriage which had given me the confidence to be alone.

Our brief time together was so intense that I did not unravel the details till later.

The weather was humid and claustrophobic and most evenings the thunderstorms turned the overhanging eaves into waterfalls. We spent hours in the cafés around Plaza del Castillo, especially the Iruña, where Hemingway's narrator, in *The Sun Also Rises*, Jake, drank between bullfights. We read, and we talked. Pamplona was still hungover from the Fiesta of San Fermín, and one or two young men still sported their bandages from the bull-running. Hemingway cleverly succeeded in collecting a bruise during San Fermín. Pamplona is a town with a testosterone complex. Ever since Pompey founded Pompaelo in 75 BC so that he could keep an eye on the northern tribes, Pamplona has been subjected to military muggings. For any marauder coming over the mountains from France, the town presents the first opportunity to give the Spanish a good kicking. Euric the Goth took it, and Childbert the Frank; it was sacked by Charlemagne and knocked about by Napoleon and Wellington.

Too soon it was time for Annabel to leave. We planned to meet again, before the winter. My progress since Cape Finisterre had been much slower than I had anticipated. Now I was about to embark upon a range of mountains more severe than anything I'd met in northern Spain.

The day was cool, for the first time in a month. As we walked back down Avenida San Ignacio, past the flowers and fountains, giddy with impending loss, I admitted what had been on my mind for days: 'I don't think I am going to manage to reach Istanbul in a year.'

Somehow Annabel managed to smile: 'I know.'

The Pyrenees

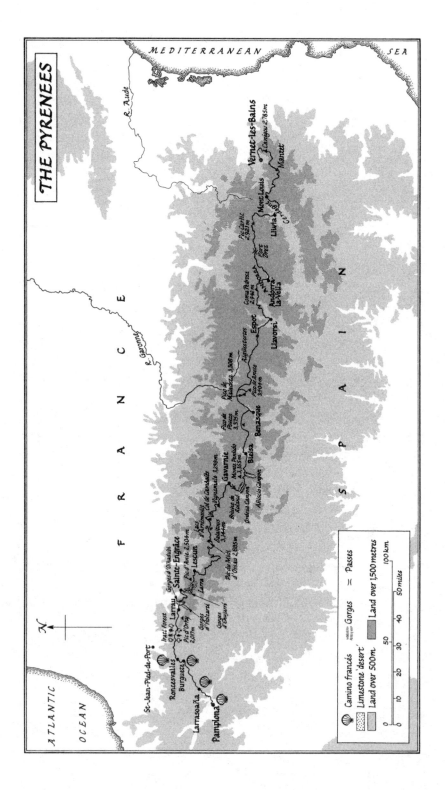

Doctor Parrot's Precedent

I lifted my rucksack off the scales in the public lavatory in Plaza del Castillo and walked out through Pamplona's walls as the bells clanged for evening Mass. So often I had been asked how much my luggage weighed but had never known the answer. Now, instead of shrugging 'Es demasiado grande!', I could reply with decimal precision: '16.6 kilograms.' My luggage was heavier than I was used to; Annabel had brought from London the set of ten maps I needed for the Pyrenees, and a large bag of film. In the mountains ahead, I would have few chances for resupplying myself. Reassuringly, I was also shod in a new pair of boots and I had exchanged my ragged trousers for a pair without a ventilated seat.

By nightfall I was back in the trees, high on a valley side unrolling my sleeping-bag beneath the stars on a ridge in the lee of a wind-bent pine. Leaving Annabel again had confused me more than our first parting at Santiago. The pull between head and heart had been almost unbearable; the logical plot of the journey and the volatile emotions of love were veering away from each other, stretching at the threads of faith that bound the whole enterprise together. On the one hand I wanted to continue my solo balancing-act along the watershed; on the other I didn't want the madness of another separation.

The sense of once again being a cast-out – albeit self-inflicted – was revived the following morning as I made my way up towards the Pyrenees through the old lands of the *cagots*, the caste of mountain pariahs whose deformities – large noses, wide nostrils, high cheek-bones and furry ears with no lobes – caused them to be abused as cannibals, lepers, heretics and cretins descended from Visigoths (the French claimed that *cagot* was derived from *canis* and *Got*, 'dog of Goths'; to the Spanish they were *agotes*, which also has Gothic hints) or Saracens, or from a strain of Albigenses allied to the Cathars of Corbières and Bogomils of Thrace. I was not in great shape myself, for I was still weary from my Basque exertions and had picked up in Pamplona a dose of Montezuma's revenge. In Larrasoaña the mayor was showing me the facilities he had installed for passing pilgrims when I suffered another convulsion: '*Tengo un dolor en el culo* – I have a pain in my bottom!' I gasped, reversing out of the room in a half-crouch, knees locked together and moving only my feet in an attempt to reach the *servicios* before importunate catastrophe spoiled the mayor's freshly painted walls. Afterwards, the mirror confirmed that I had reverted overnight from feeling clean and rested to looking wretched enough to make a *cagot* run for cover.

The yellow paint splashes of the *Camino francés* and I had converged again at Pamplona, though the flow of pilgrims had virtually dried up, for August was too late in the year to be crossing the *meseta*. The pilgrims' route climbed the bed of the Arga valley, and then the Erro, calling at Basque villages, where each massive *baserri* sat like a castle and the shopkeepers closed their doors to keep out the cold wind. I slept beneath a hedge on the Alto de Mezquiriz, just under the 1,000-metre contour, and next morning, while the dew still lay heavy on the grass, walked on to Burguete, stretched along each side of the road up to Roncesvalles.

When Hemingway brought Jake and Bill Gorton to Burguete on the roof of a bus in *The Sun Also Rises*, the place would have felt a little like the back country of Colorado, with the wind and trees and a horse paddock and the fast streams. The road has a smooth surface now which helps the tourist coaches whistle up to Roncesvalles. And there's a bank and a well-stocked store. It's not the place that Jake and Bill hiked out from each day with their rods and landing nets to fish trout in the Irati. Hemingway's haunts have a way of ageing badly.

For the mountains ahead, I bought five cans of fish, a rod of *chorizo*, a round of matured sheep's cheese and five loaves, then lurched along a footpath till the grey metal roofs of Roncesvalles came in sight. I needed coffee. 'Caffeine puts a man on her horse and a woman in his grave,' Bill Gorton had said over breakfast in Burguete; caffeine makes the meaning clearer. Ahead lay the thin reef of the Pyrenees, 400 kilometres long and 3,000 metres high.

Among the papers I carried in a plastic bag were the photocopied pages of *The Pyrenees*, the guide completed by Hilaire Belloc in 1909 and carried by English-speaking mountaineers for half a century. Belloc's ruling that 'Weight counts' was followed by a list of essentials: a pannikin, a gourd, a knapsack, sandals, a blanket and a pocket compass. Once again I was reassured that I was about to embark upon country which had been crossed many times already by people worse equipped. Indeed, the traverse of the Pyrenees had first been achieved nearly two centuries ago, in 1817, when the German explorer Dr Parrot walked from the Atlantic to the Mediterranean in fifty-three days, knocking off a few peaks along the way, including 3,308-metre Pico de la Maladeta. Parrot (commemorated by Parrotspitze on Monte Rosa) went on to make the first recorded ascent of Mount Ararat after Noah, who it could be argued, did only half the job by starting at the top.

Mass was at eight in the evening below the long-limbed vaulting of the collegiate church. I joined twenty or so pilgrims, fresh down from St-Jean-Pied-de-Port and unaware of what lay ahead of them. Eight canons in green and white vestments stood facing us as we bowed our heads before the altar. One of the canons read a medieval pilgrims' benediction. It was cold in the church and the thick mist and Gregorian chants cut back the centuries so that I knew then that my hopes and fears were identical to those who had travelled my road 1,000 years before.

I rose early and crept down the creaking stairs in the House of Beneficiaries and away from Roncesvalles along the track leading up to my first Pyrenean pass. A silver mist hid the mountain ahead. I walked slowly beside a stream, bent beneath my overloaded pack. The path soon swung steeply upwards, away from the stream, and into the trees. The only sounds were the slushing of my feet and the head-roar of my breath.

In 778 Charlemagne's rearguard had laboured up this path in a long file into the Basque ambush. The slashing demons that leapt from the trees caught the Frankish soldiers at the worst point on the climb. Slipping on fallen leaves and tree roots they fell back to the meadow below where they were surrounded and slain to a man. In the epic *Chanson de Roland*, Charlemagne's nephew, Roland, finally succumbs while summoning his uncle's help with blasts from his great horn, Olifant. So hard did he blow that blood spurted from his mouth and the veins in his temples burst.

As I climbed, the mist thickened and muffled the pass in an appropriate shroud.

Into the Pyrenees

At the crest of the pass above Roncesvalles I turned away from the solitary chapel and climbed upwards until I stepped through the top of the cloud into the fireball of the rising sun.

For three days the Pyrenees delayed showing their hand, as I walked up steadily inclining ridges through transient mists that revealed sudden images of mystical brilliance: wild horses running with manes and tails of smoke; a Virgin Mary alone with a bell; seven Bronze Age circles, all in a line; griffon vultures tearing at a sheep. In the Irati forest, whose columnar beeches once supplied the coast with oars, I lay against my damp rucksack listening for Lamiñack, the benevolent Basque Pucks who live in these western peaks.

Then the skies cleared and I climbed to a shelf above the confluence of the Gorges d'Holzarté and Gorges d'Olhadubi and lay in my sleeping-bag, cradled by pale walls which channelled the echoes of falling water into the night sky. The gorges generated their own microclimate. The air tasted almost tropical; cicadas scratched; animals rustled in the grass. I put my hand on the size of slug one would normally expect to find in equatorial jungles. A barn owl glided over the ruin I lay beside, then made several passes over my sleeping-bag, shrieking.

In this spooky nook I was preyed upon by an inappropriate bedtime story. A limestone grotto such as this, on the far side of the range, harboured the cannibal of Gargas. The story is best told by Sabine Baring-Gould, the Devon rector and author of thirty novels, various travel books and hymns (among them *Onward Christian Soldiers*), who was a contemporary of Belloc and who compiled *A Book of the Pyrenees* from entertaining (and often unreliable) anecdotes collected during his mountain excursions in the early 1900s. Living in the black depths of the Grotte de Gargas at the end of the eighteenth century was an out-of-work stonemason called Blaise Ferage, small and broad-shouldered, with astonishingly strong, long arms. Ferage had got into the habit of eating people. He shot, strangled or stabbed his victims, or dragged them alive to his lair. Unwary milkmaids or passing travellers were taken, although he preferred young women and children. No bodies were ever found. For three years peasants listened through their doors for the crackle of his footfall in the dry autumn leaves, or the rasp of his bloody breath. At night his gleaming eyes pierced the fog. He was, they said, a werewolf.

By 1780 they decided that the cannibal's appetite was getting out of hand, and called upon the Parliament of Languedoc to sentence the beast. He was captured, but escaped with the help of a talisman hidden in his hair that enabled him to break chains and open locks. The next time he was captured, they cut off his hair. But he escaped again. Nobody dared walk the streets. Finally a convicted criminal was sent out as bait on the promise of a pardon. The criminal, pretending to flee the law, cried for help outside the cannibal's cave. Blaise took him in. 'However solitary a man may be,' wrote Baring-Gould, 'he yet craves for the society of a companion . . .' Blaise and the criminal became 'intimate' and went together on hunting trips. The intimacy didn't last and finally the criminal lured Blaise into an ambush. On 12 December 1782, aged twenty-five, Blaise Ferage was convicted of murdering and devouring eighty victims and sentenced to death. He was fastened to a cart-wheel with his limbs threaded through the spokes. The executioner smashed Blaise's limbs, one by one, then dealt him the *coup de grâce* across the chest.

I woke early and crossed the footbridge across the neck of the Gorges d'Olhadubi, slung from cables tied off between two crags, then spoiled the day by attempting a short-cut down the bed of the Gorges de Kakouéta. Baulked by darkness and a dry waterfall, I had to retreat, hand over hand, up the gorge wall. The following morning I descended for lunch to Sainte-Engrâce, an irregular stone village with a cluster of knee-high circular Basque gravestones in the churchyard, planted like a garden of fossilized lollipops.

The shepherds of Sainte-Engrâce had once used the bed of the Gorges d'Ehujarré to reach their summer pastures. But the ancient path had been ripped away by a recent flood and in its place was a tangle of trees and branches, waves of shingle and immense rocks. In the gloomy depths, dusk came early. Now and again I picked up traces of the ancient track. The air was still and humid; my shirt glued to my back beneath the rucksack. With minutes of usable light to spare I came upon a section of the path which climbed steeply out of the bed of the gorge into trees, through which I caught chinks of light high above my head. I emerged into the blue darkness of early evening, on the edge of a plateau. Beside a meandering stream I lit a small fire and cooked some mashed potato in my mug. Then I spread my sleeping-bag on the cropped turf and lay back beside the embers of the fire. As I stared upwards, the mountain rim formed a perfectly circular black frame around the globe of the night sky. I felt as if I was staring through a spaceship porthole at a thousand camp-fires.

In the morning, I climbed to the skyline and crossed back into Spain. Ahead stretched the limestone desert of Larra.

'It is a clear path!' chorused the staff of the Refugio Belagua. '*Sí, sí!* You will find it easy.'

'Always it is marked . . . just follow the yellow paint.'

'Straight ahead! All the way!'

'*No tiene pierde!* You cannot miss it!'

'Four, maybe five hours . . . *máximo!*'

I wondered how many shrivelled corpses I'd find out on the desert, the victims of these blithe encouragements. I left the *refugio* with my rucksack stuffed with the full seven-litre water bag and a couple of extra litres in plastic bottles. I could hardly stand beneath the weight.

The paint-marks were not the neat two-colour stripes of red and white which I'd seen on the French side of the Pyrenees; instead, the rock-artists of Larra had chosen a mustard tone of yellow almost identical to that of dried lichen, and instead of applying the paint in precise rectangles (like the French), the Spanish waymarks appeared to have been sneezed on to the rock from a great distance. The route splashes threaded through a beech forest, shaded and quiet, then emerged on to the characteristic confusion of a limestone landscape. Without the ridge and valley pattern which fills the field of view wherever impermeable rocks lie beneath the surface, the sponge-like quality of *karst* creates this freakish, unnatural landscape. It was topographic anarchy; an unfinished mess of random lumps and bumps. Cliffs overhung a foreground of razor-like ribs which hid pockets of grass. I passed the stubs of long-dead trees whose upended roots were polished to ivory by snow and wind and sun. Chalkhill Blues trembled in the dry air. One of the butterflies landed on my finger, folding its wings upwards like a yacht's sail. The blue was the colour of a hazy summer afternoon, merged at the wing-edges into an earthy terracotta rim. Scattered about this wilderness were solitary Arolla pines, dark and sinister, with dense, tapering crowns. As I walked, the sharp rubble clinked beneath my boots, warning the lizards, who scurried with quick jerks towards the closest crevice. A breeze began to catch the clumps of yellow leopardsbane and the tall purple globes of thrift. Ahead rose the shattered cliffs of Pic d'Anie.

After two hours I crawled under the branches of a pine, out of the sun; drank some water; took off my boots. It was still beneath the tree. I lay with my head on the pine needles. Unfindable in the middle of this inhospitable rock desert, my body felt the weightlessness of complete freedom.

Five hours after leaving the *refugio*, the paint spots led up to the Portillo de Insolo, on a desolate ridge below Pic d'Anie. There was a table-top rock with a small cairn and a painted arrow to Lescun. The iris-blue sky had closed over, greyly, and I caught the crump of far-off thunder. I hurried down beside sombre screes and was chased into Lescun at dusk by a cyclone which whipped up dust then battered my back with cooling rain. By the village walls I cast a foolish taunt back at the bristling mountains: 'You'll have to try harder than that . . .'

High Life

The stone walls of Lescun clasped each other as if through stage fright before an amphitheatre of peaks which curved around the village's stepped pastures. Flaring sunlight fought bouts of slanting rain which flung themselves like handfuls of rice at the rattling slates.

The village hotel was run by Madame Carrafancq, a smiling, short-haired woman whose command-post was a desk in a wood-panelled office decorated with a stuffed woodpecker, eagles, a fox, several pine martens and the skins of two bears. Facing her desk was a gun-rack loaded with five large-bore rifles. She exuded the confident aura of a hotelier whose guests seldom quibbled over their bills.

Madame Carrafancq had recently opened a spartan *gîte* along the street, for impoverished pedestrians such as myself. I had just taken my first shave and shower for a week when I was interrupted by the arrival of a man of about fifty with a white Kaiser Bill moustache and wearing long brown shorts. Helmut was a banker from Nuremberg and he was on the eve of departing along the *haute route* armed with a gigantic Bavarian sausage. I pulled out my own shorter, slightly mottled, flaccid *saucisson*.

'It's too soft!' snorted Helmut. 'It's not good for walking.'

'It's not going for a walk; it's going to be eaten.'

'I know, I know,' replied Helmut, waving his enormous truncheon.

'But you must see that your sausage is soft. It is a soft sausage. It will not last as long as my sausage.'

'It is a fresh sausage,' I countered doubtfully, trying to hold my *saucisson* in such a way that its limpness would be minimized.

'That is why it will not last long,' triumphed Helmut. 'Because it is *fresh*. This is the problem with your sausage. You must see that my German sausage is old. That is its strength,' he continued, shaking his *Wurst* to emphasize its rigidity. 'It will keep like this for days and days. For weeks!'

Helmut was right of course. My sausage was not a high-altitude sausage. I had seen it in Lescun's *alimentation* and been lured by its unusually pallid yielding skin, which was quite unlike the chewy *chorizo* that had been my staple in Spain. I could now see that my inquisitiveness might be dangerous; when the going gets tough, the last thing you need is a soft sausage. 'Next time I go hiking,' I conceded to Helmut, 'I'll buy Bavarian.'

I woke late, noting that Helmut's bed was already vacated and smoothed. In the *alimentation* I bought food for the next eight days, the time I thought I would need to reach the next village, Gavarnie, then turned up the narrow road beside the Gave de Lescun towards the rock needles of the Aiguilles d'Ansabère.

With each day of eastern progress, the Pyrenees became grander. Bevelled grass ridges gave way to splintered stone. The skyline grew tall and fractured. Every afternoon clouds boiled up from the French side, threatening then sidling away at sunset to leave a ceiling of stars. One dusk a line of billowing cumulo-nimbus sailed past in line astern, flashing with fire as if they were raking the range with broadsides.

In this high wilderness lived the last of the Pyrenean bears, foraging from their forest lairs at the head of the Aspe valley. 'The Pyrenean brown bear is a most common beast and there is little point in describing it; few people have not seen one for themselves . . .' wrote Gaston Phoebus, Vicomte de Béarn, in the fourteenth century. Hunting accounted for early decimations but latterly the bears have been killed by sheep; with the introduction of flocks to the Pyrenees and the nibbling away of the bears' habitat by pastures and roads, bears waking from hibernation found it increasingly difficult to forage for food, so turned to eating the fluffy newcomers. Shepherds shot the predators, and later used strychnine. The sheep population rocketed.

Travelling the Pyrenees in the early 1900s, Baring-Gould found that the villages of the Couseran valleys, once famous for training dancing bears, had lost their livelihood and that the old practice of placing a stuffed Bruin in barbers' yards to advertise the sale of genuine bear grease had ceased too. By this time 2.4 million sheep were making the annual pilgrimage to the Pyrenees from Spain alone. By the outbreak of the Second World War, only 200 bears were taking refuge in the firs and beeches of the Pyrenees. By 1957, their population had fallen to seventy, then twenty by the early eighties and ten, perhaps, by the early nineties. Eight of them were still thought to roam the Aspe and its eastern neighbour, the Ossau. I watched and listened in vain. In Spain I'd sometimes sensed the eyes of wolves but had never seen them. The rarer bear I'd never even sensed; there was more chance of spotting a yeti. As a sentimental lowlander I sat on the fence: I was reassured by the notion of man's rhythmic migrations with his transhuming flocks and I needed a predatorial wilderness. The two were incompatible.

Dominating the skyline in these parts was the broken tooth of Pic du Midi d'Ossau, a steep-sided monolith 2,884 metres high, whose recognizable profile and accessibility has made it a shrine for French mountaineers. Below it is the Refuge de Pombie, a mountain hut built above a tiny glacial lake. Sitting at the only vacant table in the dining-room was Helmut. During the meal Helmut pulled out his sausage: 'Still, I have a long sausage!' he said, loudly.

'Marvellous, Helmut!'

'Yes,' he continued, grasping the tube of meat in his right hand. 'Is a *gut* sausage. A *hard* sausage!'

At the adjacent table a young Frenchwoman watched Helmut with her mouth open as a slice of veal slid backwards off her fork and slapped on to her plate.

Early next morning I scrambled up the dry cinnamon rock of Pic du Midi d'Ossau. Without the rucksack I floated up the gullies, slabs and chimneys to the twin summits. Below my feet lay the crescentic terminal moraines, like a series of smiles, of the glacier which once oozed from the mountain foot. A griffon vulture revolved on the rising air. From the summit the mountains were dull and low, like an unpainted papier-mâché model. Looked down upon, mountains lose their colour and tone. And their detail. And their sense of vertical scale. For a while I basked in the deception, knowing well that Pic du Midi d'Ossau was little more than a joke pimple compared to the peaks to the east.

Less than twenty-four hours later I was looking at the mountains from below. From Pic du Midi d'Ossau I lost 1,500 metres to cross the road descending from the Col du Pourtalet, then began the long climb back to the heights. One thousand metres above my head, the Col d'Arrious opened the door to the wild heart of the Hautes Pyrénées. Beyond the col, jammed shoulder to shoulder, were the giants of the range, Balaitous, Vignemale, Perdido, Posets and Maladeta, 3,000-metre massifs whose north-facing cirques were still locked in the Ice Age by the grip of glaciers.

On the east side of the col, the mood of the mountains changed. After edging past pocket-sized Lac d'Arrious, the path teetered along the Passage d'Orteig, cut into the sheer north face of Pic d'Arriel. Before me, the many heads of Balaitous blocked the far horizon. Below my feet was a constellation of little lakes, the Lacs d'Arrémoulit, surrounded by ice-smoothed rock. By the side of the largest lake I could see the curved roof of the refuge, and tiny figures moving slowly about its doorway.

I slept under the stars by one of the lakes and left early, before sounds began to escape from the hut. Col de Palas was still in the shade when I reached it and stared across a corner of Spain at Balaitous, the most westerly 3,000-metre peak in the Pyrenees. In the nineteenth century this mountain was hidden away in one of the least-known recesses of Europe, familiar only to the chamois hunters. When the putteed explorers from lowland Europe pushed into this region, they were sealing the fate of one of the last European wildernesses. One of the greatest Pyrenean pioneers was the barrister and squire of Stretton Hall in Leicestershire, the brusque Charles Packe. Born in 1826, Packe was one of those lost archetypes, the roving man of leisure with an encyclopaedic inquisitiveness. He was a scholar and a botanist, a cartographer and a geologist. In his early thirties he developed a devotion to the Pyrenees which led three years later to the publication in 1862 of his popular *Guide to the Pyrenees*, one of the sources used by Belloc on his Pyrenean peregrinations. When climbing alone on difficult ground, Packe roped himself for security to his two Pyrenean sheepdogs, Ossoüe and Azor.

Balaitous had caused Packe particular vexation. The 3,144-metre mountain is one of the least accessible in the Pyrenees, surrounded by ridges and subsidiary peaks which confuse the view and complicate route finding. On his first visit to the area, in 1862, Packe returned to the

The start of the journey at Cape Finisterre

Santiago de Compostela: the market after rain

Vilarello, below the Sierra de Ancares

José and his *palloza* in Piornedo

La Paredina and the Picos Blancos from the north-east

Naranjo de Bulnes in the heart of the Picos de Europa,
from Torre de los Horcados Rojos, 2,506 metres

Ordesa canyon from the Faja de Pelay

Morning on Pico de Aneto

Château de Peyrepertuse, Corbières

High wind on the San Jorio pass

A typical day in the Bavarian Alps

Hallstatt during a lull in the snowfalls

Thaw in the Salza valley, mid-March

Old Bratislava

One of the lace-makers' cottages in the Carpathian village of Čičmany

lowlands having failed even to *find* Balaitous. Afterwards he wrote that Balaitous was '. . . so completely away from the route of the ordinary traveller that the Eaux-Bonnes guides seem quite at a loss as to its exact whereabouts . . .'

When Packe returned two years later with the guide Jean-Pierre Gaspard, he spent seven days wandering about the mountain before identifying then reaching the summit, only to find it marked by a cairn; others had been there before him. The military surveyors Peytier and Hossard had reached the top in 1825, after various misadventures which had included climbing the 2,974-metre mountain Palas, under the impression that they were conquering Balaitous.

Balaitous would have made an interesting two-day excursion, but I was nearly out of food, and had no large-scale maps of the mountain. So I spent the rest of the day skirting around it to the north, traversing above the Lacs d'Arriel to a slot in the ridge linking Balaitous with its northerly neighbour, Palas, then plunging to the lovely valley of Larribet. I ambled along in the warm sun, peering into pools. The valley fed into a blue lagoon surrounded by pines and short, grassy peninsulas. I took off my clothes and waded in, standing on a single bank as my legs grew numb in the freezing current, gazing up to the granite ramparts which locked in this sliver of garden.

Below the lagoon, cataracts tumbled down to the deep valley of the Gave d'Arrens, where I turned right, to climb up to the Port de la Peyre-St-Martin, on the Spanish border. Just enough daylight remained to cross the high Col de Cambalès. The prospect to the east of the pass was one of utter barrenness. A desert of scree, vast, jumbled boulders and scattered lakes isolated by hummocks of bare granite. It looked as if the glacier had pulled out the day before. By the outflow of the furthest lake a small lawn made a perfect bed.

As dawn snuffed out the stars I lay chewing on the last of my week-old bread and the remains of the pâté I had saved from the previous evening. From this frigid beginning the day accelerated into a roller-coaster of exhilaration. After swooping down to the Marcadau valley I bounced up past the eponymous pair of peaks, La Tête d'Ours and Le Chapeau d'Espagne – the Bear's Head and the Spanish Hat – to the Col d'Arratille, then dropped back down on screes into Spain to the source of the Ara (whose sweet waters would fall to the Cinca and then the Ebro, and so to the Gulf of Valencia), where I surged up again to the Col des Mulets and a sudden view of Vignemale which brought me to an astonished, though temporary, stop. At 2,591 metres, the col was level with the glacier on Vignemale's north face. As I watched, pieces of ice peeled off the snout of the glacier and thundered down the cliffs towards the spout of water gushing from the foot of the face across the flat bed of the Gaube valley, braided into streams and gravel banks and littered with boulders dropped by the retreating ice-sheet. On the grass between the gravel banks was a scattering of coloured flecks, climbers' tents, dwarfed by the cathedral of ice. This magnificent tottering giant among Pyrenean peaks seemed to shiver like a living thing.

The couple of coffees I snatched in the refuge down by the Gaube sent me surging up again, this time to Hourquette d'Ossoue, the 2,734-metre crossing-point on Vignemale's north-eastern flank. I reached the pass at five p.m., dropped my pack behind a rock and rushed up to the summit of Petit Vignemale and bagged my first 3,000-metre peak. An eagle scored a circle above my head and a stillness had settled on this needled panorama. Back to the west I could see the split molar of Pic du Midi d'Ossau, twenty-five kilometres away as the eagle flew, but four days by boot. Ranks of ridges receded into the curvature of the earth, lit by the setting sun.

There was the Count's mountain. Count Henry Patrick Marie Russell-Killough, the *monstre sacré* of Pyrenean exploration, was eight years younger than his friend Charles Packe, but a man whose eccentricity brought him greater notoriety. Russell, born to an Irish father and a French mother, was a romantic, a man who had studied philosophy, was an accomplished violinist and, according to his contemporary Beraldi, an *effréné valseur*, a wild waltzer. He was also responsible for sixteen first ascents in the Pyrenees.

Russell fell in love with Vignemale, the highest peak in the French Pyrenees, clothed in the range's most elegant glacier. Russell's infatuation with this white-robed colossus led him to climb to the summit thirty-three times, on the last occasion at the age of seventy. But this was not a clichéd relationship between the climber and the conquered peak. On a summer night in 1880, Russell asked his two guides from Gavarnie to dig out a bed on the summit. He climbed in and spent the night buried up to his neck by a 'blanket' of rock and earth. While the cloud boiled below and the frost settled on his beard, he wondered what effect the sight of a decapitated head would have on any passing mountaineer. And at various other sites on the mountain, he excavated grottoes. An article in the *Alpine Journal*, not an organ known for sexual innuendo, suggested that there was 'something desperate about these penetrations, these determined acts of love'.

Below me lay the great smear of the Glacier d'Ossoue, the biggest glacier in the Pyrenees, split by leering crevasses. On the ice of the Ossoue, Russell, as the self-styled 'Comte de Monts', once set up a tent before the Grotte des Dames and invited guests to a banquet. Columns cut from packed snow framed the entrance to a lawn of red lichen and Persian carpets. *Jambon de Bayonne* was served with vintage wines and the mountain air was wreathed with the smoke of Havana cigars and the scent of oriental perfumes.

As dusk crept up from the valleys, I ran back down to the col, grabbed my pack and continued down the path to the Grottes Bellevue, three of Russell's caves, blasted into the foot of a short cliff, each with a small doorway, one for his guides and servants, a second for his guests and the third, with 'Villa Russell' painted above its door in red letters, for himself.

Of Russell's several grottoes on the mountain, Bellevue was the lowest, built as he approached old age and for the first time supplied with water from a spring. But Bellevue had none of the atmosphere of his higher grottoes and he soon set about creating a seventh and final home, on the summit of Grand Vignemale. Le Paradis was blasted out with dynamite. The cave was south-facing and dry and it was here, in his sixtieth year, that Russell celebrated the 'silver wedding' of his first ascent.

The path built by Russell's guides uncoiled at a dignified gradient down from the caves past waterfalls, moraines and cataracts descending to the level ground of the Ossoue valley. I followed the long, moonless tunnel till I reached Gavarnie, shortly before midnight.

Lightning Strikes

Horses woke me, trotting past my head riderless and in single file. I was lying on a bank above a footpath below the Cirque de Gavarnie, the most celebrated sight in the Pyrenees. The great cliff is 1,400 metres high and backed by a five-kilometre semicircle of 3,000-metre peaks. Down its grey face falls the 423-metre 'Grande Cascade'. I couldn't summon up a sense of wonder; in the bleary dawn the cirque was pinched and unfocused, just like the postcards that had stolen its spirit. I rolled up my sleeping-bag and walked into Gavarnie village and the Hôtel des Voyageurs.

Aside from a couple of quick dips in streams, my personal hygiene had been unattended since leaving Lescun eight days earlier. 'It doesn't matter. This hotel welcomes *les alpinistes*,' smiled the *patron*, Pierre Laterrade, as he waved me through to the dining-room for breakfast. As usual when I came down from the mountains, I was so hungry that I could have eaten a sack of old marmots. But Pierre had eggs, ham, croissants, bread, jams, cheeses and endless jugs of coffee and I ripped through the lot while my neighbours gripped their pink tablecloths with olfactory winces.

Henry Russell used to stay in room 10. The hotel's *Livre d'Or* was away with a professor in Lourdes, so I wasn't able to see the signatures of the Voyageurs' other illustrious ghosts, among them Packe and literary gypsies like Victor Hugo, Gustave Flaubert and George Sand, the trouser-wearing novelist Amandine Aurore Lucie Dupin, 'Baronne' Dudevant. The Voyageurs was also the setting for a summer's night of passion in 1807, when Napoleon's third brother, Louis, and his step-daughter, Hortense de Beauharnais, conceived Napoleon III, the emperor who regulated the price of bread, engaged Baron Haussmann to remodel Paris, misguidedly fought the Prussians, and then died an exile after a botched bladder-stone operation, in Camden Place, latterly a golf clubhouse near the Sidcup bypass. Russell had a tenuous connection with Napoleon III; the mountaineer's mother was a De Grossolles-Flammerens of Gers and the sister of Napoleon's Chamberlain.

I was always reassured when the ebb and flow of human affairs con-trived to make unlikely connections; believing in the existence of these slender threads helped me to feel a part of the greater whole, less left out, less alone. Sitting on a polished rock, I liked to think that mine was just another in an eternal chronology of aching arses to have chosen that spot for a rest. The mountains were dotted with these nodes of human inter-connection, from modern sites like the Voyageurs to the seat-worn slabs that have been rested upon since the hunters moved in behind the shrinking ice sheets.

At five o'clock I left the Voyageurs intent on sleeping beneath the stars. The streets were clogged with day-trippers. Some rode on horse-traps; most shuffled through the hedges of ephemera; the baseball caps, sheepskin waistcoats, stuffed bears, painted cow-bells, chromium-plated ice-axes, varnished walking-sticks and plastic donkeys with pannier-bags of chocolate eggs. Apart from the oleaginous smells of microwaved pizzas drifting from 'English spoken' cafés, the overriding aroma was that of horse manure.

The cairns of dung led towards the cirque, but soon I turned over the river and up the steep, east side of the valley. My pack was loaded with six days' food and was so heavy that to put it on I had to balance it on a rock or tree trunk, then crouch beneath it and attempt to stand up. By the time I reached the plateau above the cliffs, the afternoon clouds had shut out the light. I found a bivouac site in a glade beneath the cliffs of Grand Astazou and lit a small fire. The first spots of rain fell as I began to eat. I nursed the fire until falling water drowned the last embers then lay inside the bag, in the dark, while the rain pummelled the nylon.

At about midnight, the first flash of lightning seared the trees, followed by an explosive barrage of thunder. For an hour, the salvos landed every few seconds, as diffused exposures of brilliant light that filled the sky or broken javelins that split the earth. Fireballs grazed the treetops. Screwed up in the epicentre of a galactic holocaust, I waited to be carbonized by 100,000 volts of atmospheric electricity. It was little consolation to know that oak and fir trees were far more likely to be struck by lightning than pines. Since leaving the valley, I hadn't seen a single beech, which was (so I had read) the tree least likely to attract a lightning strike. I was not astraphobic, but neither had I inherited my father's ability to defy negative emotions with logic; Hol had once climbed Vignemale in an electric storm which had made his ice-axe glow purple and hum. 'Weren't you a bit alarmed?' I asked him. 'No,' he replied, 'one of the things I learned as a teenager in London in the war, when the V1s and V2s were falling, was that the statistical chances of one actually landing on *you* were very, very small indeed.'

In the quiet after the storm the rain fell steadily. I was lying part-submerged in water which had found a way into the bivouac bag. Then the second storm struck, fiercer than the first, and longer. It climaxed with a single thunderbolt which shook the ground. When the storm had dragged itself away across the cirque I bundled up my sodden possessions and set off through the trees in search of shelter. I found a hut, locked but with a front step deep enough for me to sit with my upper body out of the rain. I sat and dozed and waited for dawn. The third storm came at the hut from the side where I sheltered in the doorway.

Illuminated by lightning, I ferried my pack and sleeping gear across the clearing and crawled beneath the thick branches of an old fir.

In the morning, I found the source of the ground-shaking detonation I'd felt during the second storm. Fifty metres from my original bivouac site, a mighty pine had been shredded by lightning. Branches had been hurled into neighbouring trees and the wet grass was thick with splinters. The charge had passed along the tree's roots, which had been lifted through the grass and turned to coal. The air smelled of warm resin.

I wrestled my way into the straps of the rucksack – heavier now that everything was waterlogged – and walked up into the mist over new snow. I had climbed through the 2,430-metre notch – Hourquette d'Alans – in the sharp ridge between Piméné and Grand Astazou which would open the way to the Cirque de Troumouse and the wild country around the Lacs de Barroude, before deciding that I had crossed the line between doggedness and lunacy; if the bad weather were to continue, my wet kit would not just be uncomfortable, but dangerous. I turned around and returned to Gavarnie.

Back at the Hôtel des Voyageurs, Pierre gave me his cheapest room, in the attic. While wind and rain rattled the window, the chainsaws were at work in the village, preparing for winter; trailers passed by loaded with firewood; an old man split logs with an axe. Browsing through one of the newsagents, I came upon a series of large-scale Spanish mountaineering maps which had been drawn with a little too much confidence to be believable. I swallowed the bait. In place of my original plan, to leave Gavarnie for the Lacs de Barroude, I now switched to a southerly alternative. Hours spent with maps had revealed an exciting route over the Pyrenean watershed to the canyonlands of Aragón. The Spanish side of the crest would be wilder and weirder. And warmer.

By the fourth day in Gavarnie my sleeping-bag was dry and the clouds had moved on. With a *pan de paysan* jammed in the top of my rucksack, I walked up to the church. As I sat in the cool shadows a man with heavy spectacles emerged from a door beside the altar and sat at the organ. He let his fingers wander to and fro across the keys, picking up bars from Satie to Schubert while sunlight played beyond the open door on the geraniums and the graves and the birds chirruped a chorus. In this exquisite moment it occurred to me that beauty cannot be sought; one simply has to put oneself in the way of its whims, and wait.

The path climbed the open slopes of the Pouey Aspé valley. Parts remained of a laid stone surface, with foot-smoothed bedrock and an old embankment. Back when pilgrimages were made on foot, this was one of the converging branches of the *Chemin de St Jacques* – pilgrims who had included Lourdes on their journey to Santiago walked up the Pouey Aspé and through the 2,270-metre Port de Boucharo to Spain. In mist or snow or rain wearing a woollen cloak this would have been a terrifying hurdle, with every chance of missing the turn in the path at the foot of the Glacier du Taillon. Here I left the pilgrims' route and scrambled over the rocks to the Refuge des Sarradets, set impossibly on cliffs. The building looked as if it had fallen from the sky and lodged on a ledge.

The ridge above Sarradets was wafer-thin, eaten away from both sides by the freeze and thaw of ice. Above the hut the skyline was cut by the deep slot of the Brèche de Roland, sliced according to folklore by the dying Frank as he tried to prevent his sword, Durendal, falling into the hands of the Basques – a feat needing a long arm (or a telescopic prosthesis) since Roland was one hundred kilometres away at Roncesvalles at the time. One of the earliest trippers (who now come along a level path from the road up to the Port de Boucharo) to visit the Brèche was the widow of the assassinated second son of King Charles X, the Duchesse de Berry, who was carried up in 1822, in a chair. Henry Russell nearly lost his life here after being trapped for twelve hours by a storm. I stepped through the Brèche, into another land.

Mohammed's Bridge

Dropping away in front of me was a desert of bare rock speckled with fragments of old glacier and small lakes. Brown sierras shimmered in the distance. There was no sign of vegetation or of paths. I set the compass, then slithered down the scree. Behind me, the Brèche receded until it was a small window set in the wall between France and Spain. So close to teeming Gavarnie, I could hardly believe I'd stepped into such a bleak wilderness. Three stone-coloured animals, *rebecos*, or perhaps the rare Pyrenean ibex, appeared in the distance. *Capra pyrenaica pyrenaica* – *bucardo* to the Spanish and *bouquetin* to the French – was decimated by the hunting guns of Sir Henry Halford, the crackshot Victorian author of *Art of Shooting with a Rifle*, and Sir Victor Brooke. The animals walked slowly over the rocks and disappeared beyond Pico Blanco.

The compass led me to the Collado Blanco, a high saddle between

3,144-metre Taillon and Pico Blanco, and from here I picked my way down the loose gully on the west side of the *collado*, towards the feature marked on my dubious Spanish map as Aguas Tuertas, the One-eyed Lake. This would, I thought, make a pleasant bivouac site. But the gully ran out above a flat-bottomed bowl of grass. The lake had gone; evaporated, or drained away through some geological plughole.

The day was drawing in. I'd seldom felt so isolated: the enormous, whispering plateau was walled in to the north by Gavarnie's great ridge of rock, and cut off to the south by the unseen chasm of Ordesa. I measured isolation on a sliding scale of human decomposition, based on the amount of time my body would lie before being discovered by a passerby. Up here, we were unquestionably thinking in terms of skeleton.

Intermittent cairns led along the side of a cleft which split Pico Salarons from Mondarruego – the twin peaks dominating the northern end of the Ordesa canyon – to the brink of a cliff. Leaving my rucksack on a rock, I climbed down the cliff, on to a sloping, grassy pediment strewn with debris from the cliffs above. I was probably on the Faja Luenga – one of the ledges which separated the strata of the canyon walls. Below me was another brink. I leaned over the edge. One thousand metres down, already deep in dusk, was the floor of the Ordesa canyon.

Set back a few metres from the brink were two gigantic rocks, one of them split in two and clenching, like a nutcracker, a boulder. Beneath the rocks was a fin of limestone just high enough to protect my prone body from the wind. It would make a fine bivouac site. I fetched my rucksack and, with another thirty minutes of light left, set out to explore the ledge.

My bivouac site was in a 'bay' set between two headlands in the wall of the canyon. I followed the ledge west and was surprised to find a path which crept round beneath the cliffs of Mondarruego to the headland marked on my map as El Retablo – The Altar. The thin prow of rock jutted into the canyon, topped by a knoll of grass. I stood in the last of the sun, watching the fire of the day burn out over the western sierras, then returned to the nutcracker rock, where I lit a small fire from dead roots I'd collected on the ledge and heated a mugful of water for soup. Above the cliffs, satellites and shooting stars scored the blackboard night.

I woke once, snapped from sleep by the sound of a gunshot. Its echoes mingled with crashes and then a long rattle of stones, as a piece of cooling cliff prised itself away from warmth-retaining bedrock.

At first light I followed the Faja Luenga eastwards to the headland facing El Retablo and lay in the rising sun warming my bones beside a dwarf pine, as alone and magnificently fragile as a bonsai, balanced on a toy lawn surrounded on three sides by emptiness. In daylight, Ordesa revealed itself as a smaller Grand Canyon, with layered cliffs falling with stomach-churning verticality into the shadowed abyss.

After some false starts I found the first of the *clavijas* – ladders of metal pegs – leading down the cliff. Below the cliff, the angle eased and a path slithered down to the tree-line, then cut to and fro through the thickening layers of vegetation clinging to the canyon wall. Through box and oak and pine, the air warmed; beech and fir began to appear, and then a thickening of the undercover as ferns and rhododendrons breathed the rising humid air. By the time I stepped from the forest into the spacious birches by the shingle banks of the Río Araza, my shirt was heavy with sweat.

A 600-metre climb up the facing wall of the canyon lifted me to the Faja de Pelay. The most trodden of Ordesa's ledge-paths followed the 1,900-metre contour along a second band of strata, for about eight kilometres, towards the canyon head. I slept beside the path and continued next morning along this linear belvedere, pausing to lie among the rocks watching a flock of *rebecos* picking their way delicately across a scree. Finally the lines of strata on the canyon walls converged with the rising slope of canyon floor, then met at the canyon head where a fan-shaped waterfall, the Cola de Caballo – Horse's Tail – fell to a level meadow divided by the infant Araza. Ahead, the horizon was blocked by the highest limestone massif in Europe: Monte Perdido.

A path climbed to the Refugio de Goriz and then up to a broad pass at 2,329 metres, where I turned to the north over the flanks of Monte Perdido on a route which had been described to me in the refuge as *peligroso* and which my guidebook warned was 'awful' and 'not recommended'. The attraction of this route was that it skirted the head of the Ordesa's little sister, Añisclo.

The path (understandably, as I was about to discover) was little used. Having reached about 2,500 metres on the Pico de Añisclo (the southern buttress of Monte Perdido), the route inched nervously over screes that threatened to slide over cliffs, then scaled and descended a series of sloping slabs lubricated by grit and water. It was midday and on the south-facing slope of Monte Perdido all I could see of Añisclo was a black, jagged rent, directly beneath my boots. It was as if someone had torn a gâteau in half, clumsily. Beyond the gorge rolled the hazed waves of dusty sierras, sailed by cloud-ships.

I emerged on Collado de Añisclo, an airy thousand-metre blade falling to Añisclo on one side and to the smooth, twelve-kilometre glaciated groove of Pineta on the other, a pine-covered perfect U, framed by the parallel precipices of the Sierra de las Tucas and the Sierra de Espierba.

Descents from the heights were always weighted with small forebodings. Life down below was a lot more complicated. The plummet into Pineta was also physically painful; for over 1,200 metres, inconceivably balanced rock and scree fell so steeply that, by the time I stepped down to the banks of the Cinca, daylight was finished and so were my knees.

Among broken trees on a cone of avalanche debris I found a bivouac site behind a large boulder, and built a blazing fire. The cast of the flames on the surrounding trees and boulders formed my irregular walls for the night; walls which became familiar and cosy. If I left the firelight, to collect more wood or to piss into a downwind space, the fire winked back from the encompassing blackness, looking so tiny that it could drown in a single raindrop. At daybreak I stripped and washed beneath a nearby waterfall, then broke two eggs into my steel mug and cooked them over the rekindled embers of the fire. I filled the mug with water which I'd carried from the waterfall and placed the mug back on the embers. Over coffee, I spread the maps. In descending to Pineta, I'd left the limestone pinnacles and chasms of the central Pyrenees for the monolithic bulk of ancient granite. From here to the Mediterranean I would be walking among more isolated massifs.

Pineta's silent floor led to Bielsa. This little place had never recovered its composure since the traumatic spring of 1938. One year after Gernika was razed, the Nationalist generals launched their offensive on Aragón. One Republican division held out in the Valle del Alto Cinca under 'El Esquinazado' – 'The Dodger' – a name inherited by Antonio Beltrán from his father and grandfather who had been notorious smugglers from Canfranc, a mountain town beneath the Puerto de Somport. But the Dodger was pushed upstream by General Iruretagoyena's army, Bielsa was knocked about and 4,000 Republicans escaped over the Puerto de Bielsa and down into France. Like so many Spanish *héroes*, the Dodger died in poverty in Mexico. His escape over the Pyrenees was followed by adventures in Russia and then with the *maquis* in France. After deportation to Corsica he broke with communism and worked with US intelligence. His last mistake was to fall out with *them*.

Now it is the French who invade in thousands, pouring through the road tunnel bored beneath the pass used by the retreating Republicans, to fill their cars with cheap drink and cigarettes from Bielsa's super-markets. I bought a map in a shop selling furry animals and suede water bottles and retreated eastwards towards the Sierra Marqués. Sadly, the cartographer had muddled his ravines and I spent the night lost on the sierra and was forced to return to Bielsa the following morning.

This time I followed the route taken by the retreating Republicans, up the Cinca and then the Barranco de la Pardina, an old pack-horse route over to the Cinqueta. Warmed by a fire I spent the night in a turf-roofed hut on the eastern side of the Paso de Caballos. The nights were growing colder and longer. As I wandered down towards the Cinqueta the following morning, I passed empty *cabañas* and pastures and, on a saddle beside a pasture marked on the map as Plan des Carlistes – a rec-ollection of the days when these conservative valleys were a Carlist stronghold – a huge stone 'sofa', left by the retreating glacier. Through a sculptural quirk, the stone had a perfectly angled back, and a seat wide enough to take ten. With the *cabañas* and deserted pastures, the sofa seemed another piece of abandoned furniture.

Below, when I reached the Cinqueta valley, I met a shepherd follow-ing his flock down the dirt road. 'You're leaving the mountains?' I asked.

He nodded and said that there had been too much rain. 'The water has made their feet bad,' he said, pointing his staff at his limping flock.

Grey clouds were building to the north as I was blown up the Puerto de Gistaín the following afternoon, using Que Chova as a spinnaker to haul me up the pass. Thunder rolled as I rushed down the far side into the dusk. For two nights and a day the rain fell. In the tail-end of the storm, I walked up the valley of the Esera from Benasque with several days' food crammed in my rucksack. I arrived at the Refugio La Renclusa at nightfall. The old stone house stands just above 2,000 metres at the head of a ravine on the northern slopes of the Maladeta, the 'Accursed Mountain'. Christ, it is said, had wandered this high wilderness and turned to stone the dogs of the herdsmen. From this vast massif rose Pico de Aneto, 3,404 metres high, and the tallest peak in the Pyrenees.

Two mules and a horse stood in the mist outside the building, their loads of firewood stacked against the wall. I was directed to a dormitory jammed with rucksacks. Plastic sheets had been spread on the top bunks, to divert the rainwater on to the floor. The hut was busy with climbers and a group of geologists from Leeds University. The previous week they had found two bodies beneath a boulder. 'They'd crawled there for shelter,' said one. 'Probably in a storm.'

'How long had they been there?'

'A long time. Their faces had been eaten away by vultures.' The *Guardia Civil* had erected a pinboard in the *refugio*, on which they'd mapped the Maladeta's fatalities. The board was covered with pins. 'Lots of people die here,' said the student.

I borrowed an ice-axe and asked my Spanish bunk-mate to wake me at five.

I was the first away from La Renclusa. In the pre-dawn half-light, I climbed up the flank of the long reef of rock which splits Maladeta's glaciers. The ridge is easy to climb from the west, but hangs over the glacier so sheerly on its eastern side that there are only a couple of safe routes down to the ice. By dawn I was sitting on the crest of the ridge eating a breakfast of bread and cheese while looking across the Glacier de Aneto. The ridge was gratifyingly precise. It was also a watershed: the snows on one side of the ridge melted into the Esera, then flowed down the Cinca and Ebro to the Mediterranean, while those on the other side fed the headwaters of the Garonne at the start of its journey across France to the Atlantic.

Two men picked their way towards me, a Tyrolese guide leading his German client; one grimly looking, the other looking grim. I had seen their Porsche arrive at the road-head in the Esera valley the previous evening. The client, a banker from Frankfurt, was making a last stand against middle age.

It was on this mountain massif in 1897 that Stephen Spender's father, Harold, had a celebrated falling-out with his guide. The incident is related with polite ire in Spender's book *Through the High Pyrenees* and it neatly illustrates the pitfalls of allowing self-reliance to be subjugated by the will of the 'local expert'. Spender and his party – H. Llewellyn Smith, their French guide, Pierre Pujo, and a local man, 'Chico' ('Boy'), whom they'd employed as a porter – were standing at the foot of Pico Forcanada, an elegant double-spike to the east of Pico de Aneto, piling their unnecessary baggage on the Collado Alfred so that they could climb unencumbered to the summit. An argument ensued about the rope. Pujo, the guide, wanted to leave it behind, stating that ropes were used for crossing snow, not rocks. This was countered by his clients' insistence that this was not the case in Switzerland, where ropes were habitually used for rock-climbs.

'Never in the Pyrenees!' ruled the French guide. They left the rope at the col.

'After all,' conceded Spender, with fatalistic prescience, 'he knew the country better than we did.'

The group set off up Pico Forcanada, following an increasingly sheer line which terminated in an overhanging cave, at which point Pujo announced that he was leading them up a new route. Pujo then unlaced his boots, handed them to Chico, and continued up the rock in his socks. Following his example, Spender and Smith also took off their boots and handed them to Chico, who strung them together and draped them over his shoulders like a necklace. In climbing the pitch, Pujo found himself stuck and had to be hauled up 'hot and swearing' by Spender, a sight which so traumatized Chico that he refused to follow.

The three climbers now found themselves with no boots or rope at the top of a pitch which they could not climb down. 'I know not how this would have ended,' records Spender, 'if I had not suddenly bethought me of a woollen muffler ...' Tying the scarf to the end of Pujo's red Pyrenean waistband, the men lowered their improvised rope to Chico, who tied the six boots to the end.

They reached the top of Forcanada, but on returning hungry and tired to the col discovered that the hapless Chico had bolted for the valley with all of their food and equipment. On the long, hungry descent, the exhausted Spender consoled himself by reciting Virgil: '*O passi graviora* ... O ye who have suffered greater woes.'

Above me, the Frankfurter and his leader had disappeared into the Portillón Superior, a notch in the ridge which drops to the tongue of Aneto's glacier. When I caught them up, they were moving slowly, roped together, through blasts of spindrift. New snow lay ankle-deep on the old glacier ice. I used their steps. The three of us were soon swallowed by swirling whiteness. They were dressed for the Antarctic, in glossy over-trousers and anoraks, mitts and crampons. With my spare pair of socks on my hands, my torn cotton trousers and jacket and worn-out walking boots, I looked a likely candidate for La Renclusa's pinboard. While my two companions were wearing climbing helmets, I had my trilby lashed to my head with the hood of my jacket. The guide, a terse character, understandably viewed my presence as a threat to his client's wellbeing. The banker, suffering on the steep, deep snow, was lost in personal oblivion.

Above us, clouds tore across Aneto. The guide picked a good line to the head of the glacier at Collado de Coronas. From here, the route led up rocks awash with powder-snow towards a summit obliterated by spindrift.

The top of Pico de Aneto was defended by the Pont de Mahomet, a tottering bridge of rocks with immense drops on both sides. On the snow hummock at the lower end of Pont de Mahomet the guide was coiling the rope ready to lead out across the rocks and shouting instructions into the German's ear. They were plastered with snow.

It took the guide fifteen minutes to cajole the banker across the iced rocks while the gale buffeted his trembling legs. Through the flying snow, the two walked the few steps from the far end of the Pont de Mahomet, up to the cross on the summit of the mountain.

Watching their success through the spindrift, I realized that I couldn't bridge the gap alone. To negotiate the iced holds I needed the security of the rope. 'A barrier shall divide the blessed from the damned,' says the Koran, 'and on the Heights there shall stand men who will know each of them by his look.'

The guide didn't throw me the end of the rope. And I was not about to ask for it.

I turned around and descended to La Renclusa.

Twisted Waters

The easiest route east took me over the high granite country of Maladeta's flanks.

There was a new bite to the clear air, and as I climbed up through the crags of the Valleta de la Escaleta, I passed two shepherds, pushing their flock down towards the Esera and their winter quarters. Then I was above the vegetation and treading on ice-polished granite. The valley had opened into a gigantic rough-hewn bowl with a jagged rim over which I had to find an exit. My Spanish map decorated the Escaleta with several small lakes, and these I came to, one by one, in the wrong locations.

One cock-up led to another and when I climbed eventually to the skyline I was on the wrong pass, coincidentally the Collado Alfred, where Harold Spender and his party had taken a breakfast of bread, wine and sardines and argued about their rope. To reach the correct pass – Collado de Mulieres – I decided to take the shortest route, over the top of a 2,978-metre spike called Cap de Toro.

I was close to the summit of Cap de Toro when I found myself looking into a vertical-sided cleft. With some awkwardness (the handle on the umbrella, lashed to my rucksack out of sight behind my neck, had a habit of catching on overhanging rocks and tipping me off balance), I climbed back down until I could make my way into the bed of the cleft and thence up alarmingly slippery scree and loose rock, to the summit.

The southern side of Cap de Toro was steeper than the northern and I was hampered by my pack and the troublesome umbrella handle. I employed, as did Spender on neighbouring Forcanada, 'every variety of progress known to rock-climbers – scrambling, squeezing, and squirming, with breathless grapples with the rock-face, precarious reliances, and uncertain footholds'. Periodically I caught glimpses of the Escaleta valley, looking like the surface of the moon, between my legs. Like Spender, I was in absolutely no doubt that I should not be up there without a rope (and someone to hold it), a judgement substantiated by the tell-tale signs of incipient fear: the sensation that my genitals had been encased in an ice-bucket and the uncontrollable trembling of my legs when tensioned against microscopic toe-holds. I descended and then traversed around the rocks until I arrived at a knife-edge ridge which brought me, with some minor difficulties, to the Collado de Mulieres.

'Buenas ...' Over the edge of the ridge were two young men wedged in a crevice, eating chocolate. They were from Hamburg and were unsure how to find the way down from the Collado de Mulieres to Plan de Aiguallut, where they intended to camp. Like three men trying to stand simultaneously on a see-saw, we teetered about on the narrow ridge while I pointed down into the Escaleta at the glacial lake on which they should set their compass. My own way down was obvious. Unlike the Escaleta, the Mulieres valley was an unambiguous slot falling suddenly to the east. I lowered myself over the edge, into Catalunya.

The afternoon was all but spent by the time I reached the meadows and streams. A cold wind blew down the valley and clouds were already brushing Cap de Toro, 1,300 metres above my head. I paused by a place where the river emerged from the ground into a pool which shivered with frogs. A rowan tree hung over the water, its branches dancing with new, red berries. Warnings of winter increasingly caught my eye.

Less than an hour of light remained. I climbed onward, up into the Vall de Conangles. The valley was exposed to the increasingly fierce gusts blowing down from the west. Rain was on the way. At about 1,900 metres I reached a plateau strewn with glacial erratics – large rocks dumped by the retreating ice-sheet as it melted. In the gloom I hurriedly inspected each rock for shelter.

Under the largest rock there was a small overhang which was just big enough to accommodate a single short human. It was already occupied by a man with long, grey ringlets and a tattoo on his arm of a submarine beside the words 'HONG KONG'.

Richard Gonzalez came from a village near Bordeaux. He was forty-seven years old and had recently retired from the French Marine, in which he had served for eighteen years, mainly in nuclear submarines. From the depths of the oceans, he now found himself obsessed with the heights. He was making a solo traverse of the entire Pyrenean range by way of the *Haute Route*, the forty-five-day high-level traverse from the Atlantic to the Mediterranean. His tent had been damaged in an earlier tempest and, like me, he now slept in natural cots.

The impending storm and a spirit of Anglo-French cooperation resolved the accommodation crisis immediately. 'We will make it bigger!' said Richard, who had been a chief petty officer.

Richard ordered me to climb the mountainside and return with tree trunks. In the meantime he extended the shelter by building protective walls. An hour later, we had constructed a lean-to and walls, over which Richard lashed the remains of his tent with a multitude of seaman's knots. We stood back. '*Voilà! Le Grand Hôtel!*' said the submariner.

Inside, there was surprisingly little space. One of us would be able to lie full length in a patch of damp mud; the other would have to contort himself into an embryonic curl beneath a sagging ceiling of rock. I could not think of a more appropriate companion for a claustrophobic bivouac than a long-serving submariner. In a gesture of officer-like magnanimity, Richard insisted that, being longer than him, I should have the relative luxury of the damp mud.

By chance, we had both run low on food. Richard had some tea-bags and the end of a week-old *baguette*, which was as hard as a missile's nose-cone. I had a small cube of cheese and half a thumb-length of salami. Combined, these ingredients made a fine dinner, which we took with tea boiled on Richard's gas cooker.

Wedged into 'Le Grand Hôtel' while the storm beat outside, Richard turned to me before we went to sleep and politely asked what time I would like to rise in the morning.

'About eight, perhaps.'

'*D'accord*. I will make the tea for eight.'

In the morning we climbed together up to a misted col and performed a small ceremony, shaking hands before Richard's camera, which he had balanced on a rock.

'It is,' said Richard, 'an important place on my journey. When I was in my submarine, I was given a certificate for sailing under the North Pole, and another certificate for sailing under the Equator. Now I am standing on the place where water flows in two directions, to the Atlantic down there, and the Mediterranean down there. It is *le partage des eaux*. How do you say it . . .'

'Watershed.'

'It is unusual to have an enthusiasm for these places, *oui*?'

Beyond the col the path divided. The submariner dived into the clouded depths of the Valarties in search of provisions. I climbed up into Aigüestortes. The 'Twisted Waters' are the closest Spain has to the English Lake District, a collection of choppy fells cohabiting with chocolate-box lakes and more hikers per square kilometre than any other corner of the Pyrenees.

By one of the lakes I bumped into Begoña, the Basque mountaineer who'd overtaken me on the road to Ipazter, two months earlier. She was bouncing along like an over-active India-rubber Puck, wearing shorts and a small rucksack. Some way behind her limped Ibon, with a bandage on one arm and gashes on his knees. 'He fell!' laughed Begoña.

This was obvious. Her husband looked as if he had dropped off the top of the Matterhorn. 'Is he OK?' I asked.

Begoña nodded. 'He's fine. He just had an accident on the mountain.'

'What happened? Did he go over a cliff?'

'He tripped on his bootlace!'

That was the trouble with mountaineering. You could spend a lifetime clinging with toenails and teeth to gnarly routes then come a cropper on a pedestrian crossing. Or die of asphyxiation in a mountain hut. Heroic endings were harder to arrange than ridiculous ones.

By moonlight I cut through the back-country of Catalunya, down the valley of the Noguera Pallaresa and then up its eastern tributaries towards the Andorran border. I passed places Belloc had visited: Escaló ('exceedingly filthy') and Llavorsi ('unpleasing') and the bridge (now concrete but in Belloc's day built from timber cantilevers) he'd paid a halfpenny toll to cross. In the dead of night I stalked silent cobbles trailed by my own footfalls.

The next day I climbed up through the pines on an old smugglers' path to the Andorran border.

Golden Ages

I had to climb Coma Pedrosa without underpants. There had been rust-lings in the early hours as I lay on the concrete ledge at the back of the tiny *cabane* and marmots, or possibly a rare trumpet-snouted desman, had stolen my only pair of boxer shorts. In bare-arsed distress I scoured the burrows along the river bank, then the holes along the foot of the scree, but couldn't find the smallest shred of cotton. They were, I concluded miserably, already lining the nest of the verminous thief. Spitefully, I was glad that I hadn't bothered washing them for a day or two.

Coma Pedrosa soared above the *cabane* to 2,942 metres; the highest summit in Andorra. Way off to the west beyond the shark fins and needles of Aigüestortes, I could see the shining skull-cap of Pico de Aneto's glacier and to the north the twin spikes of Estats and Montcalm and beyond, a blue drop-off into France. Below me to the east lay the valleys of Andorra, filled with the silvery mists of car exhausts and circling on their toxic thermals, the black cross of an eagle.

'The Andorrans have all the vices and virtues of democracy,' warned Belloc. 'They are very well-to-do, a little hard, avaricious, cour-teous, fond of smuggling, and jealous of interference.' It is unclear whether Belloc regarded his rustic hosts as a reclusive criminal cult or as opportunistic free-marketeers.

A principality of 467.76 square kilometres and 60,000 inhabitants, hidden away in the high Pyrenees, with Spain on one side and France on the other, this geopolitical riddle avoided wars for 800 years and post-poned the emancipation of women until 1970, when they were allowed to vote. These two facts are unrelated. Andorra's previous cataclysm occurred in 1278, when a treaty divided suzerainty of the district equally and indivisibly between the Bishop of Urgell, on the Catalunyan side of the range, and the Count of Foix, on the French side. In limbo between this pair of squabbling freeholders, Andorra prospered in splendid, ambiguous isolation.

When I climbed back down Coma Pedrosa and returned to the *cabane* to pack my equipment, I found the missing underpants lying on my sleeping-bag. Their wanderings remained a mystery. Possibly the desman found them too repellent and brought them back. In light heart, I walked down beside waterfalls and pools and gardens of pines, to a dirt road, then bitumen lined with building-sites and hotels and restaurants, running beside a dirty river. In La Massana I turned into a bar for a beer and was halted in my step by a Yorkshire voice calling: 'For God's sake, someone buy that man a shirt!' I looked down and saw that both arms of my shirt were hanging on by a few threads and the entire garment was a blotch-work of stains and sun-faded patches. Everyone in the bar was speaking English and wearing gold chains. The bar-girl came from Harpenden, the Hertfordshire town where my mother and father had been to school.

'Poor them,' said the girl, who had come to Andorra to save money. 'There's no tax!' she grinned. 'And a three-course meal costs five pounds. We go out every night. You can't do that in Harpenden!'

Later that afternoon I walked into Andorra-la-Vella, the capital, dropped my shirt in a dustbin, pulled on the thermal vest I'd rinsed in a stream earlier in the day, combed my hair and knocked on the door of the director of the Sindicat d'Iniciativa de les Valls d'Andorra. Mrs Roser Jordana was expensively dressed and her scent filled the small office with lily of the valley.

'When the Civil War ended, Spain was devastated. In Spain you could buy nothing, not even buttons. So the Andorrans went to France and bought buttons, and brought them back over the mountains to sell at a profit in Spain.' Mrs Jordana sighed. 'Then we had the "big war" . . . Spain was rebuilt and France was in a mess. So the Andorrans reversed the direction of smuggling, bringing from Spain things which the French wanted.'

'Of course.'

'By the early fifties Andorra was looking at tourism. The sixties and seventies were our big shopping decades.'

Andorra's recent history, I learned, was remembered in a sequence of what Andorrans call 'The Golden Ages' – successive responses to post-war Europe's awakening lusts. Andorra had a Golden Age of Philishave razors, of Duralex dishes, of Stainless Steel, of Alcohol, of Electronics.

'People came here to fill up their cars, thousands and thousands of them. Last year we had over ten million visitors.'

Andorra, said Mrs Jordana, was now at a crux in its history as a *paradis fiscal*. Andorrans paid no income tax or value added tax, the principality's budget being financed from charges levied on goods imported into the country. Education and the postal service were free. The trouble was that the single European market had removed the price differentials from merchandise. Goods now cost roughly the same, whether you bought them in Spain, Andorra or France. Andorra was a victim of creeping uniformity.

Mrs Jordana smiled sadly: 'Everyone who comes to Andorra buys something; if fewer people come, less is bought; we import less, and less tax is raised.'

'How are the tiny fallen . . .'

'What worries Andorrans is that we will have to start paying tax. We hate the word "taxes"; we're not used to them.'

'How will a small place like Andorra stay on the map? What can you do?'

'We copy your country,' replied Mrs Jordana. 'We get a prince and princess, beautiful and surrounded by kids. Then we build a castle for them and then they must start being naughty.'

Over the coming days I talked to many locals about Andorra's uncertain future. The Minister of Finance – a sharp-suited Harvard economist – felt that Andorra should look to the success of Europe's other micro-states: 'Liechtenstein for example,' Josep Pla told me, 'has specialized in teeth.' In a separate meeting, Andorra's head of government, or Sindic General, the Very Illustrious Señor Jordi Farras Forne, argued that the principality's first priority was the drafting of its first Constitution. 'The *contrabandistas* are not important now,' he reassured me. 'They are symbolic . . . smuggling is finished.'

It was Josep Pla who explained to me the bizarre economics of Andorra's tobacco industry. Cigarette manufacturers wanting to export their cigarettes to Andorra had been obliged in return to buy Andorran tobacco, which was of such poor quality that it was largely unusable. To save transporting the tobacco to the cigarette factories to be destroyed, the Andorrans had offered to destroy their own tobacco. After each harvest, ninety per cent of the Andorran crop was carried to the principality's refuse dump on the mountainside above the Valira, where it was burnt, with a notary standing by as a witness. The Minister of Finance had smiled at the logic: 'It is common sense; tobacco always gets burnt in the end!'

Getting lost in this capital was impossible; the Avinguda Princep Bennloch served as the main road through Andorra and as the capital's shopping street. Neon icons – Nike, Nikon and Hermes, Sony and Panasonic, Rolex and Toblerone, Hi-tech and Zippo, McDonald's – blinked into the distance. Sentimentally, I remembered the unpretentious shelves of Spanish mountain stores, where the common brands of coffee, milk and bread were Bonka, Ram and Bimbo. In Andorra-la-Vella shoppers drifted along hypermarket aisles piled with shoes and jewellery and Jack Daniels. In basements, erotomanic men in livid nylon suits stood rooted before stacks of matt-black sound equipment inhaling the fumes of warm circuit boards and sticky credit cards. Out in the street, specialist shops catered for those in search of a titanium bicycle, or a second-hand sub-machine gun or a model of the steam-train *King George V*, in Great Western livery.

At the circus that night I watched a sad procession of animals being humiliated before a quarter-full tent of inattentive children; synchronized poodles leapt over hurdles; chimpanzees sat on chamber-pots; an elephant rolled on to its back so that a boy could throw a hand-stand on its stomach.

The motor traffic was worse than Tottenham Court Road on a Saturday afternoon. According to Mrs Jordana's statistics, Andorra had 198 kilometres of tarmac road (three fewer kilometres than it had of ski-runs) and a total of 38,201 registered cars and trucks. So if every Andorran was to hit the road simultaneously, there would be one vehicle for every 5.18 metres of tarmac; a nose-to-tail traffic jam throughout the entire principality.

I went to the Casa de la Vall. The seat of the General Council of the Valleys, Andorra's governing body since the fifteenth century, was a fortified stone house two doors down from the Unisex Perruquería on Carrer de la Vall, much sanitized since Spender's visit, when he noted that the building had 'that sordid air which hangs about every Andorran dwelling, and suggests a national dearth of manners and style . . . beauty or cleanliness'.

The twenty-four three-cornered black beaver hats and robes which Spender saw hanging on the wall of the chamber had been replaced by dark panelling, but the framed pictures of the pope and the two co-princes still hung on the end wall, and the wooden box containing the archives was there. It had seven keyholes, with the names of the seven *parròquies* – parishes – scratched into the wood above each hole. Only in the presence of all seven representatives could the box be opened. The floor of the chamber was occupied by an oval-headed table surrounded by seven chairs, with a further twenty-eight seats for the general councillors around the perimeter. Daylight percolated through the single window at the end of the room. The Basque Casa de Juntas looked imperial by comparison. Standing back from the Casa de la Vall, Spender had graciously conceded that the place had a 'pigmy majesty'.

In 1929 my maternal grandparents, Ruth and Jack, had visited the Casa de la Vall, when part of the building was still being used as a school ('very grubby', wrote Ruth). There was no road in from France in those days, and the two of them had walked over the mountains on mule-tracks. Ruth was ninety-four when I left Finisterre. She had spent most of her life travelling the world, either as a doctor or as a habitual nomad. Her father, George, used to send manuscripts and carpets back from Constantinople, until the money ran out. Ruth always said that George owned an island in the Sea of Marmara, but after he died they carried all his papers into the garden of 94 Belsize Avenue and burned the lot. So we could never be sure. My earliest memories of Ruth are of sitting on the end of her bed listening to the latest episode of her travels; a shaky take-off from an Andean ledge (I always loved the bit when the melons fell on the fat lady's head as the plane banked); passing through the Panama Canal on a freighter; treating crocodile bites in the African bush. It was Ruth who introduced me to Henry David Thoreau, giving me the copy of *Walden* that she'd bought second-hand at the age of fourteen, in 1912. I've often imagined us dwelling on one particular passage: 'If a man does not keep pace with his companions, perhaps it is because he hears a different drummer. Let him step to the music which he hears.'

I left Andorra-la-Vella one evening and walked up the valley to Les Escaldes, where Ruth and Jack had stayed in the rickety Hotel la Pla. I had with me a photocopy of Ruth's travel journal. The Valira river had thundered so loudly beneath their window that Ruth had dreamed that the sea-front at Hastings was being washed away in a storm. 'The lavatories are on tiny, rotten, flimsy looking balconies overlooking the torrent . . .' she noted. 'Investigated from outside, they looked decidedly unsafe. Think we ought to be tethered on a rope when there.' Ruth and Jack had dined on pigeon and prunes.

From Les Escaldes I followed my grandparents' footsteps up

through the forest to the tobacco fields around St Miguel d'Engolasters, a tiny, rough-hewn twelfth-century church which in Ruth's day said only two masses a year. I found it locked and seemingly unused.

Beyond the fields I picked up the mule-track again, through the trees to the lake where Ruth had bathed, then switchbacked down to Encamp. Ruth found the village served by a single shop selling rope-soled shoes and chocolate. Encamp was now a small town whose shop-windows were stuffed with everything from chainsaws to toothbrushes. It was also the home of Andorra's cultural attraction, the Museu Nacional de l'Automòbil, notable for its unique collection of 141 different types of sparking-plugs.

The museum also kept seventy or so motor-cars dating from the dawn of motoring. About the oldest was a quadricycle which had been converted into a one-cylinder, pedal-assisted, quarter-horsepower De Dion Bouton in 1898, the year Spender made his second visit to the Pyrenees. It was difficult, looking at this eccentric contraption, to believe that this was the prototype for a species which would have taken over the world in less than a century.

Beyond Encamp, the road-builders who had obliterated the mule-track used by my grandparents had made no allowance for old-age pedestrians. As the road snaked through the defile I had to share the bitumen with cars that careered past my elbow snatching at the soiled air like vacuum cleaners. I walked for two days up the main valley, hunting out the mule-tracks trodden by Ruth and Jack, Spender and Belloc. A few sections remained, fragmented by new roads, overgrown and disused, the sanctuary of basking snakes. I saw none of the vermilion caps, breeches and waistcoats worn in the valley a century ago.

I left the principality over Port Dret. For the first time since arriving in Andorra, I was looking at a landscape which had changed little: streams still trickled through clumps of broom and ivory mushrooms shone in the grass like pocketfuls of spilled buttons. Crossing earlier in the year, Ruth had found the valley thick with blue gentians and anemones, orchids and white buttercups.

The morning was clear and sunny. The valleys were hidden from sight. I stood on the top of the pass and looked for a last time across the crests of Andorra to the suede-coloured sierras of Spain. Then I turned and walked down into the green Ariège, and France.

First Frost

At the end of the long summer, the grass was yellow with thirst on the Portella de Lanos. I slept with rats and a father and son from Barcelona in a stone *cabane* overlooking the dammed lake below the pass. Rustlings of the *cabane*'s wildlife kept waking me and eventually I lit my candle and picked up a rock. The bag of food which the father had suspended from the roof was swaying.

'*Señor!*' I said, at the neighbouring sleeping-bag. 'There is a rat in your bag!' The Catalan sat up and gingerly lowered the bag to the floor. The rat climbed out of the neck of the bag and the man and his son laughed with delight: '*El ratón! El ratón!*' The rat had eaten all of their food. I was less amused, for they'd promised to leave me their left-overs in the morning, as they were returning to Barcelona.

I was woken by cold coming through the stone floor. Outside, the first frost had turned the grass a brittle silver. The frost ran up to the screes at the foot of Pic Carlit. I climbed quickly to warm up, emerging into the rising sun on the summit ridge. Off to the east rose the silhouette of Canigou, marking the end of the Pyrenees. The valleys were filled with morning gauze and in the foreground the lakes on the Désert du Carlit glittered icily. Away to the north, a tidal-wave of cumulo-nimbus clouds charged towards Carlit. I added a stone to Count Henry Russell's cairn, built when he made the first ascent in 1864, then rushed down the eastern ridge and across the desert, a wild parkland of ruffled lakes surrounded by cranial granite and stunted pines that shivered in the quickening wind. After a couple of hours, the edge of the plateau dropped sharply to Lac des Bouillouses, where knots of fishermen dressed for the Yukon, in khaki trousers and waistcoats covered with pockets, sheath knives and bush hats, were hunkered down behind boulders, sheltering from the cold.

In the gusts of the wind there was an incipient violence and by the shore of that high lake I changed my plans: instead of heading straight for the heights of Canigou, I dived down to the south, hurrying on a thin path down the valley of the Angoustrine towards the shelter of Cerdagne. Just before dark I found a hut with a stained mattress and a fireplace. I chased out a rat, lit the fire and listened to the gale build.

By morning the tempest had still not broken. Chased by rain squalls and granite clouds tumbling down from Pic Carlit, I was blown out of the Angoustrine into the great hull of Cerdagne, the biggest open space in the Pyrenees; twenty-six kilometres long and six kilometres wide and entirely above 1,000 metres. Of Cerdagne's several peculiarities, the oddest was Llivia, a fragment of Spain measuring six kilometres by three kilometres, surrounded by French territory. This bizarre state of affairs arose from the messily drafted Treaty of the Pyrenees of 1659, which placed the lower half of Cerdagne in Spain and the upper half in France. Under the terms of the treaty, Spain had to cede to France thirty-three Cerdagne villages but because Llivia was technically a town, it was overlooked and thus remained Spanish, smirking beneath its Gibraltarian rock and dominating the broadest part of the valley. Llivia made an interesting port in a storm.

Entering Llivia was an informal affair: in the village of Angoustrine a shopkeeper directed me down a lane blocked to vehicles by a *Route barrée* sign. The lane led down to a mill and over the river and then became a track up a gently rounded hill dotted with hay-bales, like the edge of a Wessex down. Somewhere on that hill I crossed the border from France into Spain again.

The roofs of the one-time capital of Cerdagne (population 923) came into view as the storm arrived. I stayed two nights above a bar in a room with one window-pane missing, while the rain battered the slates and the street outside became a torrent. *La Vanguardia*, the Catalan newspaper, carried reports of drownings. Near Puisserguier, 200 sheep were carried away by the floodwaters. The body of Mme Juliette Sanso, who had disappeared in Rennes-les-Bains, was found the following day in Château des Ducs de Joyeuses. Michel Vieule of Lezignanais described how a puddle beneath the door had suddenly inundated his house beneath ten metres of water. In Couizo, 300 houses were damaged. It was, everyone agreed, as bad as the floods of 1940; even as bad as 1891. 'Aujourd'hui', concluded the Midi newspaper *l'Indépendant*, 'les populations n'accusent personne, si ce n'est la nature' – today people don't blame anyone, it's just nature. In the bar, the men sat through *La Mountañera Familia Robinson* and *Charlie Chan and the Curse of the Dragon Queen* on the television. I'd missed a major adventure on the basis of a decision which at the time had seemed whimsical; had I not turned around at Lac des Bouillouses I'd have been caught in the open, north of Pic Carlit.

I occupied myself locally while the storm blew itself out. Llivia's *farmacia*, claimed to be the oldest chemist shop in Europe, had been converted into a museum. Above the books on the apothecary's desk, a framed family tree charted the seven generations of Estevas who had owned the shop and who would have worked with the glass distillation apparatus and the bucket-sized mortar, mixing their drugs with powdered human skulls and the dried excrement of dog and rat.

When I asked the museum's custodian whether there was a drug available to assist ailing walkers, she pulled in her grey cardigan and led me to a cabinet whose drawers were painted with the faces of saints. She pointed to the tired, bearded image of St James, scallop shells on his hat, shoulder and staff: 'That one is the best for you,' she said, pointing at the label: B JUNIP. LAUR. 'Yes,' she continued, 'juniper and laurel. It is for walking; for pilgrims like you.'

How many pilgrims suffering *en route* to Santiago had been tempted by St James's potion, only to buckle into incontinent spasms? Juniper's diuretic properties and the poisonous effect of laurel seemed unlikely to benefit a man with several hundred kilometres to walk. Maybe they believed, like the ancients, that munching Apollo's leaf would provoke prophetic inspiration.

I said: 'I think I'll stick with the vitamin pills.'

Before leaving Llivia I climbed its hill, hummocked with fragments of wall and a water-filled cistern, all that remained of the castle blown up by Louis XI in 1479 to prevent it being reoccupied by the Spanish. The storm had washed the air and soaked the land. In the low, early sun, the long, straight road running down the centre of Cerdagne shone like a ribbon of mercury in the black valley, a sight which would have been familiar to the legionaries who had watched from this hilltop 2,000 years ago, when this was a Roman highway and Llivia was Julia Lybica. Off to the west, with a ring of thin, white cloud around its base, rose Olympian Canigou, my last Pyrenean milepost.

I left Llivia on a track which ran as straight as a blade between pollarded willows and ash towards the villages of Err and Llo; other cryptic villages lay close: Ur, Hix, Ger, Alp and Das. Basque, say some, or was it just that Cerdagne had labelled itself with codes, to confuse incomers? In a field of stubble, I re-entered France.

Tracks led me on towards the head of the Cerdagne and the Col de la Perche, where a car felt its way through the mist, its headlights dulled and yellow. Some way behind, a flock of sheep shuffled along in the half-light, goaded towards Eyne by two shepherds down from the mountains. 'They look good sheep!' I called across the road.

'Not sheep any more,' one of them laughed. 'Mutton!'

Summer had emphatically ended.

Shortly after sunrise three days later, I stood on the summit of Canigou. The ridge ran away to the Peak of the Thirteen Winds, and beyond it to Red Peak and the Peak of the Seven Men. Cloud surrounded the base of the spreadeagled massif, obscuring the Mediterranean coast. Two Catalan flags cracked in the wind, tethered to a steel crucifix. To stand alone on this holy mountain floating, so it seems, on a silver ocean, is one of the prizes waiting those who complete the Pyrenean traverse. Noah stood here first, say the shepherds, cast ashore in the Ark on Canigou's shores, though it was (irritatingly for the Catalans) an Aragonese, the conqueror of Sicily, Peter III, who made the first recorded ascent at the end of the thirteenth century.

Nevertheless, the mountain is a unifying emblem for French Catalonia and Spanish Catalunya, visible from both and the home of myth and mountain sprite, most famously Queen Snowflower 'Flordeneu' and her fairies. But it's a graveyard too, and 300 or more have died in the shadows of Canigou's fanciful summits in electrical storms or in aeroplanes which strayed from Perpignan's runways, sometimes in clear weather which, say the Catalans, is Canigou striking back against modernity.

I walked slowly, heavy legged, down the mountain to a still lake set in pines. Through the trees lay the Chalet des Cortalets, the famous old hotel built at over 2,000 metres on the northern side of the mountain as a staging post for tourists conveyed from the valley by horse. The Chalet was shelled in the Second World War by the Germans, who correctly suspected it of being used by the Resistance. The place was deserted but for the *patron*, who was stacking chairs. He brought me chicken and potatoes.

'This is the last meal I cook at Cortalets this year,' he announced.

'You are going to the valley then?'

'Tonight.'

The Paradise of the Pyrenees

At the foot of Canigou I marked the completion of my Pyrenean traverse by spending a night in the worst hotel I'd ever stayed in, a shambolic guest-house with cardboard walls and paralysed plumbing. The English called Vernet-les Bains 'The Paradise of the Pyrenees' and came here each winter for constitutional walks and for the sulphur springs. The sun, observed Alfred Emberson, who founded Vernet-les-Bains' Notes and Queries Society in 1912, would be good for his countrymen 'in these days when the Gulf Stream, the vagaries of the moon, or some other occult influence has demoralized the English'.

The English were between wars: the Boer War had ended in 1902 and there would be a twelve-year intermission before the start of the First World War. They came with their bottles of Chlorodyne and Condy's Fluid by ship with the General Steam Navigation Company from London to Bordeaux and then by train to Villefranche, completing their pilgrimage in three-horse diligences, or hotel automobiles, up the hill to Vernet.

The colonists were led by 'Lord Bobs' – Frederick Sleigh Roberts, Earl of Kandahar, Pretoria and Waterford. Lord Roberts had won his Victoria Cross single-handedly capturing a standard at Khudaganj during the Indian Mutiny and ended his career as the victor of the Boer War. *En route* to immortality, he had led 10,000 men out of Kabul's gates on the famous march of 1880 through the heat and dust of an Afghan August to relieve Kandahar, covering 313 miles in twenty-two days and fighting the battle for the city the following day. The feat gripped the nation. The embryonic Ski Club of Great Britain associated itself with the victory by naming its principal downhill trophy the Kandahar Cup and Rudyard Kipling wrote his doggerel ode to 'Fightin' Bobs'.

I got hooked on Vernet's seedy sentimentality and instead of leaving, transferred my custom to the Hôtel Moderne, where I took a room smelling of coffin linings and equipped with a bidet on wheels. The bidet was plumbed to the wall with long, flexible pipes, like umbilical cords, so that it could be rolled about the room. While it rained, I sat at the table, on the bed or in the plastic armchair, with my aching feet soaking in warm water.

I went to the Sunday service at St George's, whose foundation stone had been laid by Lord Roberts. The church fund, administered by the Reverend Ferris, raised 16,941.25 francs from a cross-section of Vernet's Edwardian visitors. The names were listed on the church wall: Mr Two-penny; Miss Micklethwaite; Mr Lewelyn Twentyman; Miss Butterworth; Admiral Sir Francis and Lady Bridgeman; Lord and Lady Haversham; Sir Maurice Fitzgerald, Knight of Kerry; General Sir Robert and Lady Stewart; Lord and Lady Talbot de Malahide.

The casino was taken over each winter by the English Club, who provided English newspapers and periodicals for its members, who could also use the English billiard table, the card room and the ladies' drawing-room. A cinematograph plant was installed in the gallery, showing varied programmes of films supplied by Pathé Frères. Twice a day a band played and there were whist drives, bridge and amateur theatricals. On the first floor, beside the baccarat room, silenced through the winter, the library was stocked with 3,000 books; 'one of the most up-to-date on the Continent', wrote Eustace Reynolds-Ball FRGS, in his seminal guide, *Mediterranean Winter Resorts*.

To sweeten the locals, the English invited the school children of Vernet to the Club on the first day of each January. Bearing French and English flags, and accompanied by their teachers and the Mayor of Vernet, the children marched to the casino and listened to speeches. After the speeches, the children were invited to sing Catalan songs and to dance. Then they circled a lit Christmas tree. On leaving the Club, each child was presented with a toy, an orange and chocolate. 'It was,' records Emberson, 'a good expression of Entente Cordiale.'

During the day, one could walk to the Cascade des Anglais, or take an excursion up Canigou, returning to the Nouveaux Bains Mercader for a one-franc *bain de pieds* or, for an extra 25 centimes, a *douche ascendante au vaginale*. One might see Lady Kipling, or HRH the Princess Henry of Bat-tenberg or Darwin's son, Sir Horace, taking a break from designing his scientific apparatus. With afternoon tea, one took the cakes and jams of old Monsieur Jules Mercador, one of Vernet's droller characters in his white cap and apron; his *gâteaux de milles-feuilles* and jam of *framboises du Canigou* were especially popular. Only the occasional appearance of a wild boar, carried into town slung from a pole, would send a *frisson* across the terraces.

Readers of *The Times* saw the end approaching; on the first day of August 1914, the Foreign Office issued its 'Warning to Travellers on the Continent'. The following Wednesday, 5 August, brought the inevitable news; WAR DECLARED ran the headline, followed by a centre-page advertisement: 'Your King and Country Need You. Will you answer your Country's Call?'

The old regulars left and the flow of names in the visitors' books trickled to a standstill. One of the last entries in the *Livre d'Or* of the Grand Hôtel du Portugal was an epigraph composed by Ella Butterworth of Milford Cottage, Surrey:

> Oh! Vernet lovely Vernet!
> Land of the sulphur springs
> How can we ever thank thee
> For all the health it brings
> With deep regret I leave thee
> But the hope to return 'ere long
> To mingle with the happiness
> The laughter and the song.

Ella's poetry remained unpublished.

Few came back. Field-Marshal Roberts died in France of a chill while boosting the troops' morale in 1914. V.C. Scott o'Connor, whose book about the Pyrenees had been published in 1913, returned in January 1920. 'Vernet Revisited', he scrawled in the Portugal's *Livre d'Or*: 'I find it dead, but it will live again.' But Vernet never recovered. The great storm of 1940 destroyed three of the hotels and by the time war ended the English had other priorities.

The storm had cut the telephone lines, so I was unable to tell Annabel that I'd safely descended from the Pyrenees. I made the pilgrimage up through the hamlet of Casteil and the woods of chestnut and oak to the abbey of Saint-Martin-du-Canigou, balanced on its crag above the tree crowns. The abbey had been heavily restored. The work was in progress in 1911 when Lord Roberts and Rudyard Kipling led a party of twenty-eight up to the ruins. One of the party, an Irish lady visitor, had to be restrained from removing one of the abbey's columns to her home, where she wanted to use it for a sundial.

To gain entrance to the abbey I had to join a party of pensioners, who poured through the cloister pungent with bath salts and face powder, then congregated in the abbey shop to buy 'Jesus de Nazareth' video-cassettes. The rock tombs of Count Wilfred of Cerdagne, who had endowed the monastery 1,000 years ago, and his wife, Elisabeth, lay side by side, filled with rainwater.

Back in Vernet that evening I found that I'd missed the week's only social event, the annual *Journée Mycologique*, organized by the Federation of Mediterranean Mushroom Associations.

I polished my boots and the following morning set off towards the Alps.

The Cévennes

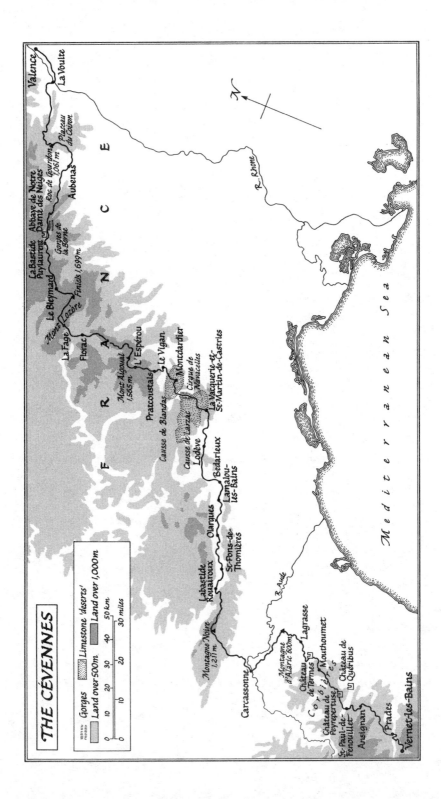

THE CÉVENNES

Gorges
Limestone 'deserts'
Land over 500m.
Land over 1,000m.

0 10 20 30 40 50 km.
0   10   20   30 miles

N

Valence
La Voulte
Plateau du Coiron
Aubenas
Roc de Gourdons 1,061 m.
Abbaye de Notre Dame des Neiges
La Bastide Puylaurent
Gorges de la Borne
Le Bleymard
Mont Lozère Finiels 1,699 m.
La Fage
Florac
L'Espérou
Le Vigan
Mont Aigoual 1,565 m.
Montdardier
Pratcoustals
Cirque de Navacelles
La Vacquerie-et-St-Martin-de-Castries
Causse de Blandas
Causse de Larzac
Lodève
Bédarieux
Lamalou-les-Bains
Olargues
St-Pons-de-Thomières
Labastide Rouairoux
Montagne Noire 1,211 m.
Carcassonne
R. Rhône
Montagne d'Alaric 600m.
Lagrasse
Château de Termes
Mouthoumet
Château de Quéribus
Corbières
Château de Peyrepertuse
St-Paul-de-Fenouillet
Ausignan
Prades
Vernet-les-Bains

F R A N C E

Mediterranean Sea

R. Aude

The Dead Zone

Ripe apples hung under a bruised sky which loosed fretful showers as I walked the sixteen kilometres down to Prades. It was market-day, a Tuesday. A cold October wind snatched at the racks of leopard-skin trousers and Superman T-shirts as Bob Dylan sang 'Hot chilli peppers in the blistering sun . . .'

The stalls filled the *place* around the foot of the church of Saint-Pierre, whose original Lombard tower had been crowned inexplicably by a cast-iron lattice, tapering to a weather-vane. It looked like an absent-minded piece of rocket-ship marginalia by Leonardo da Vinci and was abused in the town's own tourist literature as 'an unspeakable edifice'.

I left town past a bust of Pablo Casals, the refugee Catalan cellist, who put Prades on the map by settling here after crossing the Pyrenees at the outbreak of the Spanish Civil War. Beyond the fruit trees of the Têt, paths led me up into Les Fenouillèdes, the worn-out granite foothills of the Pyrenees which took their name from the fennel which grows on the warm slopes. Small holm oaks rattled in the wind as my way climbed and fell from stream to stream and my boots brushed briars heavy with blackberries. In that desynchronized way of the mountains, the season of fruitfulness was coming late, just ahead of the snows. Looking south, I could see the peaks I'd crossed the previous week, already wrapped in white.

On the wooded Col de St Jean, three men collecting mushrooms showed me their bulging bags of *cèpes*. 'It's a good year,' said one of them. 'These are worth 150 francs a kilo.'

Gusts of wind tore at the trees.

'Do you think it will rain?' I asked the mushroom collector.

'No. This wind is the *tramontane*. It comes every year. It blows, some-times at one hundred kilometres per hour. It will not rain here. But on Canigou! On Canigou it is already snowing!'

I came down from the pass at the end of the day to Trilla, a small village in the grips of the annual *vendange*. Grape-pickers were walking in from the vines behind tractors pulling carts loaded with bins of wet black grapes. The doors of the *caves* breathed sugary fumes of fermentation. The village dogs were unsettled by the grape-pickers, men and women in muddy trousers from Spain.

The dogs saw me walking down the centre of the street. I unsheathed Que Chova and repelled the first animal, but another dog rushed in unseen from the opposite flank. Involuntarily I jumped forward, which startled the dog. It lunged and closed its jaw around the back of my thigh.

Que Chova fell from my hand and I turned circles in the road, hopping on my good leg and clutching my thigh. The grape-pickers were laughing. A farmer in a cloth cap crossed the road. 'Did you speak to the dog in German?'

'No. I said nothing. I'm English.'

The farmer looked nonplussed. 'The dog only bites Germans.'

I pulled down my trousers. The dog had bitten while the muscle had been taut. Three rows of bruises crossed my thigh like smudged tattoos. The skin was barely broken, but my leg felt as if it had been crimped by a blunt guillotine. For the next four days I hobbled north towards the haven of Carcassonne, helped on my way by a relay of Good Samaritans.

The first was Cati, an Armenian girl working at the Benedictine abbey in St-Paul-de-Fenouillet. Like the churches, the ninth-century abbey had been used as a stable after the Revolution and it was now being reconstructed, room by room. Accompanied by fresh coffee and the voice of St Paul's choir at practice, I was shown the artefacts from the village's past: a pegged table for making rope-soled shoes; wooden clogs; scissors for docking horses' tails; a wooden mallet for treating leather; chisels and planes and pieces of polished *bruyère*, used for tightening the string on hay-bales. St Paul even had its own *boules*, made by Augustin Paris, who collected the wood of the box-tree root during a waning moon. His trade mark was *Supérieures aux Meilleures* – Better than the Best. These relics from the Handmade Age always looked too recently discarded to be museum pieces. We were still in the 'sentimental phase', unable to accept that we'd left behind the tools and skills we'd used for hundreds of years.

I asked Cati whether Saint Paul was busy with tourists in the summer.

'Saint-Paul-de-Fenouillet!' she laughed. 'This is the dead zone!'

The film showing that week at Saint Paul's tiny cinema was *Le Dernier des Mohicans*.

From the top of the abbey's bell-tower I could look north to the limestone wall of Corbières, a spur of the Pyrenees running north to the Aude, thick with forests and gorges and pierced by pale fangs of rock topped by the bloody battlements of the Cathars, the heretic sect of the twelfth and thirteenth centuries whose strict moral asceticism had found a fertile following at a time when wars, crises and civil disorder had created an acute fascination with evil. In the way of so many quasi-religious cults, the Cathars retreated to hidden sanctuaries – the castles of Corbières – where they died gruesomely in mass suicides and on flaming pyres lit by the Crusaders of the established Church.

Above the abbey, a path squirmed up through box and juniper, overhung by ramparts of limestone, then emerged on a little plateau crossed by a gritty path. The Château de Peyrepertuse perched on the end of a long, rocky ridge. Battlements and towers stood in relief against the darkening sky. No lights showed. Night had fallen by the time I reached the foot of the ridge. A narrow path climbed steeply over rocks and tree roots, and using Que Chova to drive back the briars, I passed beneath a cliff, or a wall, then scrambled over boulders to the brink of a void. Deafened by the rise and fall of my own breath I wondered where the castle had gone, then found the path again, cutting unexpectedly along a shelf on the north side of the ridge. The path led to the castle gate. Steps climbed to a courtyard. By candle-light I prowled the turrets and flooded cisterns, then followed the flights of steps to the uppermost keep and peered over cliffs at the village lights cowering far below.

The castle was built along the crest of the ridge for about 300 metres, but was hardly more than fifty metres wide. The older eastern complex, with courtyards and the ruined chapel, was surrounded by high, crenellated walls and dominated by a circular tower and the western keep, built on the highest part of the ridge in the 1240s and reached by a precarious flight of steps cut into the sheer rock of the northern cliffs. Up here, there were the remains of another small chapel, with the stubs of six dressed columns and a high arch at its western end. Between the two keeps was an exposed section of ridge with a roofless building – perhaps the barracks – standing alone on the edge of the cliff. Bats flitted through the gaping window. I unrolled my sleeping-bag and, by the light of my candle, settled down to read the previous day's *l'Indépendant*. Afterwards I lay looking up at the square of stars above the ruined walls, sure that I could smell the lamp fat and greasy leather of medieval soldiery.

Distant church bells and the sounds of swifts scything through the battlements woke me. Over to the south-east, the massive walls of the Château de Quéribus stood sharp against the morning light. Half a kilometre underneath the battlements, the villages of Duilhac and Rouffiac were waking up and the bent backs of the grape-pickers advanced in lines through the vines like aphids. There was a secret path down the castle's northern cliffs to Rouffiac, empty but for sleeping dogs, and the village street was black with grape juice, as sticky as blood.

I met nobody all day, limping north on tracks through the Forests of the Dead Elm to emerge at dusk from the trees before a small village which sat like a full stop in a deserted valley. The village was perfectly concentric and focused on a small, central *place* darkened by plane trees. Most of the houses were shuttered. Some had broken windows or *A Vendre* signs. Nothing in Mouthoumet moved apart from the water which spilled from the fountain in the *place*.

Around Mouthoumet spread the pastures once grazed by the enormous flocks of *mouton* which gave the village its name, flocks which would have relied on this oasis in the forest for grazing during the long seasonal journeys between the Pyrenees and the plains. Now the flocks travelled by truck and Mouthoumet had died for want of custom.

Looking for food and shelter I walked on to the next village, La Roque de Fa. La Roque was as decrepit as Mouthoumet, but a light showed from the window of the bar. The Auberge du Griffon looked as if it had been sucked skyward from the American Midwest by a whirlwind and dumped in the empty heart of Corbières: two yellow-painted wagon wheels were suspended by chains from the ceiling above a bar with a padded red vinyl fascia. Players in attitudes of rigor mortis stared wide-eyed at the ceiling from the table-football game; a mute budgerigar gazed out of the window at the night outside.

'Where have you come from?' asked the *patron*, a dark-haired woman.

'From Peyrepertuse.'

'Peyrepertuse, ah yes. So you slept at Duilhac?'

'No, I slept in the Château.'

'The Château is very dangerous.'

'No, I think it is a beautiful place. It has a special . . . ambience.'

'You are mistaken; this year a woman was killed in the castle. By lightning. She was holding the metal rail and *phisstt*! She was burnt to a cinder this big.' The *patron* extended her arms to illustrate the dimensions of a log. 'You would like something to drink?'

'Please. And to eat . . .'

The only other people in the bar were two grape-pickers; young men with long hair and worn-out army clothes, thick with mud. They slumped exhausted over their glasses of *pastis*. Madame Altimiras brought me a bottle of Corbières, from Paziols, over on the Mediterranean end of the range. The wine was heavy and warm and chased away the fainter flavours of omelette and fresh *champignons*.

I slept in a room above the bar and when I came to leave in the morning, Madame Altimiras asked whether my rucksack was heavy.

'I don't know.'

She left the bar and returned bearing a bottle. 'Please take it. It's from Domaine de la Salce, from the vineyard of Simon Miquel. It is good Corbières wine. Better than last night's.'

Rain had fallen in the night and the road north from La Roque was covered with puddles and the mace-heads of fallen sweet chestnuts. Berries nodded in the hedgerows; black clusters of buckthorn and oval whitebeam, long tendrils laden with blackberries and the maroon stipple of hawthorn. Acorns hung in the oaks and a heavily laden fig tree reminded me that the Mediterranean was less than one day's walk away to the east.

In these empty hills I passed the remains of other Cathar strongholds: Château de Termes, lonely on a crag, where Raymond de Termes had held out against the catapults and siege machines of the Crusader Simon de Montfort, till he was defeated by dysentery and died three years later in a Carcassonne dungeon. The ruins had been abandoned since 1562 when the king commissioned a master stonemason from Limoux to pull down the towers and walls. And beyond Termes the stumps of Château de Durfort glared from a wooded outcrop looped by the Orbieu. I lit a fire in a *bergerie* on the mountainside overlooking the castle and drank the Corbières while the rain fell outside and the dogs howled in the valley below. They were more than one kilometre away, but they knew I was still in the valley.

In Corbières the ghosts outnumbered the living. The Orbieu led to St Martin des Puits, a neglected hamlet set on a rock slope with a thousand-year-old church whose frescoes showed a knight on horseback and another falling backwards with his lance slipping from his grip. Spectators stood before what appeared to be marquees. Downstream, the little gorge uncurled until the bell-tower of Lagrasse's abbey appeared over the vines on the floodplain. The plane trees were shedding big, brown, papery leaves. The only other movement in Lagrasse that lunchtime was the arms of the *boules* players, swinging slowly like the hands of the old town clock. The arcaded market-place was deserted; the shops closed. Every able-bodied inhabitant was out in the vines.

Over the twelfth-century high-arched bridge I poked about the empty abbey. Recognized in one of Charlemagne's charters, the abbey was once so powerful that its domain embraced six abbeys, twenty-five priories and sixty-seven churches. Donations came from as far away as the Counts of Barcelona. But now *la capitale des Corbières* lay shipwrecked and abandoned on the rocks.

Ahead, the horizon was blocked by the black bulk of the Montagnes d'Alaric, the northern wall of Corbières. By the light of the stars I climbed until the land ahead was filled with twinkling constellations. Below lay the vast plain of the Aude, suffused on my left by the orange glow of Carcassonne and to my right by that of Narbonne. Behind me, Corbières lay in utter darkness. I slept on a mattress of box branches in a stone bee-hive hut whose diameter was so small that my legs projected through the doorway into the rain. The following day I walked along the crest of the Montagnes d'Alaric. This was limestone and I found no streams in which I could wash. Mud covered my trousers and the silk shirt I'd bought in Andorra was ripped across the back. The heels on my boots were worn away and Que Chova had been bent into a scimitar-curve.

The forests had been replaced by low scrub which clung to the limestone in defiance of dehydration and the *tramontane*. Bereft of flowers, every plant had taken on a deathly blue-grey pallor. Unkempt leopardsbane straggled across the pocked rock; hyacinth and rockroses, lavender, thyme and wild asparagus occupied pockets of grit between the silverbarked amelanchier, the scraggy broom and box and holly oaks.

I came down from the hills by night, passing silently through ranks of vines. Ahead, the spotlit turrets of Carcassonne floated like a dream on the black bed of the Aude. The walls of the city rose as tall and smooth as granite cliffs, their battlements deserted against the starlit sky. A flight of steps led up to an arched doorway, through the wall to a curving yard before another wall. I walked in both directions, till I found another small doorway. Steps led upwards towards a glow of light and a telephone-box.

I dialled our number in London.

'Nicholas Crane is away for one year. Please leave any messages for Nicholas, or for Annabel Huxley, after the beep.'

Down and Out in Languedoc

My arrival in Carcassonne coincided with the 500th anniversary of Columbus's landfall in the Americas and with the opening of the city's first McDonald's. To entice customers into the new *burgerie*, the management were offering two McChickens for the price of one. This would not have quickened my pulse had I not just made two momentous discoveries: that I was one-quarter of the way from Finisterre to Istanbul and that I had spent half my money. A McChicken was a roundel of chicken-flavoured burger in a soft bun with a piece of lettuce stuck in place with a mucus-coloured lubricant, and it provided more calories per franc than any other food-source in Carcassonne apart from dead leaves. I ate thirty-four McChickens during my stay.

Annabel's work had prevented her from meeting me in Carcassonne, so she had posted me a pair of replacement boots which had failed to arrive, and a letter which had. The letter began: 'I am nearly in tears . . .' and went on to explain how she had stayed up till midnight writing a letter to me on my antique computer, which had digested her labours then refused to regurgitate them into the printer. In exhausted frustration she had scratched out a few lines by hand, ending 'I do love you', the 'do' suggesting that I might be in need of reassurance. I was. The letters that I'd written daily to Annabel as I crossed Spain had petered out in the Pyrenees, where I was often several days from the nearest letter-box. In Carcassonne I redressed the balance by writing to her three times a day, on one occasion penning a poem on the back of a McDonald's paper mat, which began promisingly with 'My darling wife . . .' but ended when I became distracted by hunger.

> Hark sweet love,
> My heartbeat quickens.
> Time again
> For two McChickens!

With each day getting colder, wetter and shorter, and missing Annabel more than I dared admit, I waited for the boots to arrive and fretted about my dwindling resources; unless I cut back on spending, I hadn't enough money to reach Istanbul. I was staying in the cheapest room in town. Each day I checked the post office and spent hours exploring the old Cité, a warren of crooked streets encircled by Viollet-le-Duc's mock-medieval walls.

My stay in Carcassonne was enlivened by two odd relationships. The guest in the room adjacent to mine was a large woman of about fifty, who always wore short white socks and heavy shoes beneath a tent-like dress. Each morning she woke me with her dawn ablutions, which were accompanied by gurgles and spits of fluid from the drain-holes of my own bidet and basin. Twenty minutes later, she would leave her room and lock the door, then try the handle three times before unlocking the door and repeating the procedure. Then she would struggle along the narrow lead-floored balcony accompanied by the sound of scraping plastic, as she dragged several dustbin sacks. At five p.m. she would return with the bags, now shrunken, muttering '*Seize . . . seize . . . seize . . . seize . . .*' (her room number). I would hear the long-drawn-out scraping of the bed being dragged across the linoleum and wedged against the door. We never spoke to each other, but the proximity of our quarters and the intimate knowledge we each had of the other's movements, meant that we were, by our second week together, closer than many a man and wife. We communicated once, late one evening. I was undressed and lowering my shivering body gently downward (since I had to pay for the shower, I bathed in the bidet), when I inadvertently farted. For a minute I hung poised in embarrassment above the bidet until, eventually, the awful silence was broken by a plaintive answering fart from the other side of the thin wall.

I'd have gone mad in Carcassonne had I not met Monsieur Seyte, the bellringer of St Vincent's cathedral, who kindly invited me to join him at the top of the tower. Monsieur Seyte was a man of grace and dedication whose civic duty it was to sit high above the town in a belfry thick with cobwebs playing his American clavier. For twenty years he had climbed the dusty stone spiral staircase to the belfry, then pulled back and folded the plastic sheet which protected the clavier from the bird droppings, hitched his trousers at the knees, pulled leather gloves over his little fingers, checked his watch, and begun to play. The cathedral's forty-seven bells were connected by an intricate web of rusty springs, cables, levers and pulleys to the clavier pedals and the polished wooden pegs of the keyboard. The pegs were depressed by short chops with the side of the hand and knuckle.

While Monsier Seyte stamped and chopped, I perched on the floor above, among the flying bells. In the brain-battering din of that heavy-metal music the air trembled and each time I climbed down I felt ten years younger. One of the clappers had once snapped off and the metre-length of cast-iron had crashed through the ceiling and landed beside the clavier. The clapper was still propped in the corner of the belfry. I could look down through the splintered hole to Monsieur Seyte's head or out over Carcassonne to the storm clouds on the Montagne Noire – the hills I'd have to cross on my way across Languedoc to the Cévennes and then the Alps. When Monsier Seyte played *Greensleeves* for me I wondered for a moment whether the residents of Carcassonne would complain that St Vincent's bellringer had lost his mind, but *Greensleeves* brought no running figures. I sometimes wondered where everybody *was*.

The boots arrived and I wrote to Annabel warning her that I'd be out of touch for a while. Plane leaves lay deep on the towpath of the Canal du Midi as I followed its green water out of the city. I slept in the rain under a tree and then crossed the Montagne Noire in a gale. The land had entered a cycle of perpetual gloom, alternating between night and the crushing overcast of the bruised sky. On autopilot I pressed on beneath Que Chova, tramping deserted tracks ankle-deep in beech leaves or taking short-cuts along disused railway lines – on one occasion feeling my way through a long curving tunnel step by step, by the light of my candle.

By wet roadsides I passed sad memorials to Second World War catastrophes: the four policemen and their driver executed by the Germans on 21 August 1944; the five *patriotes* (three miners, a commercial salesman and an *adjutant active*) who died in a battle the following day when one hundred *maquis* ambushed 4,000 Germans; the airmen who came down near Roc de Peyremoux. Sometimes it seemed as if every rock I passed, or col I crossed, had been the site of a desperate last stand. And out in this black country I was reminded that the war went on: on the road outside St Etienne d'Albagnan somebody had painted: L'EUROPE MORT VOTEZ NAZIS.

Above me, the seasons battled for possession of Haut Languedoc. Each day brought violent changes of fortune as autumn fought to drive a wedge between summer and winter. Within any one hour I found myself blinded by a surprise attack from the sun, or buffeted by squalls. Rain had fallen every day since I'd climbed Canigou, one month earlier.

'It's the *année bissextile*,' stammered a newsagent. 'Normally the end of October is warm and dry. But each leap year, we have a terrible autumn.'

The weather precluded a return to the heights and so I walked along the valleys, drifting away into extended dreams. It was neither unpleasant nor pleasant, walking for hour on hour along wet roads beneath the umbrella. On paths in the mountains I always had to concentrate, on navigation, the weather, the food supplies. On these valley roads the mind could afford to wander. I prepared speeches for the day when I'd be a cabinet minister, I designed ecological houses, ate dinners by firelight with Annabel, planned how we'd accommodate the children (children?) in our tiny house.

I knew that I was never lonely because I had once known its true meaning. Years earlier I had lived on my own in a single room in the centre of London. On bad days the room felt like a bare cell in the vortex of the spinning world, itself a centrifuge of mixing and merging urban atoms that I could not reach from the still, dead centre where I sat despairing and immobilized by exclusion. *That* was loneliness.

The doors closed in the villages. I slept in a horse byre, on a raft of damp hay in a lake of rain and dung. And I turned experimentally to a bus shelter, but found that the luxury of a sheltered body-length bench was outweighed by the twin drawbacks of traffic noise and of having to relinquish my bed early in the morning to villagers laden with baskets and briefcases. In the thermal resort of Lamalou-les-Bains, the woman running the information desk told me that I wouldn't get a bed in the spa unless there was something wrong with me; I'd have to book in for a treatment. What would I like? An *irrigation nasale*? Or a *pulvérisation*? Perhaps an *insuflation de la trompe*? Then a *douche pénétrante*. Suddenly the bus shelters looked congenial.

Six days out from Carcassonne, I ran out of available valleys and found my way blocked by the vast plateaux that defend the southern approach to the Cévennes. The Jurassic limestone has been cut into blocks by gorges formed by rivers such as the Tarn, Tarnon and Lot, which pour down from the Cévennes. The smaller plateaux are known locally as *causses* – from the French word *chaux*, for lime, changed by the locals to *cau*. Each *causse* is several days' walking wide. They are almost waterless, for the rain filters underground, and the few *Caussenards* who eke out a living on the plateaux have historically had to survive on potatoes and rye, and milk from sheep which crop what little grass grows between the bony rock.

Loaded with two days' food, I left the small town of Lodève and climbed up through the trees following the red-and-white dashes of a long-distance footpath, the GR7. The day was cold and still; the ground puddled with the night's rain.

Along the forest track I passed men dressed in camouflage suits and holding rifles. From the trees came the faint baying of hounds and occasional crack of a rifle-shot. The hunters were cold and surly. They were stationed at intervals around the perimeter of the forest, waiting for the dogs to drive the boars out on to the track.

I stopped to talk to a pair of men resting their backsides on the bonnet of a pick-up truck. They said that they had shot six boars the previous day, one of them weighing seventy kilograms. They thought that there were another four boars still in the forest. The younger of the two hunters, a youth with hollow eyes wearing a forage cap and a bandolier of ammunition, sneered: 'Be careful.'

'Why?'

'Just be careful. Of the *fusils*.'

'But this is a public footpath. A *sentier de grande randonée*. It is for everyone. For recreation.'

He shrugged and his psychopathic eyes seemed to be sighting his cross-hairs on my wary arse. His rifle butt sat against his hip, the barrel twitching like a fishing rod snatched by a catch; he needed to shoot something. *Anything*. I beat a retreat up the track with a prickling neck.

The rain fell all day. Beyond the forest the path dropped down to the crumbling village of la Vacquerie-et-St-Martin-de-Castries, then struck out north-eastwards across the Causse de Larzac. It was a bleak desert, filled with stones and wind and isolated farms. *Garrigue* stuck to the desiccated rock like mould.

Darkness had fallen when I walked into St Maurice Navacelles. Water shone in the light cast from a window. Inside, an elderly couple were pulling up trays of food before a fire. The warmth and shelter of their secure little haven, with its companionship and plenty, was on the other side of an unbridgeable gulf. I was comfortable with my tramp's life, for it brought freedom and full-time relief from restlessness, but it was still difficult to pass a lit window at dusk without wanting to be on the warmer side of the glass.

Beyond the houses I passed through a hedge to a ruin and cleared away the broken brick and dust to make a space large enough to unroll my sleeping-bag. I lay in it to keep warm, eating sardines and bread with water while the candle kept blowing out in the draught. It was the first day of November.

I woke in the ruin before dawn and lay listening to the wind bluster and waited for the church clock to strike six. But it was seven chimes before there was enough light to move from the ruin down into the gorge.

A path zigzagged into the depths until the plateau lay one hundred metres above my head. What little light percolated through the clouds was reduced by the narrow roof of the gorge. The rock was old, 170 million years old, marine deposits. Fans of scree ran up to the base of the cliffs and scrub gripped the grit. It was a desolate, claustrophobic place. All morning I followed a path which clung to an irrigation channel on the western wall of the gorge. The gorge writhed intestinally, cut by a river that was travelling four times the distance it needed. The roar of the river far below my boots played discordantly with the roar of the wind battering the plateau above my head. Between the two I walked in a vacuum of still, damp air.

Navacelles appeared below my feet in the bed of the gorge. Seen from above, the gorge here was shaped like the Greek letter Ω, with sheer 300-metre walls. The river had cut across the 'neck' of the Ω, leaving an abandoned meander now occupied by the village fields of Navacelles, which huddled on the gorge-bed beside a dashing cataract. A single strand of smoke crawled from a chimney. A high-arched medieval bridge linked the village to the northern wall of the gorge, up which zigzagged a path. I climbed steadily till I stepped over the lip into bright sunshine. While I'd been deep in the ground, the sky had cleared of clouds. The rains had ended and the leaves of an old oak pattered in applause.

Into the Cévennes

Between the trees of the Causse de Blandas, huge piles of stones stood in rough pastures; heaped through the centuries to make space for grass to grow. The stone heaps looked like tumuli, and maybe some were, for this *causse* was dotted with menhirs and dolmen left by megalithic grave builders 3,500 years ago.

At the end of the day I came to the northern edge of the *causse* and, beside a great wood whose shadows were filled with the shufflings of sheep, I looked across the 400-metre deep Arre valley to the smooth crests of the Cévennes. Tidal waves of clouds tumbled through gaps in the crests and poured over the bald *causse*. The Arre divided limestone from granite, the *causses* from the Cévennes.

An old track switchbacked down through the chestnuts, sunk three metres into the valley side and lined with drystone walls. I passed a *clède*, one of the stone huts used for storing and drying chestnuts. More drystone walls, the *traversiers*, crossed the slope holding back the terraces of soil on which the chestnuts had been planted. These walls went back to the tenth century, when Benedictine monks came up the Hérault from the lowlands of Marseilles and Aniane to found the priory of Saint Pierre, bringing with them the skills of chestnut cultivation.

'Le Vigan,' the old bookseller behind the Place du Quai told me, 'is not a village. And it's not a town. It is something in between. For us it is perfect.'

And it was for me too. Le Vigan gathered itself resolutely about each end of the slender-arched Pont Vieux, with a disproportionately long roll-call of local heroes: the Marquis de Montcalm, who fell to Wolfe's guns on the Plains of Abraham; the Chevalier d'Assas, bayoneted leading his troops at Klostercamp; Sergeant Triaire, who blew himself up – and his fort – when 30,000 Turks overran his garrison in Crimea. And Marcel Fernand Bonnafoux – 'Marceau' – killed by the occupying forces in 1944.

I sat under the planes in the *place* and drank coffee while the deep aches of the trail slowly dissolved in the warm morning. Since coming down from the Pyrenees, I felt as if I'd been walking through a long, dark tunnel. From my table on the carpet of fallen leaves at the Café Les Cévennes I could see that the Place du Quai was neither square nor rectangular, but a long, gentle crescent of the same radius that the Cévennes make on the map, as they curve north-east from the Arre past Mont Aigoual to their northerly tip beside the youthful Loire.

The night I left this heroic little backwater I slept with conscientious objectors, in the hamlet of Pratcoustals, lost in the forest two hours' walk above Le Vigan. Jean-Benoît and Laurent were in their early twenties and had avoided compulsory military service on moral grounds. 'Instead of wearing a uniform,' smiled Jean-Benoît, in split jeans and a pony-tail, 'we have to work for the community; the civil service. We are rebuilding this village.'

Most of the ruined houses in Pratcoustals had been bought in 1971 by 'the Association' – Les Compagnons du Cap – whose aim was to restore the buildings and make them available for educational visits and holidays. Now Pratcoustals had twelve inhabitants.

Jean-Benoît was from Paris and had graduated in political philosophy. His special subject was Northern Ireland. One day, he wanted to buy a farm in Donegal. He had learned stonemasonry and had spent his sixteen months at Pratcoustals rebuilding walls. He would be returning to Paris in eight months. 'It will,' he said, 'be a nightmare.'

His compatriot, Laurent, a fey boy with curly hair and the habit of holding his head in his hands while drifting into long reveries, described himself as a gardener and an environmentalist.

There was a third character working at Pratcoustals. His name was Bruno and he came from Le Vigan. He had been employed to help the two conscientious objectors with their rebuilding work. Bruno was a large man with far-apart eyes, a chin like a spade and huge fingers. He was immensely strong and wore an ancient pair of dungarees which had fallen apart below the waist. He spoke in fast patois, twanging his word-endings so that '*maintenant*' and '*demain*' became '*mainten*aing' and '*dem*-aing', while '*putain*', an epithet which he used unsparingly, emerged like a twanging bowstring as '*put*-taing!' Bruno went out of his way to be kind to me. While the other two were out planting and rebuilding walls, Bruno cooked me dinner. I helped him mend his tractor.

Bruno hefted the axe as if it was a strand of balsa. 'You can make some firewood,' he suggested. Later, when I had finished with splitting logs, Jean-Benoît returned and saw the axe. He rounded on Bruno: 'Where did you hide it?'

Bruno shrugged.

'I could not find the axe two weeks ago and when I asked you where it was, you said you didn't know!'

Bruno shrugged again.

'You lied, Bruno. You lied!'

Bruno drank from his glass.

The next morning Bruno took his motorbike down to Le Vigan to buy cigarettes and Jean-Benoît asked: 'Was Bruno OK last night?'

'Fine, yes. Very kind.'

'He lied to me about the axe. I was very angry.'

'I could see that.'

'I suppose you could say that it's a typical problem between a Parisian and what a Parisian would call an ignorant country person.'

The mulberry trees of Pratcoustals were planted on sunward terraces and harvested for their leaves, which were fed to silkworms laid in trays in the upper storeys of the houses. Fireplaces kept the temperature warm and constant. The five *magnaneries* in the hamlet fed the ten weaving looms which made the silk stockings.

Pratcoustals also had two *clèdes*. One had been renovated by the Association, and was now a house; the other was still intact. Like the one I'd inspected in the forest above the Glèpe, the dimensions were about three metres by three metres, and in two storeys separated by floorboards with gaps to let the smoke rise. Since the *clède* was built into the mountainside, the upper floor was at ground level at the back, and pierced by a small window through which the baskets of chestnuts were tipped. The window frame was carved from granite, with a recessed lip to one side which was used for resting the base of the full basket, while it was tipped forward to send the nuts scuttling through the funnel-shaped window.

According to Jean-Benoît, the nut-gatherers would frequently carry eighty kilograms at a time; five times the weight of my own rucksack. The smoky fire would be lit on the ground floor. Being almost rot-proof, the wood of the chestnut had many applications. Beehives were made from the hollowed trunks of chestnut, with a slab of rock on top as a lid. Furniture, vine-posts, baskets were made from its timber.

Pratcoustals' clock ran by the seasons. The spring thaw would be followed by rebuilding work on the *traversiers*, and planting. Through June the track up from the valley would be busy with flocks of sheep being taken up towards the Col du Minier and the high pastures of Mont Aigoual. They'd be back down past Pratcoustals at the end of summer, fatter and shaggier. And at the end of summer the turf below the chestnuts was dug and burnt and then the ash raked back to fertilize the acidic soil. The chestnut harvest in September brought every able body on to the terraces. Winter would see the pig being killed.

In this self-contained and industrious way, Pratcoustals looked after itself. The hills provided the stone and timber for building; the sheep and silkworms produced wool and silk; there was honey from the bees and flour from the chestnuts. Chickens provided eggs, and goats the milk. Between the trees rye was grown and up on the small plateau there were tiny patches of wheat. The pig would have lived in the ground floor of the house, or in an outside sty, fed on cereals, chestnuts and potatoes, then bled and scalded for salt pork, sausages, pâtés, potted meat and black pudding.

What could not be made at home could be bought in Le Vigan. Down the hill there were silk-reelers who would buy the cocoons. The *tonnelier* had his own forge, with his saws and adzes, planes and drills and vices, used to make barrels. Le Vigan's last cooper, Paul Joseph Chapel, died in 1965. He was ninety-one. Le Vigan also had its clog-maker, and there were basket-makers, long-sawyers and an *appléchaïre* who specialized in making wagons and carts and ox-yokes.

For the men, a trip down to Le Vigan meant the chance to stock up on tobacco, or perhaps to buy a new pipe; one manufacturer offered no fewer than 170 different models of clay pipe, ranging from cheap disposables to novelty bowls shaped like the heads of Egyptian pharaohs, horses, Greek gods and (nodding towards the source of their livelihood) a pigtailed Chinaman. The tinsmith, the *estamaïre*, re-melted cutlery and sold lanterns, jugs and mugs. The glass-maker sold bottles, and glass tiles to let light into the cottages.

Pratcoustals lived not in noble isolation but as part of the heart of the Arre and the Hérault, linked to the Cévennes and the *causses*, to the Mediterranean and the Rhône. A silkworm fed on Pratcoustals mulberry leaves could produce a thread spun in Le Vigan, woven in Avignon, embroidered in Nîmes and flaunted in the Jardin des Tuileries.

Pratcoustals mattered; this hamlet – and thousands like it through the uplands of Europe – was the tiddler at the end of the economic food-chain, weakest and furthest removed from the big predators. Pratcoustals fed the mills and market in Le Vigan. Pratcoustals and its kind were a safe-deposit of Europe's rural skills and traditions.

In 1885, work began on a new road linking Le Vigan with the Col du Minier. Pressure from a local councillor took the road away from the obvious course, up the ridge through Pratcoustals, to an alternative along the bed of the Coudoulous valley and then steeply up the mountain-side to the pass. The councillor had land up the Coudoulous.

The road took eleven years to build. The first motorcars were appearing on Languedoc's roads. Pratcoustals, accessible only by foot, might just as well have been on the moon. There were no more passers-by. People began to leave the hamlet, removing the tiles from the roofs of their houses as they did so, to avoid paying tax. Rainwater dissolved the granite walls; joists rotted. By 1946, only Julien Reilhan remained. For thirty years he lived alone in the deserted hamlet. He died in the winter of 1976.

'There were about fifteen descendants who had a stake in Julien's house,' sighed Jean-Benoît, 'but one of them was a nun, and she left her share to God.'

'And the lawyers can't get in touch with God?'

'It has complicated matters.'

So Julien's house was left as it was the day he died, with half a bottle of *pastis* on the table and, on the wall, the calendar on which he used to note the weather.

Mont Aigoual

The old track up the ridge from Pratcoustals towards Mont Aigoual was paved with granite setts which had been buffed by centuries of toiling boots. Not a cloud marked the sky. Red berries hung in the indefinite forest and the track became one of many which vein the outer reaches of the Massif Central. In the dusk I took a wrong turn; it was soon dark and I was still among the trees.

A rifle-shot blasted a hole in the darkness. From the star shadows a man in a jerkin and cap stepped out and grunted, and my heart raced as I grunted back and told myself never to move after dusk in this killing season. The hunter set me right for the village and when I arrived the shop was still open and the women told me that there was a *gîte* in the village where I could stay. I bought food for several days: bread, honey, *brebis* – dry, chalky sheep's cheese – and *chèvre* – its smellier caprine equivalent. And I couldn't resist a tin of *haricots blancs cuisinés à la Toulousaine*, the most exotically disguised can of baked beans I'd ever seen. The *gîte* was closed for the winter but the guardian gave me the key nevertheless. It was so cold in the room that I sat inside the sleeping-bag fully dressed.

I left the village in the dark, while the roofs were cloaked with woodsmoke and frost crusted the fences. The sun came up while I was still climbing up through the black firs. On the summit, the duty meteorologist leaned towards his thermometers below the viewing platform.

After all the rain, the air was so clean that I could see the curve of the globe, wrinkled like a big orange.

Both horizons were encrusted with a reef of diamonds. Two hundred and fifty kilometres back to the south-west I picked out Canigou and Carlit, Maladeta and Posets, Monte Perdido and a twinkle I believed was Vignemale. Two hundred and fifty kilometres in the opposite direction were the Alps. Detached from the left extremity of the range like an iceberg floated a solitary, brilliant speck of light: Mont Blanc.

Seeing the Alps sent a shiver down my damp back. To walk through the Cévennes to the Rhône would take another two weeks, which meant that I'd be climbing into the Alps at the beginning of December. I could not have timed it worse; I'd be traversing Europe's mightiest mountains through the dead of winter. How long did winter last? Four months? Five months? How, I wondered, would I move through the snow? How would I live in the cold? How would I survive the darkness? I needed warm clothes. And I needed a tent.

From Mont Aigoual, the *draille* ran north along the ridge-lines, wide enough for thirty sheep to walk shoulder to shoulder, sporadically paved and lined with stones, each one a memorial to old migrations. The flocks came to the Cévennes from the winter pastures of the lower Rhône. Transhumance had been part of the seasons' rhythms since at least the Middle Ages. The sheep were milked for Roquefort cheese, the meat made its way to Paris and the whey to the pigs.

Walking these abandoned heights on the threshold of winter I pictured autumns past when flocks, *scabots*, of 2,000 sheep or more made their way in dusty snakes down the *drailles* towards the plains, flanked by spiked St Bernards, to the music of forty different bells covering four musical scales and urged onwards by shepherds singing in Occitan:

> E buffo li, è buffo li
> Al trauc.
> E buffo li, è buffo li
> Al cuol!

And blow at him. And blow on the hole. And blow at him. And blow on the arsehole!

Like the Castilian Mesta, the French herders gained power through numbers; in the sixteenth century their rights-of-way were formalized in the *Status de la Transhumance*. The major routes, *carrairés*, were serviced by pastures and water-sources belonging to the sheep owners. *Carrairés* were up to fifty metres wide, fed by smaller twelve-metre *drailles*. Each was bound by a strip of grazing sixty metres deep and marked by cairns.

I spent two nights on the *draille*, the first beneath the stars in the lee of young oaks and the second in a cave.

Werewolves and Other Beasts

I was woken in my cave above the Tarnon by a man walking his dog who told me that it was Sunday. I rolled my sleeping-bag and ambled down the path towards Florac and a medley of bell-ringing, the peaks for Catholic Mass beginning as those for the Protestant Eucharist were dying away.

'We had the wars,' shrugged the baker, as if the bitter struggle 300 years ago between the Protestant Camisards and their Catholic persecutors were yesterday.

One of the leaders of the ragged Camisards – who had used Florac as a mountain lair – was the guerrilla genius Jean Cavalier, a one-time shepherd boy who changed sides after being defeated by Louis XIV's generals and then, by a circuitous route, rose to lieutenant-governor of Jersey under the British before being buried in 1740, now a major-general, in the parish of St Luke's, Chelsea.

On the last day of September, 138 years later, a twenty-seven-year-old lapsed Calvinist walked into Florac intent on picking up the echoes of the Camisards. He was told in the café of cousins and nephews descended from Cavalier and of bones dug up where ancestors had fought. Robert Louis Stevenson was launching his career as a writer by making a romantic journey with a recalcitrant donkey called Modestine. Over twelve days Stevenson walked 220 kilometres through the Cévennes from Le Puy to Alais. He had chosen as his thematic quest the trail of the Camisards. It was a canny judgement; from Bloomsbury as *Travels With a Donkey in the Cévennes* to Brno, where it appeared as *Putování s Oalicí do Hor*, Stevenson's well-crafted story became a bestseller, and launched a century of donkey abuse.

I took a room in Chez Bruno on the *place* (still a pleasant 'alley of planes') and spent the rest of the day ambling around Florac's dishevelled streets. The 'live fountain' Stevenson had visited still tumbled in tiers past the twin-towered chateau (now a national park information centre) to a succession of weirs patrolled by ducks. Tilted berets and Citroëns the colour of faded denim loitered outside the cafés on the *place*. The street where Stevenson lodged on his ninth night, Rue de Thérond, now teetered between Gallic quaintness and irredeemable rubble, its derelict houses exfoliating plaster and shedding fractured drainpipes.

The mist had not lifted by morning. Ahead of me lay the heart of Lozère, the poorest and most isolated of France's *départements*, and at fourteen inhabitants per square kilometre, the least populated (the figure for Paris is 21,537). To this impoverished land came a beast as horrible as the Cannibal of Gargas. Twenty years before Blaise Ferage terrorized the Pyrenean foothills, the Beast of Gevaudan was preying on this part of the Cévennes, eating sheep and young women. Bodies were found drained of blood and partially eaten. Theories blazed along the valleys: the Beast was a vampire wearing a wolfskin, or it was a wolfpack being guided by a crazed tyrant, or it was a lone wolf of enormous size. For three years the Beast caused panic in the isolated communities of the Cévennes, separated from one another by forest and appalling roads. The bishop of Mende ordered public prayers and hunts were dispatched by the *Intendant* of Languedoc. As more went missing, dragoons rode out and a reward of 6,000 livres was offered by the king. When a 130-pound wolf was shot in September 1765, the harassed population filled the churches and the Beast was sent, stuffed, to Versailles. Three months later two boys were killed near Mont Lozère. Through the winter and following spring the killing spree resumed with new ferocity until Jean Chastel found himself looking down his sights at a second wolf. After that, the killings stopped.

The Beast of Gevaudan terrorized the French psyche and fascinated Robert Louis Stevenson: 'Wolves, alas, like bandits, seem to flee the traveller's advance . . .' he noted in his journal. Risk, for Stevenson, was one of the reasons for travelling. '. . . you may trudge through all our comfortable Europe and not meet with an adventure worth the name. But here, if anywhere, a man was on the frontiers of hope . . .' A wilderness lives through its beasts, and the memory of grotesques such as the Cannibal of Gargas and the Beast of Gevaudan goes some way towards filling in gaps left by exterminated predators. Those that remained – the wolves and the bears – were with me nevertheless, a presence whose dark superiority brought a quality of scale to the mountains that was taller than the peaks, colder than the ice and deeper than the water.

Above Florac my *draille* rose towards the bleak granite *baguette* of Mont Lozère, thirty kilometres long and five wide, but rising to 1,699 metres. A ridge eased up the mountain, its spine occupied by a community of menhirs, some three metres high, frozen in the opaque mist. I stayed with the menhirs till darkness fell and the full moon cast long shadows from each standing stone. Near the uppermost menhir stood a small wood where I climbed to the top of one of the pines and howled at the moon while the tree swayed in the gale and the silver clouds sailed above Mont Lozère's petrified sentinels.

I fell asleep at the foot of the tree on a bed of pine needles and woke before dawn to find water dripping on my bivouac bag and realized that I was screwed up with cold. This bald western rump of Mont Lozère, wrecked by over-grazing and shorn of timber, was being hammered by winds that hit no higher land between the Alps and the Atlantic. I pulled on my thin balaclava helmet beneath my trilby, and then the cotton hood of my coat. The wind was too strong for the umbrella. The little black copse was still marooned in thick mist and I had to use the compass to find the track down to the Bramon, a stream that had turned into a freezing turgid little river. I had to take off my boots, socks and trousers to wade across. As I completed this bleak exercise, rain began to fall and I reassured myself that the weather would definitely improve. In about April.

Beyond the Bramon I came to the hamlet of La Fage where I rested and sheltered inside the communal bread oven, a small barn-like building which had been restored as a 'curiosity' in 1982. A plaque described the demise of La Fage: in 1861, the hamlet had had 146 inhabitants distributed between twenty-seven families; now there were twenty inhabitant and six families. With its walls of great blocks and rye roofs it must have borne a resemblance to the granite-and-thatch *palloza* villages of the Sierra de Ancares. Many of the houses had fallen down; six were now second homes and one was a *gîte d'étape*. The bread oven had last been fired in 1950.

Beyond the door of the oven stood the *clocher des tormentes*, a granite obelisk topped by a belfry hung with the bell which used to ring out the rhythms of La Fage: the Angelus, weddings and funerals. But it took its name from its task of guiding down men from the mountain on nights like the one I'd just spent, when the mist and wind were on the rampage.

The bell of La Fage has lost its tone. Children rang it one frosty winter's day and it had cracked in the cold.

The *draille* climbed up from La Fage through dripping, leafless silver birch and then heather, from cairn to cairn until 1,500 metres, when the gradient eased and I met the full force of the gale. For ten minutes I sheltered in a crevice on a weathered tor – Mad Dog Rock – while I organized my equipment for the forthcoming battle. The Col de Finiels was about twelve kilometres along the ridge of Mont Lozère from my tor, in bad weather about three or four hours' walking.

The track writhed from col to col through forest whose clearings were churned to quagmires by loggers' tractors. Wind and rain came in blasts which threatened to wreck Que Chova. From the waist down I was soaked to the skin; water squirted from the cuffs of my boots and mud reached to my knees. Checking the map, and setting a new compass bearing meant furling Que Chova while the wind tried to tear the map's plastic bag from my hand. Droplets streaming down my spectacles had to be wiped off before I could focus on the map's contours and measure distances to the next col.

In this sightless state I reached the summit of Finiels late in the afternoon. A line of wooden posts led down to the col where I met the tall stone posts that had guided Stevenson up Mont Lozère from the north. He came up the warm, dry turf on a sunny morning wearing his knitted waistcoat, with his jacket tied to Modestine's pack. The posts had straddled Mont Lozère since medieval times, spaced every fifty paces to guide travellers down from the heights. I touched each one as I passed, wondering whether Modestine had loitered to scratch a rump on the rough granite.

By evening I was in the forest on the sheltered lower slopes of Mont Lozère looking for the 'dell of green turf, where a streamlet made a little spout over some stones to serve me for a water-tap'. This was the fabled bivouac described by Stevenson in his chapter 'A Night Among the Pines', a panegyric upon the outdoor life and in particular upon the joys of nights *à la belle étoile*. 'What seems a kind of temporal death to people choked between walls and curtains', he mused, 'is only a light and living slumber to the man who sleeps afield.'

So many self-conscious Stevensonians have already poked about in this wood that I half expected to bump into knots of young men puffing meerschaums, with TWAD open on page 172 and clutching twitching divining rods. I found the dell, or at least I found a dell which would do.

The young trees surrounding his camp-site were now statuesque Scots pine and in the calm of the evening I knew why Stevenson had spliced into his chapter the sequestered-bower quote from *Paradise Lost*.

Dawn broke and I lay in my sleeping-bag postponing the moment when I would have to pull on my wet trousers.

For the next two days I was buffeted by hailstones as I followed Stevenson's route north from Mont Lozère through milder country whose roofs now wore tiles not slates. But his footsteps became fainter and less interesting. And I grew bored with his company and that of a route whose charm had now been buried by bitumen.

Hounded by a hail squall I arrived at La Bastide Puylaurent at dusk. The village grew up around the railway junction linking Mende, Paris and Marseilles and became popular between the wars as an accessible summer resort for those driven inland by the heat of the Mediterranean coast. In the winter they came to ski. Hôtel Ranc (*'Pension de Famille: Alt. 1,024 mètres'*) was built in 1926 beside the railway line.

After the Second World War La Bastide faded back into the forests. For a while the village subsisted on the custom of workers from the railway and from local dam-building projects. Hôtel Ranc became a holiday home for old soldiers who had served in Algeria. Now it was a *gîte d'étape* run by the young and immensely tall Philippe Papadimitriou Demaitre Pausenberger Vanniesbecq, a Belgian-Greek whose grandfather once owned the Hôtel de Paris in Cairo. After a series of occupations, from gold-panning in California to hod-carrying in Peru, Philippe had bought the Hôtel Ranc, complete with its contents, from the bedspreads to the oak-and-chrome Frick refrigerators, for 900,000 francs.

'It was intuition, not science!' Philippe laughed. '*Voilà!*'

La Bastide was dying. The winter population was down to 183. In summer it swelled to 2,000, with the extra railway staff and the villa-owners from Marseilles, Alès, Nîmes and Montpellier. Each year fewer residents stayed up for the winter. Philippe's girlfriend, Catou, remembered coming up to La Bastide as a girl to collect mushrooms, from her home in Alès, before all the pits closed. The branch line to Mende was losing money and, if that closed, La Bastide might disappear from the map. There was pessimism in the village; one of the other hotels had closed recently; marriages were disintegrating.

But the *gîte* was booming: the previous year Philippe had catered for 3,000 guests. Many were British, walking along the Allier in Stevenson's footsteps. It was 13 November, Robert Louis Stevenson's birthday.

Philippe cooked *pied de mouton* mushrooms from the forest and we played darts by the open fire.

'The *gîte* is too much . . . *sedentaire*; I must do something where I move.' Philippe stared into the flames. 'We are good for something, but what . . . it is difficult to know.'

'What about you, Catou?' I asked. 'Do you want to carry on travelling too?'

She nodded: '*Oui, oui.* I want to go to Afghanistan.'

'Why?'

'Because it begins with "A" and I want to visit all the countries of the alphabet.'

We all laughed, but it seemed as good a method as any, if a little ambitious; the beginning of the alphabet was populated by hotspots: Afghanistan, Bosnia, Colombia, Dahomey, Ethiopia . . . Catou said that she wanted to escape.

'For my part,' wrote Stevenson the day before he walked through La Bastide, 'I travel not to go anywhere, but to go; I travel for travel's sake.' The line is so well-worn that, like the mountaineers' aphorism 'Because it's there', it's almost lost its meaning. Stevenson's claim to fulfilment through aimlessness seemed to me a contradictory, impossible ideal. It wasn't till I read his journal that I realized he'd lopped off the end of this passage when he rewrote the text for TWAD. After 'I travel for travel's sake', he had added in the original: 'And to write about it afterwards . . .'

Across the Water

Footpaths led me into a lightless land. I followed a ridge which had been burnt to charcoal by summer fires, above the black gash of the Gorges of the Borne and below a sky the colour of wet slate. This permanent apocalyptic dusk worked on my dread of the winter ahead. With more than another month to run till the winter solstice, conditions would get much bleaker before they got better. For five days I walked east over the long swells of Ardèche. The land was wild and empty, with high moors above valleys of deserted hamlets and abandoned farms.

Then, late one November afternoon, I came to a bluff looking down on the river, shining in the wet sunlight. The Rhône lay in a trench twenty kilometres wide. I'd not had to cross such an open space since leaving Finisterre. The dark gulf was battled over by rearing cumulonimbus and spears of cirrus pierced by ladders of sunlight and harried by phantom squalls.

I came down to the riverside town of La Voulte, appended on my map with the words 'Le Camp d'Annibal'. I found the site where Hannibal rested before crossing the river with his elephants, behind a funeral parlour, entirely covered by a housing estate. Even the circus I went to that night was a let-down; their best act was a performing goat. Not a lot happened in La Voulte, but two months later the town made national headlines when a freight train derailed, spilling petrol into the sewers, where it exploded. Had the accident happened the night I'd slept in La Voulte I doubt that my beleaguered morale would have survived the megaton blast of a shitbomb. Apparently 1,000 residents were evacuated.

In the morning I walked down to the hundred-year-old suspension bridge, sat and stared across at the far bank. Not for the first time I found myself held by two familiar anchors: sentimentality towards the land I was leaving and understood, uncertainty towards the unknown land ahead. Between the river I now faced and the banks of the Danube in Vienna lay a chain of mountains 1,000 kilometres long and over 4,000 metres high. The actual distance I'd have to walk to reach Vienna – allowing for what Hol called 'the wiggliness factor' – would be closer to 2,000 kilometres. In snow and sub-zero temperatures. It was three hours before I brought myself to walk across the bridge and turn towards the Alps.

Against the current I walked north on the levée above a brimful Rhône until I was levered away from the river by an unbridged tributary. The cold floodplain was partitioned into muddy plots by poplar-lined dykes; the mountains – Cévennes to the left, Vercors to the right – watched as self-regarding silhouettes. Near the hamlet of Nazareth, a woman with bags on her handlebars fought against the long straight road; villages floated like lonely atolls, blown by the Rhône wind and prey, I imagined, to the unspeakable acts that are bound to visit those surrounded by utter flatness: a place for the unexpected axe-attack; the pot-shot with a shotgun; the missing neighbour, wedged down a well. Crazed hounds hurled themselves at the iron gates of walled properties carrying *Chien Méchant* signs.

I reached Valence in the dark, in heavy rain, too late for the post office. I was expecting a package from Annabel, containing the tent and warm clothing, and I had hoped to sort out the new gear that evening, ready for an early start for the Alps the following morning. But I got stuck in Valence for a week. Between London and Valence the package had disappeared. I was trapped; I could not afford to abandon the gear and neither did I have the nerve to continue without it. Snow was expected any day.

I stayed in the youth hostel, sharing a dormitory with passing itinerants: a German hitch-hiker; a Canadian motorcyclist; an Englishman driving round France looking for work; a Japanese student of medieval history. Apart from myself, the only other long-stay resident was a French boy who had got himself thrown out of the army by not eating for seventeen days and then presenting himself to his commanding officer as thin as a vine-post; most men, he said, tried to get out by pretending to be mad. 'Like Yossarian!' he grinned, recalling the reluctant airman of *Catch 22*.

Every morning I walked the four kilometres from the hostel to the post office, where the staff had adopted me as a pitiable itinerant. Once a day the *hôtesse d'accueil* – a young woman called Monique Masclet – telephoned the other ten towns in France also called 'Valence' (the Latin word for 'strong' is sprinkled over Gallic maps like 'burghs' and 'thorpes' litter those of England), in case my package had gone to the wrong *département*. Each morning I fought the frustration and turned again to Valence to lift my spirits.

Through no apparent misdemeanour, the town had been twinned with Clacton-on-Sea. It was also the home of Bernard Gangloff, the creator of Sergeant Popeye. And it was the place where the son of a Catalan stonemason, Joseph Pujol, who was stationed here with the First Regiment of Cuirassiers, discovered that he could drink through his backside. Barrack-room training at Valence gave Pujol – or 'Le Pétomane', as he became known – the additional ability to play musical tunes with his elastic anus. He went on to perform at the Moulin Rouge where he once took 20,000 francs on a single Sunday. The most plausible medical explanation is that Le Pétomane was capitalizing upon a congenital abnormality in which a loop of his bowel – not unlike a section of bicycle inner tube – had slithered into his chest cavity. Varying the pressure on his lungs thus allowed him to control the gas flow through his intestine. Given the wealth and fame of Le Pétomane, it is astonishing that nobody in show-business has tried to follow the old soldier by undertaking the surgery required to create a musical bottom. One of the streets in Valence was called Rue de Ha! Ha!

But modern Valence was not uplifting. In a smoky den on a housing estate I saw the City Kids, a dermatologically challenged heavy-metal band, exact vengeance on an audience of fresh-faced teenagers. On another day I sought salvation in the museum before the rust-coloured pencil drawings of 'Robert the Ruin' – Hubert Robert, the landscape artist, who broke new ground by making his ruins the focal point of a picture instead of using them as decorative accessories. His terrifying Bastille exaggerates the scale of no. 232, Rue Saint-Antoine so far beyond the actuality of its twenty-metre walls that his painting makes the prison look like an insurmountable, evil cliff. The allegory did little to contain the effect that the Alps were having on me; my next hurdle was growing taller and more hostile by the day. I took solace in the bizarre twist of fortune which saved Robert's life; locked up in the Bastille for his support of the Revolution, he escaped the guillotine when the executioners took away the wrong Robert.

On the sixth day I ran out of patience and telephoned Annabel and asked if she would come out to Grenoble – which I could reach in a week – with a bag of replacement winter kit. Next morning Monique telephoned to say that my package had arrived in Valance.

The Alps

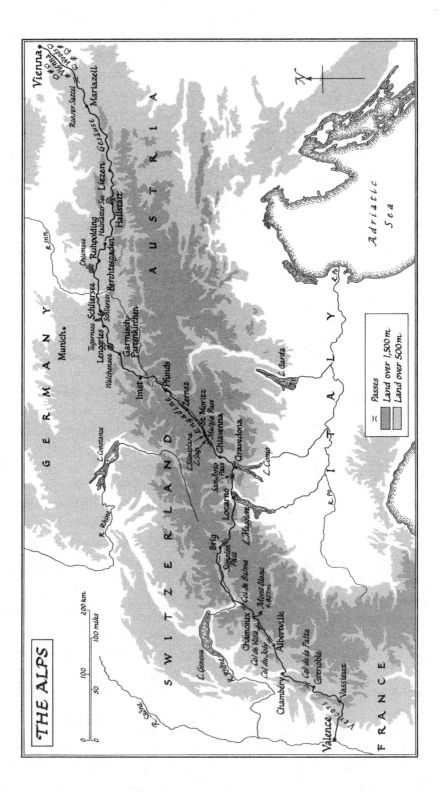

THE ALPS

Passes
Land over 1,500 m
Land over 500 m

Vienna
Vienna Woods
Rohrer Sattel
Mariazell
Gesäuse
Liezen
Hallstätter See
Ruhpolding
Chiemsee
Schliersee
Berchtesgaden
Hallstatt
Tegernsee Schliersee
Lenggries
Walchensee
Garmisch-Partenkirchen
Imst
Pfunds
Zernez
St. Moritz
L. Silaplana
L. Sils
Maloja Pass
Chiavenna
Gravedona
San Bernardino Pass
Locarno
L. Como
L. Maggiore
Brig
Simplon Pass
Col de Balme
Chamonix
Mont Blanc 4,807m
Col de Voza
Col du Joly
Albertville
Chambéry
Col de la Faita
Grenoble
Vassieux
Valence
Vercors

GERMANY
Munich
R. Inn
L. Constance
R. Rhine

SWITZERLAND
L. Geneva
Rhône
Saône

AUSTRIA
L. Garda
R. Po
R. Po

ITALY

FRANCE
Rhône

Adriatic Sea

N

0   50   100   200 km
0   100 miles

Vercors

I left Valence early, walking along the Rue des Alpes towards the rising sun and the high silhouette of the Vercors. Soon the rich alluvial soil gave way to dried earth sprinkled with fragments of limestone and by evening I was on top of a 700-metre cliff looking back across the electric glow of the Rhône. Heading east over the successive crests of the Vercors, I travelled against the grain of the country. This intimidating fortress of cliffs and forest hid bare plateaux which the *maquis* had used to receive parachute drops during the Second World War.

After six months under the stars, I could scarcely believe the luxury that a tent afforded. It was a small tent, designed for one person, with a single layer of fabric tensioned by two flexible poles. To drift off knowing that no amount of rain or snow could interrupt my slumbers produced a sense of wellbeing equivalent to a couple of large Scotches.

I crossed the frosted Plateau d'Ambel, passing the polished slab commemorating the two woodcutters, Bouillanne and Richaud, who had pulled the Dauphin's son 'from the deadly claws of a bear' in the early thirteenth century. The climb continued to 1,699 metres on the Pas de l'Infernet, a triangular peak overhanging a cliff-rimmed plummet to the valley of the Sure. The closest house was about 1,000 metres away, vertically downwards. To the south-west the smooth grass ramp of the plateau gave the impression of being poised above another world. From here I could see the full scale of Vercors, dropping in waves to the west but rising eastwards to the glistening blade of Le Grand Veymont and the platinum peaks of the Alps.

For a while I lost height, crossing old sheep *pâturages* to a deserted pass, where I looked down on the snooker-table valley of Vassieux, 300 metres below. The village sat on a little step in the otherwise level plateau, bordered by forested ridges. On the morning of 21 July 1944 the green baize of Vassieux became a killing field; in a surprise attack the Germans landed by glider and parachute and killed 700 *maquis* and a large number of civilians. On concrete supports outside the museum rested the tubular steel chassis of one of the ten-seater German gliders; outside the cemetery flapped the *tricolore*. So often since coming down from the Pyrenees I had stumbled on Second World War memorials, often hidden away in the deepest beech forests, marking the crash site of a plane, or where a group of *maquis* had been ambushed. Some were so remote that they must have been known only to the relations of those lost and to the local boar hunters. But Vassieux was different, for the Vercors was unique in the vastness of its wilderness, and only here could the *maquis* have assembled a small army – and only here did they lose so many in one action.

The following evening I reached the sixth and final wall of the Vercors. Still the snow had not arrived, but the solid cloud and stilled air threatened a change. I climbed anxiously up an amphitheatre of limestone to the highest and darkest of the Vercors forests, Le Purgatoire. The path I was following soon petered out in a confusing area of karst: sinkholes and glades. There was no topographic logic. On a compass bearing I emerged under a summit I took to be the Serre du Serpent and picked up a track running east over a low col. When this descended and met the familiar red-and-white paint dashes of a GR route, I fell down and kissed the cold earth.

The path took me north through the silent pines. Patches of fresh snow lay in sunless dips. I had the sensation that I was being followed; there was a *presence*, not animal (although coincidentally I came across a print in the snow whose splayed pads and size made me think of wolves), but human. The path emerged on to the clearing of Darbounouse, one of the ancient transhumance pastures of Vercors. The clearing was a long oval about two kilometres long and about 500 metres broad, undulating and scattered with bone-white boulders. It dipped in its centre, where the two *cabanes* had been built, and was entirely surrounded by a rim of black pines. Uncharacteristically I felt spooked by being alone up here. I waited behind a pine for ten minutes, then walked out into the open, expecting to see a figure emerge from one of the two *cabanes*. Instead, the air reverberated with a strange drone – which my hair-trigger imagination turned into 1940s Halifax engines. Later that evening, while I was collecting wood in the forest, I heard the sounds again.

Three kilometres beyond the clearing I nearly missed the Cabane de Carrette, which was hidden in a hollow, off the track. It was very isolated, surrounded by forest, with an oil drum full of rainwater under the gutter. Inside there was a cast-iron stove, a small table, and a ladder propped against the lip of the sleeping loft. There were rats, but they moved out as I made myself at home.

It was Annabel's birthday. To mark the occasion, I lit the wood-burning stove and prepared one of my more elaborate Tin Cuisine dinners. I went to some trouble with the presentation. Balancing the mug inside the wood-burning stove, I boiled a pint of water. Into this I scattered pieces of broken spaghetti. When these were *al dente*, I carefully lifted the mug from the flames and, once the lip of the mug had cooled, drank off the oil-drum water. That was the soup course. The next course was fish. With my Spanish spoon I ate two of the sardines from the tin which had already been opened. For the third course, I tipped the spaghetti from the mug into the vacated space beside the two remaining sardines. After a suitable pause for digestion and reflection, I repeated the trip outside to the oil drum and refilled the mug. Just before it boiled I tipped in a liberal quantity of Quick-lait, stirring vigorously to create an aerated froth. In went fine-sliced Mars Bar (this had been prepared earlier, for even a fractional delay at this stage allows the milk to cool beyond the temperature at which it will melt the dense toffee layer in the Mars Bar), stirring in a figure-of-eight motion (to avoid clotting) until the caramel and toffee layers were completely liquefied. Short of taking up pipe-smoking I could think of no better way to conclude a celebratory banquet than hot drinking mousse with a *soupçon* of pine smoke.

During the three hours or so spent preparing and enjoying this meal I was interrupted periodically by the lone Halifax and once by footfalls approaching the door. I froze over the stove, waiting. Nobody tried to push open the door; neither did the footsteps recede. I picked up the hut's shovel and peered outside, but only moon-shadows moved in the glade. For the rest of the evening, I took the shovel with me each time I visited the oil drum.

No snow lay outside the hut in the morning, but a film of ice had spread over the water in the oil drum. In rising winds I walked all day, and through the next, high on the flank of that final Vercors wall, detouring eventually up on to the crest so that I could look over the edge and preview the Alps. By the time I reached the top of the north-eastern summit of the Vercors, a rock called le Moucherotte, the weather had deteriorated to a sleet-driven gale. The cotton clothing which had lasted so well from Finisterre now felt thin and inadequate. The cold cut deep. I huddled in the lee of a ruin, chewing the last of my chocolate. Below me, the cliff fell away for 1,700 metres to the viscera of the Alpine city; slabs of conurbation tied up in glistening strands, pumping traffic up the Isère and Drac. Down there, somewhere, was Annabel.

Ambiance Sympathique

Night had fallen by the time I'd climbed down from Vercors and made my way through Grenoble's suburbs to Hôtel du Moucherotte, a one-star establishment run by Monsieur Lam from Vietnam. I arrived caked with mud and candlewax, bearing a handful of fuchsias. Annabel had not checked in and so I had time to clean myself up; there had been no surface water up on the limestone of Vercors and I'd not washed or shaved since leaving Valence six days earlier. I was in the hot mist of the shower massaging a body full of aches, when I heard distant banging and realized that somebody had been trying to get into the room. Annabel was standing at the door wearing an enormous rucksack on her back and cradling another in her arms. She looked radiantly beautiful.

Four months had passed since Pamplona. Strange to each other and displaced to a cheap hotel room in an unfamiliar foreign city in winter, we clung together in M. Lam's sanctuary as the heavy cloud clung to the cliffs above our room, loosing Arctic squalls on Grenoble's streets. Between downpours we made short forays to cafés and museums. This meeting was as sweet as the last had been confused. And yet our lives had diverged to the point where it was difficult for each of us to imagine the other's concerns; Annabel's continuing struggle to make progress in an industry which had more culs de sac than open roads and my prosaic concerns about snowstorms and bivouacs. December was a bad month to face another separation.

'Maybe we could start a family?' I suggested illogically.

We both now recognized that our separation had passed a critical limit; that there was more to lose by giving up than there was by extending the pain. Our longings were measured differently; for Annabel at home there were daily reminders that I was missing; for me, the anonymous foreign forests carried no echoes of home and Annabel existed as a fictional companion possessed of the surreal ability to step unexpectedly into my path, then to disappear with equal abruptness, leaving me scrabbling to recall the plot.

On the morning of the fourth day in Grenoble, Annabel closed the door of a rain-spotted Mercedes taxi outside Hôtel du Moucherotte. For a moment I pictured a desperate sprint down Rue Auguste-Gaché after the

Mercedes' receding tail-lights, followed by a nervous breakdown and a blubbing phone-call that evening to say I was on the first plane home.

Next morning Grenoble dripped with freezing rain. My new rucksack was swollen to a staggering bulk, packed with all the paraphernalia of winter survival. Annabel had re-equipped me with a thicker jacket, a Goretex coat; thicker socks, a new shirt, thermal underwear and trousers. She also left me a larger rucksack and a small gas-stove, which would make cooking in the snow easier. And a paperback to help me through the hours of darkness. A friend from London had sent a miniature thermometer 'so that I could record how cold I was'.

I crossed the Isère and climbed up past the fort into cloud-shrouded beeches, freed again from the agonizing tugs of home and the soft temptations of the city. On the mountain, life was very simple; the priority was to stay alive. This was the logic I'd learned from *les gens de là-haut*, the people from up there. As the rain and cloud thickened I reached the mouth of the Vence valley to see lights showing in a roadside bar. Madame Serges and her daughter were taking soup beside a roaring wood-burner. Bar-Restaurant La Chapelle had been in the family for 200 years. 'We are famous,' said Madame Serges, 'for our *ambiance sympathique*, our *cuisine familiale* and our *tartes maison . . .*'

'I'll have the lot. In any order.'

Ten minutes later I was presented with *champignons à la crème*, freshly picked mushrooms heated in olive oil, *crème fraîche* and garlic, with slivers of ham and bread lightly fried. The salad had a lettuce base, with ham and cubes of *chèvre*, croûtons (again, that olive oil), splashed with a mustard dressing. The cost (which included apple tart and cream, then coffee) was fifty-four francs, the equivalent in London of a short taxi ride.

Rain spattered Que Chova's crown as I followed a road up the Vence to the village of le Sappey and then the track towards the Col de la Faîta – the pass which would open the way to the heart of the Chartreuse mountains. The track climbed into light snow. I would have been wise to have fitted my new snow-gaiters to keep my feet dry, but I reasoned that the Col de la Faîta was now so close that I'd make a dash for the *cabane* on the far side. And anyway the gaiters were at the bottom of the rucksack.

The snow deepened as the track climbed steeply through the trees to 1,300 metres then disappeared in a whirling white-out. By the time I'd organized the compass and map and taken a bearing I was trembling with cold. My legs were wet from the knee down. Dusk rushed up. My spectacles clogged with snowflakes. I couldn't find my new gloves. They too must have been buried at the bottom of the rucksack. The compass led me on to a rising plateau of deepening snow. The trees fell back on both sides, then disappeared. I could see only a few metres. The map said that there would be a building of some sort. I took fifty paces to the left, then fifty to the right. Through the gloom I saw a dark angle. A roof. The building was in fact two buildings, a pair of barns. One barn was part-buried in snow and I could not find the door. The other barn was ruined and had so many planks missing that the blizzard cut straight through its interior. The floor was heaped with snowdrifts. I dumped the rucksack on the snow in the barn and dithered. Go on? Over the col? But the snow was deep. And the bearings were tricky: 122 degrees for 500 metres, then a ninety-degree left along the ridge to the col. But if I overshot the first bearing by a couple of metres, I'd go over the edge – 1,000 metres into the Isère.

At the end of the first barn there was a lean-to filled with timber and scrap metal. I climbed in and began heaving logs and sheets of corrugated iron into a protective rectangle of walls. Snow and wind whipped through the lean-to. Anticipating a draughty night, I made one last circuit of the barn, looking for a way in. The snow had drifted part-way to the eaves. I found the door, all but buried. Kicking at the drift and scooping the fallen snow with numb hands, I cleared a triangle of snowdrift and gave the door a heave. It opened. I fell inside.

All night the blizzard hammered at the roof of the barn. Several times I was woken by the rattles of ice flung from the trees at the barn roof. Inside my new, thick sleeping-bag, I was warm and thoughtful.

When I woke again at dawn I climbed down the ladder from the loft and forced the door open. Outside, the wind had dropped but curtains of thick snowflakes were still building up the drifts. My tracks of the night before had disappeared.

Snowed Under

In the opening of day, without the threat of impending darkness, the forest along the cliffs of the Col de la Faîta took on the aspect of a winter garden. The constant snowfall of the previous days had replaced the atto-detail of earth with a glaring uniformity. Even the trees looked unreal, white now and shadowed by their own limbs. Under the snow-cover I couldn't tell where paths might lie; the painted waymarks I'd often relied upon would be buried also. More than ever, I'd be relying on the compass. The edge of the snowdrifts along the cliff merged seamlessly with cloud.

My boots and trousers had got wet the day before and had now frozen. My toes were clamped by cold. I made my way slowly along the ridge, beside the invisible void. The snow was knee-deep and the weight of the pack exaggerated the imbalances of misplaced steps. When Que Chova's handle caught overhead branches a deluge of powder-snow fluffed over my head and down the back of my neck. I wanted to sit down and think what to do next. But there was nowhere to sit. I hadn't expected such an overwhelming change of rules: I could hardly move, or keep warm, or find the way, and then there were the avalanches to think about too. How, I wondered, was I going to manage another 2,000 kilometres of snow through to the end of the Alps?

I waded down the north side of the col until I dropped below the snow-line into a lightless valley. For two days I walked north through the Chartreuse mountains. Avalanche warnings were posted in the villages and I kept to the deserted roads, too unadventurous even to detour up to the Carthusian monastery of La Grande Chartreuse, a magnet over the centuries for pilgrims and those in search of solitude and wildness. Among the Romantics who came here were William Wordsworth and J. M. W. Turner, who sketched in the nearby Gorges du Guiers Mort on his first European tour in the summer of 1802. I felt a closeness with these interpreters of wild places, for it had been a visit to an exhibition by the landscape artist Richard Long which had set me thinking about lines on maps. Long had been drawing a ruled line across contours and then recording (in a suitably oblique fashion) what he found when he went out to walk that same line. Others of his lines were derived from the landscape, such as water courses or routes between summits. I liked the idea of the linear muse, of hitching up to the same nomadic thread that pulled pilgrims and *vaqueros* and land artists. But in these dark days of winter the line had become sparsely decorated; there were few signs of life in the Chartreuse; the odd column of woodsmoke or an old man probing the fog with a *baguette*. The steep-pitched house roofs that had once been thatched with rye-straw were now tiled or tinned, with eaves like hat-brims to keep the snow off the stacks of logs and kindling which doubled the thickness of south-facing walls. Close to the houses stood the *mazots*, the timber and stone lofts for stashing grain and seed; compared with the doll-temple *horreos* of Galicia these looked more like bunkers. Cattle snuffled unseen on the other side of ground-floor walls. Only the golden blocks of light cast from kitchen windows broke the greyness.

'It will not last . . .' said the *patron* of the Bar Tabac in Entremont-les-Vieux. 'Chartreuse will sleep for another ten days. On the nineteenth, that's when we wake up,' she sighed. 'Yes, that's when the skiers arrive. Then everything will change.'

At the northern end of the range I crossed the snow-covered Col du Granier and began a nightmarish 800-metre descent into the solidifying darkness. Three times I fell heavily down mud chutes lubricated by wet leaves, to reel eventually up to the gates of Rousseau's summer-house, Les Charmettes, almost incoherent with tiredness. The lights were out.

There was an hotel next door. At 110 francs for the cheapest room, it was far more than I could afford, but I was unenthusiastic about a night in the woods and anyway, I liked the idea of a room with Rousseau's view. Despite the fact that I had arrived brandishing a bent umbrella, unshaven and covered in mud, the limp, balding and terribly nice butler was good enough to ply me with free *pastis* all evening. Flatteringly, he wanted me to visit Aix-les-Bains with him. Dinner was too expensive so I made myself a pint of tea with the new gas-stove and drank it sitting with my feet in a bidet full of hot water, then moved to the window-sill to cook a meal of sardines, soup and hard-boiled egg, staring with *pastis* pupils through the trees at the lights of Chambéry.

Circumstances could not have removed me further from the possibility of tapping into the beauty that had so spontaneously inspired Rousseau. Still battered by the mountains I limped up to Les Charmettes in the morning, where Georges, who had been guiding visitors around the old farmhouse for twenty-three years, took my arm and led me from room to room.

The house was unheated – as it had been in Rousseau's day – and Georges moved stiffly beneath his thick jumper and coat, bringing the freezing house to life with all the skills of an estate agent trying to sell a ruin.

In the draughty music-room my guide held up his hands: 'Jean-Jacques! How he loved music. He played the flute, did you know? And wrote operas! Ah yes, Jean-Jacques, he was the true *autodidacte*!'

Outside the windows the lifeless garden looked wet and grey. Yet here was the orchard and the vineyard where Rousseau had spent sunlit mornings reading Huygens – who'd made the first pendulum clock – and Wallis on geometry and grammar, and Racine and Pliny and Descartes. In this garden too he had read and re-read 'at least twenty times' Virgil's *Eclogues*, an exercise which showed his mind to be a better creative organ than it was a memory bank: 'I remember not a single word,' admitted the progenitor of the Romantics, who also had the habit of leaving his books beneath the garden's trees or hedges, returning a fortnight later to find them 'rotten, eaten by ants or slugs'.

We arrived in Rousseau's room, small but facing the rising sun, with a bed occupying a curtained alcove. 'Here begins,' he had noted in Book VI of *Confessions*, 'the short happiness of life.'

At the front door, sleet was falling.

'You are travelling alone?' asked Georges as we shook hands. I nodded and he asked, 'So you do not have a family?'

'I am married.'

'Children?'

'No . . . and you?'

'I have a son.'

'What is his name?'

'We call him Jean-Jacques . . .'

The Winter Solstice

A leaden lid clamped the light from the valleys. For two days I walked along the level bed of the Isère. When bad weather kept me off the tops the consolations came in the increased frequency of encounters and in the disordered minutiae of lowland life. I'd picked up a wet tennis ball in a ditch and bounced it from Montailleur to Frontenex then noticed that my hands had turned black from the liquefied grime that had been jarred from the ball's follicles. Unwilling to throw the ball away (in case another passer-by more dedicated to salvage than myself might take on the task of shampooing the ball into a more agreeable condition), I carried it to a memorial to three *maquis* killed in a skirmish (August '44 again) and was cleaning my hands in the mist-saturated weeds when a weatherbeaten Citroën 2CV juddered to a halt on the far side of the road. An old man wearing glasses fell out and asked: 'Where are you from?'

'*Angleterre.*'

The old man's face screwed into a joyful grimace 'England! I don't believe it! I am looking for a gearbox for a 1953 Velocette motorcycle.'

'What, the single?'

'*Oui, oui!* 350 cc! Can you help me?'

'Well, not now, not at this moment.'

'Can I have your address, so that I can write to you with information about the gearbox?' The old man paused for a moment, then added: 'When will you be back in England?'

'About one year from now . . .'

'*Putain!*'

Yves lived alone in a big old house in Tournon, his wife dead and three children grown up. He said that the three *maquis* had been killed by a cannon while hiding in a small house in the woods above us, He shook his head: '*Partout la guerre . . . partout la guerre . . .*' He asked if I would like to stay with him, but Tournon was behind me. He understood that I couldn't ride in his car. 'Ah yes, I know,' he laughed. 'Once I rode my bicycle all over France. And Belgium. And Spain. I know what you mean.' As he drove away he blew a kiss from his car window.

Albertville announced itself in increments of bad taste: first the advertisement hoardings; then the petrol stations and the cubes of face-less glass. In one of the glittering stores I bought a pair of snow-shoes. They were made from lime-green plastic and each was the size of a tennis racquet. Unlike the *barahones* which the Cambridge scientist, Dr Hans Gadow, described finding in the Picos de Europa a century ago ('two flat, but curved pieces of wood, from twelve to fourteen inches long, joined together by two crossbars, upon which the boot rests, the latter being fastened by leather thongs'), my snow-shoes had separate foot-plates which were hinged at the toe, thus allowing the heel to lift with every step. The Cantabrian snow-shoe (and indeed the Eskimo one too) locked the foot down, forcing the wearer to raise the entire leg with every step, rather than to roll forward on the ball of the foot. Underneath each of my high-tech *racquets* were six *crampons latéraux*, small spikes of hardened steel for gripping on icy surfaces. I also bought a pair of pink telescopic ski-sticks.

With these lurid accoutrements strapped to my rucksack I pressed on into the heart of the Beaufortain mountains misguidedly believing that I would now be able to float across the snowy wastes in a state of miraculous levitation. But I was moving into a world that was to prove a continual conspiracy of difficulties; solving one problem simply produced another. A dog attached himself to me for an afternoon and I lost precious daylight hours taking him to a village *mairie* before I could set off up the Col du Joly, where I was appalled to feel the temperature falling far below anything I'd experienced in the Chartreuse. The dry snow squeaked beneath my boots and I could find nowhere to sleep. Eventually I unrolled my sleeping-bag on the balcony of an old wooden Savoyard mountain house, its timbers loosened by decades of dry air. The cold was so intense that I lay for an hour peeping through the puckered hole in the top of my sleeping-bag at the snow-plastered peaks with a wonder made physical by sheer exposure; a sense of anticipated hardship on a scale I had never known before. Nights like these would now be the norm. Hunger finally forced me to push both arms out of the sleeping-bag to operate the gas-stove, but the night was now so cold that for every minute my arms extended from the bag I had to spend ten minutes restoring my circulation. Neither was the tent a better option; in barns and on balconies I lay on wood and was frozen by the circulation of the night air; in the tent I lay on the snow and was frozen by heat-loss from below.

Above the old house, the Col du Joly lay between the 2,487-metre Aiguille Croche and 2,334-metre Aiguille de Roselette. In the morning the struggle to attach the snow-shoes to my boots reduced me to a gibbering psychopath. In the shop it had been so easy, with the sales assistant to help and a chair to sit on. Out in the snow I found that my heel or toe popped out of the foot-plate as I tightened the straps. My fingers turned cream with cold. Then the ratchet mechanism for adjusting the length of the foot-plates began to alter its own settings. To re-set the foot-plates required the tip of a ski-stick to be levered into a small plastic hole, while lifting a plastic flap with the other hand and sliding the foot-plate with the non-existent third hand. The whole exercise was very trying. When I finally got both snow-shoes attached to my feet, I took a tentative first step and fell face-first into a snowdrift.

Falling over happened whenever I trod on one snow-shoe with the other. I learned to avoid this by walking with my feet far apart, as if I was carrying an enormously heavy weight between my legs. In bursts of jerky waddles I made my way up the empty cirque past pretty wooden barns buried to their ears in snow. Part-way up to the col the sun broke through the *aiguilles* to my right, and in tearing off my clothes I fell over and both snow-shoes sprang off. Finally the angle of the snow eased and I stepped out on to the crest of the pass. I felt as if I'd just walked to the South Pole in swimming flippers.

Filling the view ahead of me was a single, massive mountain. Mont Blanc must have been at least fifteen kilometres away but the empty air made western Europe's highest point look within arm's reach. Intersecting crests and glaciers soared to an indeterminate summit crowned by a white beret. From this distant vantage point Mont Blanc looked too huge to be European, a spreadeagled giant out of scale with its surroundings. Shelley had been stunned at the sight, writing of 'extatic wonder not unallied to madness'. From Rousseau's birthplace in Geneva, a professor of natural philosophy, Horace Bénédict de Saussure, devoted two-thirds of his life to the mountain, putting up twenty gold thalers for the first ascent and then climbing the mountain himself in 1787, one year after the crystal-hunter Jacques Balmat and the doctor Michel-Gabriel Paccard reached the summit. Gazing across the Alps, Balmat had cried: 'I am king of Mont Blanc!' I wanted to stand there too.

But at my feet lay a view that was as depressing as Mont Blanc was uplifting. Spreading across the eastern slopes of the Col du Joly were the varicose veins of the ski industry: the crooked lines of cables and ski-pulls and pistes, dotted with black clots. Little of the original mountainside had survived; its silence, its water-sculpted flanks and its trees had all gone. A few barns remained, but skiers had used their roofs as ski-jumps. The air vibrated with an electromechanical thrum. Lumbering downhill in my snow-shoes beneath a rucksack strapped with a sleeping-mat and an umbrella I had to traverse a 'red' run while bright meteors blitzed past my elbows. I felt flat-footed, prehistoric. I moved as fast as I could, to minimize the number of minutes spent in the path of the flying flesh-bombs.

To avoid the pistes I took to the steep forest, but the drifts were thigh deep and the snow-shoes kept jamming on the branches and trunks of fallen trees, buried deep beneath the snow. Each time this happened I had to dig out my foot with my hands, unclip the two buckles on the shoe, then retrieve it and begin again. By nightfall I was still on the mountain. After a chilly bivouac sustained by mugs of tea made with melted icicles I descended a red run to Les Contamines, a sprawl of motel-type buildings jammed with cars and thousands of people dressed like Liquorice Allsorts. The mishaps continued; that afternoon I fell in a frozen stream while trying to cross a snow-choked gorge below the Col de Voza, and after ripping off the wet gaiter, boot and sock, managed to shatter the plastic zip on the gaiter while trying to chip it free of ice. By the time I had dug out a dry sock, stowed the snow-shoes and tied the broken gaiter together with a length of my blue Spanish cord, darkness was approaching. I looked back across the gorge to see that two hours of effort had gained me fifty metres of progress; in that exasperated glance I recognized that I'd have to find an easier line through the Alps if I was to have a hope of reaching Vienna.

In the half-light I followed the tracks of snow-scooters to the crest of the Col de Voza. Behind me, the sun had turned the western defences of Haute Savoie into a silhouette of broken glass. As the gradient began to ease the ice cliffs of Mont Blanc crept into view. I came out on to the bald crest of the ridge and saw how it climbed to my right, into the sky. I was standing on the toenail of Mont Blanc, the shimmering jewel I'd first seen six weeks earlier from the summit of Mont Aigoual, in an earlier season.

This was the eve of the winter solstice. For months I had been walking towards the moment in the calendar when the sun would touch the tropic of Capricorn. It was the journey's turning-point: since the summer solstice in the Sierra de Ancares, I had been walking towards darkness, reminded daily of the shortening light and lengthening night. Now the pendulum was poised to swing the other way, towards light and I'd embark on the long, euphoric swoop back towards the summer solstice. It did not occur to me that I might have to confront a third solstice.

Rather than drop off the ridge that night, I turned the other way, upwards. A piste-machine had flattened the crest of the ridge, so I climbed easily towards the cliffs at the foot of the Aiguille du Goûter, then turned off the packed snow and waded into the lee of a group of black pines. With the snow-shoes I stamped out a platform three metres long and two metres wide. On this I erected the tent, with its entrance facing due west, towards the diffused orb of the setting sun.

Mont Blanc

Chamonix, the 'World Capital of Mountaineering', is twinned with the winter-sport Meccas of Courmayeur, Garmisch-Partenkirchen, Fuji-yoshida, Aspen and Davos, but this over-developed polluted French mountain town is little more than a collection of bars and boutiques looking for a parking-space. The location of the town in the deep drain of the Arve at the tunnel entrance under Mont Blanc has cursed the inhabitants with the fumes of four million cars and 800,000 trucks which use this short-cut between France and Italy every year. Forgetting their traditional Gallic xenophobia, Chamonix's citizens had embraced imports such as 'The Pub on the Mall', 'Chamburgers' and a 'Nuit du Rock' promising English music from The Skinjobs. No fewer than seventy-four drug dealers had recently been arrested; '*Des montagnes de drogue*', read the newspaper headline. But a message left by Annabel on our telephone answering-machine gave me such an adrenaline rush that I forgot the ills of Chamonix. David Hamilton, a tall bearded Glaswegian mountaineer who always reminded me of Tintin's brave *compatriote* Captain Haddock, was by chance in the valley for some ski-mountaineering.

I found him on the edge of town on a caravan site deeply buried in snow. David's subterranean shoebox was full of human beings, skis, rucksacks and clanking bundles of mountaineering hardware. David had already climbed Mont Blanc five times so I was surprised by his cautious enthusiasm: 'It's the worst time of year to try it, but if the snow's not too loose, we can give it a go.'

David's friend John Kentish, or JK, from the Inland Revenue, agreed to complete a team of three. From the caravan window I could see Mont Blanc's summit and it looked deceptively close. 'How long will it take?'

'Better allow five days,' said David as he adjusted a ski-binding. 'At the most, seven. Though we can save a day or so by taking the *téléphérique* up the first bit.'

'I can't do that. Mechanical contrivances are out of bounds.'

'Then you can walk it. We'll meet you up there.'

'What chance have we got of reaching the summit?'

'Forty-five per cent if we start from the *'phérique*; twenty five per cent if you insist on walking up.'

Mont Blanc's difficulties, warned David, were not so much its technical challenges but its sheer scale and its reputation for multi-day storms and extremely low temperatures. 'The top's at 4,808 metres,' he nodded at the window, 'but here in Cham' we're only at 1,000 metres, or just over. So if you don't take the *'phérique* you've a climb of what . . . 3,800 metres. That's more than the height-gain from Base Camp to the top of Everest.'

Two days later I set off on the Biollay track to make a reconnaissance up through the forest to the *téléphérique* station – a climb of 1,200 metres; if I could remove the uncertainties from this section of the climb I might be able to improve the chance of success from twenty-five per cent to say forty per cent.

Nobody had used the track since the snow had fallen and it was late afternoon before I emerged from the tree-line into a bald cirque. I was wondering whether to try climbing its glazed backwall in my snow-shoes, when a man on a snow-board fell from the sky. There were two of them and they were on the way back to Chamonix after a failed attempt to climb the mountain. 'We got to nearly 4,000 metres,' shrugged the leader, a Japanese man, 'but we were tired and the snow was bad. And it was very cold.'

That evening, when I told David about this encounter, he laughed: 'Bad snow . . . bollock cold . . . Sounds like Scotland! It'll be fine.'

The *météo* was good: for the next few days the forecasters were predicting sun, with a wind at 4,000 metres of thirty kilometres per hour.

David and JK bought five days' worth of lightweight food from the supermarket. I failed to persuade them that we should take snow-shoes and instead was coerced into hiring skis, heavy plastic boots, skins and *couteaux* – detachable crampons for the skis.

We had a final drink in the Bar National, and the next morning I set off loaded like a mule. My footsteps of three days earlier guided me up through the forest and I arrived at the foot of the little cirque with enough time to pick a safe route around its steeper part, to the levelling of Plan de l'Aiguille. Following the *téléphérique* cables downhill a short way I came to the buried outline of the refuge. An hour of digging with a snow-shoe and ice-axe cleared an arc of clear space from the door and I tumbled inside. Through the evening I melted snow in my tin mug on the gas-stove; each time I dashed outside to scrape another mugful of snow I could see Chamonix vertically beneath me like an upturned casket of jewels, with diamonds flashing as headlights turned a corner. Something crystalline in the frozen air worked like a lens, multiplying the sparkles. There was no sound.

My two companions arrived on the first cable-car next morning. Beyond the *téléphérique* station I dug a hole beside a rock and buried my snow-shoes, leather boots and food for the descent. Then we snapped on the skis and David led us up the Plan and then over the edge of the lateral moraine on to the Glacier des Pèlerins.

The snow covering the glacier was silky and fast; after the initial swoop down from the moraine, we climbed gently across the glacier to the rock rib running out from the base of the Aiguille du Midi, the 1,300-metre piton of brown rock which points skywards from Mont Blanc's north-western slope. The following hour was mildly unpleasant as we edged the skis around the slope below the Aiguille above an alarmingly sheer snowfield. After so many months wearing sure-footed boots I was unimpressed by the stability of planks on steeply pitched snow and ice.

Another short descent brought us on to the broken surface of the Plan Glacier. The curved mouths of crevasses grinned each side of the snaking tramlines of the ski-tracks. Tipping over an unseen lip of bedrock, the glacier was fractured and warped into fantastic shapes: an ice finger three metres high raised in warning at a cloudless sky; a towering curl of ice shaped like a breaking wave, pierced in its centre by a perfectly circular hole large enough to crawl through. The rope tugged at my waist as David led the way through the maze.

We spent the night in the Grand Mulets hut, an aluminium shed balanced on a rock above the confluence of three glaciers. Inside, the temperature was well below zero and eating was a chore to be suffered between taking off skis and slithering gratefully into the swaddling down of a sleeping-bag. Hours were spent laboriously melting pans of snow on our gas-stove.

When I saw sunlight through the hut window next morning I realized that the chances of success had leapt. The weather was holding. David led us up a ramp of soft snow into the bed of the glacier which pours down from the summit of Mont Blanc. With the skins fitted to the underside of the skis, we also clamped on the *couteaux*. The glacier climbed steeply, drawing level, one by one, with the various *aiguilles* which form the saw-tooth profile of the mountain's defences. Progress slowed as breath came harder in the thinning air. We skirted an ice cliff, sheared by a shift in the glacier to reveal layers of strata, each marking a year of freeze and thaw. Hanging above our heads to the left were the creaking *séracs* of the ice-fall beside the Rochers Rouges. Ahead we could look up to the shallow scoop of the Col du Dôme and, on a black pin of rock to one side, the silver dot of the Vallot shelter.

Night fell as we reached the Col du Dôme. The extinguished sun was replaced by a blue half-light whose unwelcome tendrils crept across sweaty skin with the touch of ice. Fingers fumbled numbly inside rucksacks for head-torches, the skis and sticks were strapped to the outside of the rucksacks; crampons fitted to boots, ice-axe loops slipped over wrists.

With a surge David set off up the ridge towards the shelter. JK followed. The yellow blotches cast on the snow by their head-torches grew smaller as I took ten steps at a time, broken by wracked doubled-over pantings in the thin air. David reached the Vallot first and had excavated most of the snow from the entrance by the time I arrived fifteen minutes later.

The inside of the shelter was partially filled with snow. At the far end from the metal ladder at the entrance was a raised platform strewn with blankets. One side of the hut was crammed with garbage. 'Don't sneer at it!' warned David. 'There's a lot of good meals in there.'

While we yanked sleeping-bags and mats from our packs, David retold his Mont Blanc stories. He had once spent three days in a snow-hole near the summit and on another occasion survived five days in this shelter by licking out discarded tins of condensed milk. I realized again why I'd never make a serious climber: their ability to preserve their sanity in situations of claustrophobia and fear was as critical to their survival as a predilection for treading tightropes in the sky. I wasn't good at either.

The Vallot was a place of sinister dreams. Only 500 metres below the summit of Mont Blanc, its location was the second highest for a building in Europe, intended to provide emergency shelter for teams caught out by storms, darkness or injury. Climbers have managed to reach its metal door but have died of cold once inside. While I burrowed fully clothed into my sleeping-bag and tried to massage some feeling into my hands and feet, David – who claimed to be 'warm' – melted snow and made pans of tea and then a mug each of instant noodles.

It was Christmas Day.

'Wish I'd brought toothpaste,' mumbled David later, from his sleeping-bag beside me.

'Whatever for?'

'Thin slices of Mars Bar smeared with toothpaste make quite passable after-dinner mints.'

The wind hummed on the metal skin of the shelter. For a couple of hours I'd been drifting in and out of sleep, unable to ignore the thumping pain in my head. The other two had taken Diamox tablets to ease the effect of altitude. I could barely move; being fully dressed restricted movement and the inside of the bag was jammed with various items of equipment – my inner boots, a gas bottle, my water bottle – to prevent them freezing. Through the breathing hole in my sleeping-bag my eye could stare with apprehension at the hideous interior décor: snow; garbage; the stacks of skis, sticks and axes; crampons hanging like torture tools. I tried to guess at the temperature and settled on something cooler than minus twenty.

JK's voice said: 'It's 7.30.'

Nobody replied.

Half an hour later, one of the other two made tea. I didn't look to see who.

We fitted our crampons inside the shelter and clambered awkwardly up the metal ladder, through the low door and down the ladder on the far side into blinding whiteness. The sky was clear, the wind sharp. To stand in so much space and light was a contrast of heavenly release after the Arctic squalor of the shelter.

The bite of crampons, the tug of the umbilical rope and the heavy head of the axe in my hand were more reassuring than the unpredictable skis we'd left stacked in the shelter. We climbed above the shelter along the ridge towards the camel-bumps of Les Bosses. The ridge was narrow, and one foot had to be planted carefully each side of the flute of snow.

A new emotion takes over once the summit is in sight. Gone are the niggling doubts about one's capacity for failure, or for letting down the team; gone are the fears of cold, of weather, of snow conditions. Seeing the top is a panacea for all ills. The last part of that gently ascending crest passed unmeasured by time and effort, in a state of unbearably intense expectancy.

The ridge widened, then levelled. We were standing on a small dome from which the world fell away in every direction. Clouds covered Italy. The Jura mountains beyond Geneva appeared as a black reef surrounded by surf. Off to the north-east jabbed the thumb-tack Matterhorn. Beyond it, stretching into a milky-blue infinity, were thousands of peaks, glittering like shards of icy glass.

We stayed on the summit for ten minutes, taking photographs and gazing. Then euphoria began to freeze as I remembered where we were. Getting down was always more dangerous than climbing up; we had only a limited amount of daylight left to reach the Mulets hut, where a storm would be survivable. I'd developed a morbid dread of the Vallot and was determined not to be stuck there a second night.

David broke in: 'Let's get the hell out of here.'

Apart from David disappearing to his waist in a crevasse, our return down the ridge was uneventful. Less than an hour from the summit we were back in the Vallot. Precious time was lost in the laborious business of brewing tea and then thawing a tin of mackerel, which had frozen solid. By the time we had descended to the Col du Dôme, only three hours of daylight remained. What had been an even, painful slog the day before was now a dash for safety. I left ahead of the other two.

Coming around the corner into the glacial bowl below the col, my heart juddered as the air thundered. The ice cliff on the Rochers Rouges was collapsing. As the ice blocks bounded down they triggered a powder avalanche which raced across the glacier driving a bow-wave of surf. It stopped moving just before reaching our tracks.

The following morning we tilted, one by one, off the rib below Aiguille du Midi and flew back across the Glacier des Pèlerins. JK reached the rock first, and had dug out my equipment by the time I'd scrambled up the moraine to join him and David on the Plan. They left at a lope for the last cable-car with a backward yell to rendezvous that night in the National.

I came down slowly. The route down the cirque and through the trees was so familiar that I shared it as a friend. This was the fourth time I'd walked it and I ticked off the landmarks with a smile: the tree I had to clamber around; the little pebble I'd balanced on a root; the clearing with the thigh-deep snow. Five days had been squeezed into a brilliant continuum of effort and reward. Success had come with a little help from my friends; I'd enjoyed the company and the mutual reliance.

Dusk fell. The sounds of Chamonix drifted up to meet me; the roars of cars and the river; music. Then I could see the lights. Weaving through the crowds on Avenue Michel Croz, smelling the food and warmth and muttering 'Done it! Done it! Done it!' I overheard a small boy say in English: 'What's the man done, Daddy?'

Low Life

Recovery from the exertions of Mont Blanc was hampered by the traditional New Year celebrations in Chamonix. David persuaded me to join him in the annual relay race, the *Corrida de Chamonix*, in which each member of the two-person teams runs a 900-metre lap of the town centre, six times. Team 34 looked conspicuously un-professional; David wore a flashing red electric lamp on the back of his skull ('so the locals won't lose sight of me when I'm way out in front'), and for want of an alternative, I was obliged to run in my size twelve leather boots.

Dressed in skin-suits and running shoes, the other 130 athletes limbered and stretched while Haddock coughed theatrically. To reduce aerodynamic drag I tucked my mountaineering trousers into my socks. David volunteered to run the first leg, and, with Glaswegian cunning, he placed himself at the left-hand end of the jostling start line so that he could take the corner into Quai d'Arve on the inside. When the race started he shot away from the line as if he'd come down the barrel of the starter's pistol and his bearded flashing head could be seen leading the field into the first corner pursued by a tidal wave of Lycra. When he reappeared for the handover, he was lying tenth and had purple lips.

Nothing I'd experienced on the walk till then had been as excruciatingly painful as those 900 metres. The running course had slicks of water-ice on the corners and was punctuated by stretches of greasy cobbles. Runners flashed by me as if I was standing still. At the end of my first lap I collapsed into John's arms. I'd just recovered consciousness when David's flashing head reappeared screaming: 'GO-GO-GO!'

Team 34 was consistently inconsistent: on each of David's laps, we gained ten places; on each of mine we lost them. I completed my sixth lap on rubber legs and fell across the finish line to be revived by beakers of *vin chaud*. Our efforts had not passed unnoticed and during the prize-giving David and I were called forward to the podium to accept two bottles of Cuvée de la Blaitière and a pea-green T-shirt with 'Bless You' on the back. We'd won a runners-up prize for being the fastest Anglo-Scottish team. That we were the *only* Anglo-Scottish team didn't dilute our success. Winning isn't easy nowadays.

David and his crew departed for home. I gave them my post and Que Chova. Rain would be the least of my problems in the coming months and my dear umbrella was too heavy to carry as a talisman.

I left Chamonix with one of the valley's élite community of ski-bums. Wiry, unshaven, with a degree in astrophysics, Pete spoke in the valley patois; 'wicked', 'smeggy', 'funky' and 'cool' covered most descriptive needs, with 'stylin'' reserved for adjectival extremes. A fine bottle of wine was a 'good bit of kit'. Pete's work-to-play ratio was 1:4 – one week's work generating the income to ski for one month. He had two investments: his season's ski pass and his 'wheels'. He moved from chalet to chalet, living out of cardboard boxes and performing acts of quixotic chivalry. The previous week he had rescued some stranded Italian skiers from the Mer de Glace, and after they'd been helicoptered to the valley, he found himself stuck up on the glacier for the night. When he returned to Chamonix the next morning, he was too late to remove his dismantled Volkswagen clutch and gearbox from the sitting-room floor of his borrowed chalet. His landlord had got there first. Pete shook his head and grinned: 'Wicked it was, wicked.'

The ski-bums of Chamonix kept the artisan tradition alive with their industrious forging of ski passes. Skiers leaving the valley could sell their passes on the black market for a sliding scale of charges dependent on the number of remaining days' credit. The forgers filed off one side of the hollow rivet which is punched through the card for the neck cord. The undamaged stub of the rivet was withdrawn and put to one side, then the heat-sealed plastic was peeled back from the photograph, which was changed, then re-sealed with the self-adhesive plastic used for laminating maps. The set of tiny, coded perforations in the pass could be replicated with a needle; the hypodermics used by blood donors were the correct diameter. Finally the rivet-stub was pushed back into the pass and glued to the end of a second rivet cut from a discarded pass. The best craftsmen were Scandinavians; a Norwegian was turning out twenty passes a day. In an attempt to streamline production a bum had made a business trip to England, where he was able, after three months' searching, to find a rivet gun of the right size. When he returned to Chamonix, the authorities had altered the size of the rivet.

I arranged to meet Pete in Le Tour at the head of the valley. The hamlet was one of Chamonix's prettier corners and was the birthplace of Michel Croz, who died with Whymper on the Matterhorn in 1865. Pete arrived dressed in a ripped and threadbare ski-suit which he'd inherited from an American bum who'd been famous for living in garages and ruined buildings. 'Scummy guy,' grinned Pete. 'Wearing his cast-offs is worse than taking them out of a dustbin.'

Pete led the way up the snow from Le Tour, towards the Col de Balme. He'd brought mountaineering skis, spray-painted matt-black, with skins, and a frayed rucksack. Trailing in his wake wearing snowshoes and a huge pack, I followed his zigzag route around the crowded pistes and up to the skyline. The weather was changing; back down the valley Mont Blanc was suspiciously capped by a lenticular cloud. 'Not good,' warned Pete. 'Smeggy weather on the way.'

A bitter wind scythed across the ice on the Col de Balme. We pushed through the door into the skiers café on the col and were ejected immediately by the *patron*. 'Witches,' shrugged my guide as he led the way over the lip of the col in search of shelter from the icy blast. A few metres inside Switzerland, Pete chose a spot and produced a surprise picnic: kiwi fruit, bread and cheese, two bottles of beer. We sat on our packs in the snow looking at the racks of mountains while the wind thundered. 'Heat death is very bad news philosophically for the universe,' said Pete. 'You're on the way from the Big, Hot Bang, to nothing. Once you've burnt the oil and coal and stuff, it's gone. The energy density is too low for anything interesting to happen. In a million years' time there's nothing left.'

Unlike the crowded, sunny slopes on the south side of the Col de Balme, the north side was shaded, sinister, deserted and very steep. An avalanche had swept down the main gully, scouring its bed into an ice slide. Pete locked his heel-bindings and tilted over the edge. With little heart to follow I watched him jump-turn down the gully. I liked Pete; I admired his combination of knowledge and skills: the VW carburettor-mechanics, the astrophysics, the white-water kayaking and the skiing. His book box in Chamonix was filled with grimy paperbacks, among them *Arctic Dreams*, *The Fearful Void* and *Arabian Sands*. I followed him down the gully, skidding nervously as the miniature crampons on the soles of my snow-shoes lost purchase. At the foot of the gully a great tail of ice rubble fanned out towards the roofs of the Swiss village of Le Peuty. Pete said that he must set off for the road and hitch a lift back to Chamonix. He flew away, a dwindling black dot in the broad white valley.

I stamped out a platform for the tent, then buried one of the snow-shoes and the two ski-sticks as moorings for the tent's storm guys. I always took the second snow-shoe into the tent as a platform for the gas-stove which, by chance, fitted perfectly into the heel of the foot-plate.

The weather broke that night. I lay in the tent in the snow listening to the wind rage and woke in shock, dreaming that someone was shaking my shoulder. Through the tent door at dawn I saw that the snow was melting and grey cloud sealed the valley. In squalls of sleet and rain I walked the Col de Forclaz road over to Martigny in the Rhône valley. Great plans were abandoned; I had wanted to steer south to the

Matterhorn and Monte Rosa, then north to the Eiger and the great Aletsch – Europe's longest glacier. Instead, I did neither. For the next five days I walked up the grey trough of the Rhône dogged by rain and cloud.

After a month above the snow-line, I found it hard to adjust to the grubby greyness of thaw. The tones of the uncovered countryside were ugly and smelled of damp and rot. As the snow melted, the yellow grass lay slicked like wet hair. I walked on muddy tracks through the ranks of vines and along taut lanes and dismal polders beside the river. With the rain a sickly wind pushed me east up the valley.

My body was not in good shape. The intense, dry cold on Mont Blanc had split the ends of my fingers and in one of the skiing falls I had pulled a muscle in my left shoulder, which was being aggravated by the cut of the rucksack strap. My feet were in a much worse state; the toes had been battered by the days of incarceration inside plastic ski boots and had also suffered mild frost-nip. The heels were rubbed raw from the leverage of the snow-shoes. I had also picked up food poisoning.

But these were temporary inconveniences compared to the longer-term problem of coping with winter. I had come to dread the 'glooming hour', the terminal minutes of dusk. I tried to find a place for the tent, or a good barn, with time to spare; time to unpack, to wash in a stream, to eat in the light, or just to lie with the weight off my legs watching the closing light of day. But in the Rhône it was always raining and cold and the terrain was unsuitable for shelter; every square inch of land was occupied by vines, or bitumen or buildings. Sleeping one night under a motorway bridge, I found in the morning that I'd pitched my tent on a human turd. I looked into the front rooms of houses, at tables set and fires glowing; every passer-by was on their way back to a welcoming, warm home and a bed.

There were moments of respite. Arriving in the dark in the village of Riddes I was directed down to the railway tracks to a small hotel run by the Burget family. While rain slammed at the windows I subsided into an enamel bath the size of a ship's lifeboat. I hadn't been in a bath since leaving Andorra. To heighten the experience I had brought with me a bottle of chilled beer but the effect of the deep, hot water (the bath's volume was so great that I imagined the water-table of the Rhône dropping as I filled it) was so overwhelming that the beer merely complicated a sensation which was already impossibly delicious. At home I habitually ate lunch in our kitchen while reading the newspaper and listening to the radio; now I found that a coffee, or a newspaper, had to be savoured in isolation if I was to avoid sensory meltdown. I found that I had a capacity for that underrated leisure activity, thinking.

Seven days after leaving Chamonix I walked into Brig. The town had grown up at the foot of the Simplon Pass, where the Alpine watershed was pinched to less than thirty kilometres between the low-lying, flat-bottomed Rhône and the Ossola which reached north from the plains of Lombardy. Ancient passes, and now railway tunnels, radiated out from Brig to north, south, east and west; you could board a train in Viktoriastrasse for London, Rome, Vienna, Lisbon or Gornergrat – the sky-high station above Matterhorn's glaciers. Everybody in Brig was coming or going, snatching *Kalbsbratwurst vom Grill mit Rôsti* – a slimy interpretation of sausage and chips – in the *Bahnhof* buffet or frowning over timetables. 'I'm shocked we missed it!' wailed a New Yorker to his girlfriend as he stabbed at a 'train change' symbol. 'This Brig shit!'

When the woman running the station information desk said that the Simplon had been cleared of snow, I decided to bail out of the Rhône, over the watershed into Italy. But before I left for the mountains again, my feet needed surgery. I gave them a pre-med in the sink with hot water and soap then laid out the towel on the bed and opened the smaller of the two blades on my Swiss Army knife. Six toenails were black. As non-contributory luggage, these could be ignored. The left heel was raw from wearing snow-shoes, but this was already healing. The only problematical ailment was the side of one of the big toes, which had been numb since descending Mont Blanc. Now the numb area had turned black. With the point of the knife I pierced the edge of the black area, then pushed in the knife and lifted the blade, like opening an olive. Using the edges of the flap of dead skin to provide 'bite' for the knife's blade, I chased around the margin of the black area. The side of the toe fell off on to the towel, then rolled to the floor with a 'tick'. The new skin was as soft as salmon flesh; the toe oddly asymmetric.

When Goethe had limped down to this valley in 1779 he had enjoyed a sweeter pedicure: his guide arranged for the poet's feet to be bathed in a warm soup of red wine and clay and then dried by a servant-girl.

I left Brig loaded with two days' food and a couple of parcels from Annabel I'd collected from the post office. From Annabel's letter I learned that the heating in our house had packed up; a few lines later she wrote out a long list of children's names. As I climbed back towards the tree-line I had a clear picture of my wife, shivering broodily on her own, and a massive guilt attack was only averted by her last lines: 'You've written some lovely letters recently, about us and what we're doing . . . *Lebenskünstlers,* life-artists . . . That's what I hope we will be. This feels like a good start.'

Footpaths led up the dead pastures above Brig to the villages of Lingwurm and Brei, deserted for the winter, and into the forest. Escaping the Rhône – and Annabel's letter – had pulled the lead from my boots; the Simplon would open the way to Italy and its magical lakes. For a while my way followed the worn flags of the old muleteers' track. Below thundered the gorge of the Saltina – the Saltinaschlüocht. I put up the tent on a high bluff with views up the valley to the peaks of Hübschhorn and Breithorn – both now clear of cloud – and I celebrated my return to the heights with a miniature bottle of House of Lords whisky I'd found in one of Annabel's parcels, followed by a classic Tin Cuisine recipe: *Kartoffel Fondue mit Brot* – made by spreading two-thirds of a mugful of instant mashed potato mixed with cheese, on bread, thickly. Morning, I knew, would bring new fortune.

Crossing the Simplon

> Next morning we mount againe through strange, horrid & firefull Craggs & tracts abounding in Pine trees, & only inhabited with Beares, Wolves & *Wild Goates,* nor could we any where see above a pistol shoote before us, the horizon being terminated with rocks, & mountaines, whose tops cover'd with Snow, seem'd to touch the Skies, & in many places pierced the Clowdes.

John Evelyn's description of the Simplon seen from the back of a mule in May 1646 was understandably graphic for a man who grew up in the comfortable contours of Surrey. Two centuries later the poets, writers and painters were queuing up for the same experience: Words-worth, Byron, Hobhouse, Moore, Corot, Musset, Balzac, Dickens, Flaubert, Gautier and Meredith all passed through this defile separating the dark northern forests from the sunlight and space of Lombardy. The

Simplon had been tamed at the beginning of the nineteenth century, when Napoleon commissioned a new road over the pass.

From my camp above Saltinaschlüocht I dropped down into the ravine and picked up a path through the snow on the east side of the torrent. Almost immediately, I passed an old milestone propped on a cliff. The stone was cut with the number '43' (the distance in kilometres from Domodossola on the far side of the pass) and had presumably fallen down the cliff from Napoleon's road above my head. Evelyn noted in his diary that the way along the valley was marked with 'tall Masts' to guide travellers past the hazards. The bed of the ravine was locked in a blue glacial chill and there were no signs that the path had been used since the snows had arrived weeks earlier. Cones of water-ice fanned out from the base of the ravine cliff, blocking the path.

The climb to the top of the pass was no more than a 300-metre gain in altitude, but the forest was steep and north-facing and deep snow had filled in the gaps between rocks. Evelyn's party had trouble on this descent (they were crossing in the opposite direction, from the Duchy of Milan to Brig) when the irritable Captain Wray's horse fell and slid 'almost two miles' – a remarkable feat of equine glissading which the horse survived 'without any other harme, than the benumbing of his limbs . . .'

Above the Saltina I joined Napoleon's road on the broken plateau which forms the Simplon's crest. At the base of the granite eagle commemorating the Gebirgs Brigade II from the Second World War, I lit the stove and cooked a mug of soup while the crackle and crump of machine-guns and mortars echoed between the ice-fields of Tochuhorn and Hübschhorn. (The following day I stumbled accidentally on one of the Swiss Army's mountain lairs; from a section of old road I watched a slab of mountainside slide to reveal a tunnel entrance, then a team of soldiers winching a generator from the bed of a truck on my side of the gorge, to the cavern door on the other.)

The southern side of the Simplon was broader and less snowy. I came down into the Chrumm valley on frozen tracks between drystone walls which reminded me of the Lake District. The frozen soil rang like iron to the tips of my ski-stick.

It was in this high, silent valley that Evelyn met a tribe of giants with tumours on their throats as big as hundred-pound bags of silver. The weight of the tumours dragged down the flesh of the faces rendering them 'so ougly, shrivel'd and deform'd' that many were obliged to tie a strip of linen around their heads and under their chins. He added that they were further afflicted by a 'strange puffing habit' and a 'barbarous Language, being a mixture of corrupt high *German, French* & Italian.' The cause of this unfortunate malady, notes Evelyn, was the drinking of snow-water; the men, who drank more wine, were less affected than the women. They were, he adds, 'extreamly fierce & rude, yet very honest and trustie'.

As he travelled in the Alps two centuries later, Edward Whymper's fascination with cretinism included various observations on other afflictions peculiar to the mountains. Goitres, he found, were highly prized, for to be goitred exempted the sufferer from military service. Young men went to extreme lengths to grow goitres, including strapping their necks with leather belts. Whymper's solution to such shirking of duty was simple: 'Let them be forced into regiments by themselves, brigaded together, and commanded by crétins. Think what *esprit de corps* they would have! Who could stand against them? Who would understand their tactics?'

I had little chance to meet the 'Ouglies of Chrumm' since the three villages I passed – Egga, Simplon and Gabi – were deserted. In Gabi I cursed outside the locked bar, learning from a painted signboard that Napoleon had stopped here for a glass of milk on 27 May 1807 and paid for it with a five-franc piece. I'd have paid fifty francs for a coffee and a warm seat. The tent was pounded that night by gusts dropping off the Fletschhorn's glaciers and I lay in the dark imagining that this was the Alps giving me an ill-tempered kick in the backside as I scuttled south out of range.

In the Dark

A soporific wind was drifting up Lake Maggiore from the south. In the waterside gardens mothers rolled prams past ducks while octogenarians watched the white steamers slide past the mountains. Above their heads, paragliders floated like sycamore seeds off the summit of Cimetta. Locarno was enjoying that out-of-season hiatus which beautiful places experience for a few weeks in the calendar between the outgoing and incoming migrations of tourists. The only other foreigner in town was a thirty-nine-year-old Californian woman with a biological clock ticking like a cartoon time bomb: 'I'm looking for a husband,' she confided. 'A European. A count'd do.'

'They're all broke or in prison.'

'Yup, but they're not *gay*. Every male in California is gay. And anyway I don't like American men.'

I pointed to my wedding-ring and said that soon I'd have spent more of my married life away from my wife than with her.

'That's not *normal* here is it? I mean, *Jesus*! Maybe I'll stick with *Americans*.'

I spent a night in Locarno, where I was the only resident in the immaculately clean and comfortable traveller's hostel, and in the morning left my pack behind and walked up above the town to the Franciscan monastery of Madonna del Sasso, perched like one of Amalfi's palaces on a spur above the water, with sheltered terraces and alluring sun-traps. Swiss prices have changed Locarno's visitor-profile. Once it was a haven for convalescents, like impoverished James Joyce, who had come here half-blinded with glaucoma in 1917, dispatching the first part of *Ulysses* to Ezra Pound. Nowadays the cost of a coffee in Locarno would buy a whole café in the continent's poorer slums. From Madonna del Sasso I could see across the head of the lake to the silver mountains thirty kilometres away, dividing Lake Maggiore from Lake Como. Part-way along this mountain wall was the notch of the 2,014-metre San Jorio pass. It wouldn't be a legal border crossing, but it was the quickest route to cheaper coffee.

That night I put up the tent in a field between Locarno and the San Jorio and settled into a now-familiar routine of washing my feet, cooking, writing my journal, reading and finally, at about ten p.m., falling asleep. The fourteen hours or so of incarceration in the tent were always fully occupied but the long spells of near darkness were increasingly visited by weird semi-conscious thought meanders and troublesome dreams. That night I was woken again by Annabel calling my name. As I opened the tent to look outside, thick frost skittered off the nylon; the valley mist was so dense that I couldn't see the far side of the field. It was a Sunday. I walked towards the bells of Giubiasco – astride the old road down from the St Gotthard pass – and telephoned London. After the dream, I'd expected a crisis, but Annabel was at our breakfast table sorting negatives prior to a session in the dark-room.

'The *dark*-room?' I wailed. 'What an awful thought.'

'I can't wait,' she replied. 'I'll be in there all day.'

The snow on the pass was deep and untrodden except for two sets of boot-prints, walking downwards, one male adult, the other a child or a small footed woman. I followed the prints up the forest and out above the tree-line to a locked building at 1,680 metres, where both had rested. Who were they, I wondered. Illegal immigrants looking for work in Switzerland? They couldn't have been up here for fun. Nobody in their right mind would come hiking on the sombre slopes of San Jorio when there were so many more picturesque places close by.

Not enough light remained to cross the pass before nightfall, so I erected the tent outside the building. For a last time I watched the sun set over the Pennine Alps and many-headed Monte Rosa – now one hundred kilometres away but clear enough to hold in the palm of a hand. From a dying sunflower above Monte Rosa, the rings of colour radiated outwards, through a nimbus of apricot to inky blues. In the foreground, Lake Maggiore and Centovalli were covered for the night by downy clouds.

In penetrating cold I was woken by a nightmare I'd had before: I was sitting against the inside wall of what must have been a barn, at night, and was slipping into a deep sleep when something made me glance up to a mirror on the opposite wall. In the reflection was my face and, looking over my shoulder, a second male face. I woke in choking panic and lay waiting for light willing away the long hours of darkness. Most nights I'd fall asleep by nine or ten p.m., but there was no point in beginning to move until 5.30 a.m., an hour before dawn, when I began a well-oiled routine. I turned myself around in the tent, so that my head was at the entrance, where I could reach the snow outside the door. The first snowball always hissed as the flame from the gas jets heated the steel mug faster than the heat could dissipate into the powdery crystals. Once the snow-melting was under way, I dismantled my pillow of clothing and towed my trousers and shirt and socks down into the sleeping-bag, to pre-heat them prior to dressing. Each time the rising level of water in the mug came to the boil, I topped it up with a snowball. Between each stage I withdrew into the sleeping-bag. When the mug was half full, I mixed in a few spoonfuls of milk powder and then filled the mug to the brim with muesli. Once this was downed I repeated the water-creation process and made a half-mug of coffee, to be taken with bread and cheese.

With my body warmed by breakfast, I dressed inside the sleeping-bag. Since Grenoble, I'd carried two sets of thermal underwear, one for sleeping (which I always kept with the sleeping-bag, in a plastic bag, as my last line of thermal defence) and the other for walking. So my first task was to remove the thermal long johns and vest and then replace them with an identical set inside the sleeping-bag without either muddling the two lots or pulling on the garments back to front. To an observer I would have looked like a chrysalis having convulsions. Squirming into the trousers and shirt were easier. Then I pulled on my fleece jacket and Goretex coat, the balaclava helmet, and finally the trilby (in which I'd kept my spectacles for the night).

Once dressed, I lay with the sleeping-bag up to my armpits while I checked the day's route on the map by candle-light. If I was leaving the camp on a compass bearing, I set the compass in the tent. Then I pushed the map for the day into the thigh-pocket of my trousers. Leaving the sleeping-bag was the least pleasant moment. I first packed the food and candle-tin back into their plastic carrier bag and the stove in another bag. Both bags were trussed with elastic bands. Then I pushed off the sleeping-bag and stuffed it into its bag, then piled the four bags and water bottle just inside the tent door. Every stage that followed had to be accomplished quickly; a two-minute fumble could leave fingers frozen for an hour. In one move I swivelled so that my feet faced the door and pulled on my gaiters and then boots. Uncurling myself into the outdoors I dragged out the rucksack and stuffed in the sleeping-bag then the other bags, leaving the food on top. The tent came down in two minutes or so, was rolled up and wedged into the rucksack's lower compartment, with the poles pushed down the back of the main compartment. The water bottle fitted in an exterior pocket. If the timing had worked, I would be lifting the rucksack to my back as the first light showed in the east.

On this morning, on San Jorio, I was away by starlight on snow-shoes. Above my camp a broad gully led up to a gently rising traverse along the southern slope of Cima di Cugn. Daylight brought a tormented sky; over to the west, Lake Maggiore was still filled with mist, but above it the peaks were flattened by careering grey clouds. It was a wild, freezing morning, and on this sunless side of the pass I felt confident that nobody would spot a tiny single figure. An hour after leaving the camp I staggered over the pass in a wind that snatched at my legs and snow-shoes, then slithered down the far side, into the sun and back into Italy.

Winter Watershed

I came down from the San Jorio pass to Virgil's Lacus Larius – Lake Como – and spent a night in the waterside village of Gravedona, a lyrical spot, where little piazzas and old churches contemplated the lake and the baker sold *chiacchiere*, sugar dusted pastries, to complement the relay of smoking *cappuccinos* I enjoyed while the sun rose.

Just up the road, Mussolini had finally been captured on 27 April 1945 by the partisan leader Count Pier Luigi Bellini delle Stelle, then executed the following day. So often in the mountains beauty and horror shared the same views. Tyrants take refuge in mountains as well as saints and refugees. As a source of contemporary evil, the Alps were unmatched among Europe's ranges, for it was in this range that the Second World War was conceived; on the shores of Lake Como, I turned to cross the Alps from south to north, to Bavaria and the roots of Hitler's war. It was a black quest but one which had an ulterior motive; from Como I was well placed to reach the headwaters of the frozen Inn, whose long valley I could follow obliquely across the Alps. The walking would be easy and by the time I emerged on the far side of the range I was sure I'd have cracked winter; I'd have crossed the winter watershed.

So I went along the shingle beach while the wind pushed white horses past the snowy frieze of Monte Legnone. At the head of the lake, I pressed on along a cobbled path that climbed above the reed-beds into the woods. My short respite from the frozen world above the snow-line was set to last just a few hours more. In this dwindling intermission, every facet of the uncovered country stood in sharp relief. The path itself was a miracle; so easy to follow and so certain. I'd forgotten how paths had their own cognition; their way of introducing their past. They carried in their sunken beds the footfalls of long-gone travellers and in their air the smells of bridles and the ring of iron and bronze. Romans had come here, marching up from Larius to the passes of Maloja and Julier, where their stone columns still lay, buried in snow. Overgrown below the eastern shoulder of Monte Berlinghera I found their stone ramp, ten metres high and wide enough for chariots to descend the cliff to the River Mera.

I followed the Mera upstream through chilled, inward-looking villages. I no longer found myself at strangers' kitchen tables. The colder, self-protective Alpine cultures were wary of a foreigner on foot carrying luggage in winter. The insulation was mutual; the harshness of the season drove me indoors too. I pushed along a wheel divided into the four quadrants of survival – navigation, shelter, food and warmth – and the wheel was not just space but time as well, so it was always rolling and I was always having to think and plan for the next quadrant. My route was still one of digressions and whimsical detours, but now I was detached from their purpose. There was too little time, and the days were too cold, for *inquiry*. I just looked. And only looking increased the detachment, as if I was uninvolved, or as if it wasn't really me who was there. My remoteness from the here and now made me less concerned about what happened to the man with the battered trilby. Because he wasn't me.

The Mera turned a corner at Chiavenna and became walled in by the peaks of Bregaglia. For a clearer view, I climbed hundreds of steps up to the village of Savogno perched on a sunward ledge 500 metres above the valley floor.

Savogno had no road and, try as I might, I could remember no other roadless village I'd passed other than Bulnes, in the Picos de Europa. And like Bulnes, Savogno was timeless, looking much as it had 500 years earlier. Wooden balconies clung precariously to lopsided walls separated by cobbled alleys and flights of stone stairs. Every levelling had been created by painstaking terracing. The only sign of modernity was the steel cable that the villagers used to winch their supplies up from the valley below. The village had been locked for winter; the only inhabitant was a cat, the only sound the water spout. A stone lying against an alley bore the date 1535. Later I met a man on a path who said that forty people lived in Savogno, in the summer.

Val Bregaglia climbed gently towards the interior of the Alps. I passed for the third time into Switzerland and climbed once again high up the valley side, this time to Soglio, the village popularized through the centuries for its sublime light and bewitching views across to the Bondasca glacier and the giants of Bregaglia. *'La Soglia del Paradiso'*, the threshold of paradise, Soglio was dubbed by the painter Segantini. The poet Rainer Maria Rilke agreed that 'everything there was like a promise of future events . . .' But by the time I reached the village a wet mist had overtaken me and the view was cut to ten metres and the light was grey and depressing. Pension Willy, where Rilke stayed, was shuttered and closed. I spent the rest of the day on paths that tiptoed up through the contours on the steep northern slope of the valley until I passed through the snow-line. By moonrise I was standing in knee-deep snow at the foot of the Maloja pass.

A motor-road climbed the pass out of sight to my right, but I wanted to find the old Roman road up through the black pines. Wearing snow-shoes and a head-torch to read the compass I waded up through the forest till the light of the torch caught the first painted mark on a tree. The climb occupied half the night. In the deep snow and in the blackness of the forest, the path had entirely disappeared, and I could only make progress by leaving my rucksack and searching upward for the next paint-mark on a tree trunk, or other likely clues such as dips in the snow or linear clearings. Then I'd climb down and recover the rucksack. Occasionally I caught a glimpse of headlights probing the icy road far below. Few night climbs had given me as much pleasure. I felt fit and patient and was happy to spend so many hours gaining these few metres if it meant that I could wake on the crest of the Maloja. The pass was one of the points that defined the journey: it was on the continental watershed. Above the Maloja rose three rivers, one flowing south to the Mediterranean; another flowing north to the North Sea; and the third, the Inn, running the length of the Engadine to reach, by devious means, the Black Sea.

Leap-frogging upward I eventually reached the top of the cliffs, where there was a clearing in the trees. I was pressing out a rectangle for the tent, when I saw an opening beneath my snow-shoes. It was a small concrete door or window. Squirming through the gap in the snow I dropped through to a room, lined with concrete and fitted along one wall with rusting metal frames. The temperature on the miniature thermometer read minus seventeen. I slept on a wooden shelf under the frames but was woken by the cold before dawn. In the long wait for daylight to show at the slot above my head, I hugged my knees, buried in a tomb which nobody would see till the snow melted in spring.

At first light I extricated myself from my refrigerated lair and waded through the snow until I emerged from the trees in Maloja village, once a favourite base for discerning Victorian travellers who valued its isolation from overrun St Moritz, further down the valley. The explorer Sir Richard Burton stayed here in the last year of his life and Thomas Huxley liked it too: '. . . the air is splendid,' he wrote, 'excellent walks for invalids, capital drainage . . .' In this last respect, Maloja was unchanged. The lavatory of the Hotel Schweizerhaus, a gigantic parody of Swiss vernacular with balconies fretted into arboreal lace, was plumbed for the Space Age. Looking for a sink to wash my hands (and feet and head, socks, shirt, etc.) I was led to a white cabinet with a deep recess on its front surface. I put in my hands and they were sprayed with hot water, then splattered with an ejaculation of creamed soap. The machine waited while I lathered my hands, then rinsed them in a fine spray and finally blew them dry with hot air. Huxley would have been amazed. The machine's one drawback was its height above the floor, which demanded a hand-stand if one was to get one's feet into its cleansing orifice.

Unlike most passes, the Maloja had no drop-off on its far side. Instead it opened into the high snow-filled avenue of the Engadine. The morning was brilliant and clear and numbingly cold. I walked all day on the black metallic ice of the Engadine lakes. I was one of hundreds. A rabbi on skis with a long white beard, wearing a black skull-cap and greatcoat, passed me with a nod, and babies cocooned in down, lashed to pulkas behind their fathers. Two demented writers strode in shoes on the ice arguing animatedly. Skin-suited athletes swung past like flocks of swallows leaving nothing but the whisper of minimal friction hanging in the still air. Most had come up from St Moritz, where I intended to find a sheltered shop doorway for the night, a plan that was averted by Theo, a ball-bearing specialist from Schweinfurt, who insisted on taking me to the youth hostel so that I could sleep indoors 'We are shocking! . . . We are shocking!' repeated Theo's wife in approximate English over dinner in their chalet as I explained the inconveniences of winter camping.

St Moritz is better suited to ex-empresses and soccer stars than to vagrants and I left next day, at dusk, to avoid another expensive night in the hostel. Below St Moritz the trails through the snow were deserted and I walked alone for hours on end through silent forest. Until the nineteenth century these woods were full of life, but the rate of attrition was too great for the game species to survive. One John Colani of Pontresina had shot 2,700 chamois by the time he was twenty. The house steward of the *Schloss* at Zernez had shot a dozen bears. I'd seen no wildlife since disturbing a couple of deer down in Bregaglia, but one morning I woke on the edge of a wood to see a stag the size of a small horse standing a few steps from the tent. He was a twelve pointer; I hardly dared breathe. He raised his head slightly, drawing the air, then stepped on through the snow with unhurried regal dignity.

I had no spare energy for rushing up peaks, or for entertaining detours. But instead of passing life by, I found that it came to me instead. I was startled from a daydream by a girl on a white horse galloping past with snow spraying from its hooves; a hot-air balloon hung above and I could listen to the conversation of its aeronauts; the Glacier Express trundled along the Engadine at dusk with the lit windows filled with dining passengers.

Two women joined me on the snowy path up to the hill village of Guarda, teaching me Ladin, one of the Rhaeto-Romansch dialects left behind in the Alps since the time of the Romans. The language was confusing, with no fewer than five variations, two in the Engadine alone. But I remembered *Allegero!* (Good day!) and *Arrivia* (Goodbye) – which won me friends in the village shops – and I was able later to decipher the prayers and exhortations to have faith which decorated the patterned exteriors of the Engadine houses.

Fortunately the clear skies stayed through to the end of January and into February. I was losing sleep in the long cold nights. I started to make mistakes. I wrecked the water bag I'd carried since Spain by allowing it to freeze solid. The ice crystals tore it to ribbons. A buckle on the rucksack snapped. One night while floundering in the snow, I lost the pedometer – an inaccurate but entertaining gadget I'd bought in Chamonix to measure my daily distances. A piece from one of my snow-shoes fell off and was lost. The handle on the mug melted off. The arms on my spectacles worked loose and I had to remember to tighten the screws every morning. I set a sock on fire trying to thaw it over the gas-stove, then melted a boot insole in the same way. A shampoo sachet I'd liberated from a room in St Moritz split and emptied over my toothbrush and vitamin pills. My camera repeatedly froze because I kept forgetting to keep it inside my jacket. I should have stopped to rest and to mend. But I couldn't afford the cost or the chance to make progress while the sky was clear. I was a mess. As each of my little 'systems' fell by the wayside, it was replaced by a faith in momentum.

I was called down the Engadine by the bells of the churches. Between the villages I walked on tracks, snowed over, high on the valley side. Six days after leaving St Moritz I called at a village called Tschlin, having run out of food. But it was a Sunday and the shop was closed. For safety I ought to descend to the valley floor and the road. Unable to come to a decision, I spent an hour looking around the empty streets. One of the houses was painted with a Ladin prayer:

LA VIA AIS STIPA

MO PUR PASSAI

ED IN DIEU AS FIDAI!

which I approximately translated as: The way is steep but you have to take it and trust in God. I pressed on along the mountainside with just one chocolate bar remaining. The Inn was in a gorge here, squeezed between the Silvrettagruppe and the Otztal Alps. The map showed a summer path contouring along the valley at about 1,700 metres till, after about seven kilometres it zigzagged down to join the road at the border-crossing into Austria.

Normally tracks heading down a valley become wider, as they are joined by increasing numbers of feeder-paths from pastures and hamlets. This one became narrower, then disappeared. I was very hungry and tired. The snow was deep and loose. Keeping to the same level on the valley side I came to a gully coming down from a couloir beneath the summit of Pic Mundin. The gully was choked with avalanche debris. Across the valley the mountains which had recently released the body of 'Otzi' the Iceman reminded me how easy it was to make these mistakes. Otzi had been my age, thirty-five to forty they think, and had been trying one pass too many when he was caught by nightfall. He died lying down, with his head on a stone, and was buried by snow. Five thousand years later, Otzi emerged from a glacier with his bow and quiver and grass-filled shoes, entirely bald but for four pubic hairs.

The second gully was much more difficult to cross. Under new snow was a chute of ice. With stiff boots and an ice-axe this would have been as easy as a street pavement, but with flexible boots and a pair of ski-sticks, the traverse made me nervous. Below me the gully plummeted 500 metres to the Inn. A third gully had little snow but was bombarded by stonefall.

Beyond the gullies the mountainside was striated with snow ledges. On one of these ledges was the summer path, but I had no way of knowing which. Then I came on deer prints. I followed the prints for an hour as they made their way along the ledges, climbing then descending, always missing the dangerous corners. The deer had selected the only sequence of ledges which would lead them off the east face of Mundin, and they led me to safety.

I got down to the Inn at dusk. Four days later I walked down the Fern Pass towards the great tower of Zugspitze, on the northern edge of the Alps.

Fallen from Angels

'You'd like to go up Wank?'

'Excuse me?'

'Wank is a good peak,' said the girl at the information desk. 'One thousand seven hundred and eighty metres. You can use the *Wankbahn*.'

'I have a rule that I don't use mechanical contrivances . . .'

'Then you go on the *Wankweg*.'

Wank's sunny aspect and views of Zugspitze make it popular with elderly adherents of *Liegekur* – deck-chair cure – and with students on rail holidays who've already sent postcards from Condom and Craponne in France. The mountain is a gentle thing on the edge of Garmisch-Partenkirchen, the showpiece resort that hosted the 1936 Winter Olympics, but there was no hope of me reaching its summit; I'd had a bad day. Having camped in the forest below Zugspitze, I'd crossed the border into Germany up in the trees. The snow was deep and I'd tripped on the snow-shoes and smashed my knee on a rock. The damage wasn't great but the knee was swollen and bloody and I'd limped down to the town to check into an unaffordable *Gasthaus* for an afternoon's convalescence on a bed.

I could have rested longer but didn't dare stay. The cost was appalling and the high-pressure system that had brought a month of cold clear weather still sat over the Alps. While the sun strode daily across a brilliant sky I couldn't afford to waste the chance to move further east. I collected my new boots and mail from the post office and set off along the Bavarian Alps. I could already sense Vienna beyond the horizon; my half-way point to Istanbul lay only 400 kilometres away as the crow flew, or about 700 kilometres by foot. Among the letters was one from Annabel confirming that she would meet me in Vienna. 'Just let me know when you'll be there . . .' she had asked. Laughter rang in the valleys. Sledges, skis and skates whizzed and skidded. Outside Wallgau, husky-dogs raced around an eight-kilometre circuit in teams of four and six, towing their frosted riders while cheering spectators cupped steaming beakers of *Glühwein*.

This was Bavaria. Germany. Food was served for giants; a humble 'toastie' was large enough to fill a family; *Schweinemedaillons mit Rahm-champignons und Röstzwiebel* was served as a mountain of beef and pork bedded on lettuce and radish, beneath lava flows of mushroom sauce. *Konditorei* windows were stacked with baroque confections oozing kirsch or cream – or both – which could be taken with *grosse* cups of hot chocolate in the café beyond the counter. Even the cans of sardines I carried to my refrigerated camps were exotic; presented in polychromatic piscatorial wrappers printed with salivatory titles like *Sardinen in Feiner Kräuter-creme*. A can of humble bangers became *Pikant Gewürst mit Curry in Pflanzenol*.

Two days after leaving Garmisch-Partenkirchen, I arrived on the shore of Walchensee, the first unfrozen lake I'd seen since Como. Beneath a ring of steep black *Bergs* I found a place for the tent, on a peninsula facing west, then watched the sun go down over 1,700-metre Herzogstand. When I woke, the lake was hidden by a thick mist and a cold wet wind cut through the pines. The weather had at last broken.

The snow fell for a month, some days as a few weary flakes, others as long-term onslaughts. I laboured alone, day after day, through an interminable white wilderness, precariously separated from catastrophe by a combination of chance and concentration. Climbing over the top of a nondescript mountain called Fockenstein in a blizzard (for no other reason than it was in my way), I nearly knocked myself out after skidding on ice and breaking my fall with my forehead on a tree. In bare trees rooks waited like undertakers. At night the hinds barked in the forest – sharp desolate roars that never failed to make me start. My days became polarized between Breughelesque extremes; the human silhouette in the white and black forest and the bumptious hubbub of the *Gasthof*.

Since eleven minutes past eleven on the eleventh day of November – the eleventh month – Bavarians had been preparing for *Fasching*, the rolling carnival which drives out the evil spirits of winter and welcomes in the spring. In the spa of Bad Feilnbach, I'd taken a bed in the *Gasthof* in order to tend my wounds, and in the evening had settled into the bar over a colour brochure describing the spa's treatments for 'gynaecological disonders'. I was examining a photograph of a woman reclining in what looked like a tub of hot manure (a caption reassured readers that 'each bath is prepared with fresh mud'), when I was called to the adjacent table by an elderly man.

'You know,' he said, 'that it is "Nonsense Thursday"? It is *Weiberfastnacht*, Women's Night.' Karl Jahn explained that we were barred from using the restaurant and that we could expect some abuse later in the evening. The women wear masks so that no one can tell who is who. Of the various stages of *Fasching*, this was the maddest. In Köln, he said, it was much worse. There, the women exacted Freudian retribution on men by snipping off their ties. 'It is difficult for men on Nonsense Thursday,' added Karl, who had fought at Monte Cassino as an eighteen-year-old. 'No men are allowed outdoors before ten p.m., unless they dress as women. It is best to stay indoors. Or go to the forest.' The climax would be the procession on Rosenmontag, in four days' time. Shrove Tuesday would bring hangovers and the start of Lenten abstinence.

All night a female brass band reeled to and fro through the bar, yodelling and tossing back schnapps. Some of the band were men, dressed and made-up as women pretending to be men, with painted moustaches and dislocated bosoms. The abuse was more survivable than the schnapps. At breakfast I asked my neighbour, a northerner with a *Blutwurst* complexion, what he thought of *Fasching*. 'It's for the Catholics,' he shrugged. 'We are Protestants and *Fasching* means nothing to us.'

The blizzard scratched the grey sky, covering the roads with soft drifts that immobilized all traffic. Inside my layers I was warm and dry, self-contained and pleased to have the land to myself. Village names on my maps sounded like a genealogy of sprites and goblins: the warring brothers Anger and Sinning; the six crooked cousins, Hub, Eck, Ed, Moos, Heft and Zain; mean Uncle Taxa; Wart and Gugg who guarded the bog; soft-hearted Furt; and Funk who was always frightened. And wincing Rimsting. Their homes were on the map too: Sodding and Wind-Passing; Petting, Necking and Fucking.

Cloaked in white I crossed the muffled plain and on *Fasching* Sunday turned back into the mountains. In England Annabel and I would have been celebrating our second wedding anniversary; in Ruhpolding the streets were fogged with breath. Booths sold *Fasching Krapfens* – apricot-filled doughnuts – and steaming *Glühwein*, while a troupe of women in gold masks, red top-hats and black cloaks danced through the well-wrapped crowds and *Bockwurst* stalls singing and waving red umbrellas.

The next day the snow was falling so fast as I climbed the Schwarz-bach that the ploughs couldn't keep the road clear and the cars piled up at the bottom of the pass like abandoned sledges.

While avalanches rumbled in the white-out I entered the magic forest of Zauberwald and stamped out a space for the tent in the thigh-deep drifts. Local legend has it that God bade the angels distribute all the things of beauty equally throughout the world. The angels gathered up in their gowns the mountains and seas, the rivers, lakes, trees and flowers, but two of them paused to admire the beautiful things that they carried and when the Lord saw this, he let them enjoy their wonder for a while and then reminded them to be on their way. The two angels were so startled by the voice of God that they dropped the folds of their gowns and all the beautiful things fell out in a cascade and landed on one spot, which is now known as Berchtesgadener Land.

On a map, Berchtesgadener Land takes the shape of an arrow-head about one-quarter of the size of Andorra, inserted into Austria. This virtual enclave is crammed with mountains – among them Watzmann, the highest peak entirely within Germany – which focus on fjord-like Königsee, eight kilometres long and the country's deepest lake. Until it was annexed by Bavaria in 1803, Berchtesgadener Land was a separate state ruled by its own provosts.

Into this land of rustic rhythms came the unhappy son of an illegitimate minor customs official, Alois, who had lived for a while with the name of his mother, Schicklgrüber. The boy grew up across the border, in Austria, in a small place called Braunau – 'brown pasture'. His early passion for painting enraged Alois and the boy left home for Vienna, where he survived by his wits, making a meagre living drawing postcard sketches and beating carpets. When the Great War began, he volunteered for the army and fought bravely, but after the Armistice he fell under the spell of Dietrich Eckart, a guru of political extremes. Eckart was twenty-one years older than his embittered scion, a short fat man, with heavy jowls and a liking for Munich's beer halls. He belonged to one of the many small political parties of the time, the National Socialists. One thing led to another: the Austrian joined the party; Eckart bought the anti-Semitic *Völkischer Beobachter* as the party newspaper. The Austrian took over the party and changed its name, moving its headquarters to the Alps. On a mountain called Obersalzberg in Berchtesgadener Land he bought Haus Wachenfeld – the *Berghof* – with the royalties of his book *Mein Kampf – My Struggle for Four and a Half Years Against Lies, Stupidity and Cowardice*.

No other mountain in the world has inspired such terrible deeds. 'It was there,' wrote the politicized infantryman, 'that all my great projects were conceived and ripened.' Albert Speer, whose own chalet was just down the slope from the *Berghof*, wrote that the newcomer's attraction to Obersalzberg was less a love of nature than a fascination with the 'awesomeness of the abysses . . . ' Some have argued that the National Socialists, with their monuments to sun-worship, crypts for the ashes of the hierarchy and construction sites on ley lines, were less a party than a neo-pagan sect.

On Obersalzberg plans were made for the Third Reich. The *Berghof* was enlarged, barracks, gymnasiums, greenhouses and a movie-theatre were built. For his fiftieth birthday, Schicklgrüber's grandson was given a tea-house on top of the mountain above Obersalzberg.

To reach the tea-house, the six-and-a-half kilometre Kehlstein-strasse was built, curling 700 metres up the Kehlstein to a parking lot where an opening in the mountain led to sliding doors. Through the doors were four brass walls, highly polished to reduce the sensation of claustrophobia, for the owner didn't like confined spaces. After a forty-one-second electro-mechanical surge, the doors opened again and passengers stepped out on to a sunlit terrace. The vast view gave the impression of looking down upon the world.

'The Eagle's Nest' still exists. Through the Berchtesgaden tourist bureau I was introduced to Sergeant-Major Klaus Pfeiffer of the Gebirgs-Jäger – the élite mountain regiment of the German Army. We set off together one morning, with rucksacks of food and survival gear. Klaus wore skis and I wore my snow-shoes. We made good progress up through the forests at the foot of Kehlstein.

Klaus was fit. A full-time mountain instructor and guide, he had climbed Mount McKinley in Alaska and made thirty-five ascents of Watzmann. He had also made 150 freefall parachute jumps and was a qualified scuba diver.

The weather on Kehlstein was as bad as it had been for the last weeks, snow driving through mist. A skier had died two days earlier on a mountain just south of Kehlstein. He had been escaping from an ava-lanche when a branch on a tree went through his neck. We stopped above the tree-line and stared up into the white-out. Klaus pointed to a steep-ening snowfield and a line of rocks. 'We have to cross up there. I'm not sure . . . Maybe it will not be possible, because of avalanche.'

We chewed on some chocolate while Klaus talked about the time that he'd been swept 300 metres down a mountain in Austria six winters ago. 'I was buried for thirty minutes under two metres of snow. I man-aged to clear an air-space in front of my mouth and nose, so I could breathe. And lucky for me, they found me. But in another avalanche on the same mountain at the same time, a man was buried for only five minutes under half a metre of snow, and he died of suffocation.' Klaus looked up through the swirling snow at the overloaded slopes of

Kehlstein and shook his head. 'We go down. I'm sorry. It is too dangerous. It is a pity for you, but . . .'

I was disappointed. Klaus returned to Berchtesgaden and I walked
down the mountain to Obersalzberg's levelled shoulder. The half-tones
of winter had turned this infamous place into a grainy black and white
print. Up in the trees I found the rubble of the 'Leader's Prohibited Zone',
the complex of buildings which had once housed a private army, and the
chalets of Goering and Hess, Bormann and the rest of them. Speer's
three-storey wooden chalet and his architectural studio were still visible
from the road. But the rest had been flattened by 1,243 tons of bombs on
25 April 1945. (The Lancaster bombers, 318 of them, had missed the tea-
house.) In a thin wood I found the snowy hummocks of the *Berghof*'s
walls. The garage was intact and on its back wall were lines of ominous
graffiti:

DER FÜHRER LEBT IN UNSEREN
HERREN WEITER!

and in English beside a swastika:

WE ARE STILL ALIVE

Underneath the garage ran the tunnels and chambers of the *Berghof*'s
bunker.

The owner of the adjacent Hotel Zum Türken, once the billet of the
Reichssicherheitsdienst, the Reich's security service, had fitted a turnstile
to the hole in the centre of the hotel's souvenir shop. A spiral staircase
lined with brick descended like a screw-thread into the mountain. Sinister standard-bearers had been here too, scoring on smoke-blackened
walls: HEIL HITLER . . . SIEG HEIL . . . HITLER WAS RIGHT . . .
HEIL DER FÜHRER. The steps descended to a narrow, vaulted tunnel.
To the north-east it once led to Martin Bormann's private bunker but was
now blocked off. In the other direction, the tunnel descended towards the
Berghof's bunker. The tunnel was lit with electric light. I was the only
person underground and each time I stopped moving, the dull echo of
my boots was replaced by a sepulchral stillness. A line of bullet marks
starred the concrete. Small chambers and flights of steps led off at angles.
At every corner sneered the slit of a machine-gun post. To reach each gun
position meant passing the slit and entering a chamber further down the

tunnel, then climbing up metal rungs through a circular hole in the ceiling to the gun room. The place was impregnable. Eventually I ran into a brick wall, where the tunnel leading through to the Leader's bunkers and those beyond had been blocked. When the bunkers were completed between August 1943 and April 1945, there were 2,775 metres of tunnels and seventy-nine rooms, enough to accommodate 400 people for six months. Nothing had been overlooked: if poison gas had been pumped into the bunker, fans could draw out the gas and replace it with fresh air. With the 'Wolf's Lair' in Prussia, this was going to be the last refuge of the Third Reich.

Later in the week I visited the graveyard in Berchtesgaden. On the wall were the sad memorials to men whose bodies never came home, men like twenty-nine-year-old Josef Hasenknopf, from Klaus's regiment, who had been killed in Romania on a spring day in 1944.

Somebody else had visited the graveyard that morning; a set of footprints crossed the night's snow from the gate to Eckart's headstone.

Strammer Max

The snow fell as if it had forgotten how to stop. I left Berchtesgaden at the beginning of March and crossed the border into Austria in a narrow valley guarded by a solitary German policeman in a heated shack. I encouraged myself by estimating that Vienna and Annabel lay just two weeks to the east. But I was wrong, again.

Within hours of arriving in Austria the weather deteriorated to Siberian extremes. Snow covered the road-signs and drifted between the banks in knee-high waves. Occasionally a snowplough swept by behind a peeling bow-wave. Between their passing I had the roads to myself, feeling my way east between posts poking above the drifts and on one occasion where the road had totally disappeared, having to relocate it with the compass. The air was not cold, as it had been in the Engadine, but it was below freezing. Each house was protected by a portcullis of icicles.

Since my fall in the forest below Zugspitze, my right knee clicked with every step, as if a piece of gristle had become partially hooked over the edge of the kneecap. With all the ice about, hidden under new snow, I slipped often. Sometimes the snow balled up under the soles of my boots and I would not know until one foot shot forwards on a slick of ice and my legs would part, like a pair of scissors being opened too far. This did not help the knee.

Once, a motorist stopped and asked me to climb in from the blizzard and when I politely declined he lost his temper and drove away with the passenger door swinging open. Had he waited long enough I would have explained that he had nothing to offer. I'd been living on my own feet for so long that I neither needed nor wanted any alternative. I wanted to tell him of my 'mirrors of perception' – how I had learned to make the most of the here and now; wanted to be in the here and now. Cars (and TVs and planes and the lot) offered avoidance of anything that was not working out; without that option I had to make the best of every situation. Now everything worked out because I had no opt-out. All the motorist could offer me was a cramped seat in recycled air to somewhere I knew nothing about. Out in the snow I was not intolerably uncomfortable and I knew where I was going and that when I stopped at nightfall I would experience relief beyond anything he could imagine. There was something else too; my self-reliance and confidence would only exist for as long as I remained independent. Nothing was worth its sacrifice.

My daydreams became inhabited by the oddballs and toxic psychotics from the paperbacks (John Updike, Donna Tartt, Martin Amis) Annabel had been posting me. There was too little to look at or think about in the eternal whiteness. I walked along the valleys. The villages were sometimes far apart. If there was a *Gasthof* I rested, shedding my snow-caked jacket, pack and hat at the door and wedging myself against the hot ceramic tiles of the *Kachelofen*, ordering a bowl of *Gulasch*, or the Updikian *Strammer Max*, a snack of three fried eggs on a layer of bacon and a wedge of bread, covered with chopped raw onions, sliced cucumber, tomato and gherkins. Writing my journal I saw how far the journey had departed from the romantic image of a mountain odyssey:

Snow in eyes. Building on pack till I'm all white. Unseeing, white on white. I no longer exist. A pass. Down to Gosau. Another gasthof. Goulash. A beer. A large empty room. But it's not empty. A corpse-like patron with death-pallor face, skeleton & potbelly & brown nylon trousers with a shine like ice on the back of his thighs. A couple in each corner. No one speaks. The unspeaking couples create unbearable tension in the dead room. Slump with Updike, the beer glass, the radiator at my back. Walking? Inertia. Every last nano-calorie needed to lift myself for another 14 kms in driving snow. Down valley, narrows to gorge, steepening, cliffs to side & ahead, till new valley comes & the lake. Hallstattersee. New cold wind. Main road sweeps off to left. I turn right. Shiny ice under-foot. Icebergs on lake. Piercing wind. Road hugging cliff. Precipice below to black water, ruffled. Fishing sheds tiled in white. Drifts between. Sweden? Norway? The Lofoten Islands. Sheds & ripples. Aloneness. Mountains like gravestones. The village. Hallstatt. Slivers of yellow light. Wood burning. Can't face tent. Press door-bells. Nicht Nicht Nicht. Cold. Hungry. Tired. Tired of own thoughts. Decide to walk back up road to avalanche tunnel where there's a pile of grit behind a wall. Grit will make good bed. Soft. On way pass a Pension sign. One last try. Steps up. Buzzer. Door opens. Woman. Toys. Warmth. Cooking smells. Domestic chaos. She smiles! Stand in kitchen as snow melts off hat & shoulders puddling lino. Woman tells little daughter to show me room. Daughter bossy: '*This* is your key . . . *This* is the bathroom.' All this repeated three times. As if I'm a *very . . . naughty . . . boy.* The sink plug in room is solid brass, like a toy piston. Beautiful. Phone A: she picks up phone before finishing her previous conversation and the last three words she's saying are: 'a husband adrift.'

All night the snow fell and by morning avalanches had cut the road each side of Hallstatt. The police set up roadblocks to prevent anyone from leaving the village. The roadblocks stayed for four days.

My room with the family had been previously booked so I moved into 69 Gosaumühlstrasse, a wooden house with its back to the cliff and its front to the water, which Frau Zimmerman said had been built in 1599. She lived on her own in the house and was now in her sixties. The staircase had been scaled for humans half my size, narrow and steep, with treads half the length of my foot. My beamed and panelled room on the first floor sloped so steeply that I could feel my calves pulling as I walked up from the sink to the bed. The wardrobe leaned forward with its wooden doors hanging open like a pair of broken wings. I woke each morning in this ship's cabin, with its small window on to the flecked water and Frau Zimmerman's tap on the door to tell me that my break-fast tray was ready. It was the perfect place for an indefinite entrapment.

Few mountain communities have had to adapt so rigorously to the constraints of their location. In the Pfarrkirche, built on a ledge above the village roofs, there was no space for a graveyard so the bodies of the dead had been stacked in an ossuary; limbs around the walls (like the neat stacks of firewood under Alpine eaves) and the skulls on top. To aid recognition, the foreheads were painted with the name of the deceased and decorated with flower garlands for women and oak (or ivy) leaves for men.

Hallstatt's reason for clinging to its improbable site lay in the mines which gave the village its name; Hallstatt or 'salt place'. The mines had brought wealth to the villagers since the Stone Age. In 1846 the first of 2,000 graves were found on the mountainside 350 metres above Hallstatt. In the graves were the bones and artefacts of Celts who had lived on the lake in the period 1000–500 BC. So extensive were the finds that they gave their name to historical chronology; the Early Iron Age became the Hallstatt Period. In the museum I was shown a salt-miner's rucksack made from wood and skin, which incorporated an ingenious quick-release shoulder-strap; one of the straps was replaced by a long, wooden handle which could be gripped in the right hand. To release the rucksack of salt, the carrier lifted the wooden handle and the pack swung free so that it could be lowered to the ground without the squirming and shoulder-wrenching which is the modern method of releasing a rucksack.

Only 150 or so men still worked in the mines and it was rumoured about Hallstatt that the mine would soon be closed, snuffed out after 3,000 years by competition from cheaper sources of salt within the expanded European market. Hallstatt would fossilize as a museum community; many of the old wooden houses were already holiday homes owned by rich outsiders and those that came on the market were unaffordable for locals. In the summer the village was swamped by 200 coach-loads of sightseers a day.

I was woken on my fifth morning in Hallstatt by the church bells at six and looked out of the small window to see blue water and a silver mountain. After a month of daily snowfalls, the skies had cleared. On the way out of the village I slipped on the ice and slammed to the road. The blood from my hand followed me along the lake-shore like a line of red perforations in the white snow.

The Vienna Woods

By mid-March the snow was softening but still deep. Looking for the line of least resistance, I followed the Enns upstream to the confluence with the Salza and then followed the Salza to its headwaters at the pilgrimage town of Mariazell. On a low pass called the Rohrer Sattel the tent was battered all night by a strangely warm wind. Coming down the pass in the morning I found myself walking on jaundiced slicked-back grass covered with nodding snowdrops. Above me, the bare branches of the beeches scratched at a warming sky. Only Weinerwald lay before the end of the Alps, and Annabel.

I had one last call to make on my Alpine traverse. Outside Heiligen-kreuz in a cemetery on the hill is the grave of Mary Vetsera, the girl who died in 1889 with the Austro-Hungarian Empire's last crown prince, thirty-one-year-old Rudolf Habsburg. On a snowy January afternoon, deranged and syphilitic Rudolf took seventeen-year-old Mary to the royal hunting lodge at Mayerling in the Viennese woods, where he seems to have persuaded her into a suicide pact. Rudolf was entombed with the rest of the Habsburg dynasty in the Kaiser Gruft in Vienna; Mary was smuggled out of Mayerling at night and buried hastily at Heiligenkreuz.

By default, this sad episode altered world history: if Rudolf had not died, Archduke Franz Ferdinand would not have been assassinated in Sarajevo; the First World War would not have started and a surviving Habsburg monarchy would have stood in the way of the National-Sozialistische Deutsche Arbeiterpartei. Perhaps this is the reason that Mary Vetsera's headstone bears the Old Testament words: 'Man cometh forth like a flower and is cut down.' To which can only be added the previous lines in the Book of Job: 'Man that is born of a woman is of few days, and full of trouble.'

The grave was surrounded by rusting iron paling and dead ivy. Old flowers lay on the cracked, lichen-stained lid of the grave. Two silver-haired women in long woollen skirts and grey *loden* hats were arranging flowers on nearby graves. They saw me looking at the headstone, and walked over. 'She's gone,' said one of the women, matter-of-factly.

'What do you mean?'

'She's not here. Look,' she added, pointing at the crooked slab, 'the grave has been entered. They took away her skeleton.'

'Who?'

'We don't know. It is a mystery. Mary Vetsera has disappeared.'

On a footpath stile I lay on my back in the sun, looking up at the black starbursts of the pine crowns against a brilliant ceiling. In the still of those moments, spring arrived: the sounds of a woodpecker; a pigeon chortling; flies buzzing; the sigh of the warm wind in the pine needles; the smells of resin, of damp soil; the yellow butterflies toppling from the wood and cavorting downhill past the wooden water-trough; the sensation of heat on a bare forearm. It was as if the previous night's gale had blown away the last shreds of winter. There was one other curious sound, of constant, almost imperceptible ticks and creaks, as if the entire skin of the earth was being stretched by the unstoppable pressure of new shoots.

To honour the absent Que Chova I spent my last night in the Alps – and my 299th since leaving Cape Finisterre – sleeping on the summit of Paraplui mountain, a tree-crowned dome on the edge of the Vienna woods.

In the morning I left the trees and came down a long, grassy shoulder past the early-morning dog-walkers, into the suburbs of Vienna.

The Carpathians

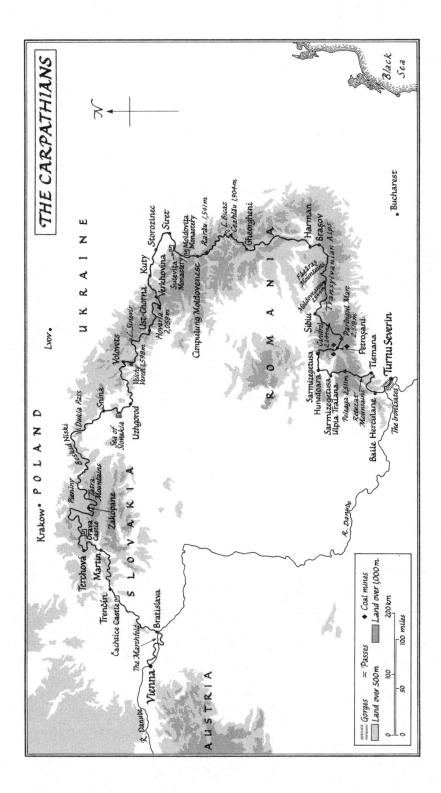

THE CARPATHIANS

Vienna

Engulfed by the city, I set the compass to 'North'. Cars snarled; pedestrians hurried by, eyes down on the gritty end-of-winter pavements. I passed the sanctuary of Heitzinger, and its celebrity cemetery. I'd forgotten how cities remember. In the mountains, triumph and despair have to be read in the rocks and snow; in the city they're chiselled in stone. The spring of Schöner Brunnen, 'beautiful fountain', which gave the palace its name, had run dry and a grimy Egeria looked askance at neighbouring statues defiled by the anti-poetry of the moment: AUSLÄNDER RAUS and METALLICA ULTIMATE WARRIOR. Up Schönbrunnstrasse I passed the hotel plaque recalling the stay in January 1913 of J.W. Stalin while he wrote *Marxism and the National Question*. When I arrived in Karfsplatz-Ressel-Park a posse of police cars had cornered a group of young men. One of them was splayed against a wall while a policeman patted the insides of his legs. *Ausländers*.

I dropped the rucksack, with its absurd appendages – snow-shoes, ski-sticks – and slumped on to a bench; a grot-covered gaberlunzie sniffing at the perfumed passers-by. I'd been sleeping in the forests for a week, and the streams had been so cold I'd washed only once. I could go under in this place, I thought. Give up on the whole thing. After all, Finisterre to Vienna was more than a Sunday walk. I'd crossed western Europe, the hard way. Annabel would have a husband again. We could start a family, after a bit of practice. I opened my eyes and dragged a row of broken fingernails across my itchy scalp. It was the balaclava that made my head rot. After four months of wearing a synthetic sock on my head, day and night, my skull had turned into a seething bacterial biomass.

Annabel arrived the following morning, by which time I had laundered my body and clothes. I ran up to the railway station on Rennweg clutching a spray of irises. She emerged on to the street under two rucksacks and wrinkled her face: 'Nick! What do you think you look like?'

'What do you mean?'

'That thing.'

'Oh. The beard arrangement.'

'If it was a beard it wouldn't matter.'

'I forgot to shave.'

'It'll have to come off.'

We stayed in Metternichgasse in a flat belonging to an old family friend; every time we turned off Rennweg I was reminded uncomfortably of Metternich's overused aphorism, 'East of Vienna, the Orient begins.' Reaching the end of the Alps had absorbed so much mental energy that I had not considered the true weight of 'Part II'. And now, in Vienna with Annabel, the remainder of the journey hung above us like a slowly descending blade. As well as Metternich's tiresome reminder I was also nagged by the Molossian gambler, Pyrrhus, and his fateful observation upon the laws of diminishing returns: 'One more such victory and we are lost.' I had no way of knowing how much I'd pushed my luck. Annabel had willed me into the heart of the continent; but would she help me on to its furthest shore? Winter had been difficult for her, alone in London; she too was emerging, blinking into the daylight of another year. And she too was realizing that the end was still out of sight. I had said that I'd be away for one year, but after ten months I was only half-way to Istanbul. Annabel seemed to be quietly stoic. We did not speak of our independent existences and lived as if there had been nothing before, or anything ahead.

We went to the new Dracula movie and then Woody Allen's *Husbands and Wives*. And the opera. I sat through these evenings looking for guidance; watching for the red – or the green – light; I had the courage neither to prolong the agony, nor to sacrifice the ideal; the decision was out of my hands.

We had gone for breakfast with our friends Kim and Anna Nasmyth and their two daughters in a flat that reminded me of home. Then they suggested that we went for lunch in one of the *Heurigen* – wine-taverns – in the Vienna woods. Since I had to walk there, and a snowstorm was blowing up, the travel arrangements were more complicated than they would have been in a group of non-autophobics. Kim and Annabel volunteered to walk with me, while Anna and the children travelled by motor vehicle.

Through swirling snow we set out on the two-hour walk to Wienerwald. Beyond the slender pencil of St Stephen's Cathedral we joined the banks of the Danube canal, grey and flecked in the gloom, where I converged with the footsteps of Patrick Leigh Fermor, who'd entered Vienna over the Radetzky Bridge *en route* from the North Sea to Constantinople. His books had set me off twenty years earlier on my first self-propelled journey – to the Mani peninsula in Greece, by bicycle – and his sudden presence was a shock; he wouldn't approve of my wavering resolve.

Kim led us from the canal bank up the slope of Kahlenberg. By the chapel on the summit we peered through the blizzard at the line of the Danube and Vienna laid before us on the milky floodplain.

Over our glasses of *Gespritzer* I turned to Annabel and raised the subject of our continuing separation. 'I'm wondering whether it's such a good idea to carry on with this thing.'

She looked surprised: 'You've come too far. For both our sakes, you can't possibly turn back now.'

I felt rather hurt. 'You could at least have begged me to come home . . .'

While not exactly an endorsement, it wasn't a veto either. I decided to leave Vienna as planned; the point of no return would be the border-crossing into the lands of the east, on the plain beyond Vienna. I'd decide out there, in no man's land. Delaying a decision, I reminded myself, is quite different from indecision.

Annabel's departure was worse than Grenoble; worse than Pamplona. My last sight of her was through the sliding doors of her train, mute and unreachable on the wrong side of the glass. Our next opportunity to meet was so remotely distant that we had not even discussed it. East of Vienna, the Carpathians cut a sickle-shaped curve 1,300-kilometres long through Slovakia, Poland, Ukraine and Romania. The next city on my route – and the next chance for a rendezvous – was Sofia, at least six months away.

I fell to a frenzy of preparation. Each task involved hours of pavement bashing: a futile quest for a Ukrainian visa; a trek out to the free Catholic hospital in the old Jewish quarter for a tick injection; and a maddening trawl from bank to bank trying to change into ones and fives the large denomination dollar notes Annabel had brought me. Vienna's cashiers shook their heads with polite exasperation: 'You want one-dollar notes. Every day the Russians come for one-dollar notes. They take them away in suitcases.' After much begging I broke my funds into a brick-sized wad of small-denomination dollars and Deutschmarks.

The search for maps of the Carpathians took me west of the Rathaus to Krotenthallergasse and an austere block containing the *Bundesamt für Eich-und Vermessungswegen*, the Austro-Hungarian map survey. Deep inside, up stairs and along corridors, I was shown through a locked door into a windowless inner sanctum. Leaning over a map cabinet was a character with a handlebar moustache and a Franz Joseph beard overlapping a taut white shirt. *'Grüss Gott!'* he growled, holding out a hand.

I explained that I had walked from Spain and that I was now walking to Istanbul and needed maps. Peter Kretsek was unmoved, as if this was an everyday request. 'We will look first at the *Übersichtsblatt* – the over-view sheet. A "key" I think you would call it in England.'

On the map cabinet he spread a sheet titled *Generalkarte von Mitteleuropa*. I had never seen a single grid of maps covering such a vast area of the continent; from Turin in the west to 'Konstantinopel' in the east; from the Pindus of Greece to Stettin on the Baltic. Peter saw my incredulity. 'They are the maps from the empire, of course.' He smiled for the first time and added: 'They are somewhat out of date.'

'How out of date?'

'Well, one hundred years or more, naturally.'

'You have them all in stock?'

'All of them.'

The maps were colour-printed from hand-drawn originals on paper as thick as card. I left with thirty-seven sheets, rolled up like a gun-barrel, wondering how I was going to manage the weight.

The Fulcrum

East of the city the iron sun of the Prater Park's Ferris wheel rose above the leafless trees. I crossed the Danube on the Praterbrücke to the water-logged footings of Lobau Island, one of the defensive features that lined both sides of the black fen of the Marchfeld, the fifty-kilometre plain separating the Alps and Carpathians. Levelled by the Danube's alluvium, the Marchfeld was the deepest, widest gap in Europe's continental divide, the habitual battleground for emperors, kings and generals to settle geopolitical scores.

One of the greatest of these confrontations occurred in 1809, when for two spring days Lobau Island was churned to mud and slime as Napoleon used this moated marsh to strike at Archduke Charles. On the edge of a smoothed field I found the pillar marking Napoleon's *Haupt-*

quartier, the spot where the emperor must have heard the news from the far side of the island, that his *Grande Armée* had suffered its first defeat, driven back by the archduke, riding with the colours in his hand, at the head of the Austrian reserves. Close to the pillar stood a memorial from a later war, a concrete bunker covered with shrapnel rosettes. The path across the island set off through a wood whose bracken floor was drilled with the six-foot-deep inverted cones of bomb craters. A woodpecker hammered at an old beech.

Beyond Lobau Island I emerged from the trees. Marchfeld was a curious fulcrum marking my half-way point between Cape Finisterre and Istanbul. Wearied after an interminable winter and awaiting the alien lands east of the old Iron Curtain, I felt marooned between two horizons; beyond the end of the beginning but impossibly far from the beginning of the end. On this spirit-level plain, nature too was at odds with itself. The massive river had always wandered at will through this breach in the ranges. Now it was held to its meanders by dykes, along which I walked above the combed fields. Driftwood clotted in trees marked old flood levels. The wind pushed and pulled, unable to decide whether to help me east or send me back. Snaps of rain had me pulling my jacket on and off every few minutes.

In the villages, people were surprised to meet someone crossing the Marchfeld on foot. '*Why* have you come to Schönau?' asked a young man incredulously.

The village lay beneath the bulwark of the Marchfelddamm and I had stopped by at dusk looking for a meal. In the *Gasthof*, Frau Barnet fed me on deep-fried carp followed by *Palatschinken* – filled pancakes – and gave me a room for the night. In the morning she presented me with a cigarette lighter printed with the telephone numbers of the *Gasthof* and the Vatican, a message perhaps that I was looking for help in the wrong direction. Later that day, a cashier gave me a Bank of Austria bottle-opener. I pocketed these presents superstitiously, as if they were in some way contributory to the decision being made.

Beyond Schönau, hills began to form on the horizon ahead. For an hour I trod across the treeless table-top, in sight simultaneously of the Alps behind and the Carpathians ahead. My legs dragged as through water, hugged by a current flowing back west. I could still turn back. Hitch a lift to Vienna. A flight home by the morning.

Finally the Alps faded from sight and I broke free.

Vienna now slipped easily behind as did the dead-weight of doubt.

The rucksack felt lighter too; in the Alps I had laboured beneath a load of twenty kilograms. Now I had swapped my heavy winter sleeping-bag for the old 'Afghan' bag I'd slept in through to Grenoble. I had given Annabel the snow-shoes and ski-sticks and the cooking stove. On the kitchen scales in Metternichgasse I had weighed every item, tossing out the winter socks and gloves, and the extra set of thermal underwear. That my rucksack still weighed fifteen kilograms was due to the maps (1.8 kilograms), various chapters copied from books (1.9 kilograms), camera equipment (4.1 kilograms), notebooks and other papers (900 grams) and the banknotes (410 grams). I had not been able to steel the nerve to leave the tent; it would be another two months before night temperatures rose above freezing. To save a few grams I'd cut the borders off Peter Kretsek's beautiful maps and left behind the nail-brush which I used to scrub my clothes.

On the far side of the Marchfeld I crossed the Danube once again and then doubled back downstream to the legionary base which had looked across the water to the barbarian forests of the Quadi and Marcomanni, 'the men of the mark' – the border – at a time when the Roman Empire was sealed in by a great crescent of German tribes from the Black Sea to the Hook of Holland. Reaching on foot the margin of my own western European empire, I could sense the wonder and fear that this borderland must have held for the Roman civilization. Gathered by blood into tribes which depended upon fighting for their cohesion, the Germans settled matters through their *Thing* – the council of war, – and worshipped as their main deities the warlike triumvirate of Wodan, Donar and Ziu. For the Romans, it was more convenient to write off these strange peoples as barbarians than to elevate them to an equal and threatening standing. Yet the Romans copied the weapons and clothing of the northern tribes, and enlisted the fair-haired, blue-eyed warriors into their army. Two thousand years later, distrust and misunderstanding still divides Europe in two. Of the various governors of Europe since the demise of the tribes, the only one that made sense was the Roman Empire; only under the Romans did the full width of the continent function as a unified body. Perhaps the Romans peaked too quickly; we've had to wait 2,000 years for conditions to bring us to the Treaty of Rome in 1958 and the genesis of the European Economic Community.

I spent the afternoon under a stony sky looking unsuccessfully for toga pins and coins among the old walls and ways of Roman Carnuntum, once a city of 100,000. At nightfall I put the tent on the highest point on the bluff, just back from the forty-metre cliff down to the Danube. About me were Roman culverts and the rubble of the legionary barracks. From the door of the tent I could look across the darkening lands of those German tribes.

I fell asleep thinking about the border I'd cross in the morning. But in the early hours I was woken by voices and lay with a thumping heart listening to a conversation between several legionary centurions. One of the voices, more strident than the others, was recognizable as Annabel's father, a colonel who had served in the King's Own Yorkshire Light Infantry. There was a pause in the exchange as they turned their faces towards the tent and I heard the unmistakable tones of my father-in-law. 'Nick!' he commanded. 'Get a bloody move on!'

Into the East

Fleeing west trailing grey smokescreens was a non-stop stream of decrepit Skodas and Ladas. In the other direction moved slow convoys piled high with carpets, mattresses and miscellaneous furniture. The westward verge was clean but for its banks of old snow; the eastward verge was littered with the detritus of consumer binges: beer cans, condoms, ice-cream spoons, cigarette butts, chewing-gum wrappers, turds, orange peel, Pepsi tins, perfume boxes and packets of rare export brands of fag: Memphis, West, HB, Hobby and Philip Morris of Andorra. A broken Trabant smoked dejectedly, so overloaded that it had sunk to its cardboard haunches, its four occupants staring at the panting engine like forty-niners contemplating the death throes of their last horse.

The Austrian police waved me through to a booth occupied by men in green uniforms bearing the Slovakian coat-of-arms, the white cross rising from three blue mountains against a red sky; a rather more benign symbol than the Lion of Bohemia which had greeted Patrick Leigh Fermor when this had been the West's gateway to Czechoslovakia. I passed through the old Iron Curtain with less inconvenience than it takes to cross a busy road.

Ahead of me the stubble of Bratislava's tower blocks prickled around the southern tip of the Malé Karpaty, the Small Carpathians. Bratislava had been caught with its trousers down by its overnight promotion from provincial city to capital. I wandered through cobbled backstreets whose stuccoed houses were subsiding into screes of plaster and rubble. Restaurants and hotels were 'closed for reconstruction', a euphemism embracing anything from structural collapse to financial insolvency. In the central square, Hlavné námestie, Emperor Maximilian II looked down from his waterless fountain, islanded by grit. Apart from the clattering of an old bus-shaped Soviet helicopter and the rattle of dented trams, the streets were almost silent. It took me a while to realize that there were virtually no moving cars.

The awkward proximity of the Austrian capital threw Bratislava's deficiencies into relief. The drab clothes and pasty faces, the austere stores and matted carpets were symptomatic of a place which did not know better. A 'cheeseburger' I ate turned out to contain all the usual ingredients – spongy bap, slice of plastic cheese, ketchup – except the burger. Then, just as all the clichés about the East were becoming predictable, I was wrong-footed in the Snack Bar Veterán by being served a tall glass of Pilsner and a plate of fresh noodles oozing with cheese sauce and speckled with pork crackling, the famous Slovakian workers' dish *bryndzové halušky*. I ate it many times over the coming weeks but never was it as delicious as it was on that first night in Bratislava. The least expensive source of hot food was the self-service *samoobsluha*, an eating joint run like a factory canteen, where you bought a ticket and queued at a window for a bowl of dubious gruel.

I took a room on the first floor of the Hotel Palace in Poštová ulica. The maxim that there is an inverse relationship between the grandeur of a hotel's name and the quality of its plumbing was borne out by the Palace. Needing to bathe a septic toe, I had just turned off the taps in room 124 when the entire sink peeled forward off the wall into my arms. I staggered across the room bearing its considerable weight as the plug dropped from the severed waste-pipe, followed by a column of freezing water which poured off my groin, down both trouser-legs and across the treacle-coloured carpet. In some distress I splashed down to the hotel foyer. 'It is not only the problem with the water,' I explained, 'but two of the windows are broken.' The room also smelled like an old plimsoll. 'Please,' I asked, 'may I have an alternative room?'

The receptionist's eyes looked through me to something distant and of more consequence. Without moving her eyes, she said: 'No.'

Two days later the same sightless receptionist called me to her desk and handed me a key. On the top floor of the hotel, I found that I had been relocated to a new room with a clean carpet, sound plumbing, unbroken windows, fresh flowers and a black and white television broadcasting four channels of snowflakes. This was my introduction to the bizarre contradictions of post-Communist Europe.

Yesterday

Easter in Bratislava was marked by marathon Masses and a clamour of bells. The aisles of St Martin's Cathedral were packed. Street-vendors sold painted eggs, and a few boys self-consciously stalked the streets carrying ribboned willow-switches, recalling the spring rite of whipping the legs of girls to bring rejuvenation. But nothing could bring my own legs back to life; I was tired beyond any short-term recovery. My legs looked as if they would last the distance, but they had lost their spring.

When the shops reopened after Easter I stocked up with food for the hills and visited the Slovenská Kartografia kiosk on Kyjeuské námestie. But instead of maps, the kiosk was now selling pornography and cigarettes. The unshaven young man behind the lurid covers set me off on a trail which led to golden booty: a set of *Letná Turistická* maps, drawn to a scale of 1:100,000 and overprinted with colour-coded walking trails. These opened the door to the hills of the Malé Karpaty.

For the next five days I walked north-east through the trees accompanied by squirrels and woodpeckers. Glades shimmered with snowdrops and I passed the first crocus, a purple *albiflorus*, flaming in the lee of a tree. In the evenings the sight of my shadow walking ahead reassured me that I was indeed following my own spirit. At night I put up the tent between the grey poles of the beech trunks and lay listening to the barking deer and screech of hunting owls. Once again the land became companion rather than adversary. Beneath my feet, the bruising ice and sloughy snow had been replaced by quicker beds of melting soil and spring grass. I could rest where I chose; on a sun-warmed tree trunk or a dry rock, or lie back in a hammock of crackling leaves. Since the snows had left I could see my way.

At every path junction an enamel signpost indicated the walking distances to nearby hills and passes, springs and villages. Each signpost carried its altitude and location. It was almost impossible to get lost. At regular intervals stood wooden weather-shelters, *besiedkas*, with seats and a fireplace. My Slovak maps marked a network of paths spreading across the uplands of the entire country, chiselled out of the forests by youth groups and Scouts and Committees for Recreation, measured, labelled and mapped so that families could walk at weekends. If all the Communist countries had similar networks, I speculated, it would be possible to walk right the way across the old Eastern Bloc without seeing a car, from the conifers of the German Harz to the parched stones of the Bulgarian Stara Planina. Not until my second day in the Malé Karpaty did I realize that there was something very strange about this formidable network of mountain trails: nobody was using them. I didn't find out why till some time later.

As I walked north the hills gained in height and began to sprout castles placed to defend the watershed between Moravia and the Danube basin. Beyond the ruins of an old Hungarian castle called Plaveck I came to a *chata* – a mountain hut – in a clearing. Adults and children played handball on the grass. Pleased to see a sign of life in the forest, and assuming that this was a typical mountaineers' hiking hostel, I asked if I could stay the night.

'Of course! Of course!' called a tall, bearded man in English. 'Come inside for some food.'

Filling half of the hut's dining-room was a banqueting table laid with roast chicken and a bewildering assortment of salads.

'Sit! Please!' said the man, pulling back a chair and handing me a glass of wine. 'This is just a snack. We are eating properly tonight.'

'What marvellous service!' I laughed. 'In England the hikers' hostels never serve lunch.'

'Oh,' smiled the man apologetically, 'this is not a place for walkers. It is a private *chata*. We are celebrating the fortieth birthday of our friend. He is a dentist, from Bratislava.'

Having gatecrashed the dentist's birthday party, I was not allowed to leave. At dinner that night I was made the guest of honour and given a seat beside a professor of history from Bratislava University. The twenty or so adults had grown up through the sixties and seventies on the Beatles, whose harmonies and iconoclastic lyrics had represented every-thing that was absent from Communist ideology. John, Paul, George and Ringo were idols; their songs learned by heart. At midnight, after the fireworks and plum brandy, I was invited to rise from my seat at the head of the table to sing McCartney's *Yesterday*. Alone. The birthday dentist, who had in a previous incarnation been a folk musician, would accompany me on guitar.

I cannot recall ever seeing so many faces simultaneously crumpled. The idea that an Englishman neither knew the words to *Yesterday*, nor could sing in tune, was so inconceivable that the shattered audience were unable to disguise their disappointment. I soldiered on to the finish, inventing rhymes, humming sections and repeating too many times the only line I could remember (*All my troubles seemed so far away*) while the dentist steered the way with encouraging chords. I finished off-key, bowed and sat down. The silence that followed was eventually broken by Madonna's *Erotica* exploding from the tape machine, and the shouted request that I should now dance.

My turn for amazement came the next morning when Adrienne, a lecturer in business studies, told me that she had never heard of a 'cheque-book'. 'You know what we used to say about socialism?' She laughed. 'That it was like a merry-go-round: the Slovaks turned it round; the Czechs sat on the seats and the Russians took the money!'

It was Adrienne who explained to me why I was alone on the marvellous network of hiking trails. 'Everyone is too busy working,' she said. 'Trying to earn money. We do not have evenings and weekends any more. Just work.'

The first cuckoos called me on towards the most sinister castle in the Carpathians. Čachtice's battlements rose above an outcrop surrounded on three sides by a bend in the River Jablonka. Clusters of primroses nodded conspiratorially in the wind on the banks of the barbican, where a gateway opened to the inner fortifications and a keep twenty metres high. It was in this tower that Countess Alžbeta Báthoryová died in 1614.

Intermarriage among her Transylvanian forebears had probably corrupted Elizabeth's genes for she was prone to faintings and rages exacerbated by the boredom of being cooped up in a castle while her husband, the 'Black Knight' František Nádsady, was off fighting Turks. Slow servant-girls were hurried along by being stuck with pins, or reprimanded with a cudgel. She took up torture and murder, and pursued an unconventional relationship with her two maids. All this would have remained a Čachtice secret had not František died and given Elizabeth the space to pursue her perversions without restraint. She turned her attentions to daughters of noble birth and before long rumours began to circulate and her son began to worry about his inheritance. It was said that 600 young girls had died in the castle. Stories that Elizabeth bit into the throats and breasts of some of her victims gave rise to the legend that she bathed in the blood of young virgins to preserve the milky translucence of her own skin. To protect the family name Count Thurzo rode into the castle on a freezing day at the end of December and locked her in her own keep, where, after four years, she died.

I was able to crawl into the keep, through a small hole in the base of the tower. Among the tumbled blocks was one carved with a Latin cross. I'd often slept in places where I sensed old spirits might roam but I was unsure about Elizabeth. I walked the ramparts till midnight, looking down on the vulnerable triangle of my tent. Elizabeth had been fond of this castle, she liked its wildness and its thick walls, which muffled every sound. Superstition finally got the better of valour and I whittled a stake then drove it into the earth by my head. Sleep came slowly.

Down in the village, the museum was closed but a svelte restaurateur next door, a graduate in 'maths, biology, psychology and pedagogy' from Nitra University, had the key and showed me in. On the wall was a repellent picture of Countess Elizabeth sitting fur-clad in a chair watching five peasant women, prostrate in the snow, being dashed with water from an icicled fountain, while a sixth shrieking peasant was dragged across the courtyard by one of Elizabeth's maids. The museum's star exhibit used to be a portrait of Elizabeth looking coy in a lace collar and long dress but the painting had been stolen months earlier.

'Where do you think she is?' I asked Ivan.

He shrugged. 'Japan? Austria? Germany? She has been . . . *exported.*'

The Duellist

Sometimes I did not find what I was looking for; or I found it but it fell flat. Other times I was looking the other way and something found me.

Outside the industrial town of Nové Mesto I visited the only soap factory in Slovakia. On a site like a mad scientist's nursery, tubes and chimneys protruded from windowless blocks surrounded by a concrete apron. The gateman telephoned the head office and ten minutes later I was being led by a white-coated technician to the office of the director, Mr Kollar, who refused my request to see the production line because the processes were 'secret'. Over coffee, the technician told me that the main ingredients were cattle and pork fat, 'with just a little coconut oil', and it was this image, of pensionable milch cows and geriatric pigs being tipped by the truckload into smoking vats while a chef wearing a nose-clip flavoured it with a dash of tropical nectar, that made me less sad about Mr Kollar's intransigence. For some time thereafter my infrequent encounters with soap were slightly less pleasurable.

That day the larks sang and the sun shone from a clear sky, and I walked up the floor of the Váh to Trenčín. Proud above the old red roofs and tower blocks rose a bulwark of rock topped by Trenčín's castle. Ten metres up the face of this rock, 2,000 years ago, a mason attached to the II Auxiliary Legion chipped an inscription to commemorate a Roman victory against local tribes during the Marcomannic War. The mason was one of 855 soldiers who spent two winters here in 'Laugaricio', four days' fast march up the Váh from the safety of Carnuntum. The legion had been operating well beyond the bounds of the empire. Perversely, the Hotel Tatra had been built against the rock-face. The hotel was 'closed for reconstruction' but a workman led me through the drifts of cement dust and broken breeze-blocks, then helped me remove a rear window from its frame. The six-line inscription was about two metres away; close enough to hear from that far century the tap of the mason's mallet, the creak of his wooden scaffold and the clink of falling stone chips.

V . . . . . T O R I A E

A V G V S T O R V

E X E R . . Q V I L A . .

G A R I C I O N E S E . .

. . . .

. . . .

Above the inscription rose the twelfth-century castle which used to pro-tect the old trade route up the Váh to Poland. My guide was a twenty-four-year-old, bearded d'Artagnan called Dušan, who slept alone in the castle as caretaker. He split his days between working as a tourist guide in the castle and teaching English to factory seamstresses, but his passion was sword-fighting. Dušan belonged to a group who were trained in medieval combat.

'There are small accidents,' he said, showing me a scar on his palm. 'We all have cuts to our hands and fingers, but only two of our members have had a blade pass through a hand.' Dušan agreed that he'd been born too late: 'Yes, I would have liked best to have been alive for the Thirty Years War . . .'

'Didn't that wipe out half of Europe?'

'Yes, because the sword-fighting was at its best then. Come to the castle tonight. I will show you something.'

After dark I walked up the ramp to the iron gate at the first portcullis and waited. Dušan emerged from the shadows on the far side. He unlocked the gate and led me up the cobbles into the castle.

Dušan's room was a small stone cell. Against one wall was a bed and in the corner beneath a crucifix stood a tiny table laid with two candles and a quill. On the walls were a crossbow, a sword and two shields. He handed me a handerchief-sized rectangle of metal mesh. 'I am making a chain-mail shirt, but it takes a long time. Nowadays it is difficult to get the original materials, so I am using steel washers. I can fit 200 washers in one hour.'

'How many washers do you need for the whole shirt?'

'Thirty-five thousand. It takes a long time to make chain-mail.'

Dušan led me out to another locked door in the wall of the keep. Inside were racks of medieval clothing and swords. Dušan chose a sword and handed it to me. It was surprisingly heavy. He saw me fingering the sharp tip. 'We keep them sharp because the wounds are cleaner when we make mistakes. So they heal quicker.' He patted his stomach: 'Our trainer has told us that these swords can go through three bellies at once. Now, we'll go outside.'

Underneath the floodlit castle wall, Dušan stopped and turned. He had a sword in his hand. 'Now! Arm out! Point the sword at my belly!'

I lunged forward. Steel clashed and my blade caught the light as it was swept upward by Dušan's parry. My shoulder felt as if it had been dislocated. The tip of Dušan's blade was absolutely still, at my throat. My right arm, with the sword, hung limp behind my back; my left hand was spread across my crutch. My eyes ran down the ruler of steel to a pair of narrowed eyes and black beetling brows. 'You see how I used my feet?' asked Dušan from behind his hilt.

'Actually, no.'

'Feet are insurance; I parried your attack. But I also moved backwards, out of your reach. Now, try again.'

Under the stars above the Váh, the clang of steel on steel echoed from the stone battlements.

Dušan knew as many ways of kebabbing a body as a chef knows recipes. He was unflinching. As the tip of my blade leapt towards him he parried and stepped then struck. When I reopened my eyes, his sword-tip was always parked a finger's width from the skin of my neck.

'Good!' announced Dušan as I began to tire. 'Now I'll show you something dangerous!' He drew breath. 'I invented it myself. It's a variation on the Italian *stesso tempo*. Do you want to know why it's dangerous?'

'I'm not sure . . .'

'I'm going to set up a move that will make you fall on to my blade. Once you have begun your parry, there is no way you can stop yourself becoming impaled. It is the momentum of your own body!'

The move involved a pirouette, as if Dušan was turning from my attacking thrust, the catch being that while turning his body, his sword remained extended forward over his left shoulder.

I submitted when I was no longer able to lift the weight of my sword.

I left at midnight. Dušan showed me down the ramp through the sequence of locked gates. Above us the vast bulk of the castle loomed over the silent town. In the centre of the darkened main tower of the castle burned a tiny yellow rectangle of light.

'My room,' nodded Dušan. 'The people in the town have told me that they like to see the light up there, alone in the night.'

Malá Fatra

Slovakia sold sardines I'd never seen before. The most common were the Sarda brand. They were supplied with the little flipover can-opener which I remembered from my childhood. The only drawback with Sarda was the olive oil, which smelled as if it had fallen out of the bottom of a truck engine. The more palatable Delamaris sardines were suspended in an unspecified 'special sauce with oil' whose volatile aroma varied with altitude. Delamaris were labelled as having come from 'Izola, Yougoslavie' (a small port in what is now Slovenia) and Sarda from 'Croatia', yet both 125-gram cans were identical and both were stamped with the same date: 22 January 1992. It was, well . . . fishy.

Before leaving Trenčín, I also bought one sample of every variety of Slovak chocolate bar so that I could identify the brand most suitable for mountain rations. Of these the fifty-gram Kama bar was unquestionably the most revolting, with a coarse, almost gritty texture and an aftertaste like old cardboard. Figaro's milk chocolate, *Mliečna čokoláda*, came in a dandelion wrapper but left the mouth lined with grease. The mocca sandwich of the Diana bars looked promising, but if eaten too fast it anaesthetized the back of the palate. The cheapest bar of all was Figaro's cooking chocolate, *Čokoláda na varenie*, dark, rich and not too sweet; after swallowing it left lingering, sensuous scents of sun-dried cocoa-bean in the gutters of the mouth. Irritatingly, the vile Kama offered the best source of energy, packing a whopping 2,270 kilojoules of energy per hundred grams.

My strict dietary regime – to eat anything whenever I saw it – had so far spared me any digestive problems other than occasional twenty-four hour bouts of food-poisoning which could always be traced back to urban restaurants. In the mountains I drank from springs and streams and subsisted mainly on bread, cheese, sardines and vitamin tablets. Since leaving Finisterre, I had swallowed 660 tablets.

These were the inconsequential thoughts which entertained me as I made my way out of Trenčín early on a sunny April morning. From their beginnings outside Bratislava railway station, the Carpathians grew in steps. The Malé Karpaty, which I'd followed as far as Nové Mesto, had reached 700 metres. Now I had crossed the Váh, I was about to traverse the Malá Fatra, which would top 1,000 metres. After the Malá Fatra came the 2,500-metre High Tatras, the tallest part of the Carpathians.

The hills hadn't been trodden since autumn. At lunchtime I dropped down into Trenčiánské Teplice. Like most spas, it was populated by people who'd come to damage their health without being spied on; the supermarket shelves groaned beneath more biscuits and chocolate than I'd seen anywhere in Slovakia and the *samoobsluha* was packed with customers tucking into fatty *guláš*. Beyond a concrete sanatorium called the Krym, I was drawn toward the smell of melting chocolate and found a knot of people propped up on sticks waiting to collect their boxes of fresh *kakaové oblátky*, circular chocolate-wafer sandwiches the diameter of a discus that were being turned out by a pair of women in white coats working at a revolving table of hot presses.

'You can only buy these at the *kúpele*, the spa,' said my neighbour sagely. 'They are good for the stomach,' he added, patting the inner tube hanging over his belt. Each box contained ten discuses. I bought a box and ate the lot as I climbed up through the forest above the spa. Afterwards my mouth felt as if I'd chewed through a crate of cork tiles, but my stomach, miraculously, was still absolutely empty.

The nights had ceased to be frosty and darkness no longer stilled the forests. I slept on a 700-metre ridge looking down into the valley of the Teplička. Deer stood in the last of the sun and later, as I wrote by candlelight, an owl patrolled to and fro along the brow of the ridge.

In the morning I ambled on along the ridge through posies of primroses that had pushed up through the golden bedding of the beechwood. The fecundity of the hills reached down to the valleys. I came off a hill called Slopsk into the head of the Porubsk valley to buy bread, and found a long thin village stretched along the stream. Vegetable plots were being spring-cleaned, and I drank fresh milk while old men wearing blue pillbox hats sipped tankards of foaming beer. A ten-year-old boy with a flock of foraging goats and a jersey full of holes showed me the path out of the village towards Vápeč, the highest peak in this south-western corner of the Malá Fatra.

The two boys I met on the summit of Vápeč came from a world the ragged young shepherd could only dream about. Lúbor and his friend were attending Trenčín high school and had taken advantage of the clear weather to carry their *parapentes* – parachutes that fly like wings – up to the top of Vápeč. As soon as the breeze settled they were going to run off the mountaintop and float down to the valley.

The timing of the Revolution had been perfect for this pair, coinciding with their last years at school. They'd had the stability of Communism for their childhood and yet could look forward to the opportunities of a market-driven democracy. 'Sure it's good for us!' shouted Lúbor, who wore an aerofoil haircut. 'We're free!'

'What if the Communists come back?' I asked.

'They won't . . .' But Lúbor sounded uncertain, and added: 'You know many people still say that life was better under the Communists. Since the Revolution, all the prices have gone up. But life will get better.'

'What do you plan to do?'

'Me? I'm going to join the Slovak Air Force. Then I'll convert to civilian airliners.' And with that, he spread his wings and flew off the mountain.

Beyond Vápeč I crossed an architectural watershed; in the villages, timber began to replace rendered brick. Log-cottages in faded blues snuggled in soft market gardens and in Čičmany, set in a wide bowl at the head of one of the Malá Fatra's longest rivers, the Rajčanka, every cottage was painted with stylized birds and hearts and repeated geometrical bands, triangles and diamonds, crosses and zigzags, the hieroglyphs of the lace-maker's art.

A small museum described the familiar history of dependence on cattle and sheep and then depopulation in search of work. But Čičmany was not a normal mountain village. Its reputation as a source of felt slippers and later, its lace, kept the community alive. The house-painting began two centuries ago, although most of the original pictograms were destroyed when Čičmany was razed by fire in 1921. In the museum alongside the carved milk jugs, butter churns, cow-bells and old boots was a wooden hay rake identical to those used in the hills of Galicia, 2,500 kilometres to the west.

From Čičmany I followed the Rajčanka valley then climbed through larches to the summit of Klak, at 1,351 metres. Off to the northeast rose the snows of further, higher Carpathians. The far-off Váh was just a misted trench in the receding waves of hills. The high sun burned the detail from the land; turned it to a grey washboard of ridge and furrow. I slept up here with the deer, above the twinkling lights of distant villages, then walked down the long valley of the Slovianska Dolina until the steep-pitched forest fell back and was replaced by the smooth slopes of enormous collectivized fields that ran down to the willow-fringed banks of the Turiec.

Martin was Slovakia's cultural kernel. In 1861 intellectuals drew up the Martin Memorandum, arguing for a Slovak district within Hungary. And it was here in 1918 that the Martin Declaration formalized the federation with the Czechs. More recently Martin's engineering works had manufactured tanks for the Warsaw Pact countries. Now the demand for tanks had dropped and the town's main function was as an ethnographic repository. In 1961 when the programme of collectivization in Czechoslovakia was complete, only thirteen per cent of the land remained in private hands. The landscape was hoovered clean to make space for 6,300 cooperatives. After the strip-fields and hay-stooks had gone, some of the old tools and buildings were collected here in Martin. Beyond a housing estate south of the town stood a *skansen*, an entire village of cottages, barns, churches, shrines and wells. Unsurprisingly, the museum was 'closed for reconstruction' but the caretaker showed me around. Every building had been painstakingly disassembled on its original site and transported by truck to the edge of Martin, then rebuilt. All that was missing were people.

In the town itself, built like a cultural palace at the head of flights of steps, stood the Slovenské Národné Múzeum. Displayed in gallery after gallery were thousands of rustic artefacts gathered from forest, river and farm throughout the Carpathians. There was an eight-metre dug-out canoe, fish traps, bear traps, guns and knives; castle hardware that included punishment stocks, leg-irons and a torture table; fiddles, flutes and alp horns which once played at country fairs; tools that had seen many a harvest – scythes and rakes, pitchforks and ploughs; and there were children's toys, a wicker crib, a rocking horse, a wooden sledge. And the straw-man, like a Bavarian Krampus, who came in the night and stole the spirit from the land.

It was impossible not to be struck by the aesthetic wealth of the traditional peasant. The tools were crafted from raw materials – wood, stone or bone – which came directly from the land they were destined to work. They were utilitarian, designed to be practical, but each had been made by hand, and each was different from the next. They were beautiful.

There was nobody else in the museum. As I walked slowly from room to room, the melancholy curatrix turned off each light behind me.

Jánošik

Juraj Jánošik grew up in the last years of the seventeenth century in a small village set between the open jaws of a gorge in the Malá Fatra. The ruling Habsburgs were against the ropes. Vienna had just been saved from the grand vizier by Sobieski's rag-tag army of Poles, and a brilliant young nobleman called Ferenc Rákóczi II was about to interfere with the imperialists' plans by launching a guerrilla war against them. Cardinal Kollonics' inflammatory dictum, 'Make of the Magyar first a slave, then a beggar, and then a Catholic', guaranteed that it was a popular uprising. With others from the Malá Fatra, fifteen-year-old Juraj joined Rákóczi's peasant band and walked east to fight. Initially there were 7,000 of them, but their numbers rose to 100,000. They were routed at Koronco and again at Nagyszombat, then at Pudmerics and finally at Trenčín.

Rákóczi's rebels scattered to the hills. Jánošik went north towards the Tatras and the town of Kežmarok, where he settled to train as a priest. While he was there, his mother died from illness. Jánošik's father built a coffin, but because he had taken time off work to do so, he was lashed one hundred times. He died. At this point the embroidery of folk-heroics begins: angered by the treatment of his father, Jánošik took to the hills again and gathered about him a band of good rogues who spent the next few years robbing the rich to feed the poor. Woodcuts show this Slovakian Robin Hood with a flintlock pistol jammed into the top of his *opasok*, the deep, five-buckled belt still worn by Carpathian shepherds, and a *valaška*, the hatchet-headed walking stick, in his hand. The hold-ups, skirmishes and improbable leaps from castle walls were woven into the poetry and prose of Slovak history. Only Jánošik's beginnings – and end – are unequivocal. On a spring day in 1713 he was captured by the lords of Liptov near the headwaters of the Váh and hung from his ribcage in the square of Liptovsk Mikuláš. It was Terchová, Jánošik's birth-place, that I now circled on my map.

Outside Martin the hills rose to snow-dusted crests. I followed the road out of town, buffeted by filthy buses, while loudspeakers hanging from lamp-posts broadcast Communist advice on potato planting. Out-side the villages, men and women shuffled along in a crouch, dropping seed into furrows cut by horse-drawn ploughs. More horses brought carts of silage to be pitchforked on to the rich soil. The horses wore red tassels and woollen balls on their bridles and silver discs on their collars, as they had since Jánošik's day.

Beyond Turany I found the path over the 1,200-metre summit of Chleb – bread. The track was paved with old stones and must once have been a short-cut between Jánošik's birthplace on the far side of the range, and the Váh. The beeches on this south-facing slope were already in bud and I was dallying in this waking forest when the cumulo-nimbus cloud that that been been sailing up the Turiec like a man o' war collided with Chleb. A blast of wind was followed by rods of rain which turned the mountainside into a single shining stream. With no umbrella, I sat under a bush while dead wood and water tumbled earthward. This was the first time I'd seen a Carpathian storm. Some time later I discovered how much more vigorous they could be.

I slept just below the summit of Chleb, putting the tent on a patch of grass between the slabs of old snow. Far below, Martin and its satellites were constellations of orange dots, joining at their focuses in a fur of diffused sodium.

In the morning I climbed to the top of Chleb and then walked around the horseshoe ridge to a promontory overhanging Vratna dolina. From here I could look down into Jánošik's homeland; the two secret valleys funnelling down to the sheer-sided gorge and beyond it the roofs of Terchová.

The heart of this northern, highest limit of the Malá Fatra was desiccated by gorges and cliffs. In here, it is said, Jánošik buried his treasure. I left my rucksack in a guest-house and spent the morning scrambling through lightless canyons looking for wooden caskets.

There were six engineers staying in the guest-house. They were surveying a route to lay fibre-optic cables across Slovakia, from Žilina to Bratislava. Each cable, they said, contained forty fibres, and each fibre could carry 10,000 calls simultaneously. I asked them whether they believed in the existence of Jánošik's treasure. There was laughter and one said, 'Yes, yes! There is buried treasure. But it is *we* who are burying it!'

Borderland

North of Terchová the mountains grew taller and wilder. I had to cross the Malá Fatra range again, so that I could reach the Tatra Mountains, the refuge for a sizeable proportion of the continent's larger wild animals, among them bears, wolves, stags, boars, moufflon and lynx. A booklet I'd picked up in Bratislava listed the hunting season for forty-two species, among them hedgehogs and hamsters. I had never met a hamster hunter and speculated idly what such an individual might be armed with. A net perhaps. Certainly not a blunderbuss. Crossbows fired from horseback seemed to offer the twin benefits of spectacle and good sport. But I finally settled on the probability that a Slovakian hamster hunt involved beaters who drove the shy rodents towards the waiting barrels of hidden blowpipes.

Up here I fell into a frozen pond near the summit of Mincol after mistaking a smooth-surfaced glade of snow for a short-cut. The snow suddenly gave way and I dropped through to my thighs, floundering frantically beneath the weight of the rucksack and cursing the irony of drowning on a mountaintop. The water was bitterly cold.

I descended into a paradise. The morning's sun had cooked the eastern flank of the Malá Fatra and my trousers quickly dried. On the shaded forest floor the brilliant white petals of cinquefoils shone like cats' eyes beside the path and the purple bells of primroses reached toward the light. Below the trees the path cut across pastures which could have been landscaped by Capability Brown; monumental pines framed the misted mountains and the grass was spangled with heart-shaped crocuses, constellations of buttercups and tall oxlips hanging like limp windsocks in the still air. I lay with my head on the warm rucksack watching the insects loop-the-loop around the tilted dishes in the grass.

I reached the valley as a thunderstorm struck. Fat drops of rain smacked the hot tarmac of the road as I hurried upstream to the castle of Orava. The lair of the Thurzu clan occupied a giddy eyrie on a fin of rock which rose one hundred metres sheer above the river. To see inside the castle I had to tag on to the back of a coach party from Poprad, an experience made bearable by the guide, a young man whose imagination had been infected by the outrageously dramatic location of the castle. Among the exhibits was the skin of a bear which had eaten a toxic plant and fallen asleep on the railway track. The train had been derailed. From an upper battlement we were invited to lean over the abyss and appreciate the void into which women suspected of being witches had been dropped; if they survived the awesome fall they were proclaimed to be genuine witches and were then finished off by being impaled with a stake; if they died in the fall they were redeemed as 'good women'.

The fixtures and fittings of a medieval home were all there: a torture room with a table fitted with iron hoops, and a handy pair of giant tongs. There was an armoury with pikes and helmets and so on, and 'drinking chairs' with a hinged bar which locked the incumbent into place to prevent him falling to the floor. The women's dining chairs had especially narrow seats designed to pinch the hips and so discourage them from hanging round too long at the dining table. There was also a dummy woman, Morena, who was set on fire and thrown over the battlements each spring, to bring in the new growing season. All things considered, it was not an easy time for women.

There was an inn below the castle and I rashly decided to spend the night there so that I could eat a hot meal. I was the only guest in a dining-room for ninety. Net curtains blocked the view of the castle and any risk of romance was removed by a radio-cassette machine blasting out Rod Stewart. The waitress must have seen a fifties' copy of *Woman's Own* because she'd covered her head with lipstick and ringlets, and through some kind of implanted revetments in her brassière had succeeded in jacking-up her bosoms so that they trundled around the dining-room ahead of her like a pair of siege cannons.

'I'll have the local speciality, please,' I said. 'And a Pils.'

Thirty minutes later she returned with a plate containing a boiled frankfurter, a brown extrusion of mustard, and a slice of bread that curled at each corner. 'Local speciality!' she said with a proud smile, standing back to pour a bottle of Martiner Pils from a great height into my glass. Predictably – at least to me – the beer turned into a tidal wave of froth that surged over the lip of the glass, across the tablecloth and over my crutch. Starved and tired and sitting in my wet pants staring at a limp frankfurter bobbing on a lake of beer, I grappled for a response. For a very small fraction of a nano-second my impeccable credentials as a politically correct male slipped as my eyes alighted upon a suitable subject for the castle's giant tongs.

I followed the serpent-coils of the Orava upstream past impoverished villages of low timber cottages festooned with May Day bunting. Tied to front gates or to the top of tall poles along the roadside were finials of fir trees, hung with streamers that fluttered like prayer flags. I turned up a side valley towards the Tatras, but found my way blocked by the village of Zuberec, where a young couple in a garden took me to a modern house where, they said, I would be given information about my onward route. Too late, I realized that I was in the police station.

'It's not permitted,' said the policeman when I explained that I was walking up the valley to Poland. 'If you go up there, you will come back in handcuffs!'

He added that I would have to walk to the town of Trstená where there was an international road crossing to Poland. To reach Poland on foot from Zuberec was a fifteen-kilometre hike over a pass; to walk around by road was over fifty kilometres.

'What about Suchá Hora?' I asked. This was another road crossing, much closer than Trstená.

'Suchá Hora is for Socialists only.'

'I'm sympathetic to Socialism.'

'But you are not a Slovak Socialist.'

I walked from Zuberec back down the valley. Out of sight of the village I turned right, up another valley, the Blatna, which climbed through dense forests to a low pass. Above rose the rock and snow of Osobitá. I came down the far side of the pass to meet a stream called the Oravica. It was dusk. The border lay along the ridge right in front of me.

I climbed quickly. From the valley to the ridge was a height gain of only 300 metres. I emerged from the forest beside a hut. The door was open. Inside were pieces of furniture used by the border patrols. Beyond the hut was a broad swathe of open ground straddling the ridge. I moved along the edge of the forest. Every few hundred metres stood timber watch-towers. I waited for ten minutes but nothing moved.

I reached the first watch-tower and left the rucksack at the foot of the larch-pole ladder. The rungs of the ladder were scuffed and muddy. Inside the tower was a military sleeping-bag. Looking along the ridge I could see the watch-towers to each side. One of them had partially collapsed and was leaning three-legged towards the ground. A movement at the forest edge made me start. I crouched in the watch-tower, panting. But it was just deer.

Poland lay three minutes away. It would be easy to cross, but what would I say to the border police when I tried to leave Poland without an entry stamp in my passport? I delayed the decision by walking on, along the edge of the clearing. The trees parted and I could see the main wall of the Tatras – an intimidating barricade of rock and snowfields running from Salatin, to Spálená, Banikov, Tri kopy and Ostr Rohác, all five peaks over 2,000 metres. I pottered on, up to the summit of nearby Magura, but the view was blocked by pines. This was another defining watershed: the mist that dribbled off one side of Magura would run down the Czarny Dunajec, out to the Vistula and then the Baltic, while the puddle a few inches away would trickle down to the Oravica and the Danube to the Black Sea.

By the time I got back to the clearing it was nearly dark. I put up the tent, ten metres inside Slovakia. In the last minutes of light, deer began to emerge from the forest until there were twenty or so, grazing beneath the watch-towers. An owl glided silently past the door of the tent. I lay in my sleeping-bag, warm and tired and unaware that in ten hours' time I would be running for my life.

Exit, Pursued by a Bear

At dawn I looked out of the tent at the mist in the pines and decided that coffee in Suchá Hora was a more appealing way to start the day than an illegal border crossing. I shook the water from the tent and began walking along the forest cutting that separated the two countries. Granite marker posts, painted with a red 'CS' on my side and a 'P' on the other, stood at hundred-metre intervals along the centre of the cutting which ran along the crest of Magura's northern ridge.

So early in the morning I had not fully woken, and I was watching my feet rather than the track ahead. Trees which had been brought down by the weight of winter snow still blocked the way, and the wheel-ruts were deep with snowmelt. I was thinking about coffee and hoping that Suchá Hora would also field a plate of steaming *bryndzové halušky*. So when I looked up, I was surprised to see a bear.

We stared uncomprehendingly at each other. For so long I had dreamed of this meeting. In disbelief I ran through all the animals that this might be. But nothing else looked like a bear. It *was* a bear. Then I saw that the bear had started running. 'That's odd . . .' I thought slowly. 'All the wild animals I've met have always run in the other direction. Away.' This one was running towards me. I felt confused and mildly indignant; I prided myself on my ability to watch animals unseen, often from quite close. They only ran away when the wind altered or when I was forced to ease an aching muscle. This animal had not even thought of running away; it had looked up and leapt forward.

The bear ran with a relaxed, shaggy gallop, like a second-row rugby forward heading for the line. I was familiar with the sliding scale of wilderness emotions, from wonder to terror, but I'd never travelled so quickly from one to the other. For such a shambolic creature, the bear was moving incredibly fast.

I pulled off my trilby to prevent it catching on the branches of trees, then ran into the forest and up the mountain in zigzags, hoping that the dense foliage would break the bear's line of sight, and the sudden alterations of course would throw him – or her – off my scent. I did not get very far. As I crashed blindly through the underscrub a series of traumatizing fates tripped through my mind: claws, teeth, torn skin, falling and, worst of all, *no one knowing*. That I should lie for ever undiscovered and of unknown fate in this black forest was far more frightening than the battle that was surely about to take place.

Sprinting uphill wearing a rucksack proved surprisingly strenuous. After less than 200 metres I could no longer breathe. I clung to a pine trunk. For several seconds I hung retching, feeling the sticky bark on my cheek. I tried to listen above the rasps of my own throat. But I could hear no sounds from the trees. I wondered whether I should stay still or put further ground between myself and my pursuer. I stared into the trees, searching for movement. But the forest was as still and damp as it had been several minutes earlier. I stumbled back southwards through the trees until I reached the clearing where I'd camped, and fell to the grass feeling ashamed and ridiculous. The bear, coming out of hibernation, must have been hungry and confused. Had I dropped my rucksack the animal could have mauled it while I watched from a safe distance. And taken a photograph.

To continue my journey I had to pass the same spot again, but the bear had gone. I consoled myself that I had at least met 'The Beast', albeit with little dignity. But perhaps that was the nature of a predatorial encounter.

Later that morning I met an army truck full of foresters and asked them whether they had ever seen bears on Magura.

'Yes! Yes!' they laughed. 'But they cannot hurt you. They eat grass, not Englishmen! They're from Zakopane! They're Polish bears. They're harmless!'

My Slovakian was not good enough to point out that any wildlife would seem harmless if you are one of eight burly foresters in an army truck filled with chainsaws and rifles. For self-defence the most I could muster was a month-old rolled-up copy of the *Daily Telegraph*.

I reached Trstená that evening and the next morning crossed into Poland. My border difficulties had now brought me too far north, too far west and too low. Instead of a watershed that could be crossed by a single step across a mountain ridge, I was now separated from the lands of the Vistula by the great bog of Jabłonka. To get back to the Tatras I must either extend my detour by continuing north to the bridge at the town of Jabłonka or make my own short-cut across the bog.

The first Polish village north of the border was Chyzne, a ribbon of houses along the top of a ridge that projected into the wetlands. To keep to the dry ground, Chyzne's cottages had been built in a single line one kilometre long, facing their barns on the other side of the lane. Painted shrines hung with May bunting stood at intervals and there was a bustle of activity I'd not seen often in Slovakia: carpenters hammered at new houses and in the fields below the barns jack-knifed figures worked the soil. A woman leaning against her gate told me that a path ran all the way to Podczerwone on the far side of the bog.

'How far?' I asked.

'Five kilometres only!' she replied.

I could see from the map that it was at least ten kilometres.

The lane ran out into the fields beyond Chyzne and became a muddy track that led to a forest and a watch-tower. Signs read WSTĘP WZBRONIONY – No Entry. I had not expected to find the border so close.

Inside the forest the track showed little signs of use. When it divided I took the right-hand option, which kept me closer to an easterly bearing. But the track curved through the trees taking me southwards, towards the border and into a calf-deep swamp. Splashing through water I reached a familiar line of granite posts. This time the 'P' was on my side. Again, the posts ran along the centre of a clear-felled cutting. I hadn't committed any major misdemeanours but it would not look that way to bored soldiers were they to come across a foreigner floundering in no-man's-land. In places wooden footways had been built above the water for the border patrols. Using these, and wading, I made my way east along the strip of cleared marsh between the two countries. At any moment I expected to hear a shout or a shot.

Nearly three hours after leaving Chyzne I emerged from the trees on to a grassy plain. Far off to the east rose the needle of a church tower. Podczerwone. I sat on the grass and wrung the water from my clothes while a fiercely mewing kite wheeled and rolled above my head.

I followed the logging carts up the long valley of Chochołowska into the heart of the High Tatras. Peaks hidden by the previous day's mist now stood clear of the trees, jagged and streaked with old ice. The valley ended in a huge pasture – the largest *polana* in the Tatras – set beneath an immense cradle of rock and snow.

In the mountain refuge I learned that local bears, a mother and her cubs, had recently taken to raiding the rubbish bins behind the refuge. The girl who took my bunk fee for the night added more gossip: 'They say there are some new bears up here, from a zoo. The authorities released them because they had no money for food and now these bears are in the forest and very angry. They don't like people.'

'I think I met one of them . . .'

Apparently the nuns in Zakopane's convent had been woken recently by thumps on the convent door. Undoing the latches they found a bear, which had let itself in through the convent's outer gate. They chased it away with brooms, but the bear returned the following night and woke them again with its insistent door-thumping. Later, a Zakopane schoolteacher reassured me that the bears were the innocent victims of bad publicity. 'They are not dangerous,' she smiled. 'They are just a nuisance. They all come from Slovakia.'

Krupówki Street

I came down from the mountains and took a room on Krupówki Street. Carnival came every day to Zakopane's main thoroughfare. Gypsy troupes danced for Silesian tourists clutching repro icons. A portraitist from Shanghai knocked out five-minute sketches. Shepherds sold smoked sheep's cheese. Next to the kiosk selling the new magazine, *Businessman* (the May cover showing a shifty character with a crewcut and narrowed eyes, hands shoved in trenchcoat pockets), women in from the villages set up stalls heaped with knotty jumpers and patterned butter-presses. Further down Krupówki lurked the fat man in the polar-bear suit roaring: '*Photograph! Photograph!*' And at the bottom, beyond the concrete arches, sprawled the flea-market where Russian merchants with beat-up Ladas, boots open, sold second-hand screwdrivers, Zenit cameras and the dress-uniforms of Soviet admirals.

The gold rush was on. Poles were returning from the United States with wads of dollars. One evening I watched a mobile crane lift an entire wooden shop off the back of a truck. The shop came from a village outside Zakopane. It was lowered into the last available slot on Krupówki like the final piece of a jigsaw puzzle. 'You see!' laughed one of the spectators. 'It is quicker than building a new one!'

One end of Krupówki ran into green fields and the other end rose to the cliffs of Giewont, the 'Sleeping Knight' of the High Tatras. From my table in the Heineken (the bar had a more ethnic name, but everyone called it after the brewers' umbrellas which shaded its terrace), I could walk to the foot of the Tatras in fifteen minutes. Street-eating was diverse; fast-fooderies advertised *hamburgery*, pizzas and the ominous-sounding *drobburger*, which turned out to be a delectable snack of bread and chicken. The Redykołka and Obrochtowka served specialities such as tripe soup, fried potato pancakes and *pierogi* – pasta envelopes filled with sheep's cheese. And in Zakopane's last remaining Communist-era coffee-house, Kawiarna Europejska, a sombre hall with thick net curtains and a decor of integrated mud tones, brown-waistcoated waiters served *ekspresowa*, or coffee fortified with rum, beside big helpings of *jabłecznik* – apple purée sandwiched between decks of filo pastry glazed with icing and corniced with cream.

Near the foot of Krupówki was a heavy-metal music store called 'BUM'.

'Why do you call your store "BUM"?' I asked the manager.

'In Polish,' he explained 'it means BANG!'

I hesitated. 'In English, it means . . . this,' and tapped my backside.

The colour drained from his face. 'No. No. You are saying that my shop is called "Bottom"?'

I nodded.

'Bum is bottom?' His cheeks crinkled into an entrepreneurial smile. 'A bumshop!' he laughed. 'That will be good for English business!'

One day in the Heineken, I fell into conversation with a bare-footed woman who turned out to be a teacher at Zakopane's high-school, the Liceum Szkół Ogólnokształcących. She asked if I would take one of her classes. The school was up on the slope at the edge of town. Class 3A were seventeen- and eighteen-year-olds and they wanted to be ski-instructors.

The day was sunny and they sat on the grass in a semicircle. I spread the map of Europe that I carried in my rucksack and told them about using snow-shoes, and about skiing up Mont Blanc. I described the *pallozas* in Galicia and the Roman road up Bregaglia. I showed them my jet-fighter compass. I told them that I had walked 6,000 kilometres, from the Atlantic Ocean, especially to speak to them. They listened with polite disinterest and after a while I became distracted by my own map. Each week I had been extending the black line. From Finisterre to Zakopane the line had always headed generally east, but now it was about to inscribe a gigantic inverted 'S' down to the bottom corner of the map. Together with my Rubicons (the Rhone and Danube) and my successive watersheds (Mediterranean, North Sea, Baltic, Black Sea), I'd measured my progress in fractions of the total distance to be covered. Now, in Zakopane, I could see that I was at six-tenths. For the first time, I knew that it was possible, that I might reach Istanbul. I'd never before understood why six was a magic number.

In London a mountaineering friend, Jon Tinker, had told me about Maciek Berbeka. 'If you ever get as far as Zakopane,' Jon had said, 'look up Maciek. He's a good bloke. A really good bloke.' They had climbed together in the Himalayas.

I had arranged to meet Maciek who lived with his wife, Eva, and three sons by flower-filled pastures beneath the cliffs of Giewont, at an hotel just off Krupówki.

'There was no chance of a different life,' said Maciek. 'Look,' he added, pointing beyond his house to Giewont's cliffs. 'Look at the mountain. I was born with this view!'

Maciek was a boy when his father died in a Zurich hospital after a climbing accident. He took up speleology, spending every weekend with friends in the western Tatras looking for new caves. At fifteen he began climbing on top of – rather than underneath – mountains. After school Maciek went to the Fine Art Academy in Krakow. The climbing trips became more ambitious: twice to the Caucasus and then, in 1978, to Chamonix. He had fifty dollars for one and a half months, and took with him tins of food from Poland. His climbing partner in Chamonix was Dobroslawa 'Mrufka' Wolf, who later died on K2. When western European climbers asked why they always walked rather than take the cable-cars, they laughed and said: 'We're training.' They lived cheaply, picking blueberries for their pasta and collecting bottles for supermarket deposits.

Maciek put up new routes on the South Face of Annapurna, the South Pillar of Cho Oyo and the South Face of Dhaulagiri and made winter ascents of Manaslu and Broad Peak, where frostbite claimed half a toe. He was Poland's greatest surviving mountaineer.

Learning to climb with the sudden storms of the Tatras had – like the Scottish Highlands – encouraged a hardy breed of climber, used to operating in savage weather. Sudden thunderstorms could unleash blizzards and winds too strong for a man to stand. In the Tatras there was also the *halny*, a curious wind which sprang up when warm air on the southern, Slovakian side of the range was sucked over the watershed by the lower temperatures and lower pressures on the northern, Polish side. Tornado blasts of warm wind tear down the *dolinas* into Podhale and at sunset the clouds can take on weird hues of purple and green. The *halny* is said to turn people crazy.

Too many Polish mountaineers had died over the last three years. Maciek called it the 'black time'. The Zakopane Mountaineering Club, which had produced so many world-class climbers, had ceased to function. Under Communism the club was relatively wealthy. Now the members did not pay their subscriptions or did not have the time. Maciek was thirty-nine; another imminent quadragenarian. I saw him on the grass in front of his half-built house, with his leaping sons, and wondered whether his mountaineering was at an end. 'Are you thinking of giving up?' I asked. 'Settling down, here, with the family?'

Maciek smiled. 'Ask me later in the year . . . after I've been to Everest.' He was going to attempt the mountain from the north, from the Tibetan plateau, with Jon. Later, I often thought of Jon and Maciek, waiting breathlessly for dawn in tents at 7,000 metres with the spindrift scratching at the nylon. You have to be there to understand why it's worth it.

Half-way down Krupówki was the office of Związek Podhalen. The Górale Federation was established to encourage and preserve the region's highland culture, a spectrum of surviving idiosyncrasies from music and dress to the *Góralski* dialect. Running like a river of continuity through Górale history is the annual transhumance – the seasonal migration of sheep from their winter quarters in Podhale southwards into the High Tatras and eastwards along the Carpathians. It is an old ritual; sheep came to the High Tatras in the sixteenth century. In the 1930s there were 36,000 sheep in Podhale. The migrating flocks filled the stony roads with streams of wool. At the head of the flocks marched the shepherds, their broad-brimmed black hats tilted against the sun, each swinging a *ciupaga*. Running ahead were dogs which could take the leg off a wolf.

By the late forties Podhale's sheep population had doubled to 70,000; Socialist planning demanded too much of the grasslands and as they became overgrazed, the shepherds were forced to move further and further from Podhale, to new pastures far to the east. On 7 and 8 May 1948 an enormous flock of 6,000 sheep departed for the far hills of the Beskid Sądecki, several days' walk away. The following year, the great migration gathered momentum as flocks were herded on to trains and taken still further east, into the Beskid Niski and the lands taken from the Łemks. Each year the migration reached further along the Carpathians, further from Podhale, further from home. From the sidings at Nowy Targ, the trucks rattled east through Nowy Sącz, Jasło, Krosno, Sanok to

Ustrzyki Dolne on the border with the USSR, where the flocks were run down ramps and taken out to the wild hills of the Bieszczady. It was a device, say the Górale, to keep the independent-minded highlanders out of the way. Finally, in 1962, the Górale were banned from using their traditional *polanas* in the valleys of the High Tatras. The authorities told them that sheep-rearing was incompatible with the flora and fauna of a national park. Now the sheep were back in the High Tatras. In six experimental *polanas*, flocks had been re-introduced. A maximum limit of 2,000 sheep had been set for the entire park.

One morning Góska Karpiel, an ethnographer working for Związek Podhalen, walked with me up Dolina Bystrej. The Kuźnice *polana* lay beside the road, a half-hour's walk from Zakopane. Near the stream stood a wooden cabin oozing smoke. The door was open. Inside, a fire burned on the earth floor. Chains from the roof-beams supported a copper cauldron of milk, which was being stirred by one of the three shepherds. The *baca*, the head shepherd, was a tall, good-looking man called Jan Staszel-Furtek. He waved us to the bench along the back of the hut and cut us each a slab of white sheep's cheese, *bunc*. Jan spoke expressively from the centre of the hut, an apparition wreathed in smoke: 'When they closed the park to sheep we all lost our jobs. The Communists wanted to kill a generation of strong people, strong people who loved life.'

Now they were back in operation, albeit in a small-scale way, with fewer than 200 sheep, close to the edge of town. Jan's *szałas* produced about twenty cheeses a day. He expected to move to a new *polana* each month, taking the sheep on to fresh grass. When Jan paused the only sound was the crackle of burning logs. I asked about the fire.

'We lay it in May, in the shape of a cross. It must never go out, all summer. If it does go out, we will have bad luck. One of us will get injured, or a sheep will die.' He pointed to the two huge logs which lay on each side of the fire. 'They burn very slowly, for one night and a day.'

Jan changed into his Górale clothes: the thick cream felt trousers, embroidered down the thigh, the white shirt, embroidered waistcoat and the black-brimmed hat trimmed with a band of cowrie shells. At his neck he pinned a silver filigree brooch. 'The *spinka!*' he laughed. 'It is traditional. Before the days when shirts had buttons, we used it for closing our shirts. And it is good for cleaning a pipe.' He lifted the *spinka* and inserted its spike into one nostril, miming a drill: 'And it's good for cleaning the nose!'

Later I met a fourth-generation Górale *kowal,* a blacksmith, who made *spinkas.* 'There are four elements to every *spinka,* explained Andrzej Gąsienica-Makowski. 'First the eagle, which represents power, then the heart, for love. That's love for people and for your country. And there is the cross to symbolize our Christian faith. And the sun.'

'Why the sun?' I asked, suspecting some pagan connection.

He smiled. 'Every *spinka* has these things.'

Through Góska, I met Yasiek, a big man, thirty-nine, and in need of more than one life. By profession he was an architect, but he was a musician too and his collection of twenty Górale songs, *Muzycko Piknie Gros,* had sold well in Zakopane's music stores. He took me to the house he had just built.

'Did you design it?' I asked.

'Yes, of course. And I built it.' He held up his hands: 'With these.' He showed me the joints that he had cut, and the wooden dowels that held the house together. 'We still use the old ways. There is no need to change.'

The main room in Yasiek's house was crossed by carved beams and decorated with Górale clothes and musical instruments. His brother had made the furniture. 'They are Górale,' Yasiek said, pointing at a row of pipes and fiddles.

'You play them all?'

He picked up an alp horn over two metres long and fed it through the corridor into the kitchen. He tipped the kettle into the horn's spout. 'Hold the end,' he said.

We stood at opposite ends of the room. Yasiek pursed his lips around the horn's mouthpiece. Through the window I watched a boy on a bicycle stop and look up at the house as Zakopane's sky was filled with a long sonorous blast. Once, we would have heard an answering blast from a far-off *szałas;* today, from somewhere in Zakopane a bus hooted in response.

Yasiek played the other instruments. 'This,' he said, putting down a fiddle after sawing through a jig, 'is the *złobcoki.* It is the most important musical instrument for the Górale.' He played a selection of pipes, among them the wistful *piszozałka dwojocka,* a twin-barrelled flute with a painfully sad tone. Finally he picked up an animal skin sprouting several stiff legs. 'You know why it is called *koza*?'

I shook my head.

'It is the Górale word for "goat" . . .' grinned Yasiek, going on to list the frequency with which the bagpipes have popped up across the continent: as the *piffero* in Italy, the *cornemuse* in France, the *cabrette* in the Auvergne, the *biniou* in Brittany, the *zampoña* in Castile and the *gaita* which I'd seen played on the steps of Santiago de Compostela's cathedral. Indeed, it was even possible that it was the Poles who brought the bagpipes to western Europe, for Haydn's friend Dittersdorf found that nearly every village around Vienna played the *Polnischer Bock*, the Polish goat. Perhaps the second century BC *askaulos* of Greek shepherds had been passed along the Carpathian chain, to arrive at the Tatras long before other Europeans had thought of stuffing tubes into an inflated bladder. Like so many disappearing species, the bagpipes (depicted in Hittite carvings 1,000 years before the birth of Christ, and therefore one of the oldest surviving instruments on earth) seemed to have found their last refuge in mountains.

On the grass in front of his house Yasiek filled the air bag and the whines of several strangled goats carried across the trees to the cliffs of Gwiewont.

Yasiek was playing that evening at a school prize-giving, and after the children's poetry recitals had petered out in desultory applause, I walked with the musicians through Zakopane to the house of Yasiek's sister. Soup, bread and vodka appeared and the six musicians took their seats at one end of the long table.

They opened with a slow *ozwodna* then accelerated into a medley of dances. Girls in crimson skirts spun like tops before a young man whose buckled shoes beat a tattoo on the wooden boards. Later, during the *kyzesane*, Yasiek's sister 'fled' with her hands on her hips to the kitchen, while the fiddler's fingers danced a frantic hopscotch on his strings. The vodka bottle and tumbler circulated around the table, the tumbler thrown back in one without the glass touching the drinker's lips, then refilled and passed to the neighbour. Round and round went the tumbler. Bottles came and went. The wood-panelled room creaked and banged. Cigarette smoke threaded the strings of the impassive bassist. Yasiek's beautiful sister swirled and sang like a bird. The tumbler revolved. The room revolved . . .

Ascension Day

I woke up feeling as if I'd undergone a clumsy lobotomy.

That afternoon, Maciek and I were walking down Krupówki when I saw my father. As we hugged, Hol said: 'You didn't receive my message?'

I hadn't. I knew that Hol and Naomi were on holiday in eastern Europe and we'd agreed by letter that Zakopane was the most likely place for our paths to cross. He had left a letter for me in the post office, and a miniaturized message stating an 'RV' and an 'ETA' on a stamp-sized piece of paper under a rivet on the post office door, in case I found the building locked. But while my father had been checking the post office every hour, on the hour, I had called once every two days. Thoroughness was one of many aptitudes I had failed to inherit from Hol. He was a great believer in 'failsafes', an insurance I had generally ignored, often to my cost. A rendezvous, for example, should be backed up by a pre-arranged phone number that all parties could call if circumstances altered. When we went sailing, every loose item in the dinghy was secured by a length of string to prevent it floating away or sinking when we capsized, which was often. To avoid ambiguities when communicating through a telephone answering machine, Hol always signed off with 'Message ends'.

Hol and Naomi were staying on a camp-site outside Zakopane. Being with them brought the journey back from the fantastic into the ambit of a family outing; to them, nothing could be more normal than this Carpathian encounter. The three of us left town together for the lakes of the eastern Tatras, following family footsteps that stretched back two generations. My parents knew the Tatras well, having brought young Poles here on selection courses prior to Hol's leadership expeditions along the Pyrenees. And my grandparents, Ruth and Jack – whose path I had taken through Andorra – had walked through the Tatras in May 1936, seven years after their Pyrenean jaunt.

Hol led the way up through the forests to the lake of Morskie Oko and then over the rocky ridge of Opalone. The snow-filled gullies up here had caused Ruth a few heart-stopping moments as their guide Stefan teetered ahead of them. One of the gullies 'appeared to end in nothing', noted Ruth in her journal. Part-way across, clad in her 'sensible walking shoes' and long skirt, Ruth looked up as Stefan called encouragingly, '*Unter ist Tod!*' – Below is death! Sixty years on, the same gully still looked fairly precipitous. Some way behind my parents, I saw Hol hand Naomi a sharp rock and say: 'If you slip, roll on to your stomach and dig it into the snow.' We met no other old-age pensioners on that path.

The purpose of the expedition was to visit the Valley of the Five Polish Lakes, a ladder of tarns that sat in ascending glacial hollows through the heart of the eastern Tatras. But when we reached the high point overlooking the valley, we saw a wilderness of snow and ice. The upper three lakes were still frozen over and the entire valley was zebra-striped with snow.

'I don't think we're really kitted out for winter climbing,' I said, as a picture flashed before me of the three of us sitting all night in a snow hole with our feet in rucksacks.

'Pity. . .' said Hol.

We arranged to rendezvous again at the Pieniny, a small range to the east. The following morning, Ascension Day, I walked out of the Tatras through Bukovina, the highest village in Poland. Dressed in their dark suits and pork-pie hats, serious farmers led their wives in print frocks and head-scarves through an avenue of sunlit blossom to their new church. I stayed for the eight o'clock Mass, then walked down the hill and across the Białka, its braided streams dashing between shingle banks and willows.

Larks beckoned me up a track towards a shrine on the skyline, where I had breakfast lying on the cool grass looking back at the silver points of the Tatras, arranged like a centre-spread in a picture-book beyond a painted foreground of viridescent pastures. Rashly, I told myself that I'd see no more snow; the rest of the Carpathians were wilder, but lower, and the season would be warming now, all the way to the Balkans.

The Cheesemakers

The *szałas* stood behind trees on the first slope of the Pieniny, surrounded by smoke and dogs. Inside, the *baca*, a *juhas* and a boy were making cheese while a transistor radio sung *Hey Jude*.

In the far corner, the fire's embers were heating a bucket of water, hung from a chain. The three shepherds had arranged themselves into a production line. Their eyes sparkled in the firelight. The *juhas* sat with his legs splayed around an enormous wooden tub with his sleeves rolled to the elbow, kneading the whey from handfuls of curd. After cramming the curd into an enamel mug and packing it tight with his thumbs, he tipped it out as a cylindrical block and handed it to the boy, who delicately teased it into a ball, then dropped it into his copper tub of water ready for the *baca*.

The *baca* sat beside the fire. He was older than the *juhas*, a thin man with a small scar on his chin and a gold tooth. Only his forearms moved as he worked like a human lathe to manipulate each pale globe into a decorated spindle, driving a steel wire through its heart, squeezing the cheese into a lozenge. Then the *baca* withdrew the wire and placed the lozenge back into the bucket. From the crumbling consistency handled by the *juhas*, the cheese left the *baca*'s hands soft and smooth like skin.

The final stage of manufacture was also handled by the *baca*. Into the puckered navel at one end of a lozenge drawn from his bucket, the *baca* re-inserted the wire, easing it through until it reappeared at the far end. Then he fitted two semi-circular wooden moulds over the lozenge's waist, clamping them tight with a belt of plaited string. Holding the cheese in both hands, by its two tapered ends, the *baca* tossed it lightly in the air, catching and squeezing so that the cheese was pressed against the interior of the mould, and so that the last droplets of whey ran out along the wire. For a last time, the *baca* withdrew the wire. Turning to his bed, he picked up two wooden plugs and pressed one into each end of the tapered cheese, rolling the cheese in his hands so that it closed about the barrels of the plugs. With his fingernails, he picked the plugs out of the cheese, leaving a star-shaped socket at each end. Finally he eased off the plaited belt and then prised away the two moulds. Lying across the *baca*'s palms, about twenty centimetres long, was an ivory fusiform cheese, tapered at both ends, with a single band of quadricones about its waist, flanked by two bands of hatching. Looking pale and naked, the *oscypek* rolled in the *baca*'s big hands. Caressingly, he stretched the two tapers a little and with a series of light touches smoothed the points from the quadricones and effected a slight twist to the hatched lines.

Then he dipped the cheese into a bucket of clear cold water.

Beyond the door the Dunajec flowed, sealing in the Pieniny on three sides. I left the *szałas* with a wave from the *baca* and enough *oscypek* on board my rucksack to see me through the week. The *polana* sloped up to the first ramparts of the Pieniny.

Hol and Naomi had joined me for a ramble through this little Carpathian rock-garden. The Pieniny is an outcrop of limestone not quite 1,000 metres high, ten kilometres long and four kilometres wide. Its name, 'Foaming,' refers to the rapids that trip along the bed of its nine-kilometre gorge. The shelter and relatively low altitude of the Pieniny have given it a warmish micro-climate that has attracted a wide diversity of species. 'Jack not back till 8, having done well with his birds (38 varieties)', wrote Ruth in her journal of June 1936. My guidebooks noted an extraordinary diversity of local species: 300 types of *Ichneumon* fly; eagles, boars, wolves, the rare red-roundled butterfly *Parnassius apollo*, the endemic treacle mustard, *Erysimum pieninicum*. I wouldn't have known one *Ichneumon* from another, but I couldn't have missed the purple orchids that covered one slope, or the armies of frogs, or the black and yellow salamander that blocked our path.

We wandered on to the high point of the Pieniny, the triple-headed crag of Trzy Korony – Three Crowns. It wasn't much of a summit. Hol, I knew, was disappointed. He likes to reach the top on all-fours, crawling nose-first into a blizzard with the challenge of a bivouac to follow. Just short of the top of Trzy Korony there was a queue of trippers waiting to buy tickets to the summit from a national park official wearing a uniform and peaked hat. We filed up to the top, but the exercise was so distressing that I forgot to note the view. In one of those quaint human contradictions, half a million visitors a year cram into a national park set aside to protect rare species.

Not until we reached the far end of the range, at the tip of a brittle ridge, did we escape. On the outcrop of Sokolica, a prow of rock hanging 300 metres above a U-bend in the Dunajec gorge, we could look down on the wooden rafts which were the cause of the Pieniny's popularity, drifting like dead leaves down the rapids.

The next day Hol and Naomi took the raft trip (I thought about joining them, but, while they were not 'mechanical', they were nevertheless too fast-moving for my liking; I'd convinced myself that anything quicker than walking pace would make me giddy), while I sat on the river bank at our camp below Trzy Korony. Just downstream I could see the mouth of the Dunajec's gorge. In the other direction the landscape was soft and striated with thousands of strip-fields, an anachronistic imprint of medieval farming, in this case caused by the eternal subdivision of land as it passed from father to sons. Opposite me, on the Slovakian bank, was the Red Abbey, Červen Kláštor, the one-time home of Friar Cyprian, the eighteenth-century would-be aviator who became a legend with his hang-glider. Local folklore relates that the flying Friar once crossed the Tatras in his machine.

Another Dunajec bridge carried us from the limestone of the Pieniny into the next Carpathian range: the sandstone country of Beskid Sądecki. We walked up the valley of the Grajcarek past log-cottages until the wooden onion dome of Jaworki's church poked above the trees.

The clock on Jaworki's church gave the time as nine. Like several other church clocks I'd seen in the Carpathians, this one was painted on to its tower. In Trencin there was a clock whose minute and hour hands had been reversed. 'Because the old people do not need to know the exact time,' I was told, 'we put up the big hand for the hours, so that they can tell the approximate time more easily.'

'It's because it's always time for Mass . . .' a man in Jaworki nodded at the church clock. He was sweating, bespectacled and overweight and said that he was a tank-turret designer from Łodz, taking a short holiday. He wore a jungle hat and a camouflage suit draped with cameras and an armoury of lenses. We'd met him up a side valley, the pretty Dolina Homole, which climbed to a viewpoint overlooking Slovakia. 'Definitely spying!' whispered Naomi.

The spy insisted on acting as our guide. Taking the lead, he struggled up steep slopes, seeping perspiration and feeding us mango-flavoured boiled sweets. On the descent to Jaworki, he took Naomi's arm on the steeper scrambles and when we regained the road he bowed low, kissed her hand and said in perfect English: 'Thank you so much. It was my greatest pleasure to accompany you on your touristic excursion.'

No roads linked the valleys of the Dunajec and the Poprad but several paths crossed the hills of Beskid Sądecki. Naomi arranged to meet us on the far side of the range the following day and Hol and I set off into a thunderstorm. The mist was thick and the map imprecise. We climbed up to about 1,000 metres and were in dripping forest with half an hour of daylight remaining when I had to announce to Hol that I had made a mistake. 'We may be slightly off-course . . .' I warned him. 'Or possibly lost.'

Rainwater dripped from the end of Hol's nose. 'Far be it for me to pass comment on the navigation,' he replied. 'But if I might contribute, not that it particularly matters since I'm enjoying myself immensely, I would suggest that if we turn through 180 degrees and retrace our steps along this path for approximately eleven and a half minutes, we will see a cutting at about two p.m. to our original course, and although it has been known for me to be wrong, I am ninety-three per cent certain that the alternative I'm suggesting will lead us north-north-west towards the summit of Radziejowa.' He was of course right.

We slept on Radziejowa. I put up my tent in the falling rain while Hol lit a fire using two damp paper bags. My tent was only large enough for one of us, so Hol volunteered to sleep with his upper body out in the rain. The last time we had shared such cramped quarters had been on a mountain called An Teallach in Scotland, one January night fifteen years ago. A group of us had become benighted on the summit ridge and had spent the dark hours balanced on ledges cut from the snow. There were not enough bivouac bags to go around, so we all had to double up. Hol and I spent the night like a pair of shrink-wrapped mummies, soaked to the skin. I had never been so cold in my life and by dawn I eventually cracked and began complaining. 'Are you uncomfortable?' asked Hol, surprised.

My nagivation made us four hours late for the rendezvous with Naomi in Piwniczna, a small town that derived a living from straddling a border-crossing with Slovakia. Signs bearing the words *Uwaga! sły pies* covered gateways throughout the town. Why, we wondered, were we being warned of sly pies? And if we were, what were sly pies? Poisonous pasties? Sneaky steak-and-kidney puddings? Killer quiches?

'*Nie!*' laughed the man who served us lunch. '*Pies* is dog. Dangerous dog!' We left town; Hol dislikes dogs even more than I do; sleeping on a beach in Italy, he had once been selected from several thousand sun-bathers by a mongrel which urinated over his feet. Hol had run into the sea as if his legs were on fire.

We camped on the banks of the Poprad and in the morning followed the river's meanders upstream, with the wooded slopes of the Beskid Sądecki on our left and gentler contours of Slovakia on the far bank of the river. Hol took the car on ahead, leaving Naomi to walk with me. Cottage gardens were dappled with the blossoms of lilac and hawthorn. We passed beehives, cut from tree-trunks. One had been carved into a bear, standing on his hind legs. Others were totemic heads with the bees crawling through the mouths.

At lunchtime, Hol and Naomi left for Krakow. They said that they might try to intercept me as I crossed the Dukla pass, in about one week's time. It was hot, that day. Walking down the road beside the Poprad, my boots left their prints in the softened tar. I wondered wistfully whether my own children might one day walk these mellow uplands, following *their* father's footprints.

The Black Stork

Beyond the Poprad river lay the land of the Łemks, the people who once occupied the northern curve of the Carpathians from the Beskid Niski to Bukovina, descendants perhaps of nomadic Vlach herdsmen who began migrating north in the fifteenth century. The mountains they eventually ran up against were the outer bend of the strategic wall that defended Europe from the steppes. They might as well have set up camp on a firing range. Over the centuries armies and borders have shifted to and fro across the watershed, cutting the Łemk lands into random scraps, re-stitching them, tearing them apart again. The trench-lines of two world wars criss-cross the range. After the Second World War, troublesome Łemks were shipped off to Siberia; the poor ones emigrated to America; those that stayed were collectivized, urbanized and now democratized. One of the Polish maps I'd found in Zakopane was dotted with the crosses of ancient Łemk churches, the wooden *cerkwi* once used by the Greek Orthodox congregations, with their separatist Uniate liturgy. Most had been taken over by the Catholic Church. These churches are the symbolic totems of a lost culture, and over the following days my route came to be dictated by the sad little crosses on my map.

I turned away from the river, following its tributary, the Kryniczanka, upstream towards the Beskid Niski. Powroźnik's *cerkiew* peeped from the trees. A circular wall, and then the circle of grey trunks, surrounded the church. I tried to sketch it, but found its angles impossible to tame. Three onion domes descended in height from the top of the tapered tower at the west end of the church to the tiny octagonal stub on the eastern end of the roof. The central tower had three progressively smaller pagoda roofs and on top of each onion was a miniature octagonal tower, with a tiny onion above. Each tower was topped by a cross and, around the foot of the church, the walls flared in a skirt. There were no windows on the north side and just three tiny glazed windows on the sunward side. The entire exterior of the church, including the domes, was clad in a skin of wooden shingles. In its sylvan curves and delicate scales the church possessed a loving magicality, as if it had grown from the forest floor, drawn upward by some celestial calling, moulded into its exotic contours by craftspeople who felt the grain of the wood as keenly as the wrinkles in their own hands.

In the remains of that hot afternoon I continued up the Kryniczanka to Krynica, 'the pearl of Polish spas', a string of sanatoria and gardens strung along the floor of this gentle valley. Lawn-mowers filled the air with the smell of English cricket-pitches. Old folks shuffled along the *deptak* beside the river cramming in ice-creams, pizzas and hot-dogs.

Taking the waters was more ritualized here than in previous spas I'd happened upon. One hour before meal-times, residents converged on the pump-room clutching their personal water jugs. The back wall of the pump-room was lined with copper troughs and a row of labelled water-taps. Girls in green uniforms took water orders at counters. *Habitués* had favourite cocktails that the girls mixed then heated in a steaming copper tray. Boards listed the chemical constituents of the various waters, and their proportion of solids, from Zdrój Jana, which contained a delicate 0.071 per cent of suspended minerals to the mighty Zuber at 2.14 per cent. Zuber put Krynica on the map. If Krynica's literature was to be believed, it was the most concentrated mineral water on the continent.

Disregarding the 'are you sure you're old enough' expression on the counter-girl's face I bought a cup of Zuber and took a tentative sip. It tasted like volcanic saliva, a tectonic cocktail of rotting rocks and school-boy stinkbombs. I was about to sling the contents into the pot plants when I saw a sign forbidding it. With the eyes of the counter-girls boring into my back, I drank the entire cup. The girls watched, professionally impassive, as I gasped back the tide and, in a show of ill-conceived gamesmanship, returned to the counter and ordered another.

Breakfast in the Pensjonat Wisła was salted semolina. Not for the first time I reeled out of a health-spa holding my stomach.

Beyond Krynica lay the quiet hills of the Beskid Niski. My route eastwards took me against the grain of the country, from valley to valley. A track struck upwards from the top end of the spa, then rose and fell across fields speckled with purple orchids. Architectural pines lent a sense of parkland.

The first valley I came down to had a sad little *cerkiew* that had been painted mustard yellow. But in the next valley, Banica's *cerkiew* sat like a wooden ark, moored to a flowering horse chestnut. A low wall surrounded the church, interrupted by the separate wooden belfry. Evening was settling on the valley and I lay on the hill above the church while the cows were brought down to the village. Eventually the congregation filed out on to the lane. Three elderly men wearing suits led a flock of children, the girls with lace in their hair, dressed in white-petalled dresses, white shoes and little lace bags at their wrists, the boys as stiff as guardsmen in black suits.

In these poignant valleys, tradition clung by its fingernails to the crumbling economics of the Communist–Capitalist watershed; roads were broken; houses in ruins. In Hańczowa, the shops' shelves were barren, or occupied by a single rank of the same product: string, tinned fish, buckets, jam. They had no cheese, or bread, or sausage. But Hańczowa had a beautiful *cerkiew*, clad entirely in shingles. Even the three onion domes were scaled with wood. A new stone cross inscribed with Łemk Cyrillic and dated 1988 stood in the churchyard, marking a return of its Łemk congregation.

The ridge between the Ropa and its easterly neighbour, the Regetóroka, was higher than the Beskid Niski's earlier hurdles. The path climbed through old beeches over the top of a hill called Kozie Zebro. Part-way up, shutters were thrown across the sky and spots of rain began to smack my hat. Several seconds later I stopped dead as a tremendous roar tore into the hill. The beeches bowed before the tempest. I had no time to pull on my jacket. Rain beat down. Thunder and lightning crashed. I crouched on the sodden ground with my head under my arms. Branches and dead wood spun down. Two minutes later the wind was gone, but the hammering rain continued. Between the bursts of lightning, I dashed down the hill till I found a space between the trees where I settled into a crouch while the water filled my boots. Between the flashes the forest was as black as night.

After the lightning flickered out I made my way back up the hill. The wood looked as if it had been shaken by a giant hand. Foliage and broken limbs lay across the path and the wet air was heavy with the sweet smell of sap. A few steps from where I had been when the storm struck, two statuesque beeches had been felled across the path. Splinters of wood, ripped branches and leaves littered the ground. The trees had not been struck by lightning, but blown down.

By the time I reached the Regetóroka, the sun was blazing from a clear sky and the meadows were steaming. People were emerging from cottages, blinking. Cattle strolled back to the fields. In the last of the day I hurried over the ridge to the Zdynia valley and then up once more on to the heights of Popowe Wierchy. The woods up here were full of deer. In a glade beside the path, two bucks were jousting. Their panting and the bone-crunching thuds of their colliding foreheads carried through the forest. As I held my breath behind a tree, a wildcat slunk across the path I'd just left.

In these hollow hills I met few signs of human life; sightings were notable for their rarity: two girls marching hand in hand to school along the dirt road to Kryzwa, miniature rucksacks bobbing on their backs; a *szałas* – the only one I'd seen since leaving the Pieniny – with the *baca* lifting muslin bags of *bunc* on to a massive set of see-saw scales, watched by a buyer from Nowy Sącz; a charcoal-burner whose eye-whites shone like pearls from a face that looked as if it had been dunked in a tub of soot.

Beyond the charcoal-burner's wood I crossed a hill to the head of a valley which might have been lifted from Hardy's Wessex; swaddling hangers wrapped their arms about handkerchief fields and a scattering of roofs. The only sounds were the larks and the lowing of cattle. It was a picture of pre-desecration England.

The houses belonged to Bartne. Some were old *hizhas*, the Łemk cottages. The village had two *cerkwi*, one in caramel gloss (curiously with a taller central dome, in the style of the Boyks, further east) and the other a little gem, hidden by trees, shingled on its triple domes. Beneath gravestones inscribed in Łemk Cyrillic lay the men who had cut the millstones and grindstones for which Bartne had been known. Above the church, three men were tearing old thatch from a *hizha* roof and replacing it with timber. The only other thatch *hizha* had been abandoned. Prompted perhaps by satellite dishes he'd seen in some far-off town, the cottage's last incumbent had nailed an enamel wash-bowl to the eaves. The bowl was tilted to the heavens and around the rim he had painted in black letters BARTNE TV. Ironic fantasy was a Łemk trademark. Two days earlier I'd passed a scruffy barn daubed with blottesque capitals advertising the improbable existence of a SEX SHOP. And one of the few cars I saw in the Beskid Niski was a ubiquitous Polski Fiat 650 E, with brushed-alloy MITSUBISHI 2.3 TURBO D auto-badges riveted to its engine cover.

While I was at Bartne the clouds stole up again and the village became shadowed and sad. In a fragility of mood which I would later find familiar, I felt the gloom cast by the collective tragedies of these troubled hills and I was soon spreading the maps looking for a way out.

I left Bartne on an ancient cobbled track over Przełęcz Majdan, the 600-metre pass which opened the way to the Wisłoka valley.

The skies cleared and the shadowy land burst with brilliant colours and heat. As the valley widened I began to pass shrines poking above the undergrowth. Old plum trees fought with briars and the dates on two of the shrines – 1883 and 1894 – recalled a time when this valley would have been lined with Łemk farmsteads. The shrines were all that remained; flaking Madonnas, a Christ, St Nicholas. The farms must have been burnt during the migration, or dismantled.

But this was not another valley of ghosts. Further downstream, a horse was ploughing, women hoeing, timber was being cut and crops planted. Chickens and geese strutted in farmyards. Tractors stood in driveways. Świątkowa's *cerkiew* rose like a little cathedral surrounded by a nebula of buttercups.

I reached the valley's main village, Krempna, at dusk. It was a Friday night and in the shop a queue of men waited to swap wads of screwed-up złotys for half-litre bottles of vodka which they stuffed down the front of their trousers, or wedged into the waistband at the back, and then covered by tugging a pullover over the bulge. The shop had no bread. I loaded up with tinned meat and sardines for the weekend. By the time I had been served a thunderstorm was shattering the dusk.

In the bar next door the men muttered and fought beneath the sickly glow of low-wattage light bulbs. Through the grimy net curtains and rain-smeared glass, the lightning scratched at the black sky. Most of the men were waiting for the bus. There were about twenty of them and they'd been drinking for some time. I sat exhausted. I had nowhere to sleep. That was normal, but this night I noticed it more than usual. A long and beautiful day was disintegrating into chaos and there was nothing I could do to stop it.

I bought another coffee. A man in a sports jacket was shouting in the face of a farmer. The farmer punched him and Sports Jacket tottered backwards into a table occupied by four men staring at an empty bottle. They pushed him away and he continued his hapless ricochet, crashing into a chair which splintered into pieces. The back of his jacket had become streaked with lime or white-wash. The farmer's son was banging a table with his fist and shouting at another young man who was wearing a red baseball cap. They both stood, maddened faces closing. The farmer tried to drag his son back. Sports Jacket was collared by the bar-woman about the broken chair.

I walked outside and stood under the eaves on the concrete terrace listening to the calming hiss of the rain. A short man fell through the door. He bounced off the terrace rail, then the bar wall, then the railing again, before falling back and head-butting the plate-glass of the shop window. The glass jangled in its frame as the man reeled sideways to the top of the steps. Just in time, he saw the abyss and stopped. Slowly and deliberately he lowered himself to the concrete and, like a child entering a swimming pool for the first time, he bumped down the flight of concrete steps on his backside while the monsoon slicked his hair into a tight black bathing cap.

An hour later the bus arrived and there was a panicked evacuation of the bar. Double-jointed marionettes jerked and collided through the puddles, bawling at the driver to wait. I took one more coffee to give the rain time to ease, then set off to find a bed.

In the light rain the fields outside Krempna appeared to be steaming. I stopped to chat to a man wearing oilskins and a cravat. He was carrying a small milk churn. He suggested that I walk on to the next village, Polany, where the priest would let me sleep in the churchyard.

I didn't reach Polany. The steam I'd seen in the fields turned out to be smoke from a charcoal-burners' furnace in the woods. As I passed their camp, their dogs went crazy and I swore bitterly in the dark and rain, wanting the company and shelter that the charcoal-burners could provide but incapable of summoning the courage and energy to get past the dogs and to tackle the uneasy introduction with the men of the forest, in the night, alone.

I left the road and climbed the valley side till I found an easy slope behind a tree. Another thunderstorm struck as I crawled into the tent. Later, the rain moved on and clouds like smoke raced across the moon. I ate the tinned pork, drank some water, wrote my journal. At about midnight, there was another storm. The headlights of a vehicle moved slowly along the valley road, while somebody played a searchlight to and fro across the hillside. There was nothing I could do except bless the tree I'd put between myself and the road. Through a slit in the tent door I watched the beam probe the woods and sloping fields. The clumsy arcs drew closer. The beam rushed at the tent. I was blinded. When I regained my night-vision, it was the vehicle's tail-lights I saw. They searched the whole valley. I could not help thinking that I was the quarry, reported perhaps to the police as a suspicious foreign vagrant.

In the morning I walked back to Krempna to find the man in the oilskins.

'It's Lithuanian,' said Jerzy Butwiłło when I asked about his surname. 'But we live in Warsaw. And here, in Krempna. This is where we come in the summer. To the Beskid Niski.'

He was seventy and retired. He had been a radio journalist. Jerzy and Teresa's cottage in Krempna stood outside the village, raised slightly on the valley side. They had taken the cottage from the village of Grab, an out-of-the-way place at the end of a cul-de-sac valley down on the border with Slovakia. They had the cottage dismantled and transported to Krempna, which had a shop and a good road.

I asked Jerzy about the Łemks.

'Before the civil war sixty-five per cent round here were Łemks. After the deportations, it went down to thirty or thirty-five per cent. Now many of the young Łemks are in Polish cities. They speak Polish, think Polish.' He sighed. 'They love the mountains and fields. And they feel the love that their grandfathers and grandmothers felt. But these things don't buy bread.' Jerzy looked out of the window. 'Some of the Łemks who left have become very successful. The Rector of the Faculty of Art in Krakow is a Łemk. To understand this country,' he continued, 'you must understand the politics of Great Emotion. One-and-a-half million Poles were deported from eastern Poland to Siberia. One million died there. My cousin was deported to Siberia. Then he went to Tehran with General Anders and then he fought at Monte Cassino. Now he lives in England. But he has never been back to Poland.'

How strange it was that Jerzy's cousin would have been attacking the position on Monte Cassino held by the teenage Karl Jahn – the Bavarian pensioner I'd shared a *Fasching* drink with, back in that long winter.

Jerzy poured another coffee and I asked: 'What if the original Łemk owner of your cottage came to your door?'

'Sixteen years ago a Ukrainian came here and said that this was the land of his father. They had been deported in 1947, when he was a ten-year-old boy. We had a good conversation here in this room. I told him that Teresa was born in Lvov, which is now Ukraine. The Ukrainian man understood. We all know the emotions of being moved. This man felt the same as my wife, like the Germans feel about Stettin ... Stalin moved everybody. But you know something,' added Jerzy. 'This man, this Ukrainian, he thought our way of living was very strange. He asked us: "How can you live here without cows?" I explained that we only came here in the summer, but he couldn't understand it. Couldn't see why we had no cows. He was working in Ukraine in an electrical factory.'

Oddly it was the Górale of Podhale, not the Łemks, who reminded Jerzy and Teresa most of local customs. 'They still bring the sheep in spring from the Tatras to Bieszczady. They bring them by train. But when they go back in September, they walk. We watch them go by. The *baca* in the front in his Górale clothes, and the sheep with their bells, and the big white dogs. Then at the back are the other shepherds.'

Life in the valley changed when the state farm closed. The farm was still there, beside the road. Behind the locked gates the giant silo stood empty, the barns and machinery repair yard still, the diesel pumps rusting. Grass had pushed through the joints in the concrete and the red lettering on the front of the main building was fading away.

GOOD ORGANIZATION AND SENSIBLE WORK
MAKES ECONOMIC PROGRESS

The farm gave people work and a place to live. There was a sense of order and control. The coupons were the control. You needed coupons to buy shoes, sugar and meat, soap, vodka, chocolate. The workers' quarters were across the road from the farm, behind some trees. Around the quarters was a three-metre fence overhung by barbed wire. When the farm was built there were not enough workers in the valley, so they brought in prisoners and to keep the prisoners in, they had to build the fence. The fence never got taken down.

Inside the fence were rows of off-white cubes separated by concrete slips. Each cube contained three rooms: kitchen, sitting-room, bedroom. In one of these cubes lived a school teacher and her husband, a vet.

When I arrived, Barbara Mielczarek was working in the garden she had made beside the front door. She was a good-looking woman, strong, tall, with long dark hair. We went into the kitchen.

'What bothers people here is unemployment,' she said, as she cut some mushrooms for soup. 'With the government farms they had work. Now there is none. There are families with five, six, seven children. Some children come to school looking as if they have had no breakfast.'

Warm fur squirmed about my ankles. 'They belong to Dariusz,' smiled Barbara at the litter of puppies.

'Under Communism everyone was almost the same,' continued Barbara,' but with not very much. Under capitalism, a few have a lot but most have nothing.' She sprinkled salt into the pan. 'People wait for the state to give them money. They don't understand that you must make life yourself.' She shrugged. 'You can change politics and economics as much as you like. But you can't change the thinking.' She thought for a moment, then added: 'The children who go on to university, who leave Krempna, will change. Those who stay will not change.' She looked out of the window. 'It is beautiful here, but Beskid Niski is still one of the poorest parts of Poland. You must understand that what you see is not always the truth . . .'

A black stork flew overhead with slow pterodactyl flaps.

Barbara laughed. 'You see . . . that stork has built its nest on top of the chimney from the central-heating plant. So it is black from the soot. But actually it is a white stork!'

Shock Therapy

After a year of momentum I was finding it harder to leave places. Every day I was confronted by the big question: to stay or to move on. It might apply to prolonging a picnic by a trout stream, or stopping off for a day in a village. They were incompatible needs; it was the old battle between root and branch, digging in or reaching out. The nomad in me was beginning to develop sedentary aspirations.

Jerzy walked with me down the footpath from his cottage to the road, then he climbed on to his bicycle and pedalled towards Krempna. I turned the other way, towards the Dukla pass.

The day was bright and the south wind filled the valley with sun-warmed air from the Hungarian plain. Doors hung open on the long low log-cottages. Most were painted, with black timbers separated by indigo plaster. Under the eaves stood stacks of firewood. But all had traded their thatch for corrugated metal.

I paused to photograph one of these cottages and was called through the broken gate by a tall man wearing dungarees. He was as thin as a pitchfork, with a rhamphoid nose and a partially closed left eye that swam in a puddle of tears. He pulled me into the centre of a lilac bush. 'Our *kapliczka*!' he shouted, pulling back the branches from a two-metre shrine. In the lower of the two niches, a megacephalous St Nicholas peered out. One of his arms had snapped off and he was hemmed in by plastic flowers, old birds' nests and a jam jar of lilac blossom. The man broke a twig from the tree and used it as a crutch to balance the arm in place then he grabbed my hand and towed me towards the cottage.

The right half of the cottage was for the animals; the left half for Stanysław Fajks and his wife. He was not a true Łemk, but the grand-son of a Pole and a German. They had two rooms. The front room had an oven and range, a table, two chairs and two single beds, on opposite walls. The floorboards were bare. There was a white-painted dresser occupied by crockery and utensils, a transistor radio and a cuckoo clock. Six buckets of well-water stood beside the cooking range. The back room was similar to the Górale 'White Room' – with a spare bed and a dining table laid with cotton cloth; shelves lined with a few possessions. The room smelled unlived-in. Beyond the house stood the hay-barn.

Stanysław's wife poured boiling water on to two small glasses quarter-filled with coffee grounds, then tipped in two spoons of sugar. After the grounds had settled she handed Stanysław and me the glasses and then sat on the end of the bed, pulled off her shoes and washed her feet in a bowl of water.

The cottage had been built in 1917, two years after the Russians had been driven from the Carpathians, but the *kapliczka* dated from 1720, so Stanysław's plot may have been occupied for three centuries.

Stanysław drained his coffee and said: 'Come to see the cows!'

The five cows were ten minutes along the valley, in a pasture surrounded by an electric fence which Stanysław successfully persuaded me to grip, using a piece of cow-parsley as an insulator. The shock threw me on to the grass and when I came round Stanysław was weeping with hysterical laughter and kissing my neck. As I waved goodbye with my good arm, I reasoned that, in the absence of television, electrical shocks administered to strangers provided all the ingredients of comedy: the set-up; the theatrical mishap (I bawled very convincingly) and then the farcical pretence by the victim that the injury had been deliberately self-inflicted; an experiment to see what happens when low intellect comes into contact with high voltage. It had been a long time since I had been kissed passionately, and although Stanysław's unshaven chin, black chipped fingernails and vodka-charged breath were far removed from my memories of Annabel, the unsolicited intimacy and the electric shock led to several hours of hormonal disquiet.

Beyond Polany, the road became less travelled. I picnicked by the river. The only passer-by during a three-hour siesta was an ageing Autosan bus, which bumped along the unmade road and splashed uncertainly through the ford. The bus was going to Olchowiec, the valley's last village.

The walk to Olchowiec was exquisitely melancholic. As the valley narrowed and the trees closed in the certainty of loss grew stronger. I was about to leave Poland. Olchowiec was a few buildings clustered about a track junction by the river. A farmer with cowshit up his trousers responded to my wave and took me into his kitchen while he changed his clothes. People came and went from the kitchen. The farmer's name was Teodor Tomaszuyk and he had seven children. Teodor had been born in Ciechania, a remote border village south of Krempna. In 1942 he was taken off to Bavaria to work in a labour camp and at the end of the war his village was razed. In a brown suit Teodor led me back along the white dust road down the valley and then up into a side valley to an isolated cottage.

Tadeusz Kiełbasinski lived in a thatched Łemk *hizha*. He was slight, with a silver moustache and given to dancing whenever the tempo of the Łemk music on his tape machine became irresistible. Instead of animals, Tadeusz had a collection of Łemk clothing and domestic tools. Among them was the *czucha*, a thick, tasselled smock and the *hunia*, a thick brown jacket and baggy white trousers. With the help of clothes-pegs, Teodor dressed me in the full Łemk kit, with the black boat-shaped *krysak* on my head. 'These will not fit you . . .' he said, lining a pair of *kyrpci* against my feet. The Łemk shoes were little more than a single flap of leather, folded over and stitched.

The most beautiful of the Łemk clothes was the *kozuszanka*, a thick waistcoat embroidered with flowers. The women's hat, the *czepec*, was white also, with a densely embroidered band of geometric patterns in orange and red, lifted by touches of yellow.

'It was,' sighed Tadeusz, 'another world. Another time.'

Round the walls Tadeusz had arranged various other Łemk artefacts, all crafted from wood: cattle yokes, a butter churn, a potato strainer, a primitive loom, woodworking tools (including a wooden plane identical to one my grandfather Jack had given me), a massive cabbage grater.

He pointed at a pile of rusting sub-machine guns. 'You know where these come from?'

'Dukla?'

'You know about Dukla?'

'A bit.'

'Dukla was terrible.'

'Yes.'

'Ninety thousand Russian soldiers died. Six thousand Czechoslovak soldiers died. And Germans. How many Germans I don't know. The fighting was here. Outside Olchowiec. I picked up these things in the woods. You can find them everywhere.' Tadeusz pointed out Russian and German helmets, drilled by bullets and shrapnel, and a rusting Russian sword, ammunition boxes, mortar bombs and a shell one metre long. 'Yes. It was here. In these woods. You will see.'

Dukla Pass

Above Olchowiec the road up the Wilsznia was just a farm track. There was little to see of the village of Wilsznia. My pre-war map recorded a population of thirty-five and a string of cottages and a *cerkiew*, extending 500 metres up a side valley. In the long grass I came on rotting purlins and a few blocks of stone, nettled mounds and outlines of field terraces. The only standing object was a weathered shrine and rusting cross that could have marked the site of the *cerkiew*. Wilsznia, like Ciechania and so many other Łemk villages, had disappeared.

Subsiding into morbidity I wandered off into the woods behind Wilsznia. I'd meant to continue along the old valley track, over a small pass to Tylawa, on the Dukla road. With nowhere in mind, I climbed through the beech woods. There was a track of sorts that made its way ambivalently up the side of a ridge. The woods were as still as winter and laid with a carpet of bronze leaf-mulch. After a while the track went off somewhere else and the ridge became a narrow crest pocked with gun-pits. I thought perhaps that I had strayed south to Slovakia, but compass bearings through the trees fixed me on the summit of 702-metre Studeny Wierch, the highest point in the Dukla area. From the lip of one of the gun-pits I could peer down to the 'Valley of Death', the killing-fields of autumn 1944.

The Soviet plan had been to trap Army Group South, the First Panzer and Hungarian First armies, in a pincer movement by launching the Red Army and 1 Communist Czecho-Slovak Corps as a spearhead through the lowest gap in the Carpathians. The Soviet divisions were worn down by the long summer offensive and low on men, weapons and ammunition, but without the Dukla breakthrough, there was no pincer. The ridges of the Beskid Niski acted as ready-made ramparts for the Germans, who were well dug in and knew the lie of the land. The Soviets threw men and machines at the Germans until they broke through the pass.

I could find no path down the south-east side of Studeny Wierch. Lower down, the spacious beeches gave way to a jungle of scrub that had colonized an obstacle course of unnatural hummocks and holes. Suddenly every shadow on that torn ground hid a *doppelgänger*. I began to run, ploughing through brambles and bogs, compass clenched, dragging myself over fallen trees, tripping on roots, snagged by my own hysteria. I skidded and fell into a hole and found my legs in a dug-out, its bulging log-walls and sagged roof, home yesterday to boys who had the bad luck to be in the wrong place at the wrong time and who would die because they had orders to hold the pass. I felt as if I'd crashed through the lid of a tomb.

I stumbled from the foot of Studeny Wierch scratched and soaked and made my way by road up to the pass and through the border. The Slovaks on the south side of the pass had turned the entire valley into a grisly theme park. There were memorials to the mine-clearance teams and busts of men whose youthful features rammed home the futility of an eighty-day battle for a pass that, fifty years on, would belong to neither of the principal combatants. I wondered whether the relatives of tank commander Frantisék Urána or Sergeant Ivan Vasilievič Babin knew that their boys had been cast in corrosion-proof alloy and set in a wall at the head of a quiet valley in the Carpathians. Did they even know they'd died at Dukla? A pyramid of stone rose from the spot used by the Czechoslovak general, Ludvik Svoboda, for his observation post when his troops blasted their way down the south side of the pass on 6 October. Svoboda subsequently became the president of Czechoslovakia.

Parked on the verges for the next five kilometres was an incongruous collection of war traffic: tanks, field guns, mortars, fighter-bombers. Dug-outs and gun positions had been restored in a field of orchids and a transport-plane sat chin-up in a sea of buttercups.

Compared to Roncesvalles, remembered by a single stone and an epic poem, Dukla looked so clumsy.

Roads to Nowhere

At Dukla I had to depart from my cherished line. My natural route would have taken me east through the old Łemk lands of Bieszczady and into the Ukrainian Carpathians. But there were no border crossings in the Bieszczady, and Ukraine was still surrounded by a ring of steel. So I would have to walk south, out of the Carpathians, to the nearest border-crossing, at Uzhgorod, then climb back to the hills beyond the wire. What would have been a depressing detour was saved by the appearance at Dukla of Hol and Naomi, who'd accurately estimated when I'd be crossing the pass. For the next few days I had their company while I descended the Carpathian piedmont.

Requited nostalgia for Slovakia, company and a downward gradient lengthened my weary stride. But this eastern corner of the country, hard up against the inward bend of the Carpathians and two sealed borders, was not the same country I'd ambled through in the spring. After Poland, it all looked run-down. The sad *hostinecs* had empty shelves; Communist public-address speakers dangled off telegraph poles like old skulls; cottages slumped into beds of cow-parsley; unkempt fields strangled deserted collective farms. There was so little traffic on the roads that I treated them as my own.

According to a map Tadeusz had shown me, Łemkówie extended well south from the border into the Laboreck hills. Here, between the mountain and the plain, the Łemks merged with people known variously as Rusyns, Ruthenians, Rusnaks and Ruthenes. Their churches are as lovely as those on the Polish side of the watershed.

In Bodružal, a small village up a side valley south-east of Nižn Komárnik, the woman entrusted with the key refused to let us see inside the exquisite wooden church. There had been a robbery. St Basil's rose from this reclusive glade in 1658 and conformed to the Greek-Catholic style of the Łemk *cerkwi* across the border, although its central tower was unusually heavy around the hips and there were no fewer than five ascending roofs and 'onions' on its smallest tower; less the work of an architect than of a topiarist.

We had more luck at Prickra, twenty minutes on, up a cul-de-sac below the Polish border. Here, a woman bringing in a barrow of nettles opened up the tiny church and switched off the electronic intruder alarm. Julia Brenišinova saw my surprise. 'They steal everything now. Everything.'

Sadly the top of the iconostasis had been damaged by a leak in the roof but St Nicholas was intact and the colours on the panels were a glorious combination of terracotta, aquamarine and gold; the black irises of the saints seemed to watch from every angle. Julia said that the church's six benches were regularly used. The screens in these tiny places of worship were as vividly descriptive as TV pictures and must have filled their populations with awe and amusement; in the next village, Mirol'a, the Last Supper (always over the central 'Holy' door in the iconostasis) depicted Judas as a gypsy, clutching a cartoon swag-bag labelled '13', while the Resurrection icon showed Jesus shooting towards the ceiling like an indoor firework.

We crossed the hills on tracks marked on the 1904 edition of my Austro-Hungarian *Generalkarte*, wading through uncut pastures and woods which had been left to the deer; we came upon a tiny fawn, frozen with fright in a bed of dead leaves and lay beside it till it gathered its breath and pushed itself upright on rickety legs, then bounded into the beeches mewing like a baby.

One hot afternoon we walked into Miková, a village whose ordinariness would have guaranteed indefinite anonymity were it not once the home of Andrej and Julia Varchola. Andrej had emigrated to America and worked in a Pennsylvanian coal pit, and some years later, in 1921, Julia crossed the Atlantic to join him. She bore three sons: Paul became a scrap-metal merchant; John became a clerk at Sears, Roebuck; Andy became a pop artist. 'I come from nowhere,' Andy once said in America.

'Which was the home of the Varcholas?' I asked a man in his yard.

'Number 106, down the road.'

Number 106 was an abandoned cottage with exfoliating paintwork. Through the windows we could see a black and white TV with a cloth on top, a wash stand, a fifties radio and a single bed.

While I took a photograph, Hol had met a neighbour who told him that the Varcholas had lived in number 103. This was a small bungalow surrounded by apple trees, chickens, vegetables and a wire fence through which the owner was urinating. 'Oh yes . . .' said the old man. 'The Varchola cottage was here, before our house.' He said that the tree outside his cottage had been planted by the Varcholas. Miková, was a little too far from Manhattan for it to have benefited as a destination for pop-art pilgrims, but as we were leaving the village, we were hailed from the *potraviny*, the local grocery shop, by a man who claimed to be Andy Warhol's first cousin. The house beside the shop had once belonged to Warhol's aunt, Eva Bezeková.

The next day, while I was hiking on a hot road south down the valley of the Vyrava, Hol and Naomi drove into the town of Medzilaborce and visited the Múzeum Moderného Umenia Rodiny Warholovcov. Outside the museum were a pair of outsize Campbell's soup-cans (one Cream of Celery, one Tomato) and by good chance the director of the museum, Dr Michal Bycko, was available to take Hol and Naomi on a tour of the works of art produced by various of the Varchola family – the paintings by the scrap-metal brother, Paul, that he made with hens' legs, and one of his rare works in oil, listed in the catalogue as 'Heinz Tomto Ketchup'. Andy Warhol's baptismal shirt was there, and a gramophone record reputed to be the only known example of Julia Varchola singing in Ruthenian.

'I don't know . . .' concluded Naomi. 'Maybe I'm too old for modern art.'

Four days' walking south-eastwards from the Dukla pass I emerged from the hills into the glaring space of the Cirocha valley. Wedged into the upper reaches of the valley was Snina, the first town I'd seen since Zakopane. White tower blocks rose above the trees. It was market-day. Sellers of socks and nylon bathmats competed with hawkers of bras and car parts, old tomatoes and clothes-pegs. One man was selling four aluminium pistons from an internal combustion engine, but he had no idea which engine they would fit.

'I might have bought them if he'd known . . .' said Hol thoughtfully. 'Always useful to have a few spare pistons.'

Hol did, however, buy a set of Russian feeler-gauges. 'You know that the blades in European feeler-gauges increase in increments of thickness such that an intelligent engineer can use combinations of the available blades to create every step up in size?'

'Ur, no, I didn't know that, Dad.' (Although, now I thought of it, Hol had given me a set of feeler-gauges for my fourteenth birthday. But I hadn't investigated the method of blade sizing.)

'Well . . .' continued Hol. 'These Russian feeler-gauges have a differ-ent blade for every step up in size, the implication being – unless I'm mistaken, which on balance I think unlikely, there being no obvious alternative explanation – that Russian engineers are assumed to have a low level of mental dexterity.'

'I can sympathize with them, Dad.'

Sending parcels also required a certain level of mathematical ability. The Slovakian government was still using old stock Československo stamps, and all denominations had been exhausted except for the three and two crown. Hol quickly produced a formula for calculating the least number of stamps for a given parcel. 'Divide the total needed by three. Call the result x and call the balance left over y. If y equals nought, use x three-crown stamps; if y equals two, use x three-crown stamps plus one two-crown. And if y equals one, use x-minus-one three-crown stamps plus two two-crowns. It's really very simple.'

The two-crown stamps depicted a flight of Spitfires shooting down a twin-engined Luftwaffe bomber, which seemed a curious choice of sym-bolism at a time when both Czechs and Slovaks were trying to foster trade relations with Germany.

The following morning we climbed over the 1,000-metre granite tor of Sninsk kameň and came down past the kidney-shaped lake of Morské Oko on to the plain of Už. From the V-shaped valley, choked with beech woods, we burst abruptly into the bright light of unshaded slopes, the view ahead empty of mountains. An avenue of walnuts led down the south-facing slope of Virhorlat, past vines and orchards, to-wards the silver surface of the Sea of Slovakia, an incongruous mirage in the heart of the continent. When this dip in the end of the Hungarian plain was flooded in the 1960s, it gave landlocked Czechoslovakia its own ocean. The village on the far shore was called Lúčky.

We camped on a broad sward at the water's edge. As the moon rose over the lake a nightingale sang in an olive tree. By day the intense heat turned the lake into melted glass, still but for the necking grebes and a stalking crane. The entire shore had once been a vast camp-site, with chalets and wash-blocks, showers and shops. Now it was derelict. Apart from a Dutch policeman and his wife, we were the only people on the Sea of Slovakia. On our second day we walked up to a military camp, where a retired major told us that the lake was polluted with lead from the chemical works at Strážske.

Our only visitor was a black and chrome presidential saloon which raced at breakneck speed across the grass then slewed to a halt beside us. Out fell a young man wearing Bermuda shorts. He pointed to the official Michalovce district stencilling on the car door, *Okresny Podnik Sluzieb Michalovce*, and said: 'Where are you from?'

'The United Kingdom,' said my father.

'Then you have to pay a camping charge,' said the entrepreneur.

Actually the boy was more interested in showing off the car than in collecting camping fees. 'The top speed is 210 kilometres per hour,' he said, heaving open the back of the car to reveal a three-litre V-8 motor which looked large enough to power an armoured personnel carrier. 'Rear engine. It is the 1979 model. A Tatra T613.' The boy nodded. 'Very fast.' He had fitted sheepskin covers to the seats.

Hol remembered the Tatra from before the war. Hitler ran his early campaigns from the back of a T11. 'This is the car for my roads,' the Führer had said of the rear-engined, air-cooled, independently sus-pensioned 1930s Tatra. The Germans took over the Tatra factory in 1938 and at the end of the war its brilliant chief designer, Hans Ledwinka, was locked up by the Soviets for six years on a charge of Nazi collaboration. Some of Ledwinka's ideas were used by Ferdinand Porsche to create the original Volkswagen Beetle, but the Tatra itself was left to wallow about in the antediluvian fossil-beds of eastern Europe.

'They're rare,' said Hol, admiring the T613's chunky carburettors, then turning to Naomi. 'It would be nice to have one of these, wouldn't it, darling?'

'Can't you just take a photograph?'

South of the Sea of Slovakia the land was flat and unfamiliar. Clambering roses and vines scrambled along the eaves of white-painted cottages which were disfigured by the giant ears of satellite dishes. One cottage even owned a lawn-mower, made from a slab of bent steel, a motorcycle engine and four push-chair wheels. A lawn-mower struck me as a defining symbol of civilization. I couldn't imagine mountain folk cutting grass so they could *look* at it.

Naomi and I picked up an abandoned byway that cut through forgotten fields. The yellow petals of creeping Jenny hid in damp nooks and the track was thick with Michaelmas daisies. Through the spilling hedge to our left, a sea of snow-white camomile flowers ran up to the foot of the forests of Virhorlat. Back on the roads again we walked beside field edges inked around with larkspur, poppies and cornflowers whose fine blue fronds waved in the hot plain's breath like fingers of coral deep under the sea.

In a village I bought a long oval loaf stippled with caraway seeds and a can from Latvia labelled *Atlantijas Sardines*.

'This is herring!' Mum protested.

'This is Cyrillic,' I replied, unnerved by the alternative label on the underside of the wrapper.

Ukraine lay less than a day away and I felt as if I was being led unwillingly to the brink. It wasn't just the absent visa, but the unknowingness of what lay beyond the fence. Crossing the old Iron Curtain back at the Danube had been a small step into the unknown compared to the leap I was about to make into the old Soviet Union.

Outside the next village, Sobrance, I walked off the edge of my last 1:100,000 *Letná Turistická* map. From here to Istanbul I would be relying on the one-hundred-year-old *Generalkartes* I'd picked up in Vienna. The prospects for finding my way were not good.

Hol walked with me that last afternoon, along back-roads lined with apple trees whose fruit was already half-formed. In a village called Kristy, three boys pulled up buckets of well-water to fill our bottles. I put up my tent on the dyke above the canal and all the village boys came out that afternoon, two to a bicycle, and threw themselves in the green water. A cuckoo called and a man cast a net. A cross-piece of springy willow pushed the net into a square which flashed as his catch flicked frantically in the light of the fireball sun. At dusk the boys brought us a bag of cherries and a shirt full of wild strawberries, then zigzagged back to the village. Their voices carried on the cooling breeze and the poplars rattled like falling rain. From the top of the dyke I could see across the plain to a clump of distant towers. Uzhgorod.

In the morning I gave Hol and Naomi a letter for Annabel, and my most recent journal, and said that I would see them at the end of the year. Then I walked alone up the queue of cars and trucks waiting at the border. An unsmiling Ukrainian policeman glanced at my British passport.

'I'd like a visa please, for one month.'

'*Nyet!*'

Sverdlova 13

The *milicia* headquarters was at Sverdlova 13. The waiting-room had bleak painted walls and a desk opposite the door. Along one wall were a few chairs. It was a room which had never known good news.

That afternoon the Ukrainian border police had eventually relented and given me a three-day visa. Soldiers had let me through the high wire fence at about three p.m. It was a Thursday. My visa expired on Sunday. Therefore I had the remains of the Thursday and Friday to find a method of extending the visa. If I failed, I would have to walk back to the border and return to Slovakia.

For the first two kilometres towards Uzhgorod the road was lined with trucks, buses and cars. Some had broken down. Others had been there so long that their occupants had set up camps beside their vehicles.

Uzhgorod's suburbs almost reached the border. Sverdlova was on the western side of town. Inside the door of number 13 a guard inspected my passport and directed me to the waiting-room. While I waited I wrote on a piece of paper in Russian my formal request for a one-month visa and a précis of my journey.

A tall man wearing slacks and a check shirt opened the door. 'You are English?' he asked, in English.

'I am. And I would like a visa-extension please.'

'Not so fast. There is no hurry.'

Sasha was a police captain. He talked for an hour, about Somerset Maugham and Tibet. He was relaxed and beguiling. He sat on my side of the desk, at forty-five degrees to my chair. Periodically he would pause and say: 'What is your point of view, forgive me. . .' or ask rhetorically about my motives: 'Why are there so many Englishmen coming to Ukraine now? You must understand that you cannot help us.'

'I am not trying to help you. I am trying to help me. All I want to do is walk through the corner of your country. Through the Carpathians.'

'Transcarpathia has . . . military installations.'

'I'm not interested in anything military.'

Sasha shrugged sadly. 'In the mortuary I have an English corpse.'

'You talk like a psychologist.'

'I *am* a psychologist; a *service* psychologist.' He had been born in

Siberia, educated in Moscow and had served in India, Russia, north-west Tibet. He had hunted Romanian Securitate men who had fled across the border after the fall of Ceauşescu.

'Are you in the secret service?' I asked, with nothing to lose.

'No. I'm a *serviceman*. I am just here to help you. There are some things you must understand. You say that you are used to climbing mountains. Let me tell you that Ukrainian mountains are much harder than the ones you are used to; they are *bureaucratic* mountains!' Sasha leaned forward. 'Your visa. Yes. I want to help you. You must believe me. What you must do is find a tourist organization to adopt you. To sponsor you. To write a letter to me, saying that you are their guest.'

In the morning I visited Intourist, who had an office in my hotel. They were not interested. 'We organize group tours only,' said the woman manager. 'We cannot help you.'

I returned to Sverdlova 13. Sasha was busy. 'We have some slaves to release . . .' he explained.

'I am in a desperate situation.'

'I really want to help you.'

'Today is Friday. If I cannot get my visa today, I must walk from Uzhgorod on Sunday morning, back to Slovakia.' I spread my map of Europe on the desk in the waiting-room. 'Look. My journey will be ruined. I have followed the mountains all the way from the Atlantic. If you cannot allow me to walk through the Carpathians in Ukraine, I have to walk across the plain in Hungary, to Romania. The plain is not on my line . . .'

'Wait . . . I will telephone.' He left the room. When he returned he said: 'Come.'

Outside the police headquarters, a car was waiting at the kerb.

'Get in the car, Nick.'

'I can't. I don't travel in cars.'

'Why not?'

'It's against my principles. I have to walk everywhere.'

'OK. No problem. We will walk. But we must hurry.'

The police captain's long legs, and my tiredness, made it an unfair race. We tore along hot pavements into the centre of town to a block of offices. Sasha ran up several flights of concrete stairs to a narrow corridor and told me to wait in an ante-room. There was an unoccupied desk with five coloured telephones. He knocked on an inner door, waited, then slipped inside, closing the door behind him.

Sasha emerged at a lope. 'Come quickly.'

We sped through the streets to a ruined warehouse, which turned out to be a school. Sasha reappeared after five minutes, saying: 'I am looking for a specialist. A mountain specialist. Come!'

He let me across town, to the east. On the road up to the castle he turned into a courtyard. In a small room to one side of the courtyard, a man was sitting behind a desk eating a sandwich. They talked quickly in Russian, then Sasha said: 'This is Piotr Nikolayovich Nazarenko. He is chief of the Zakarpatskaya mountain rescue service. You must make a private arrangement with him. He will write the letter for you. But first you must agree how much you will pay him per day to accompany you.'

'Accompany me . . .?'

'Piotr Nikolayovich will be walking with you. Across Ukraine.'

Piotr was tanned, balding, with a grey moustache. An oxygen bottle and a rucksack blocked the floor. On the wall was a poster of the Tatra National Park. He looked an agreeable companion, not that I appeared to have any choice. It was difficult, on such a short acquaintance, to judge whether Piotr's stunned expression was one of incipient horror or pleasure. We agreed on one dollar a day.

Margareta

While I waited for my passport to be 'processed' at Sverdlova 13, I had time to visit the only contact I had in Uzhgorod.

Margareta lived in a one-roomed apartment with her son, daughter-in-law and two grandchildren. Margareta's bed was in the short passage, with two cupboards and the desk her grandson used for his homework. She was seventy-seven and had Salvador Dali's *Memoirs of a Genius* open on the small table. 'You know,' she confided, 'he really is an odd man. He describes his . . . you know . . . what he *produces*. In awful detail. Not my cup of tea at all. But I'm pressing on with it because *it doesn't do to give up!*'

While Margareta read Dali her grandson played under the table in a bunker he'd built from cushions and cardboard boxes. He would stay under there for hours, she said, with the radio-cassette machine. We ate soup and meatballs at the table by the balcony. Margareta's son had trained a runner off a neighbour's vine, which now stretched across her own balcony and had produced its first grapes.

Margareta had worked as a teacher. Looking back, she said that the 1970s had been difficult times, but the sixties, under 'dear Nikita' had been her best years in Uzhgorod. She had been allowed to teach children of all ages and had been invited to lecture at the university and to run evening classes. 'Before that, under Stalin, we were not fully trusted.' The compulsory teachers' groups studied the history of the Soviet Union and Marxism. Everyone had to speak Russian and her Ukrainian had grown rusty.

She described her departure from England: 'We were very scrupulous. We were permitted twenty kilograms of luggage each and five pounds. We even had our trunks weighed at the local co-op and when we reached Dover, we sent our surplus money back to my mother. Weren't we naïve! But I had been brought up by the Congregational Church. My parents taught me to be honest and law-abiding.'

From France they travelled by train to Prague and then Uzhgorod. The train had been packed with returning refugees and escorted by Soviet soldiers. Since the Red Army passed through Uzhgorod in 1944, Transcarpathia had become a part of the Soviet Union.

'We were issued with new identity cards and registered at the housing office as Soviet citizens. In Prague we had bought two iron bedsteads, two tin plates and two enamel pans, which we traded for cigarettes. That was our capital to start a new life on.' Margareta sighed. 'But our trunks, with our clothing and pillows and kitchen-ware and so on, never arrived.'

'How did you come to marry a Czech husband?'

Margareta laughed. 'I was a Huddersfield girl, Margaret Sykes, born there in 1919. I met my husband during the war at the British–Czechoslovak Friendship Club in Huddersfield and we were married in 1942. Then a policeman called and told me that I was an alien. I had no British citizenship, because I had married a Czech. I didn't mind. I was young. I wanted to travel. So we decided to live in my husband's home town, Uzhgorod.'

Margareta refilled my tea cup. 'It hasn't been like living in England at all; for example, I have had so many nationalities: when I got to Uzhgorod I found I was not a Czech, but a Soviet citizen. And now I'm Ukrainian. The British Embassy in Kiev have told me that I could get back my British citizenship without any difficulty, but a British passport would cost me three months' pension and I have no savings. They dwindled to nothing with the inflation. I'm not sure whether I'll come back to England.'

Margaret asked about my route through Ukraine and was anxious about the forests. When I came to leave she pressed two tins of meat into my hands: 'Take these. There'll be no food in the villages.'

I was anxious too. The last words Sasha had said to me were: 'I don't know whether you will be able to cross from Ukraine to Romania. If you cannot, then you must walk in a circle and come back to Uzhgorod.' A 500-kilometre circle in the Ukrainian Carpathians would have been interesting, but it would get me no closer to Istanbul.

The Pole of Continentality

Uzhgorod is Europe's Pole of Continentality. It is the town in Europe most distant from the sea. As the crow flies, Uzhgorod is 670 kilometres from the Baltic, the Adriatic and the Black Sea.

When Uzhgorod's residents want to be beside water, they go to Lake Sinevir.

Piotr Nikolayovich Nazarenko

I spent my last night in Uzhgorod at Piotr's apartment, on the top floor of a well-appointed block on Sverdlova. I joined Piotr and his sons for a supper of porridge in the kitchen. Piotr lived in a different world from Margareta's. The spacious wood-tiled drawing room looked over the red-tiled roofs of Uzhgorod. There were ferns and a piano, a fax machine and TV. I slept on the Persian rug, thinking that I was in Paris. We had spent the Saturday afternoon shopping unsuccessfully for food. There was little on the shelves in the shops and we had returned to the apartment with a single loaf of stale bread. Piotr had topped up our supplies by raiding a two-kilogram slab of pork fat – *spik* – and various tins from the family larder.

We left Piotr's apartment at nine a.m. on Sunday morning. Piotr was wearing a large orange rucksack and propelled himself at tremendous speed with two ski-sticks, down through town to the banks of the Uzh and then east, past the railway lines and the clanging church to the countryside. I could barely keep pace.

As we marched towards the rising sun, Piotr learned English from a book he'd liberated from his son's bedroom while I learned Russian from my phrasebook. One of the first conversations we managed went something like this: 'Nick! Piotr walk one week!'

'*Nyet!* Piotr *pyeshkom* Romania!'

'No! Piotr walk Ust-Chorna!'

'Piotr *pyeshkom* Ust-Chorna, Nick in shit!'

'No shit! Piotr friend Ust-Chorna . . .'

'*Kharasho* . . . OK . . .'

The drift was that Piotr was unable to spend more than one week away from his office, and so he was going to hand me over to a colleague half-way to the Romanian border. As an arrangement it seemed designed to fall apart.

Exactly one hour after leaving Uzhgorod, Piotr tapped his watch, said 'Sit down!' then leapt into a tree. I lay on my back in the long grass. We had been walking almost east, along a country road that angled up into the hills. Skylarks sang and the stress of the previous days drained away into the earth. Piotr dropped from the tree with his shirt full of cherries. He looked at his watch and said 'Stand up.' The rest had lasted exactly five minutes.

We travelled in fifty-five minute sprints. The rest-halts were so precise that on one occasion he called a 'Sit down' in the middle of a bog. We debated the bog's unsuitability as a resting place and agreed, with some doubt on Piotr's part, to extend the previous fifty-five minutes by as many as were required for us to reach dry land.

Piotr's route-making followed the straight-line principle. Having fixed a point on the skyline, he would head for it undeviatingly, through ravines, over rows of planted potatoes, and on one occasion over the back fence of a property, across the garden and out of the front gate. On roads he broke the European convention of walking on the side that faces the flow of traffic. Because there *was* no traffic, Piotr used both sides of the roads – and the middle – depending on the most direct line to the next corner. I trailed in his wake trying to memorize my daily quota of nouns and praying for Piotr's minute-hand to reach the next '12'.

Part-way through the morning we came down a hill and Piotr broke the routine by leading me into a bar for beer. We had a litre each. The taste was only marginally less horrible than Zuber water and the alcohol content so high that my head was spinning as I hauled on my rucksack and tottered into the blazing sun. A few houses further along the street, Piotr asked for my water bottle, then tipped the contents over the road and disappeared into a house. He re-emerged wearing a triumphant grin: '*Veeno!*'

At one we stopped at a shack and Piotr spread a cloth on the grass, laying out the brick of pork fat and the loaf. He sliced the fat into fingers and laid it on slabs of bread, with roundels of raw onions. The wine was a rough rosé, and mixed with spring water it robustly complemented the fat sandwich.

'*Fsyo bila ochyen' fkusna* . . . that was delicious', I read from my phrasebook, hungry enough to mean every word.

We learned a bit more about each other during the lunch-hour. Piotr was fifty-five. He had been born in the Dombas and had worked for most of his life as a nuclear physicist. He had always enjoyed the mountains and in 1989 had taken the post of head of the *Kontrol'no Spasatel'naya Sluzhba* – the KSS – in the *oblast* of Transcarpathia.

On that first day out of Uzhgorod we crossed the grain of the country through woods and vines and villages and a vast military camp surrounded by watch-towers, rusty wire and patrolling guards. In the villages only about one household in twenty owned a car. Roses and vines crept round gables. There was no sense of wealth, but neither was there the grinding hardship that pervaded Uzhgorod. People in the country knew how to find food. At four p.m. on a high col, Piotr announced that we would camp. It was a delightful spot with a dashing stream, granite boulders and soft grass.

'Today . . . forty-five kilometres!' said Piotr, looking up from his map.

I prayed silently that Piotr's age would soon begin to temper his passion for knocking off the kilometres. He was determined that I should see Lake Sinevir, even though it was far off our route.

Piotr woke at six and picked some wild mint for the tea. He lit the fire again and laid his cloth on the ground, with the bread and pork fat and a clove of raw garlic each. Then he boiled some macaroni in the remains of the previous night's tinned milk. Before we left our camp-site Piotr removed his shirt and stood with his arms raised towards the sun. For several minutes he stood spreadeagled, absorbing the rays, eyes closed.

'*Malenki put* . . .' he said afterwards. 'It is tradition before travel: stop . . . think . . . go.'

When the ridges ended we dropped down into valleys. Unlike the decomposing concrete of Uzhgorod, the village houses were extravagantly decorated with ceramic tiles. Many had an ice-house in the garden for storing potatoes. Fields were filled with hay-stooks and the only wheeled vehicles we saw were horse-drawn carts. Three days' walking took us deep into the heart of the Carpathians and the village of Volovets, wedged into the pass that carries the railway from Moscow through to Budapest and Prague. Piotr said that we had to buy food here, to sustain us during the mountain crossing to Lake Sinevir.

We joined the back of a queue in the filthy bread shop. The legacy of past bread battles was that the queue was fed through metal railings. Volovets' shop was almost empty. In a building the size of a supermarket there were no more than ten products: macaroni, bottled vegetables and cans of Communist maconochie, hotpot stew with the meat and vegetable missing. At the dairy counter a single open jar of yoghurt stood beside a few plastic bags of curd. Behind the counter a pig-faced woman scowled at the cowering queue.

We slept in the office of the local KSS man, an overweight character with a bandaged finger. A pennant on the wall described him as the 'Commander of the Workers of the Fourth County, Falling Down of Tourists'. He stayed for dinner. The three of us sat at his desk eating bread and *spik* and onions, with *tvarok* and *smyetana* – cottage cheese and sour cream – which Piotr had mysteriously acquired.

As he chucked down shots of Polish *sliwowica*, Piotr grinned and said: 'Tomorrow, Nick! Tomorrow is big day! Tomorrow Sinevir.'

To Sinevir

I woke in the KSS office looking at a set of twelve gilt-framed illustrations of accidents. One showed how to bandage a head; another how to search for an avalanche victim; another how to construct a stretcher from a pair of skis and a rope. I lay in my sleeping-bag waiting for Piotr to call: 'Nick! Six o'clock!' The office wall also carried a world map showing the old Soviet Union dead-centre and the USA split on its vertical axis, with the eastern states wedged over on the left margin of the map and California on the opposite fly-spotted extremity. I had seen exactly the same map nailed to the wall of a fly-infested ex-Soviet barrack-room in the Hindu Kush, over on the far side of the old Empire. The twentieth century had not been kind to empires.

We ate the last of the Uzhgorod bread with some *spik* and the remains of the *tvarok* and *smyetana* and left the office late, at 7.15. Piotr led the way through ancient pines and sunlit glades. I was right to have regarded this heavenly vision with suspicion, for it turned out to be the preamble to one of Piotr's short-cuts: instead of gaining the heights of the Borzhava massif by the gentle circuitous path up the end of the massif, we made a frontal assault, steaming upwards for 700 metres in a straight line through the forest to pop out above wreaths of mist at 1,200 metres, where we joined a path which climbed on to Velchy Verch at 1,598 metres. 'High Peak' had a rusting A-frame on its summit and a dramatic view south-west to a cluster of three radomes, perched like giant puffballs on the summit of Stoy. The radomes occupied the highest point on this inner curve of the Carpathians. From here their microwave antennae could feel the ether for the snubbed pods pushing hotly through the atmosphere towards cities and legitimate military targets.

Piotr saw me staring. He smiled and mimed a missile with his hands. 'France, England . . . USA!'

He could have meant incoming or outgoing.

We were standing between forty-eight and forty-nine degrees north of the equator. A hypothetical hot war death ray fired westwards from the summit of Stoy would find no higher land until it seared through the mists of the Gulf of Saint Lawrence and smacked into the side of the Rocky Mountains above the Blackfeet Indian reservation. But when the unthinkable did visit these remote ridges, it struck from behind: Chernobyl's reactor number 4 exploded and burned at 2,500 degrees Celsius, releasing ninety times more radioactive material than at Hiroshima. Over 1,000,000 people in Ukraine, Russia and Belarus are registered sufferers of radiation sickness.

Piotr shook his head: 'Tsk, tsk . . .', but would not talk about it.

The gale tearing across Velchy Verch was numbingly cold. Piotr pulled on his nylon jacket and led the way along the crest of the Borzhava ridge over the peaks of Gyemba and Magura, then down over Hrab and Kuchera Kruhlaya, all territory of the transhumance shepherds. We could see them far below, vectoring their sheep across the cropped grass. Down to the east, the villages in the Repinka valley shone like sprinklings of rice grains. As we followed it south-eastwards the ridge lost height until it met the 1,000-metre contour and signs of irregular habitation: a shepherd's hut and a trench system from the First World War.

At the end of the day we came to the grassy saddle of the Prislop pass. Piotr pointed to a dark range to our east: 'Nick! Sinevir! Very beautiful!'

Three shepherds lounged in the grass with their horses and dogs. They had a camp in the woods and knew the southern slopes of Borzhava. The quickest way to the valley, they said, was to leave the pass and cut down over a spur.

We camped on the spur and rose early.

'Today Sinevir!'

'*Kharasho*, Piotr. *Kharasho!*'

Piotr led the way down to the valley. The small town of Mizhgor'ya was in such a state of dishevelment that I couldn't tell whether it was being dismantled or assembled. Trucks of cement and bricks and timber spewed dust and diesel smoke over cracked and potholed streets. House roofs were corrugated asbestos or flattened oil drums. Graffiti on a bus shelter read 'Death Angel' and 'Fuck All'.

Lake Sinevir was on the wrong side of the 1,500-metre mountain of Ozernaya, and I would have resented the effort had we not passed the lovely wood-tiled village of Strihaylna and, further up, the unusual sight of two farmers using a horse-drawn sledge to reach their potato plots. From above, Sinevir looked uncannily similar to Morskie Oko in the Slovakian Vihorlat: a small shaded lake in a hole surrounded by walls of black conifers.

'Very beautiful!' beamed Piotr.

I was too choked to reply. We had made a detour of two days to see Ukraine's most famous mountain beauty spot. What was it, I wondered, that made Eastern Europeans worship these depressingly claustrophobic pine-shaded puddles, when they had so many more panoramic beauty spots on the mountaintops?

Piotr set one of his beeline courses for the lake-edge, 500 metres below our feet, and we slithered down wet grass then dense forest and finally a mud-chute of avalanche debris. The lake was kidney-shaped with a tiny island, picnic huts and statues of Sin and Vir, the shepherd who drowned and his partner whose tears filled the lake. (More prosaically, the lake had been created by a landslip which dammed the river.)

The old *Schutzhaus* marked on my Viennese map still stood above the black water. The wooden building had been used as a guest-house for privileged Communists. We found its caretaker, Ivan Feodorovich, chasing a cow through the woods. Ivan wore a bus-conductor's uniform and peaked hat and offered us a bed for the night.

Piotr was unsure: 'Very expensive, Nick. Two thousand eight hundred coupons! We camp.' It was, by Ukrainian standards, extortionate, but in London the same amount would buy only half a *cappuccino*.

I said that the cost was manageable and Ivan gave us a twin-bedded suite with dual-aspect windows, balconies, a *Kachelofen* and a sink. Sadly the building had no running water, so we washed in spring water gushing from a pipe on the edge of the woods. The only warm room in the building was the tiny kitchen on the ground floor. The temperature, said Ivan, had fallen to nine degrees. A girl with a heavy lower lip served thin potato soup, then fried potatoes with *spik* and mouldy bread. Ivan milked the cow; we drank the milk while it was still warm and it left half-moons of cream on our upper lips.

Rain fell most of the night, and in the morning we set off on a two-day hike across the mountains to Ust-Chorna, where Piotr would hand me over to his colleague, Uri. With all the rain the river was swollen and turbid, and it dashed between the two ribbons of painted cottages, dainty with their wood shingles and sun-ray reliefs under the gables. Shrines stood in front of the cottages, with Jesus in painted sheet steel, or older statues of saints, dating back to the days when this valley lay inside Vienna's empire.

Piotr's route took us up the wild Ozeranko valley on a dirt road to one of the region's more extraordinary anomalies. At unimaginable expense, a full-scale, working logging dam was being rebuilt across the valley as a living museum. At the forest edge I found the remains of an original flume, one of the wooden chutes down which felled trunks were once tobogganed then assembled on the dammed lake before being released through the sluices to surge downstream on a wall of water which would carry them to larger rivers like the Tissa, where the logs would be tied together in rafts – *daraby* – and poled down to the mills. In the Ozeranko valley they had not just rebuilt the dam, but a covered bridge and a *koliba* – a traditional octagonal foresters' hut with a conical roof and a low extended porch. Like the Górale, the *koliba*'s carpenters were working with hand-axes, driving in the nails with the butt of the axe heads.

We called at the very last cottage in the valley, where a woman in an apron brought us a churn of *smyetana* and two enamel mugs. Piotr subsided into heavenly bliss. 'In Uzhgorod,' he grinned milkily, 'not possible *smyetana*. In Uzghorod, milk difficult; *smyetana* very difficult. Piotr happy! Very happy!'

We left, carrying our cooking pot filled to the brim with *smyetana*, and camped in a glade at the head of the valley. In the morning we climbed the watershed on one of Piotr's straight lines. Hopelessly lost in vertiginous forest, we stumbled on a shepherds' camp near the summit of Peredna. Piotr had difficulty understanding the men, who were dressed in rags. 'Boyks . . .' he said. I'd never seen such a dishevelled camp. The Boyks were living in three scrappy lean-tos, open to the weather. One shepherd stirred an immense cauldron of milk, much bigger than the Górale pots. Grubby muslin cloths hung over a rail. Piotr said that they carried their cheese down to the valley every week or so. With the Łemks to one side and the Hutzuls to the other, the Boyks were the smallest and least defined of the three tribes occupying this bend of the Carpathians.

The shepherds' directions were impossible to follow and we were soon lost again, eventually gaining the valley by slithering down a stream bed. For Piotr our adventures were over. He laughed and pointed down the valley with his ski-stick: 'Nick! Ust-Chorna. Only twenty kilometres.' Then he thought for a moment. 'No. Thirty kilometres!'

Uri Petrovich Kostyak

Uri Petrovich had been waiting two days for us to arrive. He ran the KSS office, a wooden cottage in the grounds of the *turbaza* – the Ukrainian equivalent of a youth hostel. He was younger than his boss, short and ridiculously muscular with a concavity in the ridge of his nose that suggested that his face had been involved in a violent misadventure. Such as a punch.

Ust-Chorna was an isolated spot, forty-five kilometres from the nearest major road and – discounting poor old Mizhgor'ya – eighty-five kilometres from the nearest town, Hust. There was no bus service and nobody seemed to own a private car. When Piotr had eventually finished briefing Uri on his forthcoming ordeal with the foreigner, the two of them climbed on to Uri's motorbike, with Piotr's rucksack balanced precariously on the back, and puttered off to find a man who was rumoured to be leaving that day by truck for Hust. I was sad to see Piotr go. He insisted that I take one of his ski-sticks as a gift.

In the twenty-four hours that it took Uri to prepare himself for departure, I was able to sample life in a Ukrainian backwater. The *turbaza* canteen was in a concrete block beyond a large painted sign depicting a happy hiker and the slogan: TOURISM – REST, UNDERSTANDING, HEALTH! At the head of the queue was a serving hatch. On the far side of the hatch a pair of overfed cooks ladled a splash of watery potato soup into one bowl and a dollop of mashed potato into another. But it was the third pot that everybody watched. In here was the 'meat'. The ladle emerged from the fatty liquid with a duplicitous swirl and juggle so that any misplaced bits of meat slipped over the lip of the ladle and fell back into the pot. The most you could hope for was a gobbet of fat that, through an oversight in the preparation, still carried a sliver of flesh. As I fielded my cavorting fat lump the cook snatched back my bowl and thrust it into the hands of the mite behind me. Then she filled an empty bowl with an extra dollop of potato and dredged the gravy pot for two morsels of meat, which she balanced on top of the potato. I'm ashamed to say that I didn't hand it back, or swap it with the child. And I paid for my selfishness by hating every mouthful.

It was Sunday and Ust-Chorna's weekly entertainment, the football match, was fought out on a pitch which occupied the only patch of flat land in the village, beyond the railway sidings. Ust-Chorna – or Königs-feld, as it appeared on my *Generalkarte* – had made its living from logs for nearly 300 years. The narrow-gauge railway fed the village with logs from the surrounding valleys. Coal dust lay everywhere. Beyond the river bridge, a shattered Second World War pillbox marked one of the Red Army's obstacles as they pushed towards the Hungarian plain.

Uri's home was a single-storey house at the south end of the village. Early in the evening his wife, Larissa, cooked the best meal I'd eaten for weeks: a thick vegetable broth sprinkled with fresh herbs and then spare ribs with bulgar wheat, salad and dressing, and freshly baked bread. As we took coffee afterwards, in front of the black and white TV, I thought back a week to the kitchen of Uri's boss, where we had dined on bowls of porridge; there were fewer ways of finding money in the country, but the food lay at the back of every house.

One of Uri's two young sons, Oshi, took me on a tour of the family property. Like most Carpathian village plots I'd seen, it was a strip of land only twice the width of the house, running back at right angles to the road until it met the steep slope of the valley side, in this case a distance of about sixty metres. Immediately behind the house was the herb garden, and facing it against the fence a two-room cottage where Uri's mother and one of his brothers lived. The rooms were full of Hutzul embroidery and Oshi's grandmother sat in a tent of rich fabric like the *grande dame* of folk art. Attached to the side of her cottage was the goat-house, a shack for the rabbits and chickens and the twin-hole earth closet wallpapered with pages torn from colour magazines. Facing this was a walnut tree and an outside table. Further down the plot were rows of root vegetables, beans and peas and the wooden cabin containing the sauna Uri had built. Beyond it the plot was left to grass for the three goats.

As the sun tipped below the black mountainside, Uri and I took a walk through the village. He had changed from his tracksuit into tennis whites that strained at every seam to contain his warring muscle-groups. Stiff-legged, I stood head and shoulders above Uri in my dark rags, while he bounced along beside me like a brand-new overpumped football. We promenaded from one end of the village to the other, a stroll that took an hour. Linguistically I had never been in more difficulty; Piotr and I had learned enough of each other's languages to get by. But Uri's first language was not Russian, or even Ukrainian, but Hutzul (which he pronounced 'Gutzul'). Flipping to and fro through my phrase-book I found out that Uri had six brothers and three sisters and had done his military service in the Soviet commandos.

Returning from Cuba, he had taken to mountaineering.

'Where?' I asked.

'Tienshan, Pamir, Caucasus, Crimea, Tatra, Malá Fatra, Sudetes . . .'

That's good, I thought, he's a survivor.

We walked down to the river, where a cable stretched across the water. Uri whistled and a man on the far bank climbed on to a wooden platform suspended from the cable, then levered the platform laboriously across the river by means of a metal bar which gripped the cable. On the way back, the combined weight of three of us on the platform dragged it down to water level. Midstream, with the water slapping our backsides, I was reminded of how far I was from north-west London.

In a glade on the far bank, beside the railway, a group of Ust-Chorna's younger generation were enjoying an evening barbecue. A fire smoked and bowls of salad and blackened potatoes lay on the grass with bottles and cherries.

Following the custom of new arrivals at a camp-fire, Uri and I cast a stick into the flames, and were each handed a *shishlak*. Uri ate his grilled pork with the intensity of a man who didn't know where his next meal would come from.

So close to the summer solstice, the light lasted almost to midnight. We lay in the grass through that long dusk, while I interrogated them about the mountains of Transcarpathia and they demanded the price of western luxuries from CDs to caterpillar tractors. They were all in their early twenties and had travelled widely within the old Soviet Union. A couple had climbed Elbrus.

A rusting locomotive screeched through the clearing, towing a serpent of empty logging trucks on a track which was so misaligned that the whole train looked as if it might topple sideways on to our fire.

As darkness fell, Oshi came to find us. Back at Uri's home, his mother had moved to the table under the walnut, with the brother and two friends from the village. The table was laid with bread and hard-boiled eggs, onions and jam-filled *vareniki*. It was not going to be possible to fend off a third dinner.

'Eat! Eat! This is the land of the Gutzul!' shouted Uri.

He told the table about my journey.

'Do you carry a pistol?' asked Uri's mother.

'No', I said. 'But I can run fast.'

The large man with the moustache leaned forward with concern: 'But the wolves can run faster than you! They will bite your leg!'

Second Summer Solstice

Uri was dressed for a covert operation behind enemy lines. He had dug out his striped Soviet Marine undervest and a pair of camouflage fatigues. At his hip hung a Bowie knife. His rucksack was so heavy that I couldn't lift it from the ground. From behind he looked like a tottering apartment block.

We left Ust-Chorna along one of the narrow-gauge railway lines which turned shortly up a side valley. After two hours, Uri dropped his rucksack with a thud and said that he'd lost his passport and money.

ID to *Homo Sovieticus* was like car keys to a Californian. You couldn't move without ID. Uri was white-faced and fumbling in pockets, in his rucksack. Then he began running, faster and faster, till his Popeye limbs became a whirling blur and he disappeared down the stony track. I began to be assailed by doubts. Had he really lost his passport? Was this a ruse to escape from his charge? If he didn't come back what would I find in his rucksack? Rocks? Since Piotr had given Uri the vital letter from the Uzhgorod *milicia*, how would I reach the Romanian border without being picked up by the police? What if Uri really *had* lost his passport and money . . . ?

Uri was gone for long enough for me to develop these worries into advanced paranoia. By the time he eventually returned, ruddy-cheeked and wearing a birthday-boy grin, I was a pallid stuttering wreck. He had apparently dropped his documents on the track. Reunited and closer through our recently shared adversities, we began the long climb up to Svidovets, the thirty-kilometre ridge linking Ust-Chorna's valley with that of the Tissa to the south-east.

Uri led us uncertainly up the mountainside. After an hour of ascent he turned and said: 'Problem, Nick.'

'I know. Never mind.'

We were one ravine too far north.

At about 1,000 metres we came to a camp of Hutzul shepherds. There were four of them and a saddled horse, waiting to ferry the cheese down to Ust-Chorna. Their ramshackle hut was a collection of logs and bits of scrap from the previous year's hut. Inside, the head shepherd sat beside the fire with a tub between his knees and his arms immersed to the elbows in warm curd. The sleeping platform, strewn with rugs and blankets, ran the length of the hut.

Outside the hut the shepherds had erected a row of spruce trunks from whose snapped-off branches hung the paraphernalia of cheese-making: drying muslins, galvanized buckets punched with holes to make strainers, a wooden curd masher and granular sacs of dripping cheese. From a wooden stand, roofed like a bird-box and stilted to keep it cool, the head shepherd drew off ladlefuls of cream and milk from two bowls, then mixed them in enamel mugs. The milk was thick and creamy, rich and sweet, like liquid, white butter.

My doubts about Uri's guiding abilities grew as we reached the crest of Svidovets. It was cooler up here, above the tree-line, the grass brushed silver by the wind from the steppe. Every spur off the main ridge seemed to be occupied by its own flock, moving slowly across the sloping greensward, splitting then coalescing in their foraging geometries.

'Problem, Nick.'

'I know.'

Uri held up his watch. It was five o'clock. We were at 1,600 metres. We had no water and there was no shelter or firewood on the ridge. Uri said that he knew a place where there was a lake and wood. We walked on as the sun was sucked into the haze of the Dnestr. I was mentally preparing for a windy bivouac when Uri pointed over the lip of a ridge.

We began to climb down. The lake was hidden from above by the convexity of the ridge's slope.

'*Pryekrasna!* Wonderful!'

A more beautiful spot would be hard to imagine. The lake occupied a glacial scoop, fed by a stream running between grass and boulders. From the interior of his tower-block pack, Uri produced an immense glass jar: 'Gutzul *pashtyet!*'

He cut a chunk free and laid it on a slab of bread, then handed it to me. In a pattern that was to be repeated many times, Uri's earlier misdemeanours were forgiven. The pâté was the best I'd ever tasted, made by one of Uri's brothers from the liver of a pig they'd slaughtered, and garnished with garlic and paprika.

After Uri had disappeared into his sleeping-bag I sat for a while with the fire's embers and the stars, grateful beyond measure to my companion for contriving to bring me to such a beautiful bivouac site on this night. There was a quality of tranquillity in these Carpathian backwaters that I'd not found in western Europe. Here, you could lie back and look at the stars knowing that the winking lights of an airliner would not break the spell; here, the horizons never carried the orange fur of city lights. This was peace at its purest, a peace which – in the world where I came from – was no longer regarded as a human essential.

The previous summer solstice – on the Sierra de Ancares – seemed so far back in history that my memories of that day were those of a child. And now, another turnabout in the daylight hours reminded me that I'd promised Annabel that I'd be home before the winter solstice.

In the morning we climbed back up to the skyline and continued along the ridge of Svidovets, peering uncertainly through thick mist as we gained height towards the 1,774-metre-high point. When we reached the top, visibility was down to a few metres. Uri looked suspiciously unconcerned.

Uri and Piotr approached the great outdoors from different directions. Where Piotr had adhered to a Soviet adaptation of Roman military marching, Uri progressed in a sequence of navigational errors, encounters and extrications. Uri relied on bumping into shepherds. Piotr kept his compass in his top-right breast pocket, secured to the buttonhole by a lanyard. Uri said he had a map at the bottom of his rucksack, although I never saw it. Piotr kept a set of 1:50,000 military maps rolled up inside his sleeping-mat. When we got lost, Uri used memory and intuition and Piotr took back-bearings. By default Uri followed the philosophy of Stevensonian motion to its extreme. Arriving was not just subsidiary to the travelling; it was most unlikely.

'This way!' announced Uri, setting off downwards, into the mist. I sneaked a look at my compass. We were headed in the opposite direction to the one we needed in order to reach the Tissa. Uri led us down, then over a spur, then down again. I suggested we returned to the ridge and try again. We did so, and this time Uri set off along a track which curved round in the cloud on the wrong side of Svidovets until it pointed at Spain.

'Problem, Nick!'

This time I showed Uri the compass. Emerging from the underside of cloud after being lost is always a moment of miraculous deliverance, but with Uri, these moments were doubly pleasurable, for Uri's mishaps were always followed by good fortune. This time it was a descent to a charming *polonina* above the Tissa, decorated with wooden Hutzul cottages and the most beautiful church I'd seen since leaving Łemkówie.

The carpentry of Yasinya's church was similar to that of the Łemk *cerkwi*. Fish-scale shingles covered the roof and walls, while dowels pinned the frame together. In plan the church took the form of a Greek cross, with a central 'spire' rising above eaves that sat like a hat-brim above the low walls. The bell-tower stood apart. The trees hiding the church from the valley below must have saved this delicate gem from the various armies who have fought their way over the Yablonitski pass. Uri could not be persuaded to begin a search for the church's key. By way of deterrent, he said that it was kept in Rakhiv, a town five hours' walk away down the Tissa.

Nearby was part of an old trench system, the reinforcement lines of General Freiherr von Pfanzer-Baltin's army group during the build-up to the 1915 winter offensive. My *Generalkarte*, surveyed in 1909, marked Yasinya as Körosmezo. Pfanzer-Baltin must have planned his attack on the same map.

Uri was in a hurry to reach the village, which lay in the valley floor a few kilometres upstream. Yasinya was the Hutzul capital. Uri had friends in Yasinya. This was the last village we would pass before tackling Hoverla, the highest mountain in Ukraine.

As we left the church, Uri shook his head and looked at the surging clouds: 'Hoverla problem,' he said. 'Big problem.'

The Hot-water Machine

The woods were so dark that we would not have found the way without the sound of the old man's breathing. He walked invisibly ahead. Like so many of the days since Finisterre, this one had encompassed a month's diversity.

Waking up in the rain by the lakeside up on Svidovets and our subsequent misadventures in the mist had been left in another time-zone. In Yasinya we had visited the KSS office and I had copied from their worn-out map the compass bearings we needed for Hoverla. We'd bought a kilogram of cherries, a cabbage and Uri had done a deal behind a shed for two loaves of bread. We had left Yasinya late in the afternoon and walked up the valley to Lazeshchina, passing horses and carts and painted cottages. Walking through Lazeshchina, Uri had spotted Dimitri Klimpuch watering his vegetables. Dimitri had climbed Hoverla eighty-one times. He was a big, genial man with a rubbery gut and bloodshot eyes. Dimitri had made us a light meal: salami, *spik*, onion tops and cucumber cut straight from the garden, home-made butter and bread washed down with tumblers of refined alcohol from a Yugoslav bottle labelled '96% vol'. The last house in the valley belonged to Dimitri's mother and we sat with her on her

In the High Tatras, the Valley of the Five Polish Lakes,
still frozen in late May

The strip-fields below the High Tatras – Naomi and
Hol provide parental guidance

Jan Staszel-Furtek, a Górale shepherd in the High Tatras

Cheese-making in the Hutzul country of Ukraine

(*Top row*) Hutzul shepherds of Ukraine
(*Right*) A Górale shepherd making cheese

(*Below*) Shepherds of the Transylvanian Alps

(*Below*) A shepherd in
the Pirin mountains

A shepherd's hut lost
on the lower slopes of
Svidovets in Ukraine

Sucevița monastery
and its painted church

In Bukovina, northern Romania, after one year's walking

Szeklers in a Transylvanian village

The summit of Romania's highest mountain, Moldoveanu,
with rain on the way

Rila monastery

The end of summer in
the Pirin mountains

Rozhen monastery

Across the Golden Horn

Reunited with Annabel on Europe's eastern shore

wooden steps in the last of the sun, drinking warm milk she'd just taken from the cow.

Now we were in this dark wood, walking uphill, behind the old man. The Yugoslav hooch had provoked my legs into seceding from my body and I was dimly aware of them down there, cocking things up. The darkness made the river roar louder and I began to worry a lot about falling in the water. The old man reached a building. A key rasped in a lock. He heaved open a door to reveal a massive cast-iron contraption which sneezed and spurted flames into the night. On one of its pipes was a pressure gauge that might have come from a ship's boiler-room. The old man unfolded the arms on a pair of spectacles and peered with his torch through the smoke at a thermometer: '*Da!*' he mused. '*Haryachiy voda!* Hot water!'

The old man's machine looked ready to blow a crater in the side of the mountain.

He showed us to an adjacent door then disappeared back into the forest. We took off our clothes and unscrewed the taps on the wall. A distant thunder reverberated through unseen pipes, followed by clanks, violent burps and a sudden hiss. Jets of scalding water burst from the darkness. Uri moaned. The hot water coursed off sore shoulders and puddled about bruised feet.

'Hey Uri!'

'*Shto?*'

'*Pryekrasna!*'

'*Da! Da!* Very good!'

Aches which had taken permanent residence in my unrested body and mind evaporated with the steam and alcohol, and were distilled in the cool mountain night and carried away by the healing stream. There was nothing beyond that moment.

Hoverla

The wooden cottage trembled in the heavy rain. We were sleeping on the upper floor, beneath the eaves. In the long hour before dawn the comforting sounds of the deluge quietened to a whisper. This was not the weather for Hoverla. But that was not the real problem. Porubnoe was the problem.

The closer I got to the Romanian border, the more I sensed that I was walking towards an unscalable wall. Nobody in Uzhgorod knew whether the border-crossing at Porubnoe was open, and if it was, whether it was open to pedestrians, or only to buses, cars and trains. If they refused to let me through, I would have no option but to walk back to Uzhgorod.

I had a secondary anxiety too. I had left Vienna with 1,500 dollars strapped to my leg. This laboriously accumulated stash of one-and five-dollar notes was the balance I needed to reach Istanbul. I'd forgotten about the lump on my leg until I crossed into Ukraine and realized that I had to complete a currency declaration form. Rather than advertise myself as a pedestrian Fort Knox (my dollars would have paid five years' rent on an Uzhgorod apartment), I extended the forgetfulness until I was inside Ukraine. Then I realized that, were the money to be discovered on leaving the country, I could hardly object if the authorities liberated me of the whole lot. So I had slit open the inside of my rucksack and sewn half the dollars into the lining. The more I thought about it, the more certain I was that this would be the first place a border policeman would search.

In the semi-darkness of the hut roof I floated back to the present and the mountain at the end of the valley. And Uri. Something had happened to Uri during the last twenty-four hours. In Yasinya he had disappeared for two hours. Thereafter he had avoided talk of Hoverla and of the country beyond.

At first light Uri left his sleeping-bag and said that he was going to use a radio-telephone to call Piotr in Uzhgorod. When he came back, he looked shaken, but refused to explain. Had Uri told Piotr that he was going to bail out? Had Piotr torn him off a strip and told him to continue? In crossing the Tissa, Uri had left his home turf; the big hills south of Hoverla were foreign territory for Uri. I'd seen his anxiety. The bad weather was a timely scapegoat; a plausible reason to turn back. But when the crisis came, it wasn't the weather that stopped Uri.

We left the camp late, at 10.30. I felt weak and pessimistic. I could barely keep up with Uri. The rain had passed on, leaving a cold, grey sky. Off to the right rose Petros, the most northerly of the 2,000-metre peaks in the Chornohora – the Black Mountains. Hoverla was its neighbour, five kilometres to the south-east, at 2,060 metres.

The path from the *turbaza* had been trampled into Hoverla's flank by generations of Ukrainian feet intent on standing upon the country's highest point. This day was no exception, and although the weather was rough and blustery, we shared the final slog with two school parties who were kitted-out for a disaster, in slip-on shoes and a variety of permeable windcheaters and jerseys. On a summit that was twice the height of Snowdon, the apex of Wales, teachers struggled to light cigarettes in the freezing gale.

The school parties didn't linger, but turned quickly for the valley. Our way lay in the opposite direction, along the crest of Chornohora. I was eager not to get lost up here and insisted that we follow the compass bearings I'd copied from the map in Yasinya's KSS office. We descended to the south-east, aiming for the summit of Turkul, four kilometres along the ridge. Off to our right, Romania lay in a grey haze. At intervals along the ridge we passed the granite finger-posts that marked the old border between Czechoslovakia and Poland, a 'P' on one side and a 'CS' on the other.

Remote on the outer bend of the Carpathians, the dark bulk of Chornohora felt higher and wilder than Mont Blanc. The hard sandstone had been eaten away on both sides by long-gone glaciers. For the first time in the Ukrainian Carpathians I was walking above cliffs and looking down into U-shaped valleys separated by jagged arêtes. A sombre glacial tarn lay below us. Uri pointed down into the amphitheatre. 'Bears!' he said. '. . . wolves.'

I began to enjoy myself. Uri began to drop behind.

Beyond Turcul, the ridge was dissected by the trench lines of Pfanzer-Baltin's mountain infantry. They dug in through January 1915, then attacked eastwards on the thirtieth. Temperatures dropped to minus twenty-five degrees Celsius and it took them a month to push the Russians back across the Carpathians. The defences also covered the next peak, Shpitzi, whose spur was lacerated with more trenches and pocked with gun positions and subsiding dug-outs. Where the spur dropped into the void, two excavated forts were still surrounded by tangles of rusting barbed wire.

Looking over the edge, we could see the tiny dots of sheep, and hear the echo of a shepherd's call. We came off the side of Shpitzi, scrambling down a slope booby-trapped with boulders and ankle-turning tussocks. Part-way down, the storm slammed into Chornohora and we were pinned to the rocks by hail and vortices of wind, then had to slither through dense forest to reach an extraordinary grotto of massive moss-covered rocks buried in deep-green pines. Some of the gaps between the boulders were big enough to slip through. Underfoot the thick moss yielded like wet sponge.

We came out on a pasture at the foot of Shpitzi's cliffs. Sheep browsed and a shepherd lay with his dogs on the grass, propped on one arm, a staff at his side. He wore a cape and a felt hat, and apart from turning his head as we approached he didn't move.

Ivan the Shepherd

Ivan Fyedorivich Mikhiluk spent the winters in his home village of Verkh Yasenov, fifty kilometres' walking eastwards, in the valley of the Cherniy Cheremosh. During June, July and August, he shared a hut underneath Shpitzi with four other shepherds and three boys. Their remote camp was a more solid affair than the shepherds' shacks we'd passed north of the Tissa. They had built a separate cheese-making hut, a kennel for the dogs, a rail-fence enclosure. To one side stood a large four-wheeled, wood-spoked cart, high-axled to give it clearance through the fords.

We spent the night with the shepherds and were woken at dawn by the sound of bells as the sheep were milked. There had been a series of violent thunderstorms in the night and the rain was still falling. During the night the glass bottle containing the remains of Dimitri's pork had disappeared. So had half a kilo of cherries and one of the two army canteens we used to make *chai*. The shepherds said that a wildcat had taken them. I found it hard to imagine a wildcat making regular use of a cooking pot.

At the 'neck' of a double enclosure, shaped like an hourglass, four of the shepherds sat in an open-sided shack, side by side, on stools, with buckets between their knees. One of the boys drove the sheep up towards the four slots in the shack's back wall. As each sheep squeezed through a slot, the shepherd on the far side grabbed its hind legs and hauled it backwards over the bucket, nipping a teat between thumb and forefinger and pulling down the jets of milk.

The boy wore a cape and chased the sheep with a sprig of fir. Round his waist was a five-buckled *cheress*, the broad belt I'd seen worn by shepherds in the Carpathians of Poland and Slovakia. He flapped in the enclosure like a netted bird, crying 'Hoh! Brrrrriiiiii! Brrrr! Russs!

Russs!' The sheep scattered before him in cascades of tinkling bells. When all the sheep were in the upper enclosure the four shepherds gathered the full buckets and walked across the watery mountainside towards the cheese-making hut. Every hundred metres they stopped, put down the buckets and rested. At one of these rests one of the boys pulled out a tin flute and played.

Inside the cheese-making hut the head shepherd was waiting for the milk. The milk was strained by pouring it through pine needles laid on top of a piece of muslin stretched within a wooden frame. The head shepherd had heard the pipe music and called for his wooden flute. In the far corner of the hut, beyond the fire, we took our places with the shepherds around a communal aluminium bowl of *smyetana* and *gorok*. One of the boys brought slabs of bread. A steaming maize and potato pudding arrived, with mugs of the morning's milk. The inside of the hut was crammed with wet bodies, smoke and steam and the sounds of camp breakfast: pistol shots from the burning logs, the slurps and grunts, the rustle of wet capes.

In a lair close to this spot once lurked Dobosz, a mountain robber as legendary as Jánošik. For Dobosz, Chornohora was a citadel. Walled in by cliffs and impenetrable forests of stone pines on the slopes of Munczel, south of Hoverla, Dobosz ruled from a great seat which he had carved from the rock. In the eighteenth century there was no shortage of recruits to take up arms against the gentry, but to join Dobosz, young would-be robbers had to survive an initiation: having reached the lair on all fours up a stream bed, they had to cross between two cliffs on a slippery plank and then place a hand on a rock while Dobosz's deputy, the one-time ragged beggar Iwanczuk Rachowski, pretended to take a swing at it with his pick. If the youngster didn't flinch, he would swear an oath of allegiance on Dobosz's massive Thunder-axe. He was in.

The band were a warrior carnival. Their stolen horses wore the skins of bear, lynx and bison, with gilded bridles and wooden saddles encrusted with gold and inlaid with mother-of-pearl, while the robbers themselves dressed in blood-red breeches, with polished copper on their jerkins and tricorns, that flashed in the sun like flame. Cocked flintlocks rested on the horses' necks, pistolets were wedged in belts. They carried javelins, sabres, axes, carved powder horns and other, captured, weapons: a Turkish yatagan, a Caucasian dagger, a knight's sword carved with a Madonna of Czestochowa. At their head rode Dobosz on his black horse, Little Thundercloud.

In the munificent fashion of folk heroes, Dobosz was another who robbed the rich to feed the poor. When he wasn't liberating Hungarian nobles of their wine cellars or holding up Armenian caravans, he plotted round camp-fires and dined on venison, bison fat and bears' paws. When the Armenians finally quit their trade route in terror, Dobosz cried: 'That'll save us the effort of hunting them in the forests! Now all we need do is visit their treasuries!' His greatest raid was on Zlota Bania, the Golden Dome, the heavily fortified and fabulously rich castle, treasury and gold mint perched on a cliff over on the Hungarian side of the Carpathians.

The story is a classic: Dobosz enlists the help of an old ex-robber called Zmyjenski, who knows the layout of the castle and who emerges from retirement for one last raid, motivated by a desire to rescue his imprisoned friend, Stasko. The band ride out, led by the old white-beard on a white horse and black-haired Dobosz on raven-coated Thunder-cloud. Spurred on through the night by thunder and lightning, the band cross the mountains to the castle, where a wedding is taking place. Pistolets cracking, they snatch a carriage containing a princess and a lord, then hurl aside inconvenient knights and sundry soldiers. The garrison is bound and gagged. Gold by the armful is bundled into leather bags. Zmyjenski's friend, Stasko, is found fettered in a dungeon and emerges into daylight covered in crud and completely mad. Released prisoners are running for the hills with pockets stuffed with ducats and tales of their heroic saviour. Dobosz meanwhile has fallen under the spell of a set of jewelled doves, whose gold wings and feathers of sprinkled diamond dust are possessed of such radiant beauty that he has to be snatched from his reverie with the warning that troops will be on them within an hour. The band make good their escape, dispersing into the forests of Chornohora and covering their tracks by riding up streams. Back at their lair, the booty is stashed in the caves of Hoverla and Munczel. In a valedictory speech, old man Zmyjenski refuses to accept his share of the spoils and limps off to his farm, taking Stasko with him, where the two will quietly live out the rest of their time. Dobosz is left with his jewelled doves contemplating the flames of the living fire.

My own reverie was snapped by the sudden commotion of shepherds gathering themselves for a day in the rain. Outside the hut, they split the flock and climbed slowly up through the mist into the trees with the ugly dogs. Uri and I waited a while, while the sing-song yodels of the men faded into the mist, and then we began the long walk down to the valley.

Naga Kaput!

Rain fell continuously as Uri and I splashed down the muddy track. Four hours after leaving the shepherds below Shpitzi, we emerged into the Cherniy Cheremosh valley at the site of the old *czerdak* – one of the many guard-houses set up at the entrances to mountain passes to prevent plague victims fleeing to uncontaminated lands. A *czerdak* was seldom a place to linger, for it was thought that people died here, unable to go on, or return, and that the very soil carried the plague. In keeping with the macabre airs of this shadowed junction, Uri began to complain that his feet were hurting.

The river was in spate. As we walked, we were caught by another thunderstorm and Uri began to drop so far behind that I had to stop every five minutes and wait for him to catch up. Finally he staggered to a complete halt and said: 'Problem, Nick.'

'What problem, Uri?'

'*Naga kaput.*'

'Bugger it.'

'*Naga* very problem.'

'Let's have a look.'

Uri took off his canvas boots. Inexplicably he had left them outside the tent all night and they had filled with water. Now his feet were red and swollen. Uri was shaking his head. We had no option but to press on; there was no traffic on the dirt road, and I couldn't carry him. Neither would he let me lighten his rucksack. We staggered to the village of Itsay but Uri insisted that we should try and reach the small town of Verkhovina. We covered the last kilometres in hundred-metre hobbles. If I slowed to walk with him, Uri slowed further.

We crept into Verkhovina shortly before dark. The *turbaza* lay two kilometres beyond the town. For Uri the extra distance was a painful postscript to the day, but worse was to come: in the *turbaza* we were given a room that was stained and chipped, with moraines of body grit on the beds and sticky patches on the concrete floor. Uri was so miserable that he'd stopped speaking. We emptied our rucksacks of wet gear. The contents of Uri's rucksack had hydrated then congealed into a glutinous sludge of tea-leaves, sugar, sodden socks, onions, rancid *gorok* and potatoes. The end of an expedition was writ not just in the squalor of our kit and surroundings but in the utter expiry of spirit. It was all over.

In the canteen we ate a vile dinner beside a group of raucous Czechs who were seeking oblivion in cheap Russian champagne. Back in room 2, it was time to put Uri out of his agony: 'Do you want to come on to Porubnoe, to the border, with me, Uri? Or take the bus from Verkhovina back to Ust-Chorna?'

Uri stared dejectedly at his decomposing feet. There was a long silence, and then he said quietly: 'Omnibus.'

On the Steppe

The leash had snapped. I catapulted out of Verkhovina towards the border, three or four days' walk away, down on the edge of the great steppe that stretched east to the Urals. Strange times lay ahead; I had lost my guide and forgotten to ask Uri for the letter he had been given by Piotr. And I was dropping down the Asian side of the watershed. I crossed a low pass into a valley which looked as if it had fallen from another planet. Every cottage along the puddled road was sheathed in metal, walls and roofs, pipes and doors so that they shone in the wet sunlight like an avenue of silver temples. The cladding had been stippled into fanciful foliage and solar emblems, like the intricate hurricane lamps in Moroccan souks or the tailgates on Pakistani trucks.

It was Saturday and I walked against the flow of villagers returning from the market in Kosiv. Some pushed bicycles with bulging sacks balanced on the crossbars, others rode in carts drawn by high-stepping horses or walked with panniers hung across their shoulders. A man with a toothless grimace laboured up the hill beneath a sack of squealing piglets.

Kosiv market-place was jammed. Metal tables, each with a set of cast-iron scales, were piled high with honey jars, cucumbers and cabbages, tiny new potatoes like earthy pearls and the reds of sweet tomatoes and strawberries. Under cover, chopped meat changed hands and a new kiosk tried in vain to sell its expensive Slovakian sweets, little tins of Nescafé and gas cigarette lighters.

Sucking strawberries I left Kosiv on the old highway that ran along the eastern foot of the Carpathians from Kolomyja to Kuty. I was alone on a road which once clattered to the wheel of the *balagulas*, the great carts driven by the Jews of Kolomyja, Delatyn, Kosiv and Kuty, men in calf-boots and sheepskin caps, who spoke the many languages of their trade: Yiddish and German, Ukrainian and Polish, perhaps Romanian too. The *balagulas* were the earliest buses, fitted with rows of planks lashed down with leather straps and padded with sacks of hay. They ran to set routes, from Hay Square in Kolomyja, then down to the monastery well to collect more custom, and when crammed with passengers set off with a crack of the whip for the slow fifty-kilometre journey south to Kuty, stopping at every village and town *en route*. They were famous for their incredible slowness and reliability. Now the only buses were rarely seen six-wheeled army trucks with crude windows hacked in the metal sides.

Two towns faced each other across the broad and sluggardly Cheremosh, no longer a mountain torrent but a plains river sidling towards its conjunction with the Prut and a bloated meander through Moldova to the Black Sea. Kuty, on the north bank, was once an important staging-post on the trading route over the Carpathians to the Hungarian plain. Here the Armenian caravans had prepared themselves to run the gauntlet of Dobosz and his robbers, riding out of Kuty one hundred horses at a time, loaded with morocco leather for Debrecen and returning with bags of ducats. Kuty later became notorious for its prisons and roadside gallows, built by the Austrians to punish young Hutzuls who had deserted the army or evaded conscription. Suicide and tuberculosis took a terrible toll on the Hutzul shepherds and a new generation of disaffected youth turned to the mountains. They were a motley lot: men like Martyszczuk, who'd shot an Austrian forest inspector who'd tried to imprison him for poaching, and Czuprej – 'Tufty', on account of his headdress of straw-coloured hair – who'd escaped from a military hospital with his imperial carbine, killing a few soldiers on the way. And the spindly pipe-smoking farmer called Kudil, dressed in a red caftan and a goatskin coat, who deserted the army and was famous for the great bear he killed with a blow from his club, a massive pine root studded with stones and iron. And Dmytryk Wasyluk, who'd magically survived a lightning strike and who went everywhere in a hooded, white wedding gown.

The storytellers told how the Hutzuls struck back, floating down the

Cheremosh on rafts disguised as birds and animals and driving the imperial soldiers out of Kuty. Wasyluk was elected their 'free prince' and a delegation was sent to Vienna to offer a pact to Emperor Joseph II. They presented the emperor with gifts: Hungarian church candlesticks, Turkish thalers and sacks of ducats, jewelled scimitars, skins and guns, axes and the magic doves that had been captured a generation earlier by Dobosz. With these treasures they bought their freedom – and an end to conscription – from the 'white stockings' of Vienna.

Now Kuty was a dishevelled agglomeration of Carpathian cottages clustered around a decrepit square fronted by collapsing Communist architecture and a wrecked church. The doors hung open. Inside, the floor was scattered with shattered timber and grit, the wall and ceiling pitted with hundreds of bullet strikes. The pulpit was gone and in its place a concentration of pock-marks. I started when a voice behind me said: 'It was the Russians.' An old man stood in the doorway. He said that the villagers were going to rebuild the church. The doors must have been pulled shut in 1944.

On the southern bank the lumber town of Viznitza – Vynicioara on my *Generalkarte* – lay at the end of the line. Rail sidings and wasteland backed by tatty apartment blocks and beyond, the old heart of the place, steep cobbled lanes climbed between single-storey cottages with neoclassical façades that could have been swapped unnoticed for those of the Marchfeld in the heart of that old empire.

Beyond Viznitza I took a dirt track that ran straight across the steppe with a vast wood on one side and a sea of wheat on the other. The drumskin of the plain still hummed to the hoofs of Huns, Avars, Khazars, Magyars, Pechenegs, Torks, Berendians, Polovs, Tatars and Kalmucks, the galloping plunderers of the steppe who forced upon Ukraine its name and reputation. The 'Borderland' has not enjoyed its role as a buffer between Europe and the Asian nomad.

This plain was not my space. I felt exposed, shrunken. Beyond the wheat the mountains were no longer mine. They had taken on a misleading rhythm, a wave motion of peak and valley that smoothed away the stubborn detail. I couldn't tell how fast I should walk, or whether this gritty line angled slightly upward or downward.

Instead of finding an easy pace on this undemanding road, I walked erratically, speeding up and slowing down, looking continually over my shoulders (was I being followed?) and constantly changing from one verge to the other. A weird cinematic sky played to a plains audience; out of the iron press of rainclouds came slender-spoked sunrays probing the grey land with laser spots of brilliant light.

Somewhere out in the midst of this plain I thought to break the monotony by taking a crap. I turned at random into the tangled wood and walked ten metres into the trees, waited and listened, then changed my course through ninety degrees and walked another ten metres, then listened again. A twig snapped. I turned slowly towards the direction of the sound. In a tree high above the floor of the wood, was a man, staring down at me. (So I *was* being followed!) I stared up at him. '*Dobri dyen!* Good day!'

But he didn't reply and I left the trees. Later I regretted my startled about-turn; I would never know why a man was up a tree in the middle of an empty wood on an empty plain. And he would never know why a man with a ski-stick and a rucksack zigzagged through the wood to the foot of his tree.

For two days I was out on the steppe, hugging the security of dykes and windbreaks of trees; stopping only to fill my water bottle from wells in muddy yards or to queue interminably for bread. On the Sunday the road was busy with horses dressed in red tassels as families trotted to church. On the Monday I was passed by occasional motorcycle-combinations driven by men wearing old leather tank-crew helmets with the rubber intercom leads trailing in the slipstream like strands of black saliva. The only town I passed was Storozinec, a shabby garrison with a weed-engulfed square and a bar full of drunks, where I was joined by a man wearing a suit and waving a bottle of Smirnoff. 'Where are you from?' he asked.

'*Ya iz Anglii . . .*'

'That's Russian!' he spat in English. 'Here we speak Ukrainian.'

One of his friends, a younger pleasant-looking man, joined us. The Suit filled our glasses. '*Zadruzbah!*'

The glasses were filled again.

The younger man said that he was a history teacher. 'I've been to Russia. To Moscow, to Gorky, to Lenin . . . St Petersburg. Life is better in Russia than here. Much better. Ukraine is a very poor country. Very poor.'

A third, much older man staggered over. He hit the table and began shouting.

The glasses were refilled. '*Zadruzbah!*'

'*Zadruzbah!*'

The rounds were fiercely competitive and I could see no obvious escape. Two of my companions were downing double shots. When Vassili began raging and tearing at my pack the barwoman intervened and pushed me towards the door. The history teacher looked ready to burst into tears. 'We welcomed you! You are our friend!' he cried. And then, in a traumatized *non sequitur*, he gasped: 'Tell them in England we are good to foreigners.'

I fell on to the street dragging my rucksack. Rain bounced off chipped concrete. Men slumped drunkenly in doorways. I grabbed for a lamp-post, missed and fell over a railing, where I hung, face down and pinned by the weight of the rucksack, while rainwater streamed down the inside of my trousers. In this upside-down position, fighting the urge to pass out, I extricated the compass and set it on south-east. Then I unbuckled the rucksack, disentangled the railing and swayed out of town. I felt one of the crowd.

The rain stayed in Storozinec and I was on a steaming road that ran through wheat fields with the vodka a burning band around my forehead. The sun returned. I lay beneath a frothy chestnut and woke to see a man pedal slowly past with his wife balanced on the crossbar holding a basket of strawberries. The bicycle hit nothing; it just folded in the road, throwing its passengers and the strawberries on to the wet bitumen. While the woman crawled to and fro on the road collecting the fallen fruit, her inebriated husband stood holding the bicycle, consoling her.

A second cyclist came past. He was wearing a charcoal suit and black trilby, with a black leather satchel over one shoulder. His spotless black and chrome bicycle twinkled in the sunlight and he pedalled with a straight back, like a man in the dock listening to his sentence.

I couldn't remember when I'd last eaten a meal. I was worried about the border-crossing. There were alien elements at work out here in the flatlands. People crossing the plains came from other parts. They were passing through. They did not belong. They were not recognized by the locals; they were untraceable. What happened as they passed through meant nothing. I could be robbed and stripped and dumped in a ditch and nobody would know who I was or care who did it. Nothing bound the steppe together except the strands of bitumen, the railway lines and the pylons.

I slept under a row of walnuts beside the road, then rose early and walked to the border. Beyond three sets of police barriers I came to the tail-end of a queue of sixty or so trucks. At the front was the high wire fence. The Ukrainian conscript on the far side said that it was not possible to cross the border on foot. I asked him to fetch an officer. He returned to his booth and made a telephone call. Half an hour later, I saw him pick up the phone again. Then he came to the wire and let me through the gate. He took me to a police officer.

In Russian, I said: 'I have walked through Ukraine.'

He said nothing.

I showed him the map. We talked about Hoverla and he left me in the booth with a customs officer who wanted to talk about English football and the cost of living in London. 'My salary is sixteen dollars a month,' he said. 'What is yours?'

'I don't have a salary.'

He turned to the document on the desk. 'Do you have a *pouff*?'

'A what?'

'A *pouff-pouff*!' he repeated, holding out his index finger. 'Gun.'

'No, I have no *pouff*.'

'Narcotics?'

'No.'

'Dollars?'

'No.'

A stamp thudded on to my currency declaration form. The first officer returned and studied the completed form, then said: 'Come with me.'

On the far side of no-man's-land, the first Romanian I spoke to was a young man in camouflage holding an automatic rifle. 'Problem Ukraine?' he asked.

'No problem Ukraine,' I smiled.

He looked disappointed.

I walked on and met a Romanian police officer. 'I'd like to buy a visa for Romania, please.'

'Impossible. You must go to the Romanian embassy in Kiev . . .'

'Kiev! I can't walk 1,000 kilometres just to fetch a piece of paper!'

But the officer had already walked away.

Over the next three hours I was offered a visa for thirty-one days, then ten days, then three days. The policeman and the cashier could not agree on the period of visa I should be allowed. I overheard the phrase 'fifty-fifty'. The period reverted to thirty-one days, which was ample time for me to reach the city of Braşov in the crook of the Carpathians, and extend my visa. They wanted the fee in dollars. But I had no dollars, officially. We settled for Deutschmarks. My passport was stamped and I walked through the afternoon sun to the last barrier. The two soldiers toyed with my passport, as if unable to decide to whom it really belonged.

Then they handed it back and I walked round the barrier and on to the floodplain towards Siret. There was no other traffic. I stopped and looked back. Ukraine was blocked from view behind the fence, with its watch-towers and strip of raked earth. The Iron Curtain had not disappeared. It had just moved further east.

Twenty minutes' walk from the Ukrainian border, Siret's shops were so well stocked that I could have stepped back on to my own high street. Bread could be bought without queuing. Shelves groaned under the weight of Lebanese lemonade, Turkish bubble-gum, bottles of Iranian shampoo, Slovakian sweets, Dutch biscuits, Wrigleys chewing-gum, Syrian chocolate, Greek fruit bars, Kodak boxes and Nescafé jars. Romanian products were noticeable for their drab or non-existent wrappings. Cheap shoes stood by wax tapers, tins of pork, nails, enamel cooking pots, refrigerators of ice-cream. In one shop, I could have bought a second hand Renault gearbox. In Siret's post office a girl wearing a 1940s Bakelite headset, sitting at a bank of sockets and jackplugs, put me straight through to London, an achievement which left me speechless. Which didn't matter since Annabel was not in our house.

'Beep.'

'Annabel . . . it's me. I'm out. I'm in Romania. The Promised Land. They've got food here. Only the easy bit to do now.'

Behind the scenes, Siret's cogs and pulleys had creaked to a standstill. Wrung out after the border-crossing, I stopped for the night in the town's hotel. 'May I have a room with a bathroom please?' I asked the receptionist.

'Of course . . .' she smiled.

'Is there hot water?'

'No, not today.'

'Is there cold water?'

'No, not today.'

'In Ukraine they have hot water.'

'That is impossible.'

The room was airless and hot and full of mosquitoes. Tormented by heat and bugs I sat up till four a.m. swatting, sweating and scribbling till exhaustion claimed me for two hours' sleep. I woke covered in volcanic pustules, with a lower lip so swollen that it hung on my chin like a length of flabby salami.

The Painted Monasteries

'This first view,' wrote Sacheverell Sitwell of his visit to Suceviţa in 1937, '... is among the most important revelations of the whole Byzantine world.'

Suceviţa sat like a treasure casket in its bucolic glen. Beyond the uncomplicated rectangle of its outer walls the river wandered through meadows of silver grass. Tapering firs and hay-stooks mirrored the monastery's towers and slanting eaves. A nun in black followed a flock of white geese.

The church occupied the centre of the grass quadrangle. There were in its tall, shingled ridge, recollections of a Boyk roof-pitch, and in its flared brim Hutzul carpentry, but in every other aspect, from the hexagonal pencil point of its single tower, to its Gothic windows, the ideas of strange and distant minds. The call to prayer at Suceviţa is still tapped out by a black cowled figure circling the church beating a two-metre board with a mallet, a tradition carried over from the Ottoman years, when bells – used for calling men to battle – were banned.

Christianity in freeze-frame covered the entire exterior and interior of Suceviţa's church. So unaltered by time was this sanctuary that it wasn't difficult to slide back through four centuries to the time when the best of Bukovina's painters were summoned by the Movilă family to create these spectacular frescoes. Alchemists and artists, they used powdered lapis lazuli or indigo for the blues, the roots of *Rubia tinctorum* – madder – for the crimsons, ochre, soot and charcoal for the blacks. And gold. To bind the paints and to protect their work from the steppe winds they hydrated the powders in a slime of cow bile and egg yolk.

The narrative they created had a cast of hundreds: saints and priests and cloaked philosophers (Plato crowned by a reliquary of bones) floated in ranks above an earthly landscape of mesas and buttes, cityscape and forest. On the sunward wall, the celestial ladder reached to the eaves spilling the damned into the jaws of twin-headed monsters and inside,

peering through the candle-soot, were the Pantocrator and an extrava-
gant Last Supper, processions and various saints being speared and
sawn, stretched and drowned.

Emerging from the forests (where 'art' had been an occasional iconostasis or the pattern on a flute barrel), the scale and spectacle of
Suceviţa's painted walls hit me with the power that it must have had for
the seventeenth-century foresters and shepherds. This carnival of the grotesque, the allegorical and the saintly, reaching as tall as the trees, was a
full-colour, multi-dimensional virtual-reality Bible lesson. The effect was
heightened by the times: Suceviţa was painted in 1596, when Europeans
were staring at the end of their world. The Turks were on the rampage,
defeating Serbia at Kosovo in 1389, then taking Constantinople, the capital of the Holy Roman Empire, in 1453; attacking Belgrade in 1456;
trampling the Hungarians into the mud of Mohács in 1526, and then besieging Vienna three years later. In 1538 Süleyman the Magnificent had
torched the town of Suceava, just down the river from Suceviţa. One of
the greatest to stand against the Turks was the Prince of Moldavia, Stefan
the Great, whose efforts were rewarded by the Papal appellation 'Athlete
of Christ'. Stefan, his illegitimate son, Petru Rareş, and various other
princes and boyars gave thanks for their victories by building a series
of monasteries and painted churches hidden away in the Carpathian
beech woods.

One day's walk south from Suceviţa, the turrets of Moldoviţa
monastery crept into view above the tree crowns. Moldoviţa's aspect
was less austere than Suceviţa's, with wild roses and apple trees decor-
ating its quadrangle, and a breathing space between the monastery's
modest walls and its surrounding hills. Like Suceviţa, the church was
entirely covered with frescoes: the 'Tree of Jesse', the 'Hymn to the
Virgin', 'Last Judgement', mass decapitations and so on.

The fresco I'd come to see had been painted at the foot of the south
wall. Waves as big as mushroom clouds dashed against the walls of a city
that was being attacked by siege guns and cavalry. From the battlements
archers drew bowstrings and cannon-barrels flickered tongues of flame.
Icons were paraded on the battlements. The besiegers were Persians
(although for the sake of suiting contemporary hatreds, they were
dressed as Turks) and leading the besieged from the battlements were the
patriarch, the emperor and empress of Byzantium and the banner of
the Virgin. The city was Constantinople.

The painting was the first signpost to my ultimate destination and it coincided with my 400th day since leaving Finisterre. On my dog-eared map of Europe, I measured out the remaining thumb-lengths of walking to Istanbul and saw that I could be on the Black Sea in another hundred days. The journey was four-fifths over. I left the monastery a little sad.

The Spoon Collector

'Don't go there!' begged Rusan. 'It's kitsch!' Rusan Dumitri was the conservator of the Museum of Wood and he did not think that I would find the Museum of Spoons interesting.

Rusan's museum began as the private collection of a local ethnographer, Ion Ştefureac, back when the double-headed eagle of the Habsburgs flew above the shingles of Cimpulung Moldovenesc, a small town strung out along a valley twenty-five kilometres' walking south of Moldoviţa's monastery. Ştefureac could see how the new railway up the valley was changing the old ways. Before it was too late, before the inherited arts of rural life were superseded by mass-production and economic migration, Ştefureac combed the villages of Bukovina. After his death in 1920, the collection continued to grow until, by the end of the Second World War, it contained over 2,000 exhibits.

Rusan, short and round with a grey beard, took me on a tour through his catacomb of rusticana. The collection was much the same as any I'd seen since crossing the Danube. Flails and hay rakes, sledges and dug-out canoes were arrayed and labelled alongside fish traps, spinning wheels, wetstone sheaths and a thousand other silvine treasures cut and crafted from Carpathian timber. Among the shepherds' paraphernalia was a *buciume*, similar to the alp horns further east but decorated along its two-metre shaft with a spiral of bark. There were a few specifically Hutzul artefacts: a distaff, some decorated powder horns and a *baltag* – like the *valaška* hatchet-stick I'd seen in Slovakia and the Polish Górale *ciupaga*.

Rusan saw my excitement and said: 'That's because the Hutzuls are in all these countries!'

'Countries . . . ?'

'Czechoslovakia, no I'm sorry, Slovakia. And Ukraine, which was the USSR and Moldavia, that is Bessarabia. And Poland, or Galicia.'

Not for the first time, it struck me that the only way to make sense of the cultural map was to ignore the political boundaries and go back to the oldest divide of all, between plains people and mountain people and coast people – and of course the nomads. A Romanian Hutzul shepherd had more in common with a Galician shepherd on the far side of the continent, than with the inhabitants of his own capital Bucharest.

The Museum of Spoons was around the corner at No. 1 Gheorghe Popovici in an ordinary residential house. On the front of the house was a plate bearing the name of Professor Ioan Ţugui. Ţugui had been professor of history at Cernăuţi, before it was lost to Ukraine. At the end of the war the professor began collecting wooden spoons. By the time he died, thirty-three years later, he had accumulated a collection of 5,000. The spoons were hung in rows, up the stairs and across the walls.

I was shown the collection by the forty-four-year-old husband of Professor Ţugui's niece, Ioan Mateescu. Using an extended car aerial as a pointer, he drew my attention, in French, to the most interesting spoons. There were spoons with icons on their handles; left-and right-handed spoons; softwood spoons in alder, lime and poplar; durable spoons in pear and maple; spoons whittled from walnut and totemic spoons in ancient yew; spoons from as far away as Finland and Iraq, Portugal and Wales; fiftieth-anniversary spoons of the Partie Communist Romanie; shepherds' spoons; honey spoons; hammer-and-sickle spoons; a double-ended spoon (*'pour le gourmand qui mange beaucoup!'*); kitchen spoons and Catholic spoons; spoons bearing the professor's portrait (Ioan Ţugui made an unlikely icon, with his bald dome, double chin and Clark Kent spectacles). In the professor's catalogue was the provenance of each spoon, press cuttings on spoons and a Romanian poem about spoons written in 1965.

Mateescu's sighs were those of a man reconciled to a life sentence as a spoon guide. His card described him as an *inginer*, under the Communists the most prestigious of professions. But there was less work now, especially in agricultural engineering, and his wife's uncle's spoons brought in a lot of lei. In the summer, up to 300 foreign tourists called every month. My heart went out to Mateescu. After five minutes of wall-to-wall spoons my eyes were involuntarily side-stepping to escape the repetition; it was like trying to add up a computer printout whose rows and columns consisted entirely of ones and it induced a faint, slightly hysterical psychological state best described as *spoony*.

Then I spotted something so bizarre that I had to cross the room to confirm with my finger what my eye had suspected. There, among the ranks of wooden exclamation marks, was a binary misprint: a row of forks.

'What are those doing here?'

Mateescu shrugged wearily: '*La diversité!*'

Rose-petal Jam

After three days' rest in Cimpulung I felt ill and exhausted; I'd written to Annabel, sewn my torn clothing and treated my digestive bacilli to a germ-rich diet of ice-cream sold in warped plastic tubs by street-traders in the market. As a result I'd picked up mild food-poisoning.

The total height gain from Cimpulung to the top of Rarău was only 900 metres, but it might have been Everest. Every step up the steep foot-path required a concentrated spasm of willpower. Eventually I emerged from the trees on to a saddle occupied by the Rarău Alpine Hotel, a ten-storey concrete block best known for being the place where the travel writer Dervla Murphy broke her ankle by skidding on vomit. The Alpine Hotel was closed for *reconstrucţie* but my woeful condition won me a room with a broken door and no glass in the window.

Rarău's popularity stems from the limestone towers that protrude from its forested summit. The two most admired spikes were the Lady's Rocks. I was unable to climb them but, by a rather contorted route involving a backward squirm through an eye in the rock, I did however get to the top of a third spike and was able to gaze weakly over a vast view of forested ridges, long parallel waves known locally as *obcine*. There was a seemingly infinite scale to the Carpathians, like the oceans.

All night the rain fell and the wind blew through my room in the Alpine Hotel. When I looked out at dawn the trees were shadows in thick mist. Blue paint spots marked the descent southwards off Rarău to a *poiana* where a fighting retreat before dogs from a nearby shepherds' *stîna* finally triggered the bacillary time-bomb I'd carried over the mountain from Cimpulung. I was not a happy hiker. The dogs, sensing a quarry who had dropped both his guard and his trousers, were closing in for the kill when they ran into an outward-rushing thermo-gaseous ring-cloud. Their gagging whining retreat was as gratifying as the first fateful lick I'd applied to the chocolate dairy ice that had just fired its warning shot in an onslaught whose duration would surpass by far the previous short-term gut rots I'd inflicted upon myself by indiscriminate troughing.

I slithered down to the Bistriţa valley and took advantage of its south-easterly course to cut through the heart of the Carpathians. The rains had flushed the mountain streams into the brown Bistriţa. The river was out of control, a churning rope of floodwater. Like its neighbour, the Cheremosh, across the border in northern Bukovina, the Bistriţa used to be busy with logging rafts. Every couple of hours I paused to nibble a small piece of bread and jam, just enough to keep me moving but not enough to overfeed the bacilli.

Little traffic passed me on the concrete road linking riverside villages that stood with their backs to the mountains. The land between the houses and the river belonged to the ducks and geese, and to hoovering pigs and docile milch cows that travellers had to thread through on the way downstream. My sorry state triggered an unwelcome misadventure.

Between two of the villages I was passed by a pick-up truck loaded with logs. Four loggers sat across the front seats. They called me over, but their faces meant no good and I walked on. Twice more they came past, leaning into the breeze with bloodshot eyes. They followed me to the next village. As I levelled with the first house, the valley bus drew up on the left-hand verge, between me and the loggers, blocking their view. I turned into the yard of the house behind the bus, and hurried through its front plot and round behind the building, where I bumped into the owner, a woman wearing an apron. I asked for a glass of water and she drew the bucket from the well and we went into her kitchen.

She had just cooked a pan of rose-petal jam, and brought me a saucerful and a teaspoon. 'It is good for respiration,' she said, bringing me a mug of hot milk too. 'It's from our cow,' she smiled.

The ingredients for the jam lay on the table – the petals, a lemon, sugar – and this picture of still sweet innocence helped erase the image of axes and chainsaws and a blood-spattered glade with worm-tongued hicks leafing through my passport and chucking aside the lumber-jacked leg that carried my hidden dollars. I was getting tired. The wall between caution and paranoia was hard to hold up with one pair of hands.

Back on the road the loggers had gone. I hoped that they thought I'd got on the bus. As a precaution, I found a track between the houses and climbed the mountainside, up through juniper and young firs until I was looking down on the village and the thread of road and its turbid partner.

For a couple of hours I scrambled along the side of the mountain, parallel with the road and river. Then it was dusk and I came down to the valley again and walked on through the night unable to find anywhere to sleep that wasn't occupied by a crop or a house or an animal. Near midnight I climbed back up the mountain and fell into an old trench system whose rampart had created a levelling on the slope wide enough to accommodate the tent. I'd walked about sixty kilometres since leaving Rarău that morning.

Rain clicking on the taut nylon of the tent woke me. Outside, woolly strands of mist drifted up a mountain slope dusted white by daisies. Waking in a camp that was selected in darkness is like opening one's eyes on the world for the first time. The grass, trees, water and rock look bright, clean and surprising. After two days on minimal rations I was surprised not to feel hungry. In fact I felt as if I could walk for ever.

Down the valley I came to the head of Lake Bicaz and one of the major crossroads in the eastern Carpathians. A cluster of shacks had sprung up around the crossroads and in one of these I settled weakly and guiltlessly into an inner sanctum that had been set aside for the sale of expensive imported luxuries. The bar was filled with uniformed police and a seedy character in a trenchcoat who sidled over and began chatting about Romania's tourist potential. His patronizing asides and eagerness to buy cans of Czech lager for the police (and me) convinced me that he was the local hood paying his dues to the *poliție*.

When he told me for the third time how welcome I was to visit Lake Bicaz I snapped: 'Who are you? Are you a businessman?'

'No,' he smiled congenially, 'I am a policeman. I am the boss of *these* policemen.'

Ceahlău

From the west shore of lake Bicaz I could watch Ceahlău growing on the horizon ten kilometres to the south. The rains of the night had polished the air and the Carpathian throne of the god Zamolxis rose as an isolated massif, asymmetrical, with towers and notches, purple in the evening sky and girdled by a ring of cloud. From here, Zamolxis once watched over the tribes of ancient Transylvania, Dacians whose communications with their deity were conveyed by messengers ritually thrown on to a thicket of javelin-tips – a habit which explains the vigour with which Romanians have adopted the public telephone.

At the foot of the mountain I came to the village of Ceahlău and as I walked between the houses and the river in the early evening I heard the urgent thunder of a water-mill. Vasili Diaconiţa had built the mill with his own hands. A 300-metre leet brought water from the river to his fulling-mill and to his mill-wheel, around which he had constructed a timber shed that housed axles and belt-drives that converted the gravitational flow of river water into instant, cost-free energy. He led me down into the guts of the hut, where belt-drives slapped and a gigantic grindstone pulverized maize into a rising cone of flour. By shifting the belts to a different set of wheels, an ingenious gear system converted circular motion to a vertical piston action that pumped a saw-blade up and down as tree trunks slid by on miniature railway tracks. Nearly every part of the great water-engine had been crafted from wood, whose smooth running I traced to the ball-races which Vasili had deftly inserted into the axle sockets. He saw me admiring the immaculate coronas of greased steel bubbles and smiled. 'Yes. Those were expensive.'

I slept in the next hamlet, the last before the road petered out into forest, and set off at sunrise with two days' worth of bread and jam in the top of my rucksack. On the latter part of the climb I was joined by a group of students. The tall boy with the singlet, reversed baseball cap and bone eagle on his chest carried the axe, which he swung at threatening objects such as tree stumps, fallen branches and sapling shadows. Two of the other boys self-consciously sharpened their sheath knives on wedges of sandstone, anticipating perhaps a role in hand-to-hand combat should a bear or band of robbers break past the axeman. The boy who was the bodybuilder walked with his eyes pinned to his pectorals, tripping on roots and colliding with trees. Aside from the girls' rucksacks of picnic food, the other mountaineering precaution the group had taken was to bring a massive torch that looked as if it had been made by fixing a car battery to the back of a headlamp.

They were all at middle school, sitting their final exams the following week. They had come to Ceahlău to draw strength for the greatest challenge of their lives.

'Only a few of us, one or two maybe, will get to university . . .' explained eighteen-year-old Anne Marie. 'I want to study economics, but there are sixty applicants for each studentship.'

They were all disillusioned. Democracy hadn't delivered the goods. I asked one of the boys whether he was happy that the era of Communism had finished.

'So so. Not happy. Not unhappy . . . It is not what we expected . . .'

'What did you expect?'

'Freedom. To be rich.'

For the two hours it took to make the laborious ascent the students spoke of their difficulties. Near the top they conferred among themselves and stopped once again on the forest path. 'Nicolae, we have something to ask you. A question for you. Maybe you can answer our question and help us . . .'

'I'll try.'

'The question we have is . . . we would like to know whether it is true that Jimmy Page had a wife who put a curse on the group.'

'I didn't know he had a wife . . .'

'You didn't!' They were incredulous.

The curse of Led Zeppelin was lifted momentarily when I said that I had been to Père Lachaise cemetery to see the bust of Jim Morrison.

'What did it look like?' demanded the axe-boy.

'I don't know. It's been stolen.'

The boy's face betrayed his shaken faith in the great western dream.

At the top of the forest we climbed past the rock fingers of Panaghia and up the long wooden ladder bolted to the cliffs of Toaca, the high point at the northern end of Ceahlău's summit plateau. Up here, at 1,900 metres, above the cliffs and anthropomorphic rock sculptures that ringed the plateau, Ceahlău floated like an island in the sky. Far below, the blue Carpathians rolled away in waves, the polished crests of paler green *poianas* shining in the sunlight above darker troughs of tousled forest. A distant flock dribbled like spilt cream down a bald *obcina*. The throne of Zamolxis still had a role as a forecaster of future events; balanced on the summit was a meteorological station.

My friends left me on top of Ceahlău, which was the scene over the following hours of an exhausting battle between the forces of darkness and light. On the east side of the plateau, perched on the cliff edge, was the Cabană Dochia, where I was given a bed. It was a Friday evening and the fumes from the outdoor latrine and adjacent pigpen were rent by the cries of weekenders staggering up the path from Bicaz bearing bags of alcohol. The party lasted till dawn. Crashes and squalls of drunken hysterics and horrible shrieks competed with backing tracks from

Deep Purple and screeching Romanian folk-punk. My fitful sleep was broken by the arrival in the next bed of three people who added a medley of strangled whimpers to the nihilistic ululations beyond the wooden walls.

At dawn I stumbled outside to find the dregs of the party sprawled in various stages of near-death, clad in the *de rigueur* kit of the ardently decadent: ripped jeans, baseball boots with gaping throats and trailing laces, US Marine caps, Rastafarian tea-cosy hats (handy for stashing the packets of Kents) and oversized T-shirts clinging moistly to under-used rib cages. The conscious ones coughed over cigarettes or groaned into their hands. A cataleptic skeleton slumped in the seat of a rusting orange bulldozer that I couldn't remember seeing the night before.

Across the narrow platform of grass, on the other side of the plateau, the rising sun was catching the shoulders of a monk as he inched along the ridge of his new church. At one end of the roof two carpenters trimmed shingles then flipped their axes over and drove each shingle into place with a nail. At the other end, two more carpenters fed bracing posts up the timber scaffold that was growing skyward into a tower. None of the men spoke as they worked. The only sound was the quartet of taps as each shingle was nailed into place. They were building the church on the lip of the abyss. As the sun climbed, the border between light and dark moved down the shingles until the fresh woodgrain of the entire church shone golden in the rays of the new day.

One thousand metres below, the miller of Ceahlău would be able to see a new spire rising from the crest of the holy mountain.

Into Transylvania

No land looked less like its popular image; it was Bram Stoker's introductory sketch at the beginning of *Dracula* that condemned Transylvania – the land 'beyond the woods' – to be the continent's black heart, a chthonian wilderness whose beetling pine-clad rocks were perpetually shadowed by clouds and howling wolves. Stoker was describing the Bîrgău pass, not far north of where I now stood. Yet the land below me was one of benign gorgeousness, of ripening pastures and clear-eyed brooks descending to the gentle rhythms of the Transylvanian plateau (another misleading image, since the 'plateau', while being uniformly high – most of it lies over 300 metres – is not a bleak and rocky place but a fertile mix of farmland and minor hills split by rivers, woods and little ravines). Transylvania is however one of the few parts of eastern Europe which has an unequivocal physical presence: the plateau is roughly circular, about 250 kilometres in diameter and entirely surrounded by mountains which reach their highest along the southern rim, where they form the Transylvanian Alps. This lopsided crucible contains an unstable cultural *mélange* which history periodically brings to the boil. The two largest minorities are the Szeklers (from the Turkic *sikil*, 'well-born'), who are Magyars of unclear provenance (one theory is that they are leftovers from Attila the Hun's adventures) and the Saxons, who were invited by the Hungarian King Geza II in the twelfth century to settle below the Transylvanian Alps, to guard the passes.

I came down from my airy viewpoint on the Pass of Bicaz and over the next five days made my way along the eastern edge of the plateau, from the Szekler town of Gyergyószentmiklós to Saxon Kronstadt, or, as they're known to Romanians, Gheorgheni and Braşov. The Carpathians brooded beyond my left shoulder loosing flurries of rain that cooled the long July days.

The reapers were out in the fields from dawn to dusk. I woke to the 'ting' of razor-sharp steel slicing the tall grass I slept in, and lay in the evening listening to the urgent rasp of the whetstones. Under the hot sun the women raked the hay and pitched it on to tall wooden carts that creaked along the roads behind pairs of slow-hipped oxen. In the half-light before sunrise I'd meet men on the road, asleep in the back of their carts while a horse towed them out for a day's work, or pedalling old bicycles with their scythes lashed to the crossbars, so that the long curve of shining steel protruded ahead of the front wheel giving the entire man–bike–scythe combination the appearance of a madcap post-Boadicean contraption setting off to do battle with other bizarre cavalries.

Transylvania has been invaded too many times to allow itself the luxury of expectation. Plans are always liable to change. Currently, the plateau was adapting to the notion of mass unemployment as an indirect result of the expiry of the Soviet Empire. Beyond the fields, there was little work. In Gyergyószentmiklós, a teacher called Mircea told me that 7,000 in the town were unemployed, out of a population of 22,000. 'Two years ago,' he shrugged, 'everybody had a job. In fact it was illegal not to have a job. It is all a great shock to us.' And he had explained how he tried to support his wife and two children on a monthly salary of 30,000 lei, about forty dollars. The town's thirty Russian teachers had all lost their jobs. 'Now everybody wants to learn English, but we have only three English teachers!'

I asked Mircea whether he was optimistic for the future and he lifted his arms fatalistically: 'We have a saying here: after the big rain must come the sun. I hope so!'

The villages had lost their shops. Further south, I called one afternoon at a bar for a coffee and asked if they had any biscuits I could buy. Not surprisingly, they hadn't, but the coffee was good and I forgot about the biscuits until a woman who had heard my inquiry returned to the bar with a packet of greaseproof paper. She had been home to collect for me eight freshly baked biscuits.

The biscuits were still on the table when a young man in a singlet came into the bar and said that his mother would like me to go to their home next door. I spent the rest of the day in a garden sharing barbecued pork and slabs of fresh bread. Both father and son were foresters, still adjusting to redundancy. Before leaving I hid a five-dollar note under a book in the kitchen. Two hours later, as I walked into evening along the grass verge beside a giant marigold sun, a pick-up truck came up behind me. It was the son, with two friends.

He crossed the road with his arm out. 'We do not want this,' he said, opening his hand. It was the five-dollar note. With it were other notes. 'And we want you to take this Romanian money to buy yourself a beer tonight.'

Then they were gone and I was left alone on the open plain, the notes in my hand and the salt of sweat and tears stinging the cracks in my lips. I folded the five-dollar note into my spectacle case, knowing that it was money which could never be spent.

There was a stillness in the Szekler towns and villages. The fortified churches were locked. Only at Csiknagyboldogasszony, where a circle of eight-metre walls on a rocky hillock enclosed a church which dated back to 1440, was there any activity. As I sat among the gravestones (many of which bore the name 'Székely') eating my bread and cheese, a black serpent of mourners crept up through the trees tailed by the coffin on a carriage drawn by two grey horses. Behind the carriage came the women, weeping beneath their black scarves.

Finally I crossed the muddy Olt into Alteland, the land of the Saxons. In the village of Hărman, the well-stocked grocery store sold *Apfelstrudel*, and at the end of a long dirt street rose the spire of a fortified church, surrounded by battlements pierced by six towers. Inside, sitting alone on a bench, was an old woman.

Anna Janesch shook her head: 'Our people are leaving . . .' In the church books Anna had traced her family back through 600 years of Transylvanian history.

I climbed the steps to the wooden galleries lining the inside of the walls. Cobwebs hung where ranks of *speck* – pork fat – had once been stored, to feed the population in times of siege. From the top of the church tower I could look across the floodplain of the Olt to the roofs of distant Braşov, and beyond to the pointed tips of the Transylvanian palisade.

When I came down from the tower, Anna had been joined by her seventeen-year-old son Albert, a blond boy wearing a reversed baseball cap and American jeans. 'Of course it's sad the Saxons are leaving,' he told me, 'but life here is not good. We want a new life. I want a house. Here it's politics, attitudes and prices. My mother is paid only 20,000 lei a month for looking after the church. It's shit.'

'What do you think will become of your village, Hărman?'

Albert hesitated, then pulled out a new passport and held it under my nose. 'Don't ask me! I'm German now!'

Storm in the Făgăraş

I turned an uncomfortable corner at Braşov. Since leaving Finisterre I had walked eastwards or southwards, and occasionally a little north-wards, but at Braşov I turned west, back towards my starting point. Remaining true to the European watershed, I now had to follow the Transylvanian Alps back to the Danube, 250 kilometres to the west, before making the turn south into the Balkan mountains. This month spent walking away from my goal proved to be one of the journey's more demanding perversities and I was reminded of it every morning by the unfamiliar sight of my own shadow blackening the ground before my boots.

Beyond Braşov I climbed over the knife-edge of Piatra Craiului to reach the beginning of the Făgăraş mountains – the name given to the eastern half of the Transylvanian Alps. The Făgăraş traverse is the classic long-distance mountain outing for Romanians, a sustained high-level walk lasting five to seven days. In heavy rain I climbed through the dusk on to the ridge and put up the tent in a clearing at about 1,450 metres.

Drumming rain brought me to the surface long before dawn. I felt in the darkness for the pile of clothes. They were sodden and cold. Inside the tent, the rain always sounded heavy. I lay awake for a while, listening for a pattern. It was ten hours already since I'd been hit by the first downpour, so the clouds would soon be moving on. By first light there'd still be dampness in the air but I'd be able to dry my clothes with a couple of hours of fast walking.

I drifted off again and when I next opened my eyes the tent interior was bathed in pea-green light. Peeking through the zip door I saw the mist was so thick that the trees beyond the glade were swimming in and out of focus. The rain was still falling.

Later, days later, I realized that this was the moment that I should have returned to the valley.

I packed the rucksack inside the tent, wrapping my sleeping-bag and dry thermal underwear in plastic bags, placing the food on top where I could reach it easily. At the last moment, I pulled on the wet clothes and crawled out into the rain. Overloaded with five days' food and the extra weight of the waterlogged tent, I followed a path through the spruce and then up on to the bleak spine of the Făgăraş ridge. Above the shelter of the trees, the wind rattled unchecked. I passed a *stîna*, but the shepherds and flock were out of sight. By the time I reached the top of Lerescu at about 1,700 metres, the rain was slamming obliquely into the ridge. I checked the compass again and lost a little height, then climbed once again, over Comisu at about 1,850 metres, by which time the wind was gusting to eighty kilometres per hour. Water streamed off my face.

I was still convinced that a crack of thunder would blow the clouds clear to give me the view back eastward to the shining reef of Piatra Craiului. And I knew that there was an emergency shelter ahead of me, just off the ridge beyond Berivoiu, where I could stop and wait for the storm to ease, or even spend the night.

Beyond Comisu the ridge climbed steadily through 2,000 metres to Lutele, then levelled for a while. Now the wind made it more difficult to stand. The ridge angled upward again. I was so cold that stops of more than ten seconds to check the compass set me shivering. At around 2,300 metres the ground tilted and began descending and I realized I'd missed

the refuge. I must have walked within metres of it, but not seen it
through the mist and rain. Berivoiu was behind me. The rain turned to
sleet. I came to a saddle. Beyond it the ground sloped steeply upward. I
was shivering violently and kneeling with my head to the wind. I could
hardly see.

It was midday. I was too cold and wet to continue or to turn back.
On each side of me the ridge fell away. I would have to put up the tent,
get warm, make a plan.

Putting up the tent was a desperate fight. I had to lie spreadeagled
on the fabric while pegging it to the ridge, then feed the poles through
their sleeves before waiting for a lull between gusts to ram the poles into
their eyelets, then pin the storm-guys to the rocky turf.

Inside, I ripped off sodden clothing and pulled on dry thermal
underwear then wormed damply into my sleeping-bag and tightened
the drawstring around my nose.

I lay in the sleeping-bag for five hours while the storm intensified.
The gusts came every few minutes, tearing up the flank of the ridge with
jet-engine roars that gave me a few seconds' warning to brace myself
against the end wall of the tent. Then the blasts became so frequent that I
had to squat against the tent all the time, watching in horror as the aluminium poles bent elastically into impossible shapes. I couldn't believe
that the tent was still standing. Sometimes the gusts knocked me down,
or found a way beneath the tent, slamming the floor upwards like a re-
bounding trampoline and throwing the sodden flotsam of my clothes
and gear into wet wads in the tent's bilges. Reluctantly I accepted that
the tent would not survive the night.

I had two options: I could stay where I was, saving the tent by dis-
mantling it and wrapping myself in its soaked nylon for the night. Or I
could pack up and look for better shelter.

There was, according to my Romanian hiking guide, another shelter
on the far side of a 2,302-metre peak called Ludisoru. I was fairly sure
that my saddle was a 2,122-metre dip beneath Ludisoru. So all I had to
do was climb the peak and descend to about 1,950 metres on the far side.
One hour of daylight remained.

I ate the pot of strawberry jam. A sugar surge supercharging my
bloodstream in about thirty minutes would help me down the far side of
Ludisoru, where I'd need one hundred per cent concentration if I wasn't
going to miss that shelter too. I copied the timings and bearings on to a
scrap of paper and put this inside a clear plastic bag in my pocket with

my watch. The timings added up to sixty-three minutes. Snatching a glance through the tent zip, all I could see was hurling sleet and an intimidating void a few metres downwind of the tent.

I dragged on my saturated clothes and stuffed everything else in the rucksack. Outside, the freezing wind tore through to my skin. Without my bodyweight to help hold it to the ground the tent was straining to become airborne. Pinning it down during gusts and pulling out pegs in the lulls, I worked my way around the perimeter of the tent. With one peg to go, a tumultuous blast smashed into the ridge and I threw myself face-down over the tent's crown, sure that I was about to lose everything: the tent and all my gear inside would cartwheel into oblivion. Clinging to the aluminium cross-piece I saw my fist in front of my nose, with the water running off white knuckles. In that desperate moment I had nothing left to give and the knowledge of that finality created a quick, passing calm as I stared at the wet clenched hand, frozen in its grip, as if it was that of another person, a lingering clip at the climax of a movie epic. Then the gust was gone and I was falling on the last peg and snatching the poles from their eyelets, noting dispassionately that three of the four eyelets had already ripped from their tapes and that just a few threads of nylon had prevented the tent from collapsing.

Skirting Ludisoru I found a little shelter from the wind but on the far side, descending in rapidly fading light, each lifting leg was whipped sideways. The slope lessened then levelled. Sixty-two minutes after I had left the saddle on the far side of Ludisoru, a ball took form in the gloom. Surrounded by gale-blasted tussocks was a polyhedron with a door in one of its planes. I fell inside. Hands steadied me. The interior was almost dark and crammed with bodies. Somebody pulled off my rucksack. I slumped down and a mug of steaming liquid was placed in my hand. Soup.

I said, '*Scuzaţi-mă*. Excuse me. The weather is not good.'

There was general agreement.

The boys had been in the polyhedron for twenty-four hours and were huddled damply on the two sleeping shelves. There were five of them. The shelter was leaking and one of the boys had rigged up a tent as a lining. There was just enough space on the two shelves for all of us to lie down. The boys were resigned to their privations. Brad, a chemical engineer from Bucharest, had through age and common sense become the group's leader. Radu wore a red headband and introduced himself as

'a hippy from Constanţa'. Robert was morose, with a handlebar moustache and a kind manner. Egon, or Egi, had a doll's face lapped by fair
hair pulled into a pony-tail. He was a Saxon but had little time for Germany, which he'd visited twice. 'Hungary is where I want to be,' he said.
(We all agreed.) The four of them were old friends and had planned to
walk the entire traverse in a week. The storm had wrecked their plans.
The fifth person was Mănic – 'Call me Maxim!' – a very tall thin man
with an ear-stud who smoked roll-ups.

The wind buffeted the fibreglass shelter all night. Water collected on
the floor. In the morning Brad led the way down from the saddle through
Scottish winter squalls to the Cabană Urlea, a wooden bunk-house on a
sheltered spur part-way down the northern flank of the Făgăraş. The
descent took nearly three hours.

The mountain hut was filled with refugees from the storm. For the
rest of that day the wind and sleet battered the windows while card-
schools huddled round tables and the air was thick with steam and cigarette smoke. There were about fifty in the hut and many had staggered
down from the ridge after harrowing ordeals. An American Peace Corps
worker called Brian had been set upon by dogs from the *stîna* I'd
passed, and escaped with two semicircles of tooth punctures around one
leg. Brian was one of two leaders of a group of Hungarian students
attempting the Făgăraş ridge. Later, as they stumbled down from the
main ridge at about the same time that I was hanging on to my collapsing tent, the entire group had been knocked to the ground by a gust,
close to a cliff edge. 'I was frightened . . .' muttered Brian, shaking
his head.

That evening the food in the hut ran out. For a third night the wind
and rain battered the Făgăraş and in the morning everyone began
rounding up lost kit and departing in knots for the valley.

I had little option but to follow. I'd eaten my five days' worth of food
and the cloud still sat fifty metres above the hut's roof. Egi reckoned that
to complete the Făgăraş traverse would take another three days from
Cabană Urlea, if the weather was fine. I had packed my rucksack and
was sitting outside the hut taking a final tea when Brian called: 'Hey!
Nick! The weather's clearing!'

Up on the snow-dusted ridge above our heads, armadas of clouds
were dispersing across a pacific sky. I drained the cup, pulled on my
rucksack and began the climb back up to the ridge.

The calm after the storm cast upon the mountains a blameless beauty, as if the furies of the last sixty hours were entirely another's aberration, a tropospheric tantrum for which all earthly things were irreproachable.

Two hours after leaving the *cabană* I was standing on Urlea at 2,473 metres looking eastwards along the fractured crest of Făgăraş towards the distant pimple of Moldoveanu, Romania's highest mountain. To the north, the slender wall fell steeply to the Transylvanian plateau, speckled with red-roofed villages. To the south, long tendons split by forested clefts stretched tautly away towards the Wallachian lowlands.

I completed the Făgăraş traverse in splendid, hungry isolation. The entire range had been evacuated. I picked my way along the twists and steps of that ragged blade, trying to steady a pulse that was running away with anticipation. Dry rock and a cloudless sunrise puts wings on the boots. Over two days, Moldoveanu's top flashed by, and Goat Lake, and the tangled fangs beyond Negoiu. On the third day out from Cabană Urlea, I descended 2,000 metres in hissing rain and walked briskly for fifty-five kilometres to Sibiu. Shortly before midnight, sixteen hours after breaking camp up on the Făgăraş ridge, I turned into the gilded foyer of the Hotel Împăratul Romanilor. Chris Brasher was sitting in a vast armchair making notes. He jumped up and shook my hand. 'Ah! You look as if you need a beer.'

Sartorial Designs

My mother went into labour the day that Chris Brasher helped pace Roger Bannister around the Iffley track to the world's first four-minute mile. The year before, in the week of the Queen's Coronation, John Hunt's team reached the top of Everest, and two years later Britain took a bunch of medals at the 1956 Olympics. I was born into a land of heroes. A Battle of Britain pilot lived on our village green, my history teacher's other eye had been knocked out in a naval battle and John Buchan was broadcast on the BBC Home Service.

One of the '56 gold medallists was Chris Brasher. Running had stayed in his blood and he had – along with a career in television – gone on to set up the London Marathon and then a company which manufacture lightweight walking boots, the Brasher Boots which I'd worn since Finisterre. Chris had heard of my walk and through Annabel had arranged to intercept me at Sibiu and then accompany me for a few days.

The capital of the Siebenbürgen, Hermannstadt, as Sibiu was called on my 1898 *Generalkarte*, could have been lifted straight from the banks of the Elbe. *Platz* led to *Platz*, cobbled and lopsided with churches and cafés below a skyline of witches-hat roofs pierced by heavy-lidded skylights squinting into the distance. Down side-streets, arches opened on to vine-clad courtyards. Walter Starkie, the roving collector of gypsy music I'd last crossed trails with in the sierras of Spain, had called here in the thirties. He'd found the Saxon population much diluted by 'Rouman-izing' and had characterized its flaxen-haired settlers with a description of enormous Elsa, the maidservant in his inn. She was, wrote Starkie, 'as heavy and massive as a mule' and able, he claimed, to 'carry sacks of coal up three flights of stairs without straining herself'. All the tenacity of the Saxons was seen in fair Elsa, who could apparently 'deliver a punch that would knock a man out'.

Sibiu's remaining matriarchs all seemed to work in the run-down department store, where I went with Chris to buy a new hat. After four-teen months of mountain weather my Herbert Johnson trilby was little more than a scarecrow's cap held together with surgical tape and a lattice of emergency stitches. On the fourth floor we found a counter selling for-esters' hats, olive green, trilby-shaped and thick enough to deflect a fall-ing fir tree. After my lightweight trilby, the *Panzerkappe* compressed my temples with leaden indestructibility.

We left Sibiu next morning at an Olympic lick loaded with three days' food. Our locally obtained supplies of *caşcaval* cheese and bread were supplemented by a bag of provisions Chris had brought from England. 'Absolutely essential for the mountains!' he had said, pulling out a litre of Macallan's malt whisky and a glass bottle of *The Original and Genuine Lea & Perrins Worcestershire Sauce*.

A gentle ramp of farmland led to Răşinari and the valley mouth that opened the way to the hills. The western half of the Transylvanian Alps was wider than the slim crest of the Făgăraş and composed of several separate massifs. My plan was to head for the heart of the Cindrel mountains, then move on to the higher Parîng range. Beyond the Parîng rose the Retezat mountains, the last of the Carpathians.

Having been warned by a bee-keeper to be careful of bears, we walked for two days over the turfed roof of the Cindrel mountains. Under an empty sky these wide treeless heights looked less like the

Carpathians than a sunburnt Brecon Beacons. The comparison doesn't work for Cindrel's curious topknots. The summits were crowned by piles of weathered stone that played games with the eye: they could be Dartmoor tors, or collapsed Druidical temples, or slices of bread, or body sculptures exhibited on carpets of green baize. From these high points the land curved away in a 360-degree cyclorama, uninterrupted but for the dark crinkles of the Parîng and Retezat.

These confusing ranges had defeated the surveyors of my *Generalkarte*. Rivers and ridge-lines bore the unnaturally smooth curves of a best-guessing cartographer. We steered by the compass and by the word of the shepherds whose flocks roamed these vast grasslands. Dressing just as they had done 2,000 years ago when this was Roman Dacia, the shepherds stood by their flocks in the cold of dawn, wrapped in shaggy sheepskin cloaks that reached to their ankles, more bears than men. On their heads they wore the black brimless elongated bowler hat that seemed confined to the Cindrel mountains. Only a headless man could have invented such an impractical hat: in wet weather, the rain drained down these low-friction domes on to the shepherds' necks; under the sun the matt-black felt absorbed the heat and the absent brim guaranteed maximum eye-glare and exposure to ultra-violet radiation. The shepherds – many of whom were boys – often had badly sunburnt faces. The only shepherd who provided a half-plausible explanation for such a nonsensical piece of headgear claimed that the hats were left behind by the Mohammedans, for whom brims were impractical since they knocked on the ground when the wearer prostrated himself before Mecca. Religious constraints aside, it is better to have a hat without a crown than a hat without a brim.

We slept at about 2,000 metres in the heart of the range. The rains of the previous week had washed the air and I was eager to sleep high, for the view. On a saddle between two hills, in a graveyard of dwarf trees, we strapped armfuls of dead wood to the outside of our rucksacks and climbed to a spring near the ragged crest of Piatra Alba – White Rock. As our fire flared into life so did those of the shepherds across the range, until every dark mountain had its small beacon. Normally I would have put my feet up with a mug of spring water and a slab of bread and cheese, but for Chris this unlikely spot created a culinary challenge he could not ignore. Using the aluminium pot he'd brought from London, he cooked beef and vegetable soup followed by spaghetti bolognese (with fresh garlic), then triumphantly produced a bar of Bournville chocolate. Afterwards we lay with the malt beneath a full moon by the flames on the warm grass and there was nothing wrong with the world at all.

Our camp the following night occupied a bend in the Lotru, the stream pouring down from the glaciated tarns of Parîng. A hanging valley led us under the northern cliffs, past pocket-sized puddles to the switchbacked path up to the col of Piatra Tăiată. Up here we passed a group of Romanian hikers, clad as usual in cut-off jeans and water-absorbent anoraks and carrying a radio-cassette player the size of a suitcase, a stark contrast to Chris, who wore mystical fabrics that repelled wind and rain, retained warmth, wicked away perspiration, and contained ergonomic pockets and non-jamming zips. The only thing his trousers didn't do was make tea.

Researching the subject before I left England, I'd found every writer to have adopted a different solution to the knotty problem of clothing: Belloc didn't believe in wearing socks and was adamant that every item of clothing ('except your boots') should be woollen. Patrick Leigh Fermor carried 'lots of socks' and included in his controversially large wardrobe no fewer than two ties, a tweed jacket and pyjamas. Hats (and umbrellas) obsessed me most and I had been disappointed that nobody had picked up the pioneering work of the Victorian, Sir Francis Galton, who patented a ventilating hat which lifted automatically to cool the head (a pedantic character, Sir Francis also experimented on himself with drugs, working through them in alphabetical order till he reached C for castor oil whereupon he was obliged to give up).

As we stepped out into the strong winds on Parîng's crest I discovered that Chris had not only designed a mountaineering hat, but was wearing it: a flat cap with a retractable cranial gusset which could be folded out in high winds to lock the cap to the wearer's head. The cap, like Sir Francis Galton's, was ventilated, not by a lifting mechanism (which always looked a dubious avenue of experimentation) but through its vapour-permeable yet waterproof fabric. The inverse relationship between distance walked and sartorial fastidiousness meant that I now looked as if I was dressed in a tramp's cast-offs. The new Romanian shirt I'd bought in Sibiu had already lost all its buttons and the crutch of my trousers had unstitched itself so that certain wind conditions produced alarming updraughts.

A crooked ridge of shattered rock crept eastwards, gaining height over subsidiary summits arrayed around the head of a great cirque. Fifty kilometres to the east, the Retezat had suddenly grown larger. My last hurdle before descending into the Balkans seemed uncomfortably close. I wasn't sure that I wanted to leave the Carpathians.

In a blustery wind late in the afternoon we stepped on to the summit of Parîngul Mare at 2,518 metres. Chris shook my hand: 'Congratulations, Mr Crane!' We toasted the Queen and the makers of Macallan's then turned for the valley.

Surf's Out

The mayor of Petroşani had closed the bars and restaurants to prevent the striking miners getting at drink. Instead, they were careering in trucks up and down the main street. In the evening we sat in a darkened back room because the hotel staff were worried that the miners would break in if they saw bottles of beer. The only other guests were seven Romanian journalists covering the strike, and a drunken Irish-American who was researching locations for a 'Balzac movie'.

Chris left by train for Bucharest, having bequeathed me the bottle of Lea & Perrins. The miners choked the town. They moved in grey waves, in overalls and rubber boots, wearing their pudding-basin helmets and headlamps. They had been on strike for one week and were angry. Every few hours they surged to the union headquarters where they were updated on the news from Bucharest by their leader, Miron Cosma, waving a sheaf of papers from the top of the front steps.

There were 40,000 miners in the Jiu valley. Two years earlier they had travelled to Bucharest and forced the resignation of Prime Minister Petre Roman. The year before that, 20,000 of them had rioted in the capital. In living memory, just, the miners of Petroşani had been armed and turned into three battalions of the 144th Infantry Brigade, the unit that held the Merisor pass in 1916 then drove the Romanian Army back down the Jiu towards their eventual destruction on the Danube. The miners understood their own power. On Petroşani's streets the police were out, nervously swinging their batons.

Sorin and his friend Stefan were sitting on a wall in Strada Republicii. They were mining engineers. Stefan, the older of the two, thin and fair-haired, was eager to talk: 'The conditions are very bad. Two hundred miners are killed in the Jiu each year. In my colliery, we lost twenty last year. There are hundreds of injuries.' He paused to nod at a trio of passing miners. 'The roofs collapse, there are fires and floods. I've seen many accidents. Many of the tunnels are just one metre high, so we have to crawl. And now there is a strike, there will be more problems. If the mines are not used, the roofs sink.' He shook his head and added: 'Whenever we return to work after a strike, there are accidents.' The money was not enough said Stefan: 'It takes twenty-five years to save up for a car, and then it's only a Dacia!'

Stefan had managed to get a German passport. His father was a Saxon. In two weeks he would be leaving Petroşani, first for a holiday on the Black Sea, and then to a new life in Essen. He had just handed in his notice at the mine and could not stop grinning. 'If they offered me one million lei,' he laughed, 'I would not go back to the mine.'

Another mass meeting had broken up and as we sat on the wall the grey tide of blank faces drifted by while the sun bled redly on the fogged sky.

Apart from Stefan, who had his ticket out, the only people laughing in Petroşani were the evangelists.

I had met them the day before. They had set up a drum kit and electric guitars on the pavement outside the police station but got no further than their first religious rockabilly number before they were outnumbered by uniforms. Now they reappeared in a hall. James, their Californian leader, was unrepentant: 'We didn't have a chance to talk to them. If they'd listen, they'd learn. We just want to spread the word of the Bible. You know,' he said with a smile of expensive orthodontics, 'I was smoking marijuana three, four times a day. I was *surfing*. Going *nowhere*. Then, one day, I broke and asked Jesus for help. You know *what*?' James was bug-eyed with incredulity: 'I was saved!'

I looked around the hall. A few young people had shown up. 'James, you don't have many miners in here.'

'Not yet. But they're listening. And so is Jesus. Jesus is listening.' He took my arm. 'We're all sinners,' he confided. 'But the only way to redemption is by following Jesus. *He* will show the way.'

I got badly lost trying to get out of Petroşani.

The Marching Camps

Fog shrouded the stilled pit-heads. It was the grey fog of industrial halitosis, of rotting coal and rusting iron, of weeping gaskets and gaseous seepage, insidious, as if every pore of this ravaged valley was voiding effluvium. The deserted gritty road passed silent apartment blocks covered with growths of fungal satellite dishes. In the soft-focus miasma above the roofs, the spoked wheels on the winding sheds stared down like stopped clocks.

The *Generalkarte* sheet called *Targu-Jiu* (a modern sheet, this one, updated in 1918, the year Vienna lost Transylvania to the new Romania) marked Petroşani as Petrozsény and I knew that it was going to land me in trouble the moment I left town. Beyond the pits the valley road became a *drum forestier* that squeezed through a gorge and emerged on sunlit meadows flanked by forested mountains. Women in print shawls carried hay rakes past brooks and grazing cows. I asked a whiskered forester how to reach Sarmizegetusa.

'That will take you a day,' he said. 'But there is a good path. You should take the way, to Dobrei. Past the *stîna* you will see the hill of Comărnicel.'

But I missed the forester's path and rather than retrace my steps I turned up a side valley thinking that I could follow it to its source, then climb upward until I cleared the tree-line and gained the heights of the Sebeş mountains. It was one of those impromptu decisions that are flawless in their logic but doomed by nature's irregularities.

A track took me far enough up the side valley to dissuade me from returning, then it faded away in a gully choked with fallen trees and chest-high scrub. To make progress I had to cut an oblique compass course up the steep valley side through dense forest. The sweat, the barricades of branches and the dragging pack were less of a frustration than the deep injustice of being lured into mistakes which would have been understandable when I was a greenhorn in the Spanish sierras but which had no right to entrap me a year later.

I gave up with the compass bearing and followed the steepest angle of the mountainside, knowing that this would take me most directly to a ridge-line where the going would be easier. The thread of an old shepherd's path followed the spur to the wreckage of a log-cabin and a dock-covered *strungă*. A final fight, on hands and knees beneath matted trees, took me up to open moorland on the Dobrei ridge. Giant cairns stood on the knuckles of higher ground along the ridge-crest, wayfarers' beacons on one of the oldest routes across the Sebeş.

Where the route up from Dobrei met the main ridge a tiny shack stood alone on a smooth green dome. Gligor was washing out his *mămăligă* cauldron at the spring. He wore the pointed hat of the Sibiu shepherds and his face was seared by the sun. 'Where are you from?' he asked.

'England. And you?'

'Loman.'

Loman was a village on the northern side of the Sebeş, a fifty-kilometre walk away. Gligor spent the summer up here with one other shepherd. They had 1,500 sheep. The unusually high ratio of sheep to shepherds was explained when Gligor added that these were for breeding, not milk. Without the weed-infested wounds of old pens, and the mud-patch of the working *strungă*, the crooked fence and milking paraphernalia of a *stîna*, the camp had a surreal simplicity. Twenty minutes after leaving him, I could still see Gligor, a pin-figure beside his black matchbox on the flawless lens of the down.

The open slope rose to Comărnicel at a little under 2,000 metres. Lusius Quietus had come this way with his bare-footed Moors, galloping on single-bridled horses across the hard turf to attack Sarmizegetusa from the rear. On Comărnicel, the Romans threw up three marching camps. West of here there was no higher ground in the Sebeş. They could look down upon the Dacians, waiting for Trajan's main force to fight its way up the valley of the Apa Gradistei. Beyond the earthworks I skirted the dark pine-clad flank of Vîrf Neagru – the Black Peak – passing ancient mine workings and following blocks of white rock that marked the way.

The high ground of Sebeş was covered with sheep, vectoring like clusters of iron filings drawn by an unseen magnet and guarded by packs of dogs that harried me from cover to cover. At dusk I slipped off the ridge and found a spring on a spur that was carpeted with wild raspberries. Facing me across a deep valley were the forested ruckles of the Dacian heartland.

Sarmizegetusas One and Two

'It is possible that they were practising human sacrifice . . .' said Professor Ion Glodariu, handing me a coffee. 'That would explain why the Romans dismantled the site. It's one of the few places in the west where they didn't tolerate the local religion.'

Glodariu's pinched skin and spectacles were those of a man who has spent a lot of hot summers staring intently into sieves. We were sitting at a makeshift table in the shade, on the edge of the great sanctuary at Sarmizegetusa. Here, in the secret valleys and beech-clad peaks of the Sebeş, the last of the barbarians fell before the civilizing might of Rome. The great extinction was complete. From Cape Finisterre to the Carpathians the noble savage had been brought indoors. After the summer of AD 106, no corner of the continent lay beyond the reach of a single superpower. We knew what the Dacians felt when the silo technicians began punching in the coordinates of every city and military site between Rosyth and Akrotiri. The idea of a sanctuary has become rather quaint.

The professor was camping at the dig for the summer with a group of colleagues from the University of Cluj. He inherited the job from his old tutor, Professor Constantin Daicoviciu, whose work here began before the Second World War. He turned to the young man at the end of the table and said: 'Gelu, you could show the Englishman the site . . .'

Gelu Florea was working on his doctorate on Dacian art. The man-made plateau on which we stood had been cut into the side of the hill a short way below the summit. Three of the sanctuaries on the plateau took the form of grids of column bases recurring in multiples of six; two of sixty plinths and one of eighteen. On the lower terrace was a sanctuary twenty metres in diameter, a circle of blocks arranged in sets of six, repeated thirty times. Inside this, the archaeologists had erected wooden posts to represent an inner circle and within that a horseshoe-shaped sanctum. Off to one side of the plateau lay the seven-metre circular altar.

Gelu looked down at it. 'We call it the Andesite Sun, because it has ten segments divided by lines which could be rays. It's a solar clock.' He pointed to a stone channel angling away from the base of the sun, and smiled wryly: 'This is what causes the rumour. The speculation. The canal is to drain a liquid from the altar. But was the liquid water? Or was it blood?'

Below the sanctuaries were another 200 terraces. 'That is where the civilians lived. Professor Glodariu estimates the population to have been 3,500 people.' Among the calcined seeds picked up on these terraces were those of poppies and hibiscus, rape and mustard, beans, lentils and spinach, rye, barley, wheat and millet. 'It was,' added Gelu, 'a sophisticated civilization. A coin-minting workshop was found here, and some of the limestone blocks are marked with Greek characters, which shows that Greek engineers worked here. And we have found a forge which has tools practically identical to those of the contemporary Greeks and Romans.'

Among the 400 or so iron tools unearthed were weapons and wagon components, keys, barrel hoops, spurs and one of the oldest sets of crampons ever found, used by the Dacians for reaching their citadels when the tracks were icy.

From the sanctuary plateau a ramp led up through the beeches to the crest of the hill. Here an uneven rectangle of walls enclosed over seven acres which was once occupied by log-huts. This was the final refuge, shown on Trajan's Column in Rome being assaulted by auxiliary infantrymen with ladders under the covering fire of slingers who have driven the Dacians back from the crenellated parapet which rose above the surviving walls. A Dacian is seen falling from the walls, the Romans hack down trees to build new siege machines; a breach is made. Those Dacians still in the town below torch their buildings and the fire spreads to the crops whose seeds will lie for 1,900 years until they are collected by the archaeologists of Cluj.

On Trajan's Column, Sarmizegetusa's final moments are ambiguous. Dacian warriors are seen drinking from a communal pot. They would certainly have been short of water. But they may have been drinking poison. Their king, Decebalus, fled northwards through the Sebeş. It was autumn. The days were growing shorter. Unwilling to let Decebalus escape into the long nights of winter, Trajan ordered his legionaries to hack a road through the forests of the Sebeş, defended by camps and covered by trusted troops. On the column, three Dacian chiefs are seen kneeling before Trajan. One of these three may be Bicilis, identified by Dio Cassius (not admittedly the most rigorous historian) to have been the man who betrayed the hiding place of Decebalus' treasure. Decebalus had ordered a group of his prisoners to divert the course of the Apa Gradistei and then excavate a pit in its dried bed, into which was piled the gold and silver of Sarmizegetusa. Having filled in the pit with stones and silt, he then had the dam removed, thus bringing the Gradistei back to its original course. Other perishable treasures such as the royal robes were hidden in caves.

To the north, cohorts of auxiliaries were crossing a temporary bridge that the Romans had flung across the Mures. In what may have been a final attempt to contain the invaders south of the Mures, Decebalus threw his warriors at the Roman camps. In a desperate defence of a camp being used to build barges for a more permanent Mures bridge, the three auxiliary cohorts ran out of ammunition and hurled stone blocks at their assailants. Watching this final assault from a forested hill, Decebalus saw the survivors beaten back. Some regrouped in the forest. Others turned to Zamolxis and were killed by their comrades. A few surrendered to Trajan, bearing gifts.

Decebalus and a few die-hards took to their horses and were pursued by cavalry and mounted infantry. The final scene in the Dacian tragedy is described on the tombstone of Tiberius Claudius Maximus, unearthed in Macedonia in 1965. The helmeted legionary, wielding spears and sword on a horse rampant, looks down on a fallen Decebalus, from whose hand falls a battle scythe. Rather than face capture Decebalus had cut his own throat. Maximus severed the head and delivered it to Trajan's camp at Ranisstorum, from where it was eventually dispatched, far from fresh, to Rome.

To this day the echoes of Dacians and Romans reverberate across the heights of Transylvania. Walking down the valley of the Apa Gradistei, I passed other eerie citadels, once Dacian, now memorials: Blidaru, above a 350-metre climb up a track whose bedrock still carries the scars of chariot wheels; Costesti, whose tower house (thought to have been the residence of Dacian kings) was approached by a magnificent flight of stone steps. (One of the friezes on Trajan's Column shows legionaries advancing up such a flight of steps, bowed beneath the *testudo*, the armoured tortoise shell of shields concealing sharpened *gladii*).

Leaving the Sebeş I walked over burnt hills to Hunedoara, where the battle between the forces of civilization and barbarism were still being fought: in the centre of this town, the fabulous castle is locked in mortal combat with a besieging force of steel mills. In the castle is the ghost of its White Knight, Janos Hunyadi, the Hungarian nobleman who turned back the Turk and won himself a legendary place in medieval Christian folklore. The Communists of the Conducator, Nicolae Ceauşescu, against whose interest it was to promote Hungarian symbols, particularly those in the heart of old Dacia, omitted all reference to the castle, to Hungary and to Hunyadi in the town's tourist brochure; the Conducator's brother, Lieutenant-General Dr Ilie Ceauşescu, wrote a 'history' called *Transylvania: An Ancient Romanian Land*, in which Hunyadi became a Transylvanian freedom fighter called John of Hunedoara, whose armies were fighting for 'Romanian unity' – which is rather like claiming that Eisenhower fought the Second World War on behalf of Texan separatists. The Communists erected the steel mills against the castle walls, upwind, where their chimneys poured ferric fog upon Hunyadi's battlements. The battlements and towers – and indeed the whole town – were thick with dust the colour of dried blood.

Romania's rulers wanted to believe that they were at the apogee of an illustrious lineage which had absorbed both the noble Dacian and the civilized Roman. That young men called Octavian still drive their Dacia cars down to the Restaurant Dacia in Decebal Street obscures the fact that – deep within the roots debate – the Romans and Dacians are still struggling for ascendancy. Pitted against Glodariu's archaeologists at Sarmizegetusa, were those of Colonia Ulpia Traiana Augusta Dacica Sarmizegetusa, the provincial capital established by the Romans close to the sacked Dacian capital, absorbing its name to confer a sense of continuity. The ruins were a day's march south of Hunedoara.

The city had been built on a beautiful site. Behind its walls rose the blue summits of the Retezat mountains. In front, the land sloped towards the soft bowl of Haţeg. A population of 50,000 lived in and around an eighty-acre rectangle of five-metre walls. Temples, baths and shops served the city and the traffic passing by on the Roman road to the Iron Gates. The amphitheatre seated 5,000.

When I arrived the forum looked like a quarry covered in ants. Men bent and scurried to and fro across a chaos of pits and trenches. Wheelbarrows teetered along planks. Young men picked at the mud with the tips of trowels. A knot had gathered, heads down, in a hole before a mountain of rubble. Among the men in the hole were Professor Ioan Piso and Professor Alexandru Diaconescu. Piso could not stop grinning: 'I have worked on this site for twenty years and this is the best year we have ever had.' He led me to a line of four inscribed blocks that were still sticky with mud. 'These are the most important things we've found. We found them this week.' He laid his hand on one of the blocks, running his fingers over a series of letters spelling DACICIA: 'This is the inscription that attests to the foundation of the town under Trajan. Unfortunately one piece is missing. The piece with the date.' Piso pointed to an immense Corinthian capital lying on its side: 'Also this week we found that.' The acanthus were as crisp as the day they were carved, protected through the centuries by soft earth.

Piso prowled his excavations with a proprietorial concentration, stopping to question a workman, to peer into a trench, to order the moving of the rubble mountain so that the corner of the forum could be dug. With his fourteen students from Cluj, Piso had employed another forty local workers. The contrast with Professor Glodariu's isolated labours fifty kilometres away in the Sebeş could not have been more striking.

When the Socialists fell, they took the Dacians with them. In the new order, the Romans were no longer exploitative invaders but the bearers of all that was best about Romanian culture. 'We do not speak of the Roman "occupation", but of the Roman "administration",' Piso told me one evening. 'The Turks were occupiers. The Russians were occupiers. But the Romans came here to work. People who are building the Dacian myth are ignoring the facts. The Romans who made this colony were the ancestors of all Romanians. This city is our birth certificate.'

Dacia was the last of the provinces acquired by the Roman Empire and it was the first to go. Only 165 years after Decebalus fled his citadel, the Romans packed up and left. After the withdrawal in AD 271 the natives clung to the old Roman capital, walling up the amphitheatre entrances to create an emergency fort. Sacked by the Huns, Ulpia Traiana was left to the weeds for 1,000 years, till the house- and church-builders of the last two centuries plundered the ruins for building material. Irregular-shaped pieces of marble such as statues were broken then crushed and burnt for use as house-paint.

I stayed two nights, sleeping with the students in the archaeologists' house in the village. On the first night an asteroid shower entered the atmosphere and I dreamed that I was standing before Trajan's statue in the forum. Beneath a bruised and weeping sky water was coursing down the emperor's cold cheeks and off the muscled rump of his horse. The forum was deserted but for the statues and the glistening flags. The rivers of rain running off Dacian gold and glistening marble against the black Carpathians stayed with me for days.

From dawn, the atmosphere was tense with excitement. Every day finds were coming to light. Over dinner a small bronze spatula circled the table, dropped by a chemist or a surgeon perhaps, treating the wounded from the battle with the Dacian rearguard below Blidaru. What the diggers really wanted were inscriptions. Inscriptions gave names and dates. They filled in the blanks; developed the argument.

Walking the shifting borders of eastern Europe I had become used to neighbourly antipathy but I'd not been to a country whose identity, cohesion and self-esteem depended upon the interpretation of fragments from a lost world. In Romania, historians are more important than generals.

The Retezat Mountains

With a pair of warm loaves wedged under my rucksack flap I followed the muddy lane through the old Colonia and out through the gap in the tall bank towards the peaks of the Retezat. As my paths rose above the Haţeg basin the patterns of hay-stooks and squares of corn stubble and swathes of green maize fell below. The night was surprisingly cold and I was reminded that Ioan Piso had declared that summer had ended on 6 August; the 'Changing of Face' he had called it. Images of the long autumn in the abandoned lands of Languedoc and the Cévennes began to repeat themselves. The Retezat would be my last encounter with the Carpathians. When I walked down to the Iron Gates on the far side of the range, the journey would enter its final chapter.

I left the mountain hut at sunrise, climbing slowly through dark spruce which thinned to dwarf pine then opened to a bare cirque. I could have been in the Pyrenees. Crystal brooks chuckled between cropped grass and warm rock, girdled by a vast amphitheatre dominated by 2,509-metre Peleaga, the highest peak in the range.

Blue-painted dashes led steeply up to the Curmătura Bucarei, the rocky col that marked the Retezat's main watershed. Behind me, the Sibişel fell away into the haze of the Haţeg basin. Ahead the south side of the col plummeted to the blue lagoon of Lacul Bucara, a glacial lake suspended in air behind the rock dam of its outflow lip. Rather than descend to the lake immediately, I turned left up the splintered ridge towards Peleaga and converged on the summit with young Romanians coming up from the far side.

We gazed down at the blue tarns in the ice-puckered valleys. Five hundred metres below us, the rocky terrain had split up a flock of sheep so that they moved in white winding termite columns. Off to the west I could see the declining ridges, fading into the haze above the Iron Gates. To the south, the sheer-sided trench of the Lăpuşinic cut a black gash once filled by a glacier that had wrapped its tail around the flanks of the range.

I took an unorthodox scramble from Peleaga's summit into the hidden valley that fed Bucara. Above the lake stood a wooden mountain rescue cabin painted with a red cross and surrounded by twenty or so young men and women. Most were wearing yellow T-shirts printed with the slogan 'Pro Natura'. They came from Bucharest University. Their spokesperson was a blond boy with a pony-tail who was studying cybernetics.

'We are cleaning the Retezat,' explained Lazar. 'In the last three summers we have collected forty tons of rubbish, and we are carrying this rubbish down to the valley.'

'Carrying forty tons?'

'Yes. We have rucksacks . . .'

They had collected the garbage from the lake beds and the shores.

'How do you pick up the garbage from under the water?'

'We swim.'

Later in the afternoon, when I had come down beside the cascades in the V-shaped notch below Lacul Bucara to the Lăpuşinic valley, I found the portaged garbage by the road-head. A monumental mountain of twinkling tin and glass recorded the voluntary labours of a bunch of students.

A footpath cut to and fro up the far side of the Lăpuşinic's wall, bringing me out on to the grassy saddle of Saua Plaiul Mic in the late afternoon sun. Two crescentic dewponds acted as a perfect foreground to the panorama of Retezat peaks, bunched to the north, on the far side of the Lăpuşinic. In the softening light the day's tail-enders made their way slowly down the track towards the Cabană Buta.

The ridge undulated into the evening. Peleaga and the Retezat slipped behind. Ahead rose the cleft peak of Piatra Iorgovanului, split by the sword of Iorgo Iorgovanului, the dragon-slayer. I was back on limestone and in the gathering dusk it was getting difficult to decipher the rugged landscape. Valleys were dry and the stone lay on the grass like splintered bone. I was resigning myself to a thirsty bivouac when, on the saddle beneath Piatra Iorgovanului, I saw rising smoke. On the edge of the cliffs stood an oval shepherd's shelter built from limestone rocks and roofed with spruce branches. Outside the hut a cauldron bubbled on a fire. The shepherd was a wild character wearing one of the domed black hats I'd seen in the Cindrel. With him were two Romanian hikers from Timişoara and two young Germans from Karlsruhe.

One of the Romanian boys asked where I'd started from that morning.

'Cabană Pietrele.'

The Romanians slapped my back with incredulous cries: 'Impossible! Fantastic!'

Shamelessly, I added: 'Actually I started walking in Spain!'

Their hysterical laughter rang off the rocks. Eventually one of them spluttered: 'You are young and strong!'

'No, I'm old and tired . . .'

The following day I had a long hot forty-kilometre hike, losing height down the spine of a ridge whose most prominent point was called Beautiful Peak. Underfoot, the beech leaves had been pounded to dust by a season of hoofs, and the grass combed by descending flocks. Summer felt burnt out. Bells called faintly on the breeze.

The August Fair

Smoke from a hundred fires wreathed the trees along the river bank below Tismana's fourteenth-century monastery. Every square metre of ground was occupied by sleeping children, parked hay-carts and cars, horses, boxes of provisions and ember piles of the camp-fires. The smoke sat heavy in the valley, loaded down with dew and the sweet weight of grilled *mititei* – the mouth-sized meatballs that constitute Romania's national snack.

On 15 August Romania's oldest monastery becomes the spiritual focus for Tismana's annual fair. All morning the human crocodile crept up the narrow valley from the Wallachian plain. Among the buses and bicycles, the creaking carts and smoking motorbikes, were families on foot, on tractors and in one case crammed into the cab of a cement-truck.

Mass in the monastery courtyard was followed by an exodus to a wide *poiana* above the village. A ten-piece Mexican band wearing gobstopper baubles on their calves and sombreros as big as cartwheels hooted brassily from a stage that had been erected against the edge of the forest. In my naïvety I had expected flocks of peasants wearing embroidered heirlooms, roving flautists and a bear-tamer or two. But this was closer to a British car-boot sale: the scorched grass of the *poiana* was occupied by rows of low-quality mass-produced domestic consumables: acrylic jumpers, aluminium cauldrons, Beatles tapes (counterfeit), bicycle inner tubes, bikinis, brake linings, brassières, bubble-gum, 'California' baseball caps, fishing-rods, flick-knives, fly swats, 'Malibu' T-shirts, oil paintings of nudes, ping-pong balls, pink plastic dustpans, rubber mice, scythe blades, shock absorbers, Snagov cigarettes, vodka . . .

Sentimentality for times past comes easy to those who do not have to live there. But no amount of rationalizing could lift my spirits; these August fairs used to act as showcases for local craftsmen as much as markets for the travelling salesmen. Gypsies pitched camp and hawked trinkets and wooden objects such as hay-forks, cradles, wash-tubs, spoons and mule saddles. Potters sold bird-shaped jugs and fruit bowls in burnt sienna and green. Women sold carded wool, or wove it with gold and silver thread. There were local carpets and gingerbread sweets and fruit drinks sold by Turkish itinerants. Leather-workers sold whip thongs and waistcoats; tinkers re-tinned copper pots over improvised hearths; oxen were shoed. Skills were worn in public. They sat behind their work, to be judged. Even the entertainments were personalized. Children could queue to watch the fat woman, couples could stand for the one-minute photographer, have fortunes told or play cock-shy. There would sometimes be a merry-go-round, made of wood and revolved by five men to the music of a fiddle band.

I spent the day at the fair. As dusk and depression crept up, my arm was grabbed by an old man wearing thick spectacles. 'Give me back my money!'

'Eh?'

'You stole my money!' He turned to the crowd: 'The foreigner stole my money!'

'I didn't.'

'Let me see. Show me your pockets!' The crowd gathered round.

I pulled out my two trouser pockets. Both were full of holes and empty. I said: 'I have nothing.'

The old man was patting his own pockets, unable to believe that he had been robbed. The crowd were staring at me. Suspicious glares focused on my forester's hat, scuffed boots and sun-bleached threadbare clothes.

Unconvincingly, I said: 'I'm a tourist.'

The crowd parted in silence and I walked across the field into the woods.

At the Iron Gates

Piston rods and cross-heads pumped and sweated, valves sighed and steam spurted. The train was double headed. Up in the billowing cloud a blue arm waved down at me and for a moment I saw the grinning engineer, cap tilted, hand shutting down the cylinder drain-cocks. The two engines gathered themselves for a final effort and, with a calamitous groan and a series of shrieks which might have been whistles or rending steel, they pulled their interminable cargo from the trees on to the plain. Lashed to rusting trucks were hundreds of glorious beeches.

I walked all day, back into the tail-end of the Carpathians, until the bitumen finished and a white dust road spiralled up the limestone of Godeanu. By nightfall I was back above the thousand-metre contour, sitting on a rock staring down the Cerna's cliffs into the dark watercourse that Patrick Leigh Fermor had tramped along in August 1934. In *Between the Woods and the Water*, he had turned the Cerna, with its smoking trouty waters, darting redstarts and mossy shadows, into a Carparthain Eden.

In the morning I followed the white switchbacks down the cliff to the dirt road that ran beside the Cerna. No sign of PLF's path remained. There is never any pleasure in following the bulldozer's blade. The twists and dips that footways make to find the line of least resistance have a riverine sympathy with the land. They cannot be travelled without feeling the forces of water and ice, or fault or fire. Only Romans and bulldozers can make a road dull.

The dispirited Cerna, shrunken by the long summer, eventually poured into a massive reservoir that spread between the valley's cliffs, smothering PLF's waterfalls in alluvial silt. The bland face of the dam gagged the valley. It was as if the cement-mixers had just been tipped over the watershed until the Cerna choked.

The road plummeted to bathing pools where shoals of children splashed and writhed around the waists of mothers with sunburnt bosoms. The men sat on the concrete verges of the pools, cuddling their stomachs as if they were life preservers. I descended past woods speckled with parked cars and tents to Băile Herculane. After the withdrawal in 271, the legionaries stayed on a while here, as reluctant to leave their thermae as the British have been to leave their last colonial beaches. The bubbling springs remained a local secret until the eighteenth century when reports of the waters reached foreign capitals. That sad Habsburg, Joseph II, who so irritated his mother by visiting the subversive Frenchman Jean-Jacques Rousseau, delayed a return to pox-ridden Vienna by a visit to Băile Herculane. A century of neglect was followed by the same boom that put Vernet-les-Bains on the map. PLF came just in time. I was too late.

The stucco was still there. So was lion-pelted Hercules, shouldering his club above the parked Dacias. One of the hotel dining-rooms had been turned into a canteen. For 540 lei, half the cost of a cup of tea in London, I was able to buy vulcanized steak and liver, with cold rice and a tepid slime of puréed aubergine and pepper. I searched in vain for high society. Even low society had given Băile Herculane a miss. The only signs of life were ponderous men in track suits steering their stomachs past the flower beds with the gravitas of super-tanker helmsmen.

The casino was locked. It sat – as it had when PLF had danced through a summer night to *Couchés dans le foin* – against a theatrical backdrop of tree crowns and cliffs. Cherubs cavorted above its arches, playing *Dudelsack* and tambourine. Its loggia shone in amber light, a sad half-tone of happier times. A poster on the window advertised the season's films; CHAPLIN ... PROSTITUATĂ ... ALIENS ... BĂTĂLIE DISPERATĂ ... COMMANDO ...

It can't get worse, I thought. I was wrong.

An old woman in white ankle socks was sweeping the casino terrace with a broom of twigs when I left for the Iron Gates. A short way downstream, the Cerna swung south and was joined by the highway and railway that rush down from the Porta Orientalis bound for the Balkans.

I walked on the verge, buffeted by trucks and startled by the roars of freight trains careering along the embankment beside my head. I stopped at a truck drivers' snack-stop advertising 'TURC' food.

'I'll have a plate of Turkish food, please,' I said to the fat woman.

'We have no Turkish food.'

'What do you have?'

'Kotlet . . .'

'OK. I'll have cutlet.'

Ten minutes later, when the anticipatory juices had eaten through my stomach wall and I was still staring at an empty table, I walked through to the kitchen and asked about the cutlet. The fat woman stuffed a last morsel of meat into her mouth, swallowed and grunted: 'The *kotlet* is finished.'

The Danube crept into sight sooner than it should have done. When the great river was dammed the flood-level covered the water meadows at the mouth of the Cerna. I emerged from the Carpathians on the hard shoulder of an international highway.

Below me stretched a silver inland sea, hemmed by steep black forest. The Iron Gates, once one of Europe's greatest natural wonders, were as unimpressive as a Welsh reservoir. Flotillas of Danube barges grew rusty off Orsova. Where the river traffic of Europe had diced with rapids, a single UN patrol boat drifted on the guileless gulf, watching for Serbian gun-runners. An inferno of heat shimmered on the black-top. The post holes that had supported Trajan's wooden walkway along the gorge's cliffs were underwater. Ada Kaleh, the Turkish island fortress under whose minaret PLF had spread his greatcoat, was under-water. The only reminder of this fabled rock, visited by the Argonauts and colonized by forgotten Ottomans, was the Ada Kaleh picnic site, a shelf of weed-engulfed concrete overlooking the railway and the blank lake.

All day I walked down the gorge on the road's hard shoulder. At the sign pointing across the dam to Belgrade, I stopped; I had always meant to cross the dam to Serbia, so that I could follow the natural curve of my mountain route down past Justinian's ramparts at Zajecar, to the Stara Planina. I loitered for an hour, watching the surly border police make trouble for the few travellers miserably backed up at the barrier. On the far bank Serbia looked innocent enough. But that is the nature of war zones: there's either nothing happening, or too much. One of the motor-ists lost his temper when another jumped the queue, and then engaged the overtaker in a perfunctory fist-fight. I just could not face it. I turned away and walked south instead, along the riverside, until the mountains fell away and I was standing on the edge of the plain.

I walked into Turnu Severin late in the afternoon with my sweaty rucksack glued to my back and took a room at the Hotel Parc, a monumental concrete block in the town centre, facing statues of Trajan and Decebal on one side, and the Danube on the other.

The telephone in the room did not work, so I had to rely on the telephonist on the ground floor to make the connection to London. Once an hour, I was fetched down to reception (whose catatonic staff were invariably watching the same James Bond video, rendered through some malfunction in tones of green, as if the film had been shot in a bath of algae) and handed a telephone just in time to hear the line go dead. The fourth time this happened, I returned to my room to find that the door key no longer worked. Weary exhortations produced a handyman and his assistant technician, who unscrewed the light bulb from the far end of the corridor (Romanian hotel corridors have one bulb, which is moved as required) and twisted it into the fitting opposite my door. While they beat at the door with a hammer and chisel, I sat on the corridor floor reading the tourist brochure I'd picked up in the foyer. The town's wealth, I learned, had been founded by 'a numerous and well-organized proletariat, who actively participated in and bravely led the masses in their struggle against social injustice'.

Finally the door splintered. I asked to be resettled in a room with a working door.

'It's a good door!' said the handyman as he showed me the new room.

I lifted the cover of the cistern. 'What about the lavatory?'

'Oh, that's broken,' he said, and left.

Nearly 2,000 years earlier, the view from the site of Hotel Parc would have embraced the continent's greatest feat of engineering: the twenty-one-arched timber bridge, 1,134 metres long and fourteen metres wide, built by Apollodorus of Damascus across the cataracts of the Iron Gates. Engineering – and bridge-building – have not served the Iron Gates well.

Eventually a line was opened between Hotel Parc and north London. Annabel was out, but she had left a message on the answering machine: 'Sorry to have missed you ... I'll see you in Sofia on the weekend of the 27th.'

The Balkan Ranges

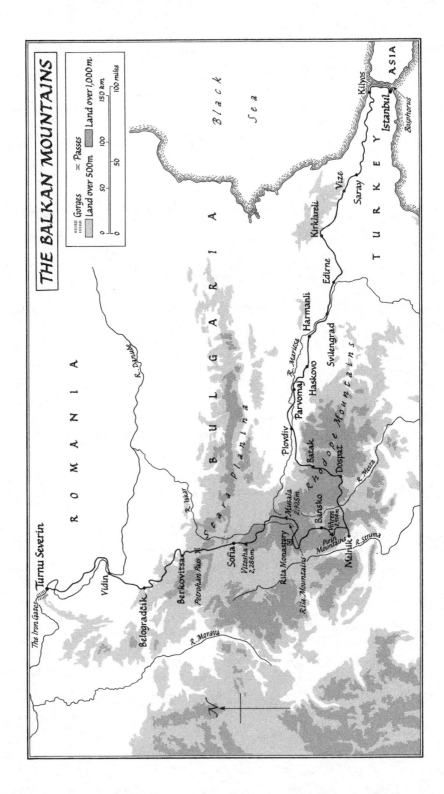

THE BALKAN MOUNTAINS

By the Danube

In turning away from the dam I had condemned myself for the first time to an assisted river-crossing: there were no bridges over the Danube between the Iron Gates and Ruse, 500 kilometres downstream. I would now have to cross the river on a ferry, two days to the south, at Calafat. I left Turnu Severin before sunrise, chewing a cheese doughnut I'd bought behind the Decebalus department store. Initially, the Calafat road followed the bank of the river, black like an equatorial lake and smelling faintly of mildew. Too quickly the sun rose and seared away the shadows. On the far bank, Serbia looked flattish and rustic, like Suffolk in a heatwave. There were few trees for shade and they made lonely companions to the watch-towers erected to deter escapees across the old Iron Curtain. Now the towers were manned by soldiers watching for smugglers. There was only the road to walk along; below the road, fishing nets dried on rocks and upturned punts basked in the sun. Flocks of birds overtook me, migrating downstream. I was unused to the flatness, and the heat. And the low altitude. And the riparian listlessness. Not since leaving the Basque coast had I dropped below one hundred metres above sea level. For a while I fell in step with a pair of creaking ox-carts and when I looked up there were fishermen balanced on drowned trees out in the river. The suffocating heat and the groan of the wooden axles and the still silhouettes balanced above the greasy hotplate of water were more Gangetic than Danubian.

I left the river where it made a U-turn to the west, cutting off as it did so a perfect ox-bow lake. The road snaked steeply up through oak woods until it hung 200 metres above the river's dry bend. Pushing into the woods along the top of the old river cliff I came on a row of deep gun-pits, leftovers from the Second World War. From the bluff they had a clear sight-line up both banks of the Danube to the Iron Gates. A German column had been attacked in these woods shortly after that extraordinary day in August 1944 when Romania changed sides and captured

53,159 German soldiers who suddenly found themselves on enemy territory.

Beyond the wood the road turned into the sun and hovered for a moment before plunging into the furnace of the Blahniţa marshes. I tottered south all afternoon, rehydrating on tumblers of chilled *suc* and a beverage peculiar to Wallachian bars called 'New York Love Cola'. 'From Yugoslavia,' I was told. I could have asked them about the escapes across the Danube; about the giant sturgeon which used to lurk in the Danube's depths; about Basarabi, a village name which ought to have been on the Prut on the far side of the Carpathians. But I was out of sorts with this landscape, and withdrew into my own concerns: would I find Annabel ready for another separation? Why was I carrying a ski-stick through a desert? Where was Que Chova? Would my worn-out boots last till Sofia? How far to the next drink, the next food?

A truck hurtled by, loaded with sheep for the *souvláki* grills of Thessaloniki and then, in a sick truckers' joke, I was crushed to the verge minutes later by a reciprocating cargo of sheepskins. The skins had been loaded facing forward, and as the back of the truck shrank on the long straight road, the sheep's tails waved in the slipstream like a crowd of tiny blackened arms.

I walked into the night and fell asleep in the early hours, fully clothed, in a field, rising after little more than a nap and resuming the march in the cool almost impenetrable blackness. Unlit carts clip-clopped through the night and then at first light the trucks started, blasting past in twos and threes in walls of wind and dust. There were cars too, and these also travelled in convoys, never stopping. The barmen said they were scared of being robbed. Now that the main road down the Sava was part of a battlefield, this was one of the quickest land routes from western Europe to Istanbul, provided you didn't get stuck at Calafat. And, they said, Calafat was a nightmare.

Two men making mud bricks called me off the road. They chatted about their work while I peeled off my rucksack and slumped under a tree. The sight of others engaged in hard physical labour was always a restorative, not just as evidence that 'knackeredness' is universal but because most repetitive manual tasks have a hypnotic efficiency that imbues the spectator with a sense of calm pleasure. Workmen lean on spades not because they're lazy but because the leaning and watching is in itself fulfilling. The brick-making was at the complicated end of the labouring spectrum. The men had excavated a trench in the field, in which they had mixed mud, straw and water to the consistency and colour of peanut butter. The younger of the two wetted the inside of two compartments in a frame and the older man used a trowel to fill the compartments with the mixture. The frame was lifted off to reveal two shining bricks.

'We'll leave them for four days to dry,' grinned the old man, showing a mouthful of silver and gold. 'Then they'll be as strong as stone.'

I met the Danube again at the next village, Cetate, which had been built along the lip of a fifty-metre river cliff. Now the military watchtowers glared across the water at Bulgaria, not Romania. As I passed beneath one of them, the soldiers spotted me and called down. I hesitated, imagining in my frazzled condition that I was about to be apprehended by bored boy-soldiers, then I realized that the voice was hailing a passing cart and telling its driver to give me a lift. We walked together for fifteen minutes, while I explained that I was unable to travel in carts.

'It's your religion?' asked the stubbled farmer.

'Yes,' I said.

He tickled his horse's rump and trotted on, calling over his shoulder: 'Liverpool! ... Manchester United! ... Peter Shilton! ... Tottenham Ospers! ...'

Under the hot flat sky monotony was held in check by oases of pleasure: I lunched in a village called Maglovit, sitting in the shade of the Orthodox church beside an extraordinary well whose winding gear looked as if it had been borrowed from a steam-engine. The axle was fitted with two gigantic iron flywheels and steel roller-bearings. The descent of the bucket was controlled by a foot-pedal tensioned by a massive leaf-spring. The minimal friction of the bearings meant that the weight of the empty bucket was sufficient to send it plummeting on its steel cable. To raise the bucket, a few sharp revolutions were enough to generate momentum in the flywheels, which then brought the water flying to the surface. I was admiring this imaginative device when a young man arrived with the key to the church. One by one, he threw a set of electrical switches. Tiny lamps began to appear on the iconostasis, inside the censers, on the foreheads of the saints and finally (and for this, he threw the switch as if swinging champagne at the bow of a new ship) the crucifix, which became entirely outlined in bright red lights.

Beyond Maglovit my road joined the highway from Bucharest for the final fifteen kilometres along a burning strip of bitumen to Calafat.

The town was built on a slope down to the river. Forty or so trucks waited to take the ferry across to Vidin, on the Bulgarian bank. Hundreds of cars simmered up and down the streets, their passengers lolling blankly on broken pavements. A Dutchman with an Alsatian dog ('It is to stop the robbers . . .') said that he had been waiting for two days. 'And some have been here *six* days!' he added. 'It is terrible. There are no lavatories. And the locals overcharge for food and drink.'

A Frenchman had been thrown in jail for trying to prevent cars jumping the queue at night. 'It is criminal,' explained the Dutchman. 'They pay a bribe and once it is dark, they sneak to the front of the queue.'

I followed the snake of scalding metal down through town to the Romanian customs, where my woodsman's hat aroused so much mirth that I had to model it for each officer, to accompanying cries of 'Eh! *Pădurar!* Forester! Over here!' News that an Englishman had arrived on foot from Bukovina spread across the dock and I was escorted with great dignity past suicidal motorists to the concrete slip.

The curiosity tingling my gut as I walked up the ferry ramp was quickly subdued by an altercation with a uniformed woman who demanded three dollars for the crossing, many times more than the 1,000 lei rate for locals.

The piratical ferry crew gathered around me. 'Let him pay the thousand!' said one.

'He's English,' said another.

'If he's walked from Bukovina, he's a guest of all Romanians!'

The uniformed woman backed away holding her thousand lei.

I never did see the Danube. Dan, Vasile, Marius, Tibi, Christi and Liviu led me below decks to a cabin where we toasted Peter Shilton and a score of English footballers I'd no idea existed.

'Do you have Bulgarian money?' asked Dan.

'Not yet. I'll get some.'

'No need. Take this.' He pulled a handful of leva from beneath the table and pressed it into my palm. 'A present from Romania. So that you don't forget.'

Into the Balkans

The stones of the old riverside fortress of Baba Vida tell most of Vidin's story: seventeenth-century Turkish battlements sit upon tenth- to fourteenth-century Bulgarian walls which were erected on the site of third-century Roman Bononia, chosen to replace the third-century BC Celtic settlement of Dunonia. The town's role as a strategic bridgehead has caused it to be overrun with seasonal regularity.

'What do you know of my country?' asked the businessman over dinner.

'That Bulgaria makes poisoned umbrellas.'

'I know . . .' he muttered, 'I know about the umbrella, the dangerous umbrella.' The big man looked momentarily tearful, then picked himself up: 'You know I did not leave my country. I did *not* leave. And do you know why? Because I love my country!' He paused for breath and repeated in a barely controlled mezzo-forte: '*I . . . love . . . my . . . country!*'

He was in salt. 'I've had a bad day, you know. This business person in Bucharest telephoned me in my office in Sofia and said, "Nicu! I have salt! You want salt?" So I said "OK" and I drive to Vidin, take the ferry to Calafat, pay a taxi 150 dollars to take me to Bucharest, then the business person says, "Sorry no salt!" So I pay the taxi 150 dollars to come back to Calafat. The Romanians are crazy!'

The businessman pointed from the terrace table to the firefly lights on the far side of the inky river. 'I'll tell you another bad joke. The taxi driver . . . I look at the taxi driver and I say to myself I know this man! You know who he was? He was a Romanian customs officer. Very crazy world.'

I'd eaten well on *sireneh po shopski*, a hot-pot of white cheese with chopped tomatoes, paprika and egg halves, baked in an earthenware pot. Vidin was bursting with food I'd not seen for months. Bulgaria, it seemed, was in better economic condition than Romania. There was even hot and cold water in my hotel room.

I left town in the pre-dawn darkness two days later, out through the Stambul Kapiya, the Istanbul Gate and into the Balkans. I took the road for Sofia, walking beside the red disc of the rising sun, then turned into the hills. By dusk I was in whispering oak woods which parted unexpectedly to create windows up to the grey peaks on the Serbian border.

In a repetition of the morning, I ran out of water again, having assumed that I'd collect my drinks from mountain streams. But the streams were dry, and so were the three springs which usually feed travellers on this long climb. After about twenty kilometres the trees parted and I looked across a wooded valley to a distant cluster of white cubes spilled around the foot of a grotesque red crag.

Belogradčik had not seen rain for five months and the town's taps were dry. Under the rising sun Belogradčik's rock formations glowed in lurid hues of orange and mustard. Above and below the town was arrayed a bizarre badland of gulfs and towers. With little enthusiasm for the extra exercise I walked slowly up the main street, past the dilapidated mosque with its pretty minaret, to the long flights of steps climbing to the castle. Like Meteora's marriage between monastery and monolith, the rocks and castle of Belogradčik have combined forces to produce a surreal architecture. The most extraordinary moment came as I crossed the grassed courtyard of the 'modern' part of the castle and looked up to see the silhouette of twin towers rising each side of a crenellated battlement, then realized that the towers were natural rock. For over 1,000 years men have defended this fantastic bastion, weaving a spider's web of walls around the existing rock towers until the total enclosed areas exceeded 8,000 square metres. I came across two cisterns, filled with water despite the drought. From the highest battlement I could look out over a wilderness of forest pierced by livid spires and the grey towers of forest fires, rising westwards to the Serbian watershed. In another season and another body I'd have liked to wander those forests, just as the *haiduks* – the forest outlaws – had, watching the Ottoman garrison of Belogradčik, waiting their moment.

The temperature in Belogradčik was thirty-seven degrees by the time I left by way of a track that snaked down through the rocks and forest into an open valley. Brush-fires blazed in the forest each side of the road. The air smelled of charcoal and dust. That night I slept high, on the watershed between the Lom and the Ogosta. The Serbian border was just a two-hour hike away, on the far side of Jazova Planina. I heard voices up on the pass and lay uneasily behind a bank of scrub, watching the road in the light of a half moon until exhaustion overcame nerves and I fell asleep.

I was walking again before light. Every hour gained before sunrise was worth two later in the day. I came down the Ogosta as the morning broke to reveal fields that were seared and cracked. Daffodil-coloured donkey carts with wood-spoked wheels rasped down the warming bitumen on steel rims, their boat-shaped beds occupied by water barrels. At Belimel I joined their queue at the public fountain, to fill my own water bottle. 'Our springs are dry. No rain. No water!' shrugged the old man as he towed me to the front of the queue.

That afternoon several drivers pulled up beside me and offered me a lift, among them two young men in a new Japanese sports car. The driver wore a revolver at his hip. Soon afterwards, I described this incident to the proprietor of a *sok* kiosk on the road up to Berkovitsa.

'This road is dangerous!' he said, drawing the blade of his hand across his throat while handing me an orange juice. 'Every day it is busy with Russian assassins and robbers.' He waited for a truck to pass. 'You know what is one of the Russian weapons? It's a kettle. For boiling water. But instead of water coming from the spout, it is *bullets*!'

I made a mental note to be wary of men bearing kettles.

'The other weapon they like is gas! Poison gas! In a can, like this: *Pssshhht! Pssht!* You sleep. They rob you!' He looked at my rucksack. 'You should not camp. And you should not stop until you reach Sofia!'

Well Met by Moonlight

There was only one potential assassin on the Petrohan pass. Part-way up the interminable hairpins, a descending Lada screeched around a corner, swerved correctively and skidded to a stop beside me. My Ukrainian ski-stick was poised when an elderly woman in a print frock fell out of the rear door and coughed up her lunch over the crash barrier.

The breeze was cooler at the top of the 1,438-metre pass. Opaque cirrus floated high over the Stara Planina and I wondered whether the weather was breaking. At the restaurant on the pass crest, I was over-charged for my meal, the first time I'd noticed it happening. Omens, like the clouds, were gathering too quickly for me to convince myself that they were meaningless.

Sofia now lay within reach, seventy kilometres away, down on its plateau at the foot of the Stara Planina. The south-facing side of the pass was as burnt as anything in Africa. I hurried down: Annabel was due to fly into Sofia the following afternoon. There were few chances to avoid the road. Only the pots of fresh raspberries and yoghurt being sold at the roadside in the first village, Gintsi, put any colour into the long afternoon.

Beyond a gorge the road burst out into the open space of a wide valley, the Iskrec (a tributary of the Iskar), according to my *Generalkarte*. I lay waiting for darkness on a rocky bluff which dominated the entire valley and the hills beyond. A few metres away was an ancient earth-work; one of Trajan's marching camps perhaps, or a temporary fort thrown up as the Getae horsemen fell back before Alexander the Great's rampage across the Danube. The sky darkened with tortured cloud. A wind sprang up. The clouds began to flash. Thunder boomed. I hadn't enough water to wash my feet, and lay with my legs poked outside the tent in the streaming rain. In the morning the land smelled of damp laundry.

The deluge had quenched the smouldering hills and cooled the air. I lost height wearily, crossing the plateau on a long straight road, fuelled by kebabs and Turkish coffee, towards the bristling outline of Sofia, set against the shadow of Vitosha.

Over the ring road I crossed the long-forgotten zones of subtopia: the railway lines and wasteland and colonizing tower-blocks with their semaphore flags of laundry in a land where normal communica-tion is impossible. Then the trams and bus-stops, the *sok* kiosks and mounds of melons, the fringe marketeers of the outer circle. Sofia was undergoing a consumer revolution: pavement vendors were selling ice-cream, pornography, cars, bras. There were more businessmen than buyers. A new car wash had drawn a queue of expensive German saloons with tinted windows and a crowd of onlookers fascinated by the spectacle of instant cleansing, achieved not by sensor-triggered re-volving brushes and pressure hoses, but by five small boys bouncing around the inside of a plastic drive-in shack wielding brushes and pails. Their customers, men with slicked-back hair, dark glasses and Hawaiian shirts, stood back from the spray fingering ostentatious watches.

There was, in the anticipation of this penultimate rendezvous, some-thing missing. Not until I'd turned the corner past Prime Minister Georgi Dimitrov's graffiti-covered mausoleum did I realize that I was not carry-ing the dread of another parting. This time it would not matter; this was the last parting.

We had arranged to meet in the Serdica, a cheap centrally located hotel beyond the Aleksander Nevski church. Annabel was standing by the window wearing a white T-shirt.

'You look young and beautiful.'

'You look absolutely terrible . . .' she laughed.

We talked and walked through the darkening evening, around sultry summer streets and parched parks, till a thunderstorm drove us back to the hotel where we found the restaurant closed and our room windows smashed by the wind. We had so little time; Annabel was out for a long weekend. Every moment was cradled for the future. We'd always convinced ourselves that our respective exiles would bring us back together with even more than we had before, but there was no way of knowing, no way of testing the theory until the thing was finished. All we could do in the meantime was nurture what we had.

We could find nowhere to eat that night and so dinner consisted of the remains of the bread I'd carried over the Petrohan pass from Berkovitsa, with a can of Bulgarian spam. This was not the romantic candlelit reunion I'd planned, but at least I'd arrived on the right day.

In the morning we went through Annabel's luggage. She had brought from London a rucksack of 'presents' from Chris Brasher. After our Transylvanian tramp, Chris had returned to London with a bad back and a list of items which he'd noticed I needed. With customary generosity, he had bought me two pairs of Marks & Spencer boxer shorts (was this a veiled criticism of my one-of-everything rule?), a new pair of size twelve Brasher Boots, plastic tubs of jam, a litre of Macallan's and a bar of Bournville chocolate (the Israeli chocolate we'd found in Transylvania had been exotically revolting). Chris had also sent me a new Herbert Johnson folding trilby to replace my heavy *pădurar*'s *Panzerkappe*. And when Annabel withdrew the last of the Brasher booty from the bag I yelped with pleasure; it was an eight-spoked wood-shafted umbrella and unlike my old talisman, Que Chova, this new one would not attract lightning strikes. When I examined its label I found that it was a Fulton, from the same Galician workshops as Que Chova.

The weekend went by in a blink. We'd seen the Thracian treasure hoards of Panagyurishte and Rogozen; we'd stood under the moon on the cobbles in front of the Aleksander Nevski church, while dead leaves had twisted in autumnal gusts through the beams of the floodlights and a wild-eyed conductor danced in front of an orchestra that sawed at gypsy dances. Then Annabel was climbing into a Lada taxi, bound for the airport.

'I'm nearly there . . .' I had reassured her. And, proportionately, I was. I had walked nine-tenths of the way from Finisterre to Istanbul. But the remaining tenth equated to 1,000 kilometres. We'd now been apart for as long as we'd spent together as a married couple. Annabel had left me a letter she'd written two months earlier, but been unable to send since she had no idea where I was. I could see all too clearly how different were our circumstances: she had written the letter on 24 June from a friend's house in Bath; that day I had woken with Uri in the rain at the shepherds' camp below Chernohora. For me, that morning had been one of fascinating absorption; for Annabel it meant loneliness; 'I don't need to question what you're doing (though I have, as you know),' she wrote, 'or worry that it isn't a good thing. So I have to sit it out and use the time usefully as a period for developing my own strengths and diminishing the weaknesses.' The difference was that I had chosen my travail; Annabel had not chosen hers. I could not sleep that night.

I was still tired from the week-long march from the Iron Gates. The physical decrepitude could simply be ignored (it was always so tedious) but I needed to kick-start the cerebral cortex one last time. So I stayed on in Sofia for another day, wandering up to the Royal Palace, now the National Gallery. The plasterwork was patched, window frames rotting and the parquet floors creaked and pinged like a three-master breaking up on rocks. Apparently King Boris III used to like the noisy floors: 'They make it more difficult for somebody to creep up and murder me . . .' he said. Boris had died mysteriously fifty years ago that week.

By chance I sat down that evening at the Pizza Palace on Bulevard Vitosha at the same table as the secretary general of the Monarchist League. He was a long British gentleman, as thin as a croquet mallet, with a clipped moustache, blazer and a Panama placed with due formality beside the pale disc of his pizza. He introduced himself with a strong handshake: 'Don Foreman, *Royal* Tunbridge Wells!'

Don had been invited to Bulgaria to witness the royal visit of Ioanna, the widow of King Boris III, and Princess Maria Luisa to Rila monastery, in the mountains south of Sofia. 'You should go to Rila,' said the secretary general, drawing on his cigar. 'It's beautiful.'

'I am. Tomorrow.'

Wandering back down Bulevard Vitosha I saw that the following night would bring a full moon. It would also be the first day of September; as good a day as any to begin the end of a walk.

Ah! Vitosha

'Ah! Vitosha . . .' sighed the girl who sold me the apple. 'Our lungs!'

I stood in Ploshtad Sveta Nedelya, the square at the city's hub, looking south up Bulevard Vitosha to the mountain that breathes life into the Sofiantsi, who use the massive loaf of granite as an extended city park. The mountain rises from Sofia's suburbs and acts as a substitute for the river which the city does not have, a lack which accentuates the impression of an arid upland outpost. Among Europe's capital cities, only Madrid occupies a higher elevation.

I walked against the flow of office workers on the way to their desks. The cool morning tasted sweet after the blistering heat of the past weeks. Summer was over, again.

As Vitosha loomed I was reminded of our first Christmas, when Annabel and I had taken the train to Istanbul. We'd stopped in Sofia to warm up (east of Vienna the trains were unheated) and climbed Vitosha on a day when Balkan thermometers had been frozen at minus seventeen degrees Celsius. Vitosha had been thick with Sunday skiers and old men tramping across the Siberian snows with miniature crampons strapped to the insteps of their heavy shoes. We'd walked all day on the snow, then warmed ourselves with tripe soup and hot wine. We had been very happy.

Beyond the tramlines I crossed the ring-road and climbed through the woods until the entire city lay below my feet, spreading out in its intricate, incremental way from the old node of Nedelya to the satellites of abrupt tower-blocks, beyond which lay the green-veined plateau and beyond that, the grey reef of the Stara Planina running east to Nos Emine, the stormy cape that troubled the *Argo* and struck fear in the hearts of subsequent generations of Black Sea Greeks.

I slept at Aleko, the clutch of hostels and hotels on the tree-line. There was a signpost here, to the E-4, the *Euro-weg* that runs from the Pyrenees, along the Alps and via Vitosha and Rila to the Peloponnese, where I had once come across a few of its painted tin signs on the forests of the Taygetos. Its middle section presumably ran the gauntlet of every battlefield between Bihač and the burnt towns of Bosnia Hercegovina. Aleko played a minor part in the emancipation of pedestrians by adopting the Christian name of the satirist Aleko Konstantinov, who led a group of 300 young Bulgarians to Vitosha's summit, in 1895. His political humour was not universally appreciated and two years later he was shot. His riddled heart is kept in a jar in his home-town on the Danube.

The morning was so cold that I delayed my climb till ten a.m. Freezing mist clung to Vitosha's moorland and I was about to resort to the methodical routine of compass navigation when I heard voices and then came upon a couple of garrulous pensioners, also bound for Cherni Vrah, at 2,290 metres the highest point on Vitosha's rocky crest.

The louder of the two was Antoni. He was seventy-seven years old and as outraged by modern ills as Agustin had been, back in the Basque Country. He and his companion, Nikolai, seemed to know the way up through the mist so well that I put away my compass.

'I love Bulgaria!' Antoni repeated. 'But it's getting worse. In fact it's total chaos. And . . . you know what is the cause? It's the young people. They don't get out of bed till seven p.m., then they go to a bar full of smoke and music and stay there as long as they can.' Antoni shook his head. 'People in that condition, they cannot climb Vitosha . . . Where are the young people climbing Vitosha? Nowhere!'

'Antoni, there's *nobody* else up here. There are no old people on Vitosha either. Except for you two.'

'That's because they can't afford the bus from town. It costs fifteen leva for the bus. And you know how much the pension is for one day? Thirty leva!'

I looked at Antoni's expensive blue anorak and cap. 'How did you get here?'

'By plane!'

'From where?'

'The United States,' he said. 'Of America.'

Antoni had been born into one of the Balkans' bad moments. The second Balkan war had just finished and the First World War had just started. Young Bulgarians were dying in the Macedonian mountains. Part-way through the Second World War Antoni was sent to Stuttgart to study architecture. 'I didn't like it,' he said. 'Then at the end of the war, I couldn't get out of Germany.' The first country to open its doors was Brazil. He stayed there seven years, then moved north, to San Mateo, a suburb of San Francisco, between the Bay and the Montara mountains.

'It's good,' he said. 'But I come back to Bulgaria pretty often. To climb Vitosha.'

Whenever we reached a stream – and Vitosha is a mountain of streams – Nikolai sang a few lines to express his happiness.

'You see,' exclaimed Antoni, 'Nikolai still sings for the stream. But the young don't sing for their streams. Bulgarian culture is destroyed. The Communists brought much to Bulgaria: the roads, the factories. But they destroyed the people and they destroyed the economy.'

When we reached Cherni Vrah – the Black Peak – the mist was heavy and wet. Inside the stone refuge the old guardian made us each a mug of raspberry tea.

'She is like us,' nodded Antoni. 'She has been making tea on top of Vitosha for thirty years.'

Musala

Nikolai knew the way off Cherni Vrah and showed me down through the mist to the col, where I picked up the markers for the valley. The change of season had been so dramatic that I woke next morning to find the tent thickly coated in frost.

I'd camped among cottony thistles on a bluff overlooking the Pala-karitsa valley and I had a clear view southwards to the grey peaks of Rila, the 'water mountains' of the Thracians. Butting above them all was Musala, the highest peak in the Balkans. I knew almost nothing about the mountain, beyond a dim recollection that Victor, the pilgrim I'd met in Santiago de Compostela, had climbed it and met a mysterious sect on its slopes. My Viennese *Generalkarte* (a Militärgeographischen Institut edition, updated at the end of 1915, presumably to coincide with the Balkan campaigns of Austria's General Conrad) marked Mus-ala's summit at 2,924 metres, only one metre adrift from today's maps, but it otherwise bore all the hallmarks of cartographic conjecture: suspiciously large blank areas and contours which seemed too regular to believe.

But as I closed on Musala, a very different picture began to take shape. Where there should have been a mule-track, a broad swathe of bitumen swept up through the forest, culminating in a colony of high-rise hotels. Beyond this winter settlement the swathe continued upward, more steeply now, and floored with the battered turf of an out-of-season ski run. After a couple of hours' climbing the trees thinned and disappeared. Bulldozers had been at work in the high valley, carving a new piste between the silent pylons. At a small lake surrounded by buildings which were half-demolished or half-built, day-trippers from the cable-car hunched breathlessly over bowls of greasy bean soup sold by a surly old man who stood behind a pot in the hut which had a roof.

Every level of this squalid rubble mound had been beaten into some kind of human amenity. Higher up the mountain a clutch of turquoise tarns below Musala's cliffs were presided over by another hut, the 'Everest'. Inside, the young warden sat in the blast of an electric fan-heater the size of an aircraft engine while Jimi Hendrix pulverized *Purple Haze*. The drought had dried the hut's spring, so there was nothing here to drink. Or to eat.

'Do you sell *anything*?' I asked the warden.

He shrugged. 'I have these . . .' he said, pointing to a bowl of enamel lapel badges commemorating the 1984 Bulgarian Everest expedition.

Above the young man, sitting at his heater with his distant sources of succour, the route to the summit of Musala had been protected by sections of railway line cemented into the rock and linked by steel cables. A meteorological station crowned the summit and inside its heated sitting-room a colour TV was broadcasting a Bulgaria–Sweden football match live from Sofia. I settled into the sofa with a mug of tea and biscuits provided by one of the meteorologists. They manned the weather station twenty-four hours a day, 365 days a year. Every three hours, day and night, one of them had to climb a spiral staircase insulated with carpet up on to the roof to take the readings, then return to the small office and enter the data in a massive ledger whose pages revealed the extremes of life on a mountaintop: a summer's day when the temperature crept up to a cool nineteen degrees Celsius, and an unimaginable night when Musala's rocks cracked as the thermometer fell to minus thirty-one. I noted uncomfortably that the night air had already fallen to minus two. The weather readings were radioed down to Sofia, and then forwarded to Munich.

I woke in time to watch the six a.m. reading. Up on the roof a sub-zero cloud drifted through the darkness. Autumn had already arrived. In a few weeks' time, the snow would be piled to the roof. Fortified by a steaming slab of macaroni pudding eaten at the highest kitchen table east of the Alps, I walked into the chilly dawn.

Out on Musala's bare rocks the sunrise melted the mists from a panorama of peaks. A brochure I'd picked up in Borovets gave a dramatic idea of the scale of the Rila mountains: 2,396 square kilometres, 140 lakes, seventy-eight peaks over 2,500 metres. A rigorous definition of 'peak' (in Scotland a 3,000-foot mountain has to be separated from its neighbour by a drop of at least 500 feet if both are to be called 'Munros') would no doubt reduce Rila's impressive tally, but as a massif it is still higher than anything in the Carpathians.

Of no dispute is the centrality of the Rila mountains in the Balkan peninsula, both geographically and hydrographically. On Musala's slopes rise the headwaters of the Iskar, the Mesta and the Maritsa, Bulgaria's three great rivers, one to flow north through the Stara Planina to Romania and the Danube; one to flow south into Greece and the Aegean; and the last and longest, the Maritsa, to flow east to Turkey, where its waters mix with those of the Dardanelles.

Across the southern horizon were the upturned stakes of the Pirin mountains. Instead of turning east from Musala to cut across to the Rhodope mountains and Istanbul, I was lured southwards, towards one of the most remote recesses in the Balkans.

Bigger the Beast

South of Musala, a high horseshoe ridge curled into the heart of the Rila mountains. Chamois, picking their way along cliff ledges, reminded me of their western cousins – the *rebecos* I'd met in Spain. Up here I floated in the clear water of Smradlivo Ezero (Stinking Lake, a slur upon an oasis from paradise), then descended a ladder of boulders puddled by bowers of foliage, to the valley and the open gate of Rila monastery.

I needed time to think, and was nervous of the journey ending. I had a simple life that I knew I would lose. The nights in the monastery were the quietest I'd known. The heavy walls shut out nature's nocturnal whispers, the cries of owls and rustles of small feet in dead grass. In Rila there was just a deep protective silence. I knew then what it must have felt like to turn into the sanctuaries of the *Camino francés*, back when trans-continental journeys were measured in months and paced out over rough tracks preyed upon by wild beasts and robbers. The sense of security was so total that everything beyond the walls was magnified to sinister extremes: trees bent in winds ready to snap and crush those beneath, cataracts thundered threateningly against bridge pilings, rocks teetered atop cliffs, the sky hid life-snuffing snowstorms. And the wolves waited.

When I left the monastery, I was still heading southwards, deeper into the Balkans. In Sofia I'd mentioned to Annabel that I might detour down into old Macedonia and she had said: 'Maybe you're adding bits on now because you don't really want the journey to end . . .' I'd denied it, but perhaps she was right.

At 2,000 metres I crossed a pass which used to mark the border of Macedonia. Beyond the pass stood a lonely stone house, built in 1924 by Macedonian prisoners, which was now a mountain hut. Vasil, the warden, cooked a cauldron of spaghetti and a mushroom stew, served with rough red wine by candle-light, while a blazing fire kept the frost from the room.

Down below, in the broad plain separating the heights of Rila from the Pirin mountains, the last potatoes were being dug and flocks of sheep tramped home past the sinking sun through orange veils of dust. On the floor of the plain slumbered Bansko. The town sat at the mountain crux of the trade route from the Aegean to central Europe, a strategic location which gave its citizens the chance to make money from the caravans of cotton, leather and wine bound for Vienna and Budapest. Bansko's merchants built fortress-houses whose high stone walls protected inner courtyards overlooked by broad timber balconies. Velyanova was fairly typical: richly woven carpets covered creaking floors bordered by wall-seats covered with sheepskins. Velyanova's owner had covered his walls with fanciful murals describing the places he'd visited, among them Constantinople. With its forest of minarets and turquoise lagoon busy with clouds of sails it looked unbelievably romantic, a mountain-dwellers' idyll.

Bansko reminded me of Potes, the first mountain town I had rested in, back in the sierras of Spain. I did not want to leave Bansko either. Racks of tobacco leaves were drying in the sun and strings of red peppers hung in semicircles like lipstick smiles on the whitewashed walls. But this was the Balkans, and life was not as it seemed.

'You are in Macedonia now,' I was told by a young man who then gave me a history lecture of such dizzying complexity that a war over it would have to be started by intellectuals or psychopaths (or both) since no ordinary person would be able to grasp the issues. Macedonia – like the Basque Country, Łemkowie and the Hutzul lands – has a historical homogeneity which has been defied by political borders drawn to follow the mountain crests. The Macedonian issue was currently dormant; but I did not have to wait long before meeting another man who pulled out a map which showed a hypothetical Macedonia glued together from bits of Greece and Bulgaria and the bottom bit of old Yugoslavia.

A shopkeeper was outraged: 'Maybe one per cent think they are Macedonian, but they are stupid. It doesn't matter whether I'm from Bulgaria or Greece or the 'Republic of Skopje'. I'm on the earth. The only people to gain from nationalism are the politicians, the chauvinists.'

His was a rare voice of reason in these parts. The patriotism of minorities could so easily be mistaken for a harmless urge to protect besieged cultural identities. But it is such a small step from protection to rejection, from preservation to partition. Civil disintegration puts power into the hands of local politicians. To me it seemed that the way forward was not through infinite subdivision, with its selfish disregard for diversity and collective responsibility, but in the opposite direction, towards a civilized kaleidoscopic whole, sheltered and nurtured beneath the big European umbrella. Ultimately, the crazed tyrants who confuse ethnic identity with nationalism cannot succeed on a continent which is coming to recognize that the dollar is mightier than the gun.

I was drawn on south, into Bulgaria's remotest range, the Pirin, ominously named after Perun, the Slavonic god of thunder. The local creation legend is oddly similar to that of Berchtesgadener Land: God was flying about the world creating places and passed over what is now the Balkans carrying a sack full of very large boulders. The rocks were too heavy for the sack and burst free, tumbling earthwards to form the Pirin.

There was in this desert of stone an unrelenting harshness. The shepherds had left and the grass was dry and brittle. The lakes had shrunk in the long drought and the white rock of the ossified mountains glared in the tired sunlight. I stood on the top of the highest peak, Vihren, in thin clouds, as dry as dust, knowing that this was the last peak I would touch.

The view from this colossal pyramid was as wild as anything I'd seen. And in the time I spent on that arid summit I realized that I could never live without wilderness, and that to destroy it and its myths would be to remove an essential part of the human psyche. The need went beyond an uplifted horizon; the need was in the storms and long dark forests as much as in the Arcadian corners where brooks bubbled by velvet turf.

*

The southern pediment of the Pirin mountains had been eroded by flash floods into a desert of sandy canyons crossed by precarious paths. I asked the way of my last shepherd, a rugose old fellow with a few thin goats. He was as thin and dry as the wind, and pointed out the path down into one of the canyons, where, hidden from sight by two crumbling cliffs, lay the village of Melnik.

'Don't you carry a gun?' asked the young proprietor of the folk-music store as he poured me a glass of Melnik's heavy red wine.

'No. Of course not.'

Julian looked unhappy: 'You should be careful . . . It is very dangerous now.'

His remark stayed with me that night as I recalled an incident at a hut in the Rila mountains. After an all-night vodka party a group of locals were singing and playing the squeeze-box when one of them snatched up a rifle and drew back the bolt. Unfortunately we were indoors at the time and the rifle was pointing at the ceiling, above which slept the hut's guests. A scuffle arrested what would have been a messy detonation. I was reminded of the Balkan gravitation to weaponry in Rozhen monastery, where I came across a pair of oriental fighting sticks lying on a table.

Expecting trouble is the surest method of getting it, and the day after leaving Melnik I was dropping off to sleep on a pass when a pick-up truck pulled up on the road below. The engine cut and the lights snapped out. Men's voices carried up to where I lay. A dog barked. The men began to climb the track. My stomach knotted into a fist of muscle. The dog was up on the mountainside, barking. The men were on the track, waiting. The dog continued searching, quartering the scrub. I tried to calm my breathing. They must be hunters, of course. Bears were hunted at night. According to the leaflet I had picked up in Sofia, there were still 780 bears in Bulgaria. But the hunting season did not begin till November. I wondered whether these were the men I'd seen in the village at the foot of the pass. A rifle shot crashed, then echoed to and fro in the tight valley. The men's voices drew closer. Then I saw the dog, on the track.

My shirt was still sweat-soaked from the walk up the pass and I was cold, but not cold enough to explain the shaking. Trussed-up in a sleeping-bag, I gripped my thighs in my fists. But when I let go to draw breath, the shaking was even worse. The dog was just standing, a dark outline, its head slightly raised, drawing at the night air for clues. I tried letting go of every muscle, relaxing. The shakes slowed, took a deeper resonance, more of a shudder. I tried thinking of home, of Annabel, of flower-sprinkled meadows, of anything soothing, beautiful. The dog began barking; repeated, sharp barks. Spasms tore my torso. In desperation I opened my eyes again. But instead of checking the dog I looked away, upward, at the punctured screen of the night sky. The patterns of stars filled in the space between the black hills. A triangle stood out with a fourth, smaller star, floating free, detached yet belonging. Here, suspended above this crazed place, was a luminous grid reference, the Holy Trinity. And the fourth star . . .? The wracking lifted from my body and I was still and loose as if floating in a salt sea. The dog stopped barking and sloped away, down the track. The men's voices receded. The sound of the truck doors opening carried up through the undergrowth; a call to the dog; the doors slamming. The engine rattled into motion and the truck's tail-lights moved up the pass, out of sight. A black form flitted overhead, a bat or a bird.

In the morning I saw in my journal that it was the autumnal equinox. Beyond the pass rose the foothills of the Rhodopes. There was a nervousness in the villages, whose populations were a mix of Christian and Muslim, many of them *pomaks* – Bulgarians who had converted to Islam during the time of Turkish rule. 'Bosnia Hercegovina is too close . . .' a worried Christian schoolteacher said quietly as the minaret above his head broadcast the muezzin's call to prayer.

I was woken again at night by gunshots and the next afternoon a van brushed past on a mountain pass and I was startled by the crack of an explosion. From the window of the van extended an arm, holding a small black object that must have been a pistol, for the explosion was not an engine backfire. The arm had been pointing at my legs. There seemed little doubt that I had just been shot at.

By the next day, my nerves were failing. At a bar in Dospat a stranger opened a conversation. He was a swarthy heavy-set character wearing sunglasses, a black shirt and camouflage trousers held up with a cartridge belt. He sat with two other men of comical ugliness and introduced himself in a long drawl: 'I'm American. Seven years in Oregon. On the ocean. I'm retired.'

'You don't look old enough . . .'

'Forty-two.' He laughed: 'I retired early. Had a share in a casino in Las Vegas. It burnt down. It gave me some retirement money. Twenty thousand dollars. Thirty thousand dollars. Hell. I can't complain.'

'What are you doing in Dospat?'

'Fishing.'

'All three of you?'

He nodded. 'I'm back to the States in three days.'

'You pleased to be going back?'

'Pleased? Shit! This place stinks! They're all idiots. They think democracy is the same as crime. Idiots! You get killed here for nuthin'. Nuthin'! They're all crazy! Bulgaria is finished.' He dropped his voice: 'Look around you . . .' At the other tables the ones and twos of local men stared into their drinks. 'Muslims! All Muslims!' Then he added sinisterly: 'This place needs a civil war. That's the only thing'll sort it out. Civil war! Only way forward!' He looked across the table. 'What you doin' here?'

'Hiking.'

'Shit! On foot?'

'Yes.'

'What you do at night?'

'Sleep in the forest.'

'Neat! No shit! The forest! You wanna be careful!'

'I am . . .'

'You carry a gun?'

I shook my head.

'I gotta gun. Smuggled it over. In the Cadillac. We got three guns here. Out in the car.'

'How did you come to leave Bulgaria?'

'Escaped.'

'Was it difficult?'

'You bet! Swam the Danube. Thirteen years ago. I was twenty-nine.' He stood up and turned around, then lifted the back of his sweatshirt and moved his finger to a small white scar. 'Bullet went in here. Right beside the spine.' He turned to face me again, lifted the sweatshirt clear of his hairy belly and pulled down the top of his trousers. 'Bullet came out here . . .' he said, moving his hand over a jagged rent across his abdomen. 'Me and my friend were in a dinghy, small rubber boat, crossing the Danube from Romania to Yugoslavia. The Romanian soldiers opened fire. Kalashnikovs or some shit: taca-taca-taca-taca-taca! First bullet goes through the boat. Second bullet goes through me. I'm swimming and saying to my friend, "Hey I think I'm cramping!" I have this sharp feeling in my gut. I put my hand down and slide it over my stomach, and this finger goes straight in! Like this! But I can feel nuthin'! There's a boat. A motor boat. I just wait for them to finish me off . . . that's what they used to do, just stab 'em with the bayonet. Let the bodies go down the Danube. Lots like that. I just wait, head down, for them to finish me. But this boat is Yugoslavs. They speak to me in a language I understand. Yugoslav is like Bulgarian. "Hey guy!", they shout. "You Romanian?" "No!" I shout. "Bulgarian!" They shout back: "Hey what you doin' here?" and pull me out on a hook. That's it. I pass out. Americans were good. Mended me good.'

One of the henchmen leaned over and whispered in his ear and he grinned and said to us: 'He's asking what we're talking 'bout.' His gold bracelet rattled on the table and he continued: 'The west's better.' He nodded at our meals: 'Ya know what the national food here is? Tell ya. It's bread! Just look at their bread!' He pointed at my plate of *kyofte*. 'Ya know how many types of bread there are here? Tell ya! One! Know how many types of bread there are in the States? Tell ya! Forty. Fifty. Seventy!' Then he leaned forward to share his last confidence: 'But not everything's best in the States. Know something? – I got two apartments in Sofia. Just fitted a new jacuzzi. Italian! Seven thousand dollars! American jacuzzis too heavy, no good. This is a nice one . . . kinda light . . . *Italian*.'

Outside the bar, in the flaring light, I decided to leave the mountains. Earlier in the journey I'd never have left the high ground but the Rhodopes were unequivocal in their warnings. I couldn't tell any more whether I was being paranoid or cautious; but I wanted to reach Istanbul alive, and the mountains had at last produced a beast which I hadn't the nerve to face. That, maybe, was what I had come looking for.

So I turned north, walking through endless forests, waking up covered in frost and passing occasional logging camps. One and a half days later, I crossed the last ridge of the Rhodopes and dropped down to the town of Batak.

Batak's story is as bloody as any in the Balkans. During the 'April Rising' of 1876 against the occupying Ottomans, murderous bands of Islamicized *pomaks* were unleashed by the Turks upon the villages of the Rhodopes. Around 29,000 Bulgarians died. In Batak, 5,000 were hacked, shot and burnt to death. A local woman showed me the interior of Sveta Nedelya church. Where the altar should have been there was a cavity filled with bones and pierced skulls. On the walls the plaster still bore bullet marks and blood-stains. The twin-headed axes used for executing Batak's citizens rested in a glass case, on a charred tree stump. The

American journalist J. A. MacGahan was the first on the scene to file a report, which was published in the *Daily News* of 7 August: 'The whole churchyard,' he wrote, 'for three feet deep was festering with dead bodies partly covered – hands, legs, arms and heads projected in ghastly confusion . . . In the school . . . 200 women and children had been burnt alive.' Disraeli found himself caught between an outraged British public and a commitment to support the Turks against the Russians. 'It is a very awkward business . . .' he observed. Very awkward indeed. Especially if you lived in Batak at the time.

On the hilltop above the town three massive stone columns bore the sculpted bodies of Batak's martyrs. Below, in the valley, the red rooftops were hazy with woodsmoke and the distant sound of a chainsaw was carried up with the children's cries.

No Sex Please

I came down to the plain by way of a gorge, relieved to be leaving my fears in the mountains, but robbed of an ideal. I'd always thought of the mountains as a refuge; a place where a niche could always be found. Now I felt ejected. And very sad. Perhaps I had come too close to Istanbul; so close to the end I was physically and mentally threadbare and the smell of the goal had sapped my belief in indefinite effort. Now that only one horizon – the low hills of the Bosphorus isthmus – separated me from Istanbul, I began to succumb to deep exhaustion. Aches I'd always ignored niggled away like grit in a sock. I felt as if I was waking from a dream and spent long reveries lost in that half-awake state, the demonical forest where the unconscious and subconscious slug it out. I became jumpy and dependent upon the benevolence of Lamiñack, the Basque Puck, to spur me eastward with goodwill and gifts: passing through the village of Isperihovo at dusk, a man cutting his vine beckoned me to the foot of his ladder and handed me two bunches of white grapes. And as I left the village I called at a house for water (the drought had dried all the roadside springs) and was given two kilograms of fresh tomatoes. A road-mending team fed me; people paid for my coffee in bars.

I slept on a dry pass and came down into the vast valley of the Maritsa, whose source I'd passed on Musala three weeks earlier and whose lazy banks I'd now follow down to the Turkish border. I walked across the Thracian plain, from town to town for five days. adopting PUMP (Piotr's Ukrainian Marching Plan – fifty-five minutes on, five minutes off) to knock back the kilometre posts. The road I walked took the course of the old Roman *Agger Publicus*, the great highway that once stretched from the Julian Alps through Singidunum – now Belgrade – to Constantinople. I suffered no more than any other who has had to cross that plain on foot, but it was enough. Between the towns there was little beyond orchards and the brittle stubble of maize. The towns were thirty or forty kilometres apart and degenerated as I descended the Maritsa.

Built on four hills and dating back to the fourth century BC when it was founded by Philip of Macedonia, Plovdiv has a history of being ransacked by passers-by. Greeks, Romans, Goths, Huns and Turks have all given Plovdiv a good drubbing, and the Christian Crusaders sacked the town no fewer than four times. The old Macedonian quarter had been tidied up since the 1928 earthquake and I spent healing hours exploring the merchants' houses, all oriels, murals and carved wooden ceilings, which sprang up during Bulgaria's eighteenth- and nineteenth-century cultural renaissance – the National Revival. But for the first time I found a town threatening; previously I'd been passing through, knowing that the infinite sanctuary of forests lay beyond the suburbs. But now that I'd forsaken the heights, this was my habitat.

In the main square a ragged man with a beaten-up three-string fiddle led a brown bear on chains from table to table. The bear wore a leather muzzle; I had to turn away from its eyes. Each time the man extorted some leva from a table he played a few notes on his instrument and the wretched bear tottered to its hind legs and paddled its forepaws helplessly.

The next town down the Maritsa, Parvomaj, was off the main road and as I walked through its decrepit centre I was ambushed by a group of boys who took me for a Macedonian tramp. Volleys of rocks followed me down the street, and taunts of '*Makedonia! Makedonia!*' Adults looked on approvingly from doorways and in that moment I knew that if I had achieved nothing else, I had made it as a *bona fide* itinerant. When I finally snapped and turned on the boys, it was a mad ragged filthy dosser who ran after them flapping his arms, raging and swearing. They hid and then re-emerged to press on with their target practice. Parvomaj balanced its books by providing me a good room for the night in the Hotel Bulgaria, where for three dollars (compared to the forty-three dollars I'd spent on a bed in Plovdiv) I was given clean sheets and a hot shower, and a wake-up knock at seven a.m. by the old man bearing a tray of hot milk, coffee, salami and a couple of delicious *banitsas* – cheese pastries – hot from the bakery. When I came to leave the staff refused to let me pay for this breakfast. They said that foreigners never stayed in Parvomaj.

As the hills beyond the Maritsa became smaller I realized that I was losing my friends; the people who'd helped me on my way, from the green hills of Galicia to this dusty Balkan backslope. Most of them I would never see again. In Haskovo I was shown inside the tiny mosque by the imam, Hadji Kadir, a short, thin man with a pinched face and soft hands. I sagged on to the richly woven rug and allowed a procession to pass by: Antoni and Nikolai, the guardians of Vitosha; the young miners, Stefan and Sorin, now parted; the sparring professors of Sarmizegetusa; Brad and the boys who'd saved me in the Făgăraş; the family – Lajos, Anna and Istvan – who'd refused the five-dollar note I still carried in my spectacle case, wrapped around the scallop shell Annabel had picked from a Finisterre beach; Anne Marie, the young Romanian economist; Vasili, the inventive miller; the Carpathian shepherds, Gligor, Ivan, Jan and the score more who had handed me a bowl of milk and pointed the way to the next pass; the woman with the rose-petal jam; the old man of Hoverla, Dimitri Klimpuch; Uri and Piotr, who reminded me of the benefits of companionship; Sasha, the Ukrainian police chief, who was a good egg after all; Margareta, the English grandmother; dancing Tadeusz; Stanysław, who shocked me; Jerzy, the journalist; Barbara, the school teacher and Dariusz, the vet; Maciek – who didn't retire, but reached the top of Everest (with Jon) after I left him at Zakopane; Yasiek, the Górale; the young ethnographer, Goska; Dušan, the swordsman; the dentist who made me sing *Yesterday*; dear Frau Zimmerman; Sergeant-Major Pfeiffer of the Gebirgs-Jäger, who tried to get me to the 'Eagle's Nest'; Pete, the quixotic ski-bum, who was to die in an avalanche on New Year's Day; Philippe Papadimitriou, looking from the window of Hôtel Ranc for passing donkeys; Jean-Benoît, who hated war; Chief Petty Officer Gonzalez, the nuclear submariner and architect of 'Le Grand Hôtel'; Helmut and his everlasting sausage; Xebe, who didn't think it strange to walk all night; and the other Basques – Begoña, Ibon, Sabin and Agustín; Julio and his Celtic ghosts; Manuel, who'd been so angry when I'd refused his food; José and Luzdivina in their draughty *palloza*; all those pilgrims . . . As one of the pilgrims myself I'd been a privileged passer-by, unencumbered by belonging, able to participate then push on. I had traded in curiosities, leaving some, taking some. But my singular theme meant that I could claim temporary residency among upland people; I'd shared their sudden adversities and their temperamental joys.

Outside the mosque, I laced up my boots and Hadji Kadir helped me on with my pack. On the street I turned to see the imam standing in the mosque's small arch, on the lintel of which somebody had sprayed FUCK OFF in green paint. I'd always treated despair as a luxury to be done without, but now, for the first time, I let go and tumbled into its black depths.

I did not try to sleep beneath the stars in this valley. The hotels deteriorated as the Maritsa widened. In Harmanli my room looked as if it had been used as a machine-gun nest in a local squabble; it had no electric light and a punch-hole in the door, whose lock had been torn off. The sink had been smashed to smithereens, leaving the taps to empty directly on to the floor, and the 'shower' was a hole in the ceiling where the pipe had been removed, presumably for recycling as a cosh or a gun-barrel.

Pain swam in waves through the bones of my feet as I walked the flat hard surfaces of the road. On the evening of my last day in Bulgaria I limped stiff-legged over the thirteen old stone arches of the Mustafa Pasha bridge into Svilengrad and checked into the town's main hotel, the Svilena. In debilitating heat I had just walked fifty kilometres. The place was thick with mosquitoes and I was apprehensive about crossing the border the next day. My feet were in such a terrible state that I could barely climb the stairs. I staggered into the room and was sitting on the bed pulling off my boots when there was a knock on the door. A woman in a low-cut black dress and mascara which looked as if it had been laid down by an asphalt gang, strode into the room.

'You, me – sex!'

I stood up, wincing. She stepped closer. She smelled of roses. Not a subtle hint of roses, but an overpowering pall which must have been applied as a body-lacquer with a high-pressure hose.

'Sex!' she ordered. 'Me . . . You!'

The temptation to bury my face between the soft curves of her cleavage was overwhelming. I swayed on my cracked feet, the intense pain below my knees countered by a kind of cerebral liquefaction at the other end. In between, things were getting out of hand. I had no strength to resist; and anyway, didn't I deserve a dose of delicious coddling? She wasn't even ugly. In fact she was pretty. Not beautiful, but hazel-eyed below the lagoons of mascara. About twenty-five perhaps. What about the transaction? Do you arrange a price before, or after? Would she take a traveller's cheque or demand dollars? Is it a flat fee or do they charge by the minute? My face was drawn slowly and involuntarily forward until I was angled like a ski-jumper above the flawless breasts. Wasn't there a Valley of the Roses in the Stara Planina? The demands of circulation had sucked the blood from my calves and head and I could feel the gentle, welcoming onrush of faintness.

'No thank you. I'm English.'

The woman looked incredulous. 'English? Polish? What the difference?'

I held up my finger, and twisted my wedding-ring. 'I'm married!'

She looked disgusted. 'Pah!'

The door slammed. By the time the dust had settled, the physiological pendulum had swung back from eye-boggling wonder to torpor. My feet hurt.

I spent the night on the lavatory, paying the full cost of my meal in Harmanli. The mosquitoes were so thick that I could knock them down with random shots from the 'Vienna Avenger', an industrial-gauge elastic band I'd bought in Austria and preserved for surface-to-air defence. By morning I was frantic with exhaustion.

Another thirty-five kilometres that day took me unhindered across my last border into Turkey and along the verge of the main road until the minarets of Selimiye Camii climbed above the dusty trees. I felt I'd been here before, and it took me another kilometre to remember where; it was Santiago de Compostela and that first view of the Obradoiro façade, rising from the steaming forests of Galicia. I was nearly home.

Sweet Waters of Europe

The muezzin's call echoed off the old stone walls of the caravanserai and I lay for a while in the white cell of my room listening to the sounds of the waking town: the bang of doors, the call of a borek-seller, the rattle of a barrow on cobbles.

The Austrian Ambassador, Ogier Ghiselin de Busbecq, stopped in Edirne's caravanserai in 1555. 'These hostels are fine convenient buildings with separate bedrooms,' he wrote, 'and no one is refused admittance, whether he be Christian or Jew, whether he be rich or beggar . . .' Nowadays the caravanserai is still open to all-comers, provided they have the money. It has been converted into a modern hotel. Busbecq was fed on barley porridge and went on to note that: 'Travellers are allowed to enjoy this hospitality for three full days; when they have expired, they must change their hostel.' The fortunes of a caravanserai rise and fall with the volume of passing traffic and for Edirne times were bad; visiting tourists had dropped from 3,000 a month before the latest Balkan wars, to 200. I ate my breakfast alone under the great plane tree in the inner of the two courtyards.

In contrast with the stagnant torpor of the Maritsa's towns, Edirne's pavements were manically active: men hawked fur coats from their arms, or tomatoes or socks; shoe-shine boys sat at corner-plots with their polished brass pots; lottery-ticket sellers competed with gypsies who squatted before sets of cheap plastic scales offering to tell your weight. Artisans sat in cubby-holes, repairing watches or video sets. And the food was so rich and varied that a year could be spent without eating the same dish twice. That tea was now the national drink, rather than vodka and beer, lent the bars an unfamiliar coherence and a conspiratorial edge. 'You must come to Kurdistan!' whispered a man over my shoulder in a tea-house. 'Yes! You are a foreigner. You will tell the truth to the outside world. Come to Kurdistan!' For a moment, I was tempted.

Edirne, once a capital city, was an apt place for me to adjust to a world where power and beauty are measured in human endeavour. In Edirne, indeed in the Ottoman world, no architect is more revered than Sinan abdür-Mennan – Spearhead the Son of the Slave of God the All-Giving. Sinan built the caravanserai I stayed in. The slave who rose to be royal chief architect under Süleyman the Magnificent is claimed to be the most prolific architect ever to have lived. His most beautiful work, Selimye camii, rose above Edirne's crowded bazaars. Each night I went to watch the moon rising on its tether above Selimye's impossibly slim minarets, the tallest outside Mecca.

Beyond Edirne I turned off the Istanbul road, the old Roman Via Egnatia, to return for a last time to the hills. For seven days I walked along the dry crest that runs the length of the Thracian isthmus.

At first the hills were bare and bleak, clear-felled centuries ago by the Ottomans, to deter Christians from advancing eastwards. With every day of progress I was reminded that I was closing on the edge of a continent, approaching a front-line. Army camps sprawled along the roadside, and tank-parks guarded by listless conscripts. Off to my right were the immense tumuli of the Thracians rising above the flat dust like so many Silbury Hills, easy to confuse from a distance with the modern military bunkers or the ten-metre mounds of sugar beet, neatly stacked with their bulbous end outward so that they looked like ossuaries of earthy skulls. Otherwise it was a caramel-coloured desert of dry soil, with hardly a tree, melting into a distant heat haze. Out here, as a lone pedestrian, I was as anomalous as ever I'd been and in every village the cost of my coffee or *çay* seemed to be covered by customers or waived by the barman. As I trod the simmering bitumen almost every passing vehicle pulled up beside me; twenty, thirty, forty a day offered me rides in taxis, tractors, cars, coal-trucks, motorbikes and on one occasion in an army staff car. As I shook my head and explained in jerky Turkish that I preferred to walk, they'd leave with a wave and I'd try to cover another few hundred metres before the next interruption.

I entered a vast forest of dwarf oaks. From dawn till dusk I walked through the trees on deserted dog-legs of bitumen which had been laid long after my maps had been drawn. My 1940 Militärgeographischen Institut sheets marked the various defensive lines across the peninsula. The oldest was the *Anastasische Mauer*, the great Roman wall stretching across the isthmus from the Sea of Marmara to the Black Sea. Again, I found myself tingling as I crossed another watershed, this time a real rather than symbolic one. This fifty-kilometre defence line of wall, towers, forts and ditches coincided with the line of high ground crossing the neck of the peninsula, and was thrown up – according to the Byzantine historian Procopius – by Anastasius I to protect Constantinople from the barbarians who were bringing fire and the sword to the Balkans. But a wall existed on this line before the time of Anastasius, constructed perhaps to defend Constantinople's drainage basin and the web of aqueducts that fed the city in times of siege. Beyond the wall I came across later lines of defence: a great ditch and embankment to deter tanks and an old concrete bunker with the sight-lines still painted on the inside of its westward-facing gun-slits.

On the sixth night out from Edirne I made my last bivouac. The day had been long and dusty and I was so tired that I could only creep a few metres off the road, slumping down against a sheltering oak and leaning back to stare for a last time at the stars. They'd been good companions, reassuringly constant, reliable. Now I was about to lose them. I didn't resent my return to 'civilization' but I didn't know how I'd live without the wilderness. Freedom on such a scale existed only in the high places and fed a quality of existence I'd never find in a city.

Leaving my bivouac in the oaks at dawn, I walked east along the spine of the hills into the rising sun on a white road through scrubby forest. On each side of the black crest lapped a silver mist, so that my pale road and its dark embankment looked like a highway in the sky.

Faintly at first, and then amplifying as I followed the slope down towards the shoreline of the cloud, came roars, metallic clangs and dull rumbles. Too soon, the road plunged to join the headwaters of Kâğith-ane Suyu, the stream which used to flow into the Golden Horn as the 'Sweet Waters of Europe', but now does so as a sewer. Ankle-deep dust as fine as flour wafted up to my waist as I struggled through the mist, deafened by the mines and terrorized by swaying trucks which lurched without warning from the gloom, swaying beneath spilling cargoes of coal and sending me sprawling into the ditch. Every twig and leaf was dust-coated, and soon I too was a pale apparition, a white wraith in a ghostly forest that had ceased to be real. I passed beneath one of Sinan's aqueducts and turned off the road, up my last hill, into the Belgrade forest. In this arboreal relic, protected from Istanbul's greedy suburbs, I found some last moments of peace, sitting back in a dell of dead leaves, dappled by beeches, and letting the feelings run. I lay back in this soft bed washed by an intense flood of fulfilment, an uncoupling so profound that everything that lay behind – this multitude of friendly faces and treasured places – fell away to leave Annabel, alone before the minarets and the circling seabirds.

I kicked through the leaves to the top of the slope and left the forest on a dirt road that dropped down through a village to a broad crescent of sand. I walked down the sand, feeling it firm up beneath my feet. It wasn't until the water broke over my dusty boots that I believed what I was staring at; in front of me was nothing: an absolutely smooth horizon; a great blankness. The Black Sea.

Across the Golden Horn

That evening I walked along the wet sand to the old fishing village of Kilyos, then watched the sun go down over the hills that marked the end of the continental divide.

Annabel was not due to arrive for another four days and so I had plenty of time to amble down the thirty kilometres or so of the Bosphorus to the heart of old Istanbul. The police in Kilyos prevented me from taking a direct route over the cliffs to reach the tip of Europe, at Rumeli Feneri. A military zone, they said. Instead I had to make a laborious detour inland on melting bitumen, passing on the way three Bactrian camels cropping the roadside trees with no regard to the coal-trucks thundering past their rumps.

Rumeli Feneri was an atmospheric spot, commanding the Black Sea entrance to the Bosphorus. Four kilometres across the water, the grey Asian shore rose in broken cliffs, punctuated by the shining finger of a lighthouse. Now that a bridge leapt the Bosphorus I could cross to Asia on foot . . . and carry on eastwards to Kamchatka; after all, I was a third of the way there already. But I was happy with ending here, on this gulf between continents. I walked out along the concrete mole and climbed one of the two Clashing Rocks – the Symplegades – between which Jason had steered the *Argo*.

From Rumeli Feneri, the road beside the European shore of the Bosphorus had to climb high above the cliffs and up here, resting in the shade of a pine and watching a Turkish patrol boat nose along the shore below me, I was startled by a blue estate-car. The rear window – and my heart – sank as a man covered in gold braid and stars leaned out and said: 'Please get in the car.'

'I'm afraid I cannot . . .' I apologized. 'Cars are a problem . . . I don't travel in cars.'

The officer's face changed from one of cordiality to impatience: 'Get in the car!'

'I'm really sorry, but I can't. It is very kind of you to offer me a lift, but I am unable to travel in cars. Neither do I travel in trains, buses, carts, or on bicycles, or . . .'

'Get in!'

I pulled off my rucksack and dropped it to the road. The two soldiers in the front of the car looked anxious. 'We're taking you to Bebek!' said the officer. Bebek was a town further along the shore.

'I'm afraid that's impossible,' I replied, hurriedly pulling out my map of Europe with its erratic black line. 'I'd like to come to Bebek, but I will walk and meet you there. In the meantime let me explain . . .'

The officer and his men climbed out on to the road. I quickly laid the map on the roof of the car and rushed through my ritual patter (watersheds, own-two-feet, non-mechanical ethic, etc. etc.), finishing with a question: 'And what is your name, may I ask?'

'Mustafa,' said the officer.

'Nicholas,' I said, shaking his hand.

Mustafa asked me to describe my itinerary for the next four days, while he wrote the details in a notebook. Then he shook hands again, smiled and left. Mustafa was the military commander of the Bosphorus. He was the highest-ranking soldier ever to have offered me a lift.

I came down to water-level and became another pedestrian, idling with fishermen and shoppers beside the deep turquoise. Boats from battered wooden sailers to air-conditioned cruisers swung at their moorings in sheltered bays backed by timbered Ottoman mansions, the *yalis*, that stood above the clear water like rows of parked caiques. The *palamut* shoals were running through the strait and in every village fishermen had set up grills and the air was silver with woodsmoke and burning oil.

With greasy fingertips I punched our home number into a public telephone. I could hear her smiling: 'The flight's booked. I arrive in two days.'

'I'm nervous . . .'

'What about?'

'Meeting you. Coming home. Starting again . . .'

'We'll just carry on where we left off.'

'What if we've changed?'

'We *have* changed!'

Landmarks crept up, registering my slow closing on a destination that had always been imaginary. I passed beneath the great bridge between Europe and Asia, climbed the ramparts of Rumeli Hisar castle, ate *palamut* at the little bay at Bebek (where I failed to find Mustafa), and took *çay* beside the baroque mosque at Ortaköy.

On Saturday, 16 October, 506 days after leaving Cape Finisterre, I came down the hill to the hook of blue water known as the Golden Horn.

Across the water rose the domes and minarets of Haghia Sofia, the Blue Mosque, Topkapi Palace, the Süleymaniye Mosque; a crown of jewels set upon seven hills.

I fell in with the flocks streaming over the Galata Bridge towards old Istanbul. Night had fallen. Up Ankara Caddesi I climbed, then left into Yerebatan Caddesi. Haghia Sofia, where we had agreed to meet, rose above me and beside it, the site of the Golden Milestone, from where all distances were measured.

A long-dreamed shadow moved from beneath a tree.

Index

Adrienne (Slovak lecturer) 211
Afghanistan 8–9, 21
Agger Publicus 355
Agustín (Basque musician) 52–4, 356
Aigoual, Mont, Cévennes 135, 137–9
Aigüestortes, Pyrenees 103
Aiguille du Midi, France 166
Aizarna, Spain 65–6
Alaric, Montagnes d', France 126
Albertville, France 160
Albigenses 77
    see also Cathars
Alcalde del Rio, Don Hermilio 51
Alcantarilla river, Spain 39
Aleko, Bulgaria 343–4
Alfred, Collado, Pyrenees 98, 100
Alps 5, 138, 149–98
Alteland, Romania 304–5
Ambel, Plateau d', France 151
An Teallach, Scotland 240
Anastasius I, Emperor 360
Ancares, Sierra de, Spain 24–31, 276
Andorra 104–9
Aneto, Pico de, Pyrenees 97, 98–100, 104
Anger, Germany 189
Aniezo, Spain 49
Anne Marie (Romanian student) 300, 356
Antoni (elderly Bulgarian on Vitosha) 344–5, 356
Apa Gradistei, Romania 319, 320
Apollodorus of Damascus 330
Aralar, Sierra de, Spain 70
Ardèche, France 144
Argo (mythical ship) 343, 362
Arre valley, France 133
Arrien, Felipe 57–8
Assas, Chevalier d' 133
Ataun, Spain 70

Austria 193–207
Azpeitia, Spain 66–9

Babia, Spain 35, 39
Bad Feilnbach, Germany 188–9
Băile Herculane, Romania 328
Balaitous, Pyrenees 86–7
Balbaran, Collado de, Spain 37
Balkan ranges 5, 331–64
Balmat, Jacques 162
Balme, Col de, France 171–2
Balouta, Spain 30, 68
Banica, Poland 243
Bansko, Bulgaria 348
Baring-Gould, Sabine 80–1, 84–5
Barnet, Frau, of Schönau 205
Bartne, Poland 244–5
Basarabi, Romana 334
Basque country, Spain 5, 51–79
    identity 53–4
Basque language (Euskara) 52, 69
Batak, Bulgaria 353–4
Báthoryová, Countess Alžbeta 211–12
Battenberg, Princess Henry of 115
Bavaria, Germany 187–93
Bealach na Ba, Scotland 4
Béarn, Gaston Phoebus, Vicomte de 84
bears 84–5, 151, 184, 225–6, 227–8, 355
Beasain, Spain 70
Beaufortain mountains, France 161–2
Bebek, Turkey 363
Begoña (Basque mountaineer) 59, 103, 356
Belgrade forest, Turkey 361
Belloc, Hilaire 78, 86, 103–4, 109, 313
Belogradčik, Bulgaria 338
Beltrán, Antonio ('El Esquinazado') 96
Berbeka, Maciek 230–31, 235, 356
Berchtesgadener Land, Germany 190, 193

Berghof, Germany 190, 191, 192–3
Berry, Duchesse de (*fl.* 1822) 93
Beskid Niski, Poland 231, 242–5, 252–4
Beskid Sądecki, Poland 231, 239–40
Bicilis (Dacian chief) 319
Bielsa, Spain 96–7
Bieszczady, Poland 232, 248, 254
Bilbao, Spain 54–6
Bîrgău pass, Romania 302
Bistriţa valley, Romania 298–9
Black Mountains, Ukraine 279–85
Black Sea 361
Blahniţa marshes, Romania 334
Blandas, Causse de, France 132
Blashford-Snell, Col. John 3
Blatna valley, Slovakia 223
Blidaru, Romania 320
Bodružal, Slovakia 254–5
Boente, Spain 23
Bonnafoux, Marcel Fernand 133
Boris III, King of Bulgaria 342
Borzhava massif, Ukraine 268–9
Bosphorus isthmus, Turkey 359–61
Bouillanne (French woodcutter) 151
Boyk people 271, 293
Brad (walker in Făgăraş) 308, 356
Brasher, Chris 20, 310–14, 341
Braşov (Kronstadt), Romania 303, 305
Bratislava, Slovakia 207–9
Bregaglia valley, Italy 182, 184
Brei, Switzerland 175
Brenišinova, Julia 255
Brian (US Peace Corps worker) 309
Brig, Switzerland 174
Brooke, Sir Victor 93
Bruno, of Le Vigan 134
Bucara, Lake, Romania 323, 324
Bucarei, Curmătura, Romania 323
Bucharest, Romania 5
    university, group from 324
Bukovina, Poland 236, 293
bullfight 66–8
Bulnes, Spain 46, 182
Bunonia 337
Burguete, Spain 78
Burton, Sir Richard 183
Busbecq, Ogier Ghiselin de 358–9
Butterworth, Ella 116

Butwiłło, Jerzy 246, 247–8, 249, 356
Bycko, Dr Michal 256

Cabrales cheese 49
Čachtice castle, Slovakia 211–12
Cadenas, Manuel and family 30
cagots (inhabitants of Pyrenees) 77
Caín, Spain 42, 45–6
Calafat, Romania 333, 335–6
Cambalès, Col de, Pyrenees 87
Camino francés (pilgrim road to Santiago de
    Compostela) 17–18, 19–20, 22–6, 78–9,
    347
Camino Real, Spain 37–8
Camisards 139
Campuliares, Sierra de, Spain 31
Canigou, Mont, Pyrenees 110, 112, 113, 121
Carcassonne, France 126, 127–9
Carcedo, Sierra de, Spain 41
Cares gorge, Spain 42, 44, 45, 46
Carlit, Pic, Pyrenees 110
Carlos (Spanish radio journalist) 39
carnival, Bavarian (*Fasching*) 188–9
Carnuntum (Roman town), Austria 206–7
Carpathians 5, 199–330
Carrafancq, Mme, of Lescun 83
Carrette, Cabane de, France 152
carro chirrión ('screaming cart') 29–30
Casals, Pablo 121
Casomera, Sierra de, Spain 41
Cassino, Monte, Italy 189, 247
Castillo, Monte del, Spain 51
Catalunya, Spain 101–4, 113
Cathars 77, 123, 125
Cati (Armenian girl in St-Paul-de-
    Fenouillet) 122
causses 130, 131–2, 132–3
Cavalier, Jean 139
Ceahlău, Romania 299–302
Ceauşescu, Lt-Gen. Dr Ilie 321
Ceauşescu, Nicolae 320–1
Cebreiro, Spain 26
Celts 196
Cerdagne, Pyrenees 110–12
Cerna, Romania 327
Cervantes, Miguel de; *Don Quixote* 52–3, 66
Červen Kláštor, Slovakia 239
Cetate, Romania 335

Cévennes, France 5, 119–47
Chamonix, France 163–4, 165, 169–71, 230
Chapel, Paul Joseph (cooper, of Le Vigan) 136
Charlemagne, Emperor 74, 79
Charmettes, Les; Rousseau's house 158–9
Chartreuse mountains, France 155–8
Chastel, Jean 140
cheesemaking 236–8, 275–6, 283
Chemin de St Jacques (pilgrim road) 93
Cheremosh river, Ukraine 287, 298
Chernobyl, Ukraine 268
chestnut cultivation, Cévennes 133, 135
Childbert, King of Franks 74
Chleb mountain, Slovakia 220–1
Chochołowska valley, Poland 227
Chornohora, Ukraine 279–85
Chrumm valley, Switzerland 176–7
Churriguera, Joaquín de 66
Chyzne, Poland 226–7
Čičmany, Slovakia 218
Cimpulung Moldovenesc, Romania 295–7
Cindrel mountains, Romania 311–12
Cinqueta valley, Spain 97
Cirocha valley, Slovakia 256
Cività Castellana, Italy 29
Colani, John, of Pontresina 184
Columella, Junius Moderatus 37
Coma Pedrosa, Pyrenees 104, 105
Comărnicel, Romania 317
Communism, fall of 5–6
Como, Lake, Italy 181
Corbières, France 122–6
Cornión massif, Spain 42–6
Cortalets, Chalet des, Pyrenees 113
Cosma, Miron 314
Costesti, Romania 320
Crane, Hol 7–8, 91, 145
    joins NC in Carpathians 235–6, 238,
    239–40, 254–9
Crane, Naomi 7, 235–6, 238, 254–9
cretinism 177
Croz, Michel 171
Csiknagyboldogasszony, Romania 304
Cubilla, Puerto de, Spain 41
Cyprian, Friar, of Červen Kláštor 239
Cyprus 4–5
czerdak (quarantine guardhouses) 285
Czuprej (Ukrainian outlaw) 287

Daicoviciu, Professor Constantin 318, 356
Danube, river 204, 206, 329, 330, 333–6
Dartmoor 7
Darwin, Sir Horace 115
Decebalus (Dacian leader) 319–20
Degrada, Spain 29
Diaconescu, Professor Alexandru 321–2, 356
Diaconiţa, Vasili 300, 356
Dingley, Ruth and Jack 108–9, 235, 238
Disraeli, Benjamin 354
Dittersdorf, Karl Ditters von 234
Dobosz (mountain robber) 283–4, 287, 288
Dolina Homole, Poland 239
Dospat, Bulgaria 351–3
drove roads 26–7, 34, 138–9, 141
Duilhac, France 123
Dukla pass, Poland 240, 249, 252–4
Dumitri, Rusan 295
Dunajec gorge, Poland 238
Dunonia (Vidin); Celtic settlement 337
Durfort, Château de, France 125
Dušan (castle guide at Trenčín) 213–15, 356

E-4, *Euro-weg* 343
'Eagle's Nest, The' 191
Eck, Germany 189
Eckart, Dietrich 190, 193
Ecuador 3–4
Ed, Germany 189
Edirne, Turkey 358–9
Egon (walker in Făgăraş) 309, 356
Ehujarré, Gorges d', Pyrenees 81
Elcano, Juan Sebastián 62–5
Emberson, Alfred 114, 115
Encamp, Andorra 109
Engadine, Switzerland 184–6
English abroad, at Vernet-les-Bains 114–17
Entremont-les-Vieux, France 158
equipment, author's walking 20–22
Escaleta, valley of, Pyrenees 100, 101
Escaló, Spain 103
'Esquinazado, El' (Antonio Beltrán) 96
Euric (leader of Goths) 74
Europa, Picos de, Spain 39–40, 42–8, 160
European Economic Community 206
Euskara (Basque language) 52, 69
Evelyn, John 175, 176–7
Extebarria, Spain 52

Făgăraş mountains, Romania 305–10, 356
Faîta, Col de la, France 155–7
Fajks, Stanysław 249–51, 356
Fasching (German carnival) 188–9
Fenouillèdes, Les, France 121
Ferage, Blaise 80–1
Fermor, Patrick Leigh 6, 202–3, 207, 313, 327, 328
Fern Pass, Austria 186
Ferrer, Jorge 15–16
fiestas, Spanish 59–61, 66–9, 70–1
Finiels, Mont, France 142
Finisterre, Cape, Spain 5, 13
Five Polish Lakes, Valley of 236
Flaubert, Gustave 90
Florac, France 139–40
Florea, Gelu 318–19
Florus, Lucius Annaeus 50
Fockenstein, Germany 188
Foreman, Don 342
Forne, Jordi Farras 106
Franco, General Francisco 32
Franks 74, 79
Fucking, Germany 189
Funk, Germany 189
Furt, Germany 189

Gabi, Switzerland 177
Gadow, Dr Hans 29, 160
Galicia, Spain 13–30, 218
Galton, Sir Francis 313
Ganaderos, Casa de, Spain 27
Gangloff, Bernard 146
Gargas, cannibal of (Blaise Ferage) 80–1
Garmisch-Partenkirchen, Germany 187
Gaspard, Jean-Pierre 87
Gavarnie, France 89–90, 92
Germany 187–93
Gernika, Spain 56–9
Gernikako Arbola (Basque national anthem) 53
Geryon, myth of 34
Getaria, Spain 62–5
Gevaudan, Beast of 140
Geza II, King of Hungary 303
Gheorgheni, Romania 303
Giewont, Poland 228, 230
Gintsi, Bulgaria 340
Giubiasco, Switzerland 178

Gligor (Romanian shepherd) 317, 356
Glodariu, Professor Ion 318, 319, 322, 356
Gobi desert 8
Godeanu, Romania 327
Goethe, Johann Wolfgang von 174
Golden Horn 363
Gomez, Julio Garcia 49–51, 356
Gonzalez, Richard 102–3, 356
Górale people 231–4, 248
Gosau, Austria 194–5
Goths 74, 77
Grajcarek valley, Poland 239
Grajos, Sierra de los, Spain 40
Gravedona, Italy 181
Grenoble, France 147, 153, 154–5
Grottes Bellevue, Pyrenees 89
Gruca, Professor 18
Guarda, Switzerland 185
Gugg, Germany 189
Guiers Mort, Gorges du, France 157
Gyergyószentmiklós, Romania 303

Halford, Sir Henry 93
Hallstatt, Austria 195–6
halny (wind) 231
Hamilton, David 164–9, 169–70
Hańczowa, Poland 243
Hannibal 145
Hărman, Romania 304–5
Harmanli, Bulgaria 357–8
Haskovo, Bulgaria 356–7
Haţeg basin, Romania 323
Heft, Germany 189
Heiligenkreuz, Austria 197–8
Helmut (sausage enthusiast) 83–4, 85, 356
Hemingway, Ernest 73–4, 78
Hercules (mythical hero) 34
herders, political power of 27, 138
Herri Kirolak (Basque trials of strength) 65–6
Hindu Kush 8–9, 21, 268
Hitler, Adolf 181, 190–1, 258
Hossard (French military surveyor) 87
Hoverla, Ukraine 278, 279–81, 356
Hoyo Verde, Spain 45
Hub, Germany 189
Hugo, Victor 90
Hunedoara, Romania 320
Hunyadi, Janos 320, 321

Hutzul people 287–8, 271, 273, 293
Huxley, Annabel 3–5, 15, 22, 348, 364
    birthday 152–3
    earlier journey to Istanbul with NC 5–6,
        343
    in Grenoble 147, 154–5
    letters and phone calls 48, 127, 164, 174–
        5, 178, 195
    in Sofia 339, 341
    in Spain 13, 14, 73–4, 77
    in Vienna 201–3
Huxley, Thomas 183

ibex, Pyrenean 93
Ibias gorge, Spain 31
Ibon (Basque, husband of Begoña) 59, 103,
    356
Iceman, Otzi the 186
Ignatius of Loyola, St 66
Iorgovanului, Piatra 324–5
Iparraguirre, José María de 53
Ipazter, Spain 59–61
Irati forest, Pyrenees 80
Iron Age, Early 196
Iron Gates, Danube 5, 329, 330
Iruretagoyena, General 96
Islam 5, 351
Isperihovo, Bulgaria 354
Istanbul, Turkey 5, 294, 363–4
    NC's previous journey to 5–6, 343
Ivan Feodorovich (caretaker at Sinevir) 270

Jabłonka, Poland 226
Jahn, Karl 188–9, 247
James (Californian evangelist) 315
Janesch, Anna 305
Jánošik, Juraj 219–20, 221
Jaworki, Poland 239
Jean-Benoît (French conscientious
    objector) 133–5, 356
Jesus, Society of 66
Joly, Col du, France 161–2
Jordana, Mrs Roser 105–6, 107
José and Luzdivina, of Piornedo 28–9,
    356
Joseph II, Emperor 288, 328
Joyce, James 178
Julia Lybica (modern Llivia) 112

Kadir, Hadji 356, 357
Kakouéta, Gorges de, Pyrenees 81
Kaleh, Ada 329
Karpiel, Góska 232, 356
Kehlstein, Germany 191–2
Kentish, John 164–9
Kenya 8, 20
Kežmarok, Slovakia 220
Kiełbasinski, Tadeusz 251–2, 254, 356
Kilimanjaro, Mount 20
Kilyos, Turkey 362
Kipling, Rudyard 114, 116
Klak, Mount, Slovakia 218
Klimpuch, Dimitri 278–9, 356
Kollonics, Cardinal Leopold 219
Köln, Germany 189
Konstantinov, Aleko 343–4
Kosiv, Ukraine 286–7
Kostyak, Uri Petrovich 271–86, 356
Kozie Zebro, Poland 243–4
Krempna, Poland 245–6, 247–9
Kretsek, Peter 204
Kristy, Slovakia 259
Kronstadt (Braşov), Romania 303
Krynica, Poland 242
Kryniczanka river, Poland 241–2
Kudil (Ukrainian outlaw) 287
Kuty, Ukraine 287–8

La Bastide Puylaurent, France 143
La Cuadra, Spain 55
La Cueta, Spain 35
La Fage, France 141–2
La Massana, Andorra 105
La Renclusa, Refugio, Pyrenees 97–8
La Roque de Fa, France 124–5
la Vacquerie-et-St-Martin-de-Castries,
    France 131
La Voulte, France 145
Laboreck hills, Slovakia 254–5
Laciana, Spain 34, 39
Ladin dialect 185–6
Lagrasse, France 125–6
Lajos, Anna and Istvan (Transylvanian
    family) 304, 356
Lamalou-les-Bains, France 130
Lanos, Portella de, Pyrenees 110
Lăpușinic, Romania 324

Larra, Spain 82–3
Larrasoaña, Spain 77–8
Larzac, Causse de, France 131
Laterrade, Pierre 90, 92
Laugaricio (Roman settlement), Slovakia 213
Laurent (French conscientious objector) 133, 134
Lazeshchina, Ukraine 278
Le Peuty, Switzerland 172
Le Vigan, France 133
Led Zeppelin 301
Ledwinka, Hans 258
Leeds University, party from 97–8
Lekeitio, Spain 61
Łemk people 231, 241, 243, 244, 247, 251–2, 254
Les Contamines, France 162
Les Escaldes, Andorra 108
Lescun, Pyrenees 83–4
Lingwurm, Switzerland 175
Llavorsi, Spain 103
Llewellyn Smith, H. 98–9
Llivia, Pyrenees 111–12
Lobau Island, Austria 204
Locarno, Switzerland 177–8
Long, Richard 157
Louis XI, King of France 112
Lourdes, France 93
Lozère, France 140–2
Lúbor (Slovak schoolboy) 217
Ludisoru, Romania 307–10

McDonald's restaurants 127
Macedonian nationalism 348–9
MacGahan, J.A. 354
Madoz, Spain 72
Magellan, Ferdinand 62–3
Maglovit, Romania 335
Magura, Slovakia 224, 225–6
Malá Fatra, Slovakia 216–26
Maladeta massif, Pyrenees 86, 97–101
Malé Karpaty, Slovakia 209–12
Maloja, Switzerland 183–4
Mampodre, Picos de, Spain 41
Mănic (walker in Făgăraş) 309, 356
Manuel (Spanish shepherd) 40, 356
Marchfeld, Austria 204–6
Marcomanni 206, 213

Margareta (*neé* Margaret Sykes) 262–4, 356
Mariazell, Austria 197
Maritsa river, Bulgaria 347, 354–8
Markina, Spain 54
Márquez, Gabriel García 14
Martin, Slovakia 218–19, 220
Martyszczuk (Ukrainian outlaw) 287
Masclet, Monique 146, 147
Mateescu, Ioan 296–7
Maximus, Tiberius Clausius 320
Medullus, Mons (Peña Sagra), Spain 50
Medzilaborce, Slovakia 256
Melchor (Basque cyclist) 24, 56
Melnik, Bulgaria 350
Mera river, Italy 181–2
Mercador, Jules 115
Mesta (Spanish shepherds' association) 27
Metternich, Prince Clemens Lothar Wenzel 202
Mielczarek, Barbara 248–9, 356
Mieres, Casa de, Spain 40
Mikhiluk, Ivan Fyedorivich 282
Miková, Slovakia 255–6
Mincol, Slovakia 221
Mircea (Romanian teacher) 303–4
Mirol'a, Slovakia 255
Mizhgor'ya, Ukraine 269
Moldoviţa, Romania 294–5
Monasterio de Hermo, Spain 32, 33–4
Mont Blanc, France 162, 164–9
Montagne Noir, France 129
Montcalm, Louis Joseph, Marquis de 133
Montfort, Simon de, Earl of Leicester 125
Moos, Germany 189
Morskie Oko, Poland 235
Moulin Rouge, Paris 146
Mouthoumet, France 124
Muniellos, Bosque de, Spain 31
Muros y Noya, Ria de, Spain 13–14
Murphy, Dervla 297
Musala, Bulgaria 345–7
Mussolini, Benito 181
Mustafa (military commander of Bosphorus) 362–3

Nádsady, František 211
Napoleon I, Emperor of France 74, 176, 204–5
Napoleon III, Emperor of France 90

Naranjo de Bulnes, Spain 46–7
Narcea river, Spain 32, 34
Nasmyth, Kim and Anna 202–3
National Socialist Party 190–1, 197
Navacelles, France 132
Nazarenko, Piotr Nikolayovich 262, 264–71,
    272, 277, 280, 355, 356
Nazareth, France 145
Necking, Germany 189
Nikolai (elderly Bulgarian on Vitosha) 344–5,
    356
Noah 113
Nové Mesto, Slovakia 212–13
Numancia, Spain 38

Obersalzberg, Germany 190–1, 192–3
o'Connor, V.C. Scott 116
Ogosta, Bulgaria 338–9
Olchowiec, Poland 251
Olhadubi, Gorges d', Pyrenees 80, 81
Opalone mountains, Poland 235
Orava castle, Slovakia 222
Orava river, Slovakia 223
Ordesa canyon, Pyrenees 94, 95
Ortaköy, Turkey 363
Ossau, Pic du Midi d', Pyrenees 85, 88
Ossoue, Glacier d', Pyrenees 89
'Otzi' the Iceman 186
Ozeranko valley, Ukraine 270–1

Paccard, Michel-Gabriel 162
Packe, Charles 86, 90
Pajares, Puerto de, Spain 40, 41
pallozas (Galician mountain dwellings) 26,
    28–9, 30
Pamplona, Spain 48, 70, 72–4, 77
Papadimitriou, Philippe 143, 356
Paraplui mountain, Austria 198
Parîng mountains, Romania 311, 312, 313–14
Paris, Augustin (of St-Paul-de-Fenouillet) 122
Parrot, Johann Jacob Friedrich Wilhelm 79
Parvomaj, Bulgaria 355–6
Pelayo (leader of the Goths) 31
pelota (game) 58
Peña, Xebe 71–2, 356
Peña Sagra, Sierra de, Spain 49–50
Peña Ubiña, Spain 38
Perdido, Monte, Pyrenees 86, 95

Pérez, Gregorio 47
Pete (Chamonix ski-bum) 170–72, 356
Peter III, King of Aragon 113
'Pétomane, Le' (Joseph Pujol) 146–7
Petrohan pass, Bulgaria 339
Petroşani, Romania 314–15
Petting, Germany 189
Peyrepertuse, Château de, France 123
Peytier (French military surveyor) 87
Pfanzer-Baltin, General Freiherr von 278,
    281
Pfeiffer, Sergeant-Major Klaus 191–2, 356
Philip II, King of Macedon 355
Piatra Alba, Romania 312
Piatra Tăiată, Romania 313
Picasso, Pablo 57
Picos Blancos, Spain 35, 36
Pieniny mountains, Poland 236–9
Pigafetta, Antonio 62, 63, 64
pilgrim roads, see *Camino francés; Chemin de St
    Jacques*
Pineta, Pyrenees 96
Piornedo, Spain 28–9
Pirin mountains, Bulgaria 349–50
Piso, Professor Ioan 321–2, 323, 356
Pisueña valley, Spain 54
Piwniczna, Poland 240
Pla, Josep 106–7
plague, quarantine during 285
Plan Glacier 166
Plaveck , Slovakia 210
Plovdiv, Bulgaria 355
Podczerwone, Poland 227
Podhale, Poland 231, 248
Poio, Alto do, Spain 25
Poland 226–59
Pompey the Great 74
Ponce, Enrique 30, 68
Popowe Wierchy, Poland 244
Poprad river, Poland 240
Porsche, Ferdinand 258
Porubnoe, Ukraine 280, 290–92
Porubsk valley, Slovakia 217
Potes, Spain 47–9, 348
Powroźnik, Poland 241–2
Prades, France 121
Pratcoustals, France 133–7
Prickra, Slovakia 255

Prislop pass, Ukraine 269
Procopius 360
Przełęcz Majdan, Poland 245
Puente Viesgo, Spain 52
Pujol, Joseph ('Le Pétomane') 146–7
Pyrenees 5, 75–117
    Corbières 122–6
    Hautes 86–96
    Treaty of (1659) 111
Pyrrhus, King of Epirus 202

Quadi 206
'Que Chova' (umbrella) 15–16
Quéribus, Château de, France 123
Quietus, Lusius 317

Rachowski, Iwanczuk 283
Radu (walker in Făgăraş) 308–9, 356
Radziejowa, Poland 240
Rajčanka valley, Slovakia 218
Rákóczi II, Ferenc 219
Rarău, Romania 297
Red Bay, Labrador 61–2
Regato Valverde, Spain 23
Regetóroka, Poland 243, 244
Reilhan, Julien, of Pratcoustals 137
Retezat mountains, Romania 311, 312, 321,
    323–5
Reynolds-Ball, Eustace, FRGS 115
Rhaeto-Romansch dialects 185
Rhodope mountains, Bulgaria 351–4
Rhône, river 144–5, 173
Richaud (French woodcutter) 151
Riddes, Switzerland 173
Rila mountains, Bulgaria 342, 345, 347–8, 350
Rilke, Rainer Maria 182
Rimsting, Germany 189
Robert (walker in Făgăraş) 309, 356
Robert, Hubert 147
Roberts, Frederick Sleigh, Earl of Kandahar,
    Pretoria and Waterford 114, 115, 116
Robles, Gil 32
Roc de Peyremoux, France 129
Rocks, Clashing 362
Rohrer Sattel, Austria 197
Roland, Brèche de, Pyrenees 93
Roland, Chanson de 79
Roman, Petre, Romania 314

Romania 291–336
Rome, ancient
    Alpine campaigns 181
    and Danube region 206, 317, 318–23, 328
    and Slovakia 213
    roads 37–8, 112, 183, 327, 355, 359
    and Spain 37–8, 49–50, 74
    wall across Thracian isthmus 360
Roncesvalles, France 78–9
Rouffiac, France 123–4
Rousseau, Jean-Jacques 158–9, 328
Rozhen monastery, Bulgaria 350
Rua, Galicia 20
Rudolf, Habsburg Crown Prince 197
Ruhpolding, Switzerland 189
Rumeli Feneri, Turkey 362
Rumeli Hisar castle, Turkey 363
Russell-Killough, Count Henry Patrick
    Marie 90, 93, 88–9, 110
Rusyns/Ruthenians/Rusnaks/Ruthenes 254

Sabin (Basque, of Ipazter) 59, 60, 61, 356
St Martin des Puits, France 125
St Maurice Navacelles, France 131–2
St Miguel d'Engolasters, Andorra 109
St Moritz, Switzerland 184
St-Paul-de-Fenouillet, France 122
Sainte-Engrâce, Pyrenees 81
Saliencia, Lagos de, Spain 36
Saltinaschlüocht, Austria 175, 176
Samos monastery, Spain 25
San Emiliano, Spain 38, 39
San Jorio pass, Switzerland 178, 179–80
Sand, George 90
Santiago de Compostela 5, 14–19, 66, 93, 234
Sarmizegetusa, Colonia Ulpia Traiana
    Augusta Dacia, Romania 321–3, 356
Sarmizegetusa, Romania 317, 318–20, 356
Sasha (Ukrainian police psychologist) 260–2,
    264, 356
Saussure, Horace Bénédict de 162
Savogno, Italy 182
Saxons, Romanian 303, 304–5, 311
Schönau, Austria 205
Schwarzbach, Switzerland 189
Scotland 8, 240
Sebeş mountains, Romania 316–17
Segantini, Giovanni 182

Sentiles, Sierra de, Spain 41
Serges, Mme, of Vence valley 155
Seyte, Monsieur, of Carcassonne 128–9
Shelley, Percy Bysshe 162
Shpitzi, Ukraine 281–2
Sibiu, Romania 310
sierras, Spanish 5, 11–74
silk cultivation, Pratcoustals 135, 136
Simplon Pass 174, 175–7
Sinan abdür-Mennan 359, 361
Sinevir, Lake, Ukraine 264, 266, 269–70
Sinning, Germany 189
Siret, Romania 292–3
Sisterna, Spain 31
Sitwell, Sacheverell 293
Slopsk , Slovakia 217
Slovakia 207–26
Slovakia, Sea of 257–8
Snina, Slovakia 256
Sobieski, John, King of Poland 219
Sobrance, Slovakia 259
Sodding, Germany 189
Sofia, Bulgaria 339, 340–2, 343
Soglio, Switzerland 182
Somiedo, Reserva Nacional de, Spain 35
Sorin (Romanian mining engineer) 314–15,
    356
Soto de Sajambre, Spain 42
Spain 5, 11–74
Speer, Albert 190, 192
Spender, Harold 98–9, 100, 101, 107, 108, 109
Stalin, Josef 201, 248
Stara Planina, Bulgaria 339, 343
Starkie, Walter 26, 311
Staszel-Furtek, Jan 232, 356
Status de la Transhumance 138
Stefan (Romanian mining engineer) 314–15,
    356
Stefan the Great, Prince of Moldavia 294
Ştefureac, Ion 295
steppe region 286–93
Stevenson, Robert Louis 139–40, 142–3, 144
Stoker, Bram 302
Stone Age 28–9, 52
Storozinec, Ukraine 289–90
Stoy, Ukraine 268
Strihaylna, Ukraine 269
Studeny Wierch, Poland 252–3

Suceviţa, Romania 293–4
Svidovets, Ukraine 275–7
Svilengrad, Bulgaria 357–8
Svoboda, Ludvik, President of
    Czechoslovakia 253
Swiątkowa, Poland 245
Sykes, Margaret 262–4, 356
Symplegades 362
Szeklers 303, 304

Tatra cars 258
Tatras, High 216, 224, 227–8, 230
Taxa, Germany 189
Terchová, Slovakia 220
Termes, Château de, France 125
Thoreau, Henry David 108
Thracian isthmus, Turkey 359–61
Tibet 8
Tinker, Jon 230, 231, 356
Tismana, Romania 325–7
tobacco growing in Andorra 106–7, 109
Tomaszuyk, Teodor 251
Torrebarrio, Spain 38
Trajan's Column, Rome 319, 320
tramontane (wind) 121, 126
Transylvania 302–5
Trenčiánské Teplice, Slovakia 216
Trenčín, Slovakia 213–15, 216, 219, 239
Triaire, Sergeant (Crimean War hero) 133
Trilla, France 121
Trstená, Slovakia 223, 226
Tschlin, Switzerland 185
Tubal (Biblical figure) 52
Ţugui, Professor Ioan 296
Turcul, Ukraine 281
Turner, J.M.W. 157
Turnu Severin, Romania 329–30

Ukraine 260–91
Umberto (shepherd, of Caín) 45–6
Urlea, Romania 310
Urrestilla, Spain 70
Urrieles massif, Spain 42, 45–7
Ust-Chorna, Ukraine 270, 271–4
Uzhgorod, Ukraine 254, 259, 260–4, 271

Váh valley, Slovakia 213, 218
Valence, France 145–7

Vallot, Mont Blanc 167, 168
Vanniesbecq, Philippe Papadimitriou
    Demaitre Pausenberger 143, 356
Vápeč, Slovakia 217
Varchola family of Miková 255–6
Vasil (warden of Rila mountain hut) 348
Vassieux, France 151
Vegebaño, Spain 42–3
Velchy Verch, Ukraine 268
Vence valley, France 155
Vercors, France 151–3
Verkhovina, Ukraine 285–6
Vernet-les-Bains, France 114–17
Vetsera, Mary 197–8
Via Egnatia 359
Victor (pilgrim in Santiago de
    Compostela) 18–19, 22, 345
Vidin, Bulgaria 336, 337
Vienna, Austria 5, 187, 201–4
Vienna woods 197–8, 202–3
Vignemale, Pyrenees 86, 87–8, 89, 91
Vihren, Bulgaria 349
Vilarello, Spain 28
Villablino, Spain 35
Villaviciosa, Marqués de 47
Vindium, Mons (Picos de Europa) 50
Viriatus 37–8
Vitosha, Bulgaria 343–5, 356
Viznitza, Ukraine 288
Volkswagen Beetle 258
Volovets, Ukraine 267
Voza, Col de, France 163

Walchensee, Germany 188
Wank, Germany 187
War, Boer 114

War, Crimean 133
War, First World 197, 278, 314
War, Peninsular 57, 74
War, Second World 129, 181, 241, 252–4, 272,
    333–4
    memorials 151–2, 159–60, 176
War, Spanish Civil 32, 57, 96, 105
Warhol, Andy 255–6
Wart, Germany 189
Wasyluk, Dmytryk (Hutzul outlaw) 287, 288
Watzmann, Germany 190
Wellington, Arthur Wellesley, 1st Duke of 74
Werner (pilgrim to Santiago de
    Compostela) 24
Whymper, Edward 171, 177
Wienerwald, Austria 197–8, 202–3
Wilsznia, Poland 252
Wind-Passing, Germany 189
Wisłoka valley, Poland 245
Wolf, Dobroslawa 'Mrufka' 230
wolves 140
Wordsworth, William 157

Yasiek (Górale architect and musician) 233–4,
    356
Yasinya, Ukraine 277–8, 280
Yves (of Tournon) 160

Zain, Germany 189
Zakopane, Poland 228–35
Zamolxis (Transylvanian god) 299
Zauberwald, Switzerland 189–90
Zernez, Switzerland 184
Zimmermann, Frau, of Hallstatt 1956, 356
Zlota Bania castle, Hungary 284
Zuberec, Slovakia 223